ROGER KAHN

★

BEYOND THE
BOYS OF SUMMER

★

THE VERY BEST OF ROGER KAHN

EDITED BY ROB MIRALDI

McGraw·Hill

New York   Chicago   San Francisco   Lisbon   London   Madrid   Mexico City
Milan   New Delhi   San Juan   Seoul   Singapore   Sydney   Toronto

The *McGraw·Hill* Companies

Library of Congress Cataloging-in-Publication Data

Kahn, Roger.
    Beyond the boys of summer : the very best of Roger Kahn / Roger Kahn ; Robert
Miraldi, editor.
        p.   cm.
    Includes bibliographical references.
    ISBN 0-07-144727-X
    1. Baseball—United States—Miscellanea.   2. Sports—United States—
Miscellanea.   I. Miraldi, Robert.   II. Title.

    GV873.K29   2005
    796.357'64'0973—dc22   2004024851

Pages 219–223: Excerpt from *A Flame of Pure Fire* by Roger Kahn, copyright © 1999
by Hook Slide, Inc., reprinted by permission of Harcourt, Inc.
Pages 229–238: Excerpt from *October Men*, copyright © 2003 by Hook Slide, Inc.,
reprinted by permission of Harcourt, Inc.

1 2 3 4 5 6 7 8 9 0   FGR/FGR   0 9 8 7 6 5 4

ISBN 0-07-144727-X

McGraw-Hill books are available at special quantity discounts to use as premiums and
sales promotions, or for use in corporate training programs. For more information, please
write to the Director of Special Sales, Professional Publishing, McGraw-Hill, Two Penn
Plaza, New York, NY 10121-2298. Or contact your local bookstore.

This book is printed on acid-free paper.

For Olga Kahn, lover of literature,
and
Edith Miraldi, lover of baseball

Books by Roger Kahn

October Men (2002)
The Head Game (2000)
A Flame of Pure Fire (1999)
Memories of Summer (1997)
The Era (1993)
Games We Used to Play (1992)
Joe and Marilyn (1986)
Good Enough to Dream (1985)
A Season in the Sun (1977)
How the Weather Was (1973)
The Boys of Summer (1972)
The Battle for Morningside Heights (1970)
The Passionate People (1968)
Inside Big League Baseball (Juvenile, 1962)

Novels

The Seventh Game (1982)
But Not to Keep (1978)

Collaborations

My Story, with Pete Rose (1989)

Edited

The World of John Lardner (1961)
The Mutual Baseball Almanac (1954, 1955, 1956)

CONTENTS

v

PROLOGUE
THE WONDER OF WRITING

I have something to report that lies beyond the imagination of mankind.
—*LONDON TIMES* CORRESPONDENT FROM BELSEN (APRIL 1945)

The distinction between literature and journalism cannot be said to be clear cut. Great journalism—Heywood Broun on Babe Ruth, Hemingway on warring Spain, William L. Shirer on Hitler—is literature. And many, perhaps most, books—pulp fiction, sex manuals, campaign biographies, ghosted memoirs—are not. When the critic Alfred Kazin tried to define literature in his profound 1995 work, *Writing Was Everything*, he wrote, "Literature is the value we can give to our experience, which in our century has been and remains beyond the imagination of mankind." That sentence, with its undertones of Holocaust and foreshadowing of Hiroshima, demands thought, but that is not my point right here. Seeking to define literature, a brilliant intellectual employs a phrase, "beyond the imagination of mankind," that he found in an unsigned story in his daily paper.

Years ago the *New York Herald Tribune* assigned me to cover a not very interesting horse race at Belmont Park near New York City. I was very young, perhaps twenty-two, and seated in the press box next to a gentle veteran from the *New York Times* named Joe Nichols. (Regardless of the individual reporters, *Times* and *Tribune* people nearly always drew press-box seats side by side.) As I labored to create an interesting lead, Nichols noticed my discomfort and said in a kindly way, "Relax, kid. It ain't *The Iliad*."

It ain't and it wasn't, but I was trying. (And so was Joe.) That I think is the key. After the painstaking business of reporting (nonfiction) or observation and imagination (fiction) you attempt, as Kazin put it, to give value to the experience of your subjects and yourself. You make a fierce effort to understand humanity. Then you try to write like hell.

Newspaper staffs of fifty to one hundred years ago were more varied than today's casts, where graduates of journalism schools tend to predominate. The idea of the old reporter always wearing a fedora, with a bottle of cheap whiskey stuffed into a desk drawer, is not a long leap from the truth. Stanley Woodward, who amassed a strong sportswriting staff at the *New York Herald Tribune*, summarized them in his 1949 book, *Sports Page*. "There were no journalism school graduates," Woodward wrote, "although one [Red Smith] made journalism his major at Notre Dame. Another taught English at the University of Michigan. Another majored in Latin and Greek at Yale. Another came to this country from Scotland as a golf professional. Another was night editor of the Paris *Herald*. Another attended City College of New York and caught on because he did an outstanding job as the paper's correspondent there. Another [Roger Kahn] started as a copy boy. Another was the son of a famous big league ball player and got the ear of my predecessor because of that. Another was a theatrical press agent. Another flew a Liberator bomber over Nazi Germany. Another was formerly an advance man for a theatrical troupe called Singer's Midgets.

The writing was uneven. Smith became one of the finest two or three sports columnists of his day. The old Paris hand, Al Laney, wrote beautiful long feature stories. The golf pro knew the game but his stuff was dry. The air force veteran was a disaster, but once Woodward hired a man he kept him. That was one reason jobs in the *Herald Tribune* sports section came hard, and it was also a reason the overall writing stayed uneven.

Woodward let his writers, particularly his young ones, make mistakes and corrected most gaffes only after they had appeared in the newspaper. The bomber pilot turned sportswriter once called a game at Yankee Stadium spine-tingling. The phrase was published the next day, which is when Woodward approached the reporter and said, "Next time you want to call a game spine-tingling, you are first going to go out in the bleachers and ask every one of those fans if his spine actually tingled." Woodward's strong voice was high-pitched, and the whole sports department heard him. I don't believe the cliché "spine-tingling" ever appeared in his section again.

Some ask what's wrong with an occasional cliché? Many things are wrong, particularly this: when a writer uses a cliché he is suspending thought and opening, as it were, an old can of words. To write well you should think every word, think every sentence, think every paragraph along the way. That's probably why Dylan Thomas called writing "a craft or sullen art." All that thinking can make one irritable.

I once watched Robert Frost, by nature a friendly sort, virtually dismember an overly aggressive student who wanted to know what a particular poem meant.

"It means what it says."

"Well," the student said, "I know what it means to me but I don't know what it means to you."

"Maybe I don't want you to."

"Could you explain the poem please?"

"Do you want me to state it in worse English?" Frost said, leaving his ardent idolater distraught but also perhaps with a first clue as to how writers function and think. Most writers look on their work as Frost did. *It means what it says.* As the wise comedian Fred Allen once put it, "If you have to explain a joke, don't."

Poetry, newspapering, novels, essays, magazine pieces are all part of that mysterious, magnificent humbling beast that we call writing. Across these pages, gathered with such care by Professor Miraldi, something like fifty years of my writing appears, recalling in some instances moments at the far borders of memory. It recalls also some who helped along the way.

Woodward was a wonder, and I remember once his asking me to write a "color" piece about a heavyweight championship fight in Miami between Ingemar Johansson and Floyd Patterson. Max Schmeling of Hamburg, an invited guest, drew cheers from bystanders as he strolled up Collins Avenue in Miami Beach. I described the scene briefly, and then, remembering that Schmeling had been a Wehrmacht paratrooper, I wrote: "Schmeling, of course, was never a Nazi. As I get the picture there were never more than six or seven Nazis in Germany. But they worked very hard." Then, sensitive to pressures I knew existed—Volkswagen advertising, for example—I put the item in the middle of my column. When next I saw Woodward he said simply, "Why did you bury your lead note?"

"I thought if you saw it, you might kill it," I said. Woodward called me a few names and declined to buy me a Scotch. I have not since consciously censored my own stuff.

After leaving the *Herald Tribune*, I signed on as sports editor of *Newsweek*, where writing was mostly anonymous and always compressed. The editorial director, John Denson, drafted me to compose the obituary of Frank Lloyd Wright and said I could have sixty lines or about 360 words to describe the epochal life and art of a man who had lived almost ninety years. A deputy said, "Don't complain. Look what Shakespeare could get into fourteen lines."

I thought (and think) that was witty and irrelevant. Newsmagazine writing is a distinct form, useful in many ways but to me at least ultimately unsatisfactory. I like the characters in my stories to have the space to take a long deep breath. The finest aspect of my four *Newsweek* years was working with John Lardner, who was as gifted an all-around journalist as I've encountered. John could write short, long, funny, moving. He was as good in *The New Yorker* as he was in his column at *Newsweek*, and he was as good at covering D-Day and Iwo Jima as he was at following the life and times of Jack Johnson, the first American black heavyweight champion, who seemed to offend society by lusting after white women, although just about half of that society did the same.

Otto Friedrich summoned me to his *Saturday Evening Post* with a dry remark over a dry martini, "Do you want to go on writing about second basemen all your life?" To this day I enjoy writing about second basemen—Jackie Robinson was one—but Otto encouraged me to write some politics and a great deal of social history, and it was his urging that led me to undertake, at the advanced age of thirty-nine, my first so-called "serious" book, *The Passionate People*. By the time Friedrich's *Post* expired, just after Christmas 1969, I was a pretty well-rounded journalist and author, comfortable across a wide variety of fields. Then in

1972 I published *The Boys of Summer*, and after that everybody wanted me to write about second basemen again.

This is my nineteenth book; all my life I've tried to write literature. I am aware that like Stan Musial or Ted Williams at bat most of the time I've failed. But the critical word is "try." That effort has been a wonder of my life.

Roger Kahn

Stone Ridge, New York

INTRODUCTION
"SLIDERS WITH SOCIAL HISTORY"

Roger Kahn's University, the *Herald Tribune*

The Unison Arts Center is nestled just outside the village of New Paltz, a mere ninety miles from the Brooklyn neighborhood where Roger Kahn was born seventy-six years ago. I drove there on a Friday night in September to hear Kahn read from his latest book, *October Men*. I was the first person to arrive in the small white-walled room where three wooden chairs had been set on a raised platform with black music stands in front of them. A Yankees hat hung nearby. No Brooklyn Dodger blue was to be seen. Three of Kahn's books were lying on a small table—*The Boys of Summer*, of course, *October Men*, and *The Era*, his 1993 book that was nominated for a Pulitzer Prize. For a while at least it appeared that no one would be there to hear Kahn read. I debated what I would do. Maybe, if no one showed up, I could drive Kahn home, stop at a tavern for drinks, and listen to him tell baseball stories. Perhaps secretly I hoped for this—to have him all alone and hear his stories. After all, as *New York Times* book reviewer Donald Hall wrote, Kahn is "masterful at retelling anecdotes." Indeed, perhaps no one in America tells sports stories as well as Roger Kahn. "Nostalgia and anecdotes," Kahn once told me, "that's what I do. I go back and I tell stories." He failed to add that he tells stories that have social and human meaning. "Sliders with social history," Kahn calls it. And so I wondered on this night what stories Roger Kahn would tell.

After many years living in Manhattan, Kahn resides today in Stone Ridge, a Hudson Valley hamlet of Colonial-era houses that is listed on the National Historic Register. The Unison Center is fifteen minutes from Kahn's home, an easy car ride over the nearby Shawangunk Mountains, whose sheer cliffs attract rock climbers from all over the East. Although in good health, Roger Kahn is no rock climber—he plays a little whiffle ball, likes to try his hand at a basketball set shot, and loves to play tennis twice a week in nearby Woodstock. And, oh yes, he likes to write. After more than fifty years in journalism, Kahn is still adding to the hundreds of magazine articles and eighteen books he has written—and he is still in demand as a speaker, as I found out. The room at Unison soon began to fill. At seven thirty Kahn entered, dressed in a blue blazer and open-necked, red-checked shirt. He was more casual than the night a few months earlier when, at Manhattan's 21 Club, he held court as his publisher, Harcourt, unveiled his book on the New York Yankees and the tumultuous 1978 pennant-winning season. After entering Unison, Kahn was escorted to a back room, out of sight of the audience. Who had come to hear him? Were these sports fans, or old Brooklyn residents here to see one of their own? Or were they—more than likely—people who had read *Boys of Summer* in 1972 and who had been touched by Kahn's poignant, poetic recapturing of Ebbets Field— "the shrine," as he called it—and the famous "Bums"—the Duke of Flatbush, Campy, Pee Wee, and the man who Kahn loved and idolized, Jackie Robinson? As I listened to people talk, all their references were, in fact, to *Boys of Summer* and where they were in their lives when its nostalgia touched them. They are not alone, of course. The book has sold nearly three million copies, is in its sixty-fifth printing, and was tabbed in 2002 by *Sports Illustrated* magazine the second best American sports book ever written. (A. J. Liebling's 1956 *Sweet Science*, a prize-fighting book, topped the list.)

Listening to the audience's whispered recollections brought me back to the spring of 1974 when, as a graduate student at Boston University, I first discovered *Boys of Summer*. I was in the throes of a love affair with the "new journalism," an engaging style of nonfiction writing in which literary techniques overshadowed facts. Tom Wolfe, Jimmy Breslin, Gay Talese—and Roger Kahn—were lumped together as a new breed of journalist. Growing up on Staten Island, across the harbor from Brooklyn, I had spent every summer playing baseball, yearning to be the Yankees' third baseman. When it was clear that the Yanks would not call, I turned to journalism. The combination of my past life and emerging interests made *Boys of Summer* a perfect match.

Ah, to write such a book. I was jostled back to the Unison Arts Center stage when the host stepped forward. Before Roger Kahn, "one of our greatest writers," emerges, he said, we will hear readings from famous baseball literature, all done in dramatic theater style. *Damn Yankees, Field of Dreams, The Natural,* "Casey at the Bat"—all to set the mood for Kahn's entrance. Finally, the host read a passage from Kahn's *The Era,* a book about the years when the Yankees, Dodgers, and Giants ruled baseball—and New York. In it Kahn recalls 1957, when the Yanks lost Game 7 of the World Series to the Milwaukee Braves. He traveled back on the Yankees' airplane as manager Casey Stengel drank steadily for three hours. As Stengel emerged from the plane, a television reporter asked, "Did your team choke up out there?" Stengel replied, "Do you choke up on your fucking microphone?" Then the sixty-seven-year-old manager turned around, faced the camera, and clawed at his buttocks. "You see," Stengel told Kahn later over drinks, "you got to stop them terrible questions. When I said 'fuck,' I ruined his audio. When I scratched my ass, I ruined his video, if you get my drift." The audience roared with laughter. Kahn's point, humor aside, was that Stengel was no dummy. He won World Series because he knew how to manage—his players and the New York media.

Enter, finally, Roger Kahn. He was smiling, waving slightly as he hopped onto the small stage to considerable applause. "I don't get applause like that at home," he said. More chuckles. But then, in answer to a question as to why he wrote about the years 1947 to 1958 in *The Era,* he became serious. Over the next ninety minutes, Kahn would show just what kind of sportswriter he is. He doesn't talk statistics or strategy, although he knows both. He follows every trade, but trades were not what he would address here. Roger Kahn likes to write and talk about social justice and about athletes facing life when they are young and old. And he likes to do it with a poetic flair. In response to a question, he quickly launched into discussing race and sports in New

York. "Two of the three New York teams discovered that people of color could play baseball," he noted, referring to Jackie Robinson's Dodgers and Willie Mays's Giants. The New York Yankees? "They were South Africa's favorite team," he said. Kahn's words can often be biting. His portrayal of Yankees owner George Steinbrenner in *October Men*—even though balanced—got him banned from the Yankees' cable television station. He delights in attacking other sportswriters. His books are filled with pokes at the late Dick Young, who was an acerbic and widely read columnist for the *New York Daily News*. In April of 2003 Kahn made headlines when he pulled out of a speaking appearance at the Baseball Hall of Fame in Cooperstown. Kahn protested the Hall's cancellation of the movie *Bull Durham* because of the antiwar stances of its stars, Susan Sarandon and Tim Robbins. "You are choking freedom of dissent," Kahn told the Hall's president, and "defying the noblest of the American spirit."

Kahn likes also, however, to praise the heroic. Jackie Robinson and Pee Wee Reese are his favorites. On this night Kahn moved quickly to a story about Branch Rickey, the Dodgers' general manager who chose Robinson in 1947 to break baseball's color barrier. While managing a University of Michigan baseball team, Rickey had a black ballplayer who was not allowed in the hotel where the team stayed. Rickey pleaded to let the young man stay in his room. They agreed. Once in the room, the young man sat on a cot, scratching at his black skin. "If only I did not have this skin," he said. The audience sat silently, engrossed. The woman next to me leaned to her daughter and said: "God, how awful it was." I wanted to whisper to her, "Social history with sliders, Kahn is good at that." Later, Kahn read an epilogue from *Boys of Summer* that recalled the death of his good friend Reese. It is a moving remembrance, added when Reese died in 1999. Kahn could not get through the reading. He was moved to tears. The audience too was moved, hushed, and feeling Kahn's pain. Kahn nodded, finally, his eyes blinking, and he said, almost apologetically: "No tears in the writer, no tears in the reader." He was paraphrasing the poet Robert Frost, one of Kahn's other heroes, with whom he studied in 1951 at a Bread Loaf, Vermont, writing retreat. The performance was over. And then the audience was on its feet, applauding, as was I, wiping back tears.

Later, over drinks at a nearby tavern (he likes Dalmore single malt Scotch whisky, with only one ice cube), I congratulated Kahn, remarking how he had the audience in the palm of his hand. He shrugged, pleased, but was more interested in telling baseball stories and recalling his early years in journalism, well before applause came his way. In 1948 Kahn dropped out of New York University, to the chagrin of his mother, Olga, an English teacher who loved poetry. He was nineteen years old. "All I wanted to do was play ball. Read a little and play ball," he says. But Kahn's playing days were clearly over. He had been only a decent third baseman on sandlot teams. It was time to think about making a living. His father, Gordon, an editor, historian, and one of the creators of the popular radio quiz show "Information, Please," contacted a friend at the *New York Herald Tribune*, one of eight daily newspapers in New York City. Kahn hooked on as a copyboy but was a bit in awe. "I admired newspaper people," he said, "but these were stars." Indeed in 1948, the *Trib* was one of America's great newspapers, literary and carefully reported, with a sweep that was both local and international. At first, Kahn was happy to be making $26.50 a week. "I put away mail and mixed paste and did the things a copyboy does," he recalled as we sat one fall day in the den of his Hudson Valley home. A ring of orange-hued trees was visible in the background, with a nearby in-ground pool where Kahn and his wife, Katharine, like to do laps all summer. A large-screen television dominated the room. Kahn has a satellite dish and a subscription to major-league baseball that enables him to see games from all over the country, although he rarely gets to the ballpark these days. "I stay up so late watching the damn games," he says, laughing. Indeed, rings circled his eyes. His hair is now gray but he is healthy and fit, and he still talks about his swing and getting back his batting eye after cataract surgery. Once, right before he left on a nineteen-city tour to promote *October Men*, I saw a whiffle ball bat and his baseball glove in his suitcase, as if he was about to make a West Coast swing to play the Dodgers and Giants. One would think that after fifty years of writing about baseball Kahn would have had enough. But he loves the game and loves to tell stories about it. "Baseball," Kahn says, "was my first gateway into the world of men. My father couldn't talk to me about sex, but we could talk about a Dodger center fielder and how he had run down a ball. Baseball was a metaphor for talking about life." When he returned from his promotional tour, a weekly newspaper in the Hudson Valley interviewed Kahn. The reporter wrote, "When I called Kahn to set up an interview I had not yet even said hello and he was regaling me with a tale of the Brooklyn Dodgers." At a recent television interview I did with Kahn, he was recounting for the audience stories of George Steinbrenner and Reggie Jackson. As we went to a commercial break, Kahn never missed a beat. Off camera, he told two more anecdotes before we came back on air.

In his early days at the *Herald Tribune*, however, Kahn almost ended up writing news. His first stories were about the playwright Sean O'Casey, then about an ice-skater at Madison Square Garden, an assignment given to him by editor William Zinsser, later to become well known as the author of *On Writing Well*. When Kahn wrote effective stories about a strike by high school sports coaches in New York City, showing how the after-school world had stopped, especially for black teenagers, he caught the attention of the sports editor, Stanley Woodward. Before long Kahn was writing sports full-time—for $48 a week. "From there [it was] sports, sports, sports," Kahn recalled. Ironically, he would have taken any job at the newspaper, "anything to become a reporter and not a copyboy," he said. Five years later, at age twenty-four, Kahn was given the assignment—in "a series of miraculous breaks," he said—to cover the Brooklyn Dodgers, the team he had grown up watching. Being on the road with the Dodgers, Kahn wrote in the *Boys of Summer*, "was a lonely, thrilling chaos, at once seductive and wild." Kahn covered baseball for four straight years, a total of about 750 games. From February to October he often wrote two stories a day. In total, he wrote nearly two thousand stories, covering the Dodgers, Giants, and Yankees. In the end, the *Tribune* taught Kahn more than how to write about baseball. It gave him lessons that stayed with him and became the trademark of his books and magazine articles, some of which are collected in this anthology.

Most important, Kahn was introduced to journalism that emphasized fine writing. "There was an abiding literacy," Kahn says. "The *Tribune* was a writer's paper. You better know who Milton is, you better have read Hardy. And everyone had. Browning, Shelley, and Keats. It was just so literary." The reason was Woodward, who had set out to collect a group of talented men who, historian Richard Kluger observed, "disdained the bizarre patois of the craft and wrote with exactness and erudition." Kahn learned by watching reporters such as Jesse Abramson, a fanatically accurate reporter whose knowledge of track and field was such that he was called "the book." Today Kahn still bristles at factual errors. He rails about how Jimmy Breslin is allowed to play with facts in his newspaper columns; how Halberstam mistakenly wrote that the Dodgers stole freely on Yogi Berra in a World Series when it was not true. He also grew angry at himself when in *October Men* he wrote—in error—that Yankees president Al Rosen would not go to the ballpark on Rosh Hashanah, when it was really Yom Kippur. In preparation for writing a Jack Dempsey biography, *Flame of Pure Fire* (2000), Kahn watched tapes of the prizefighter a dozen or more times to make sure he counted correctly the number of punches the heavyweight champion threw in certain fights.

As for erudition, Kahn had to look no further than Red Smith, the two-time Pulitzer Prize winner who for three decades was the most widely syndicated sports columnist in America. The twenty-five-year-old Kahn became a good friend of the fifty-five-year-old Smith. "Red reminded me that no matter how dramatic a ball game seemed to be it was not a battle of Titans," Kahn says about Smith, whose clear economic prose was virtually free of clichés and jargon so typical of sportswriting. Kahn still quotes leads and transitions that Smith wrote four decades ago. Of course, Kahn also often quotes Yeats and Shakespeare, almost as if they are in the same league with the adroit Smith. "In the end," Kahn says, the *Tribune* "was my university. I found an amazing world, a great cosmopolitan world."

As exciting and formative as the *Tribune* years were for Kahn, however, he left in 1955 when he was the highest paid baseball writer in New York City, making $10,000. The reasons were cumulative. The first strike against the *Tribune* came in 1953 when Kahn called the Dodgers' locker room a "sarcophagus" after the team suffered its fifth World Series loss to the Yankees since 1941. Kahn was getting too close to the Dodgers, some editors felt. As a punishment of sorts he was sent to cover the crosstown Giants in the Bronx, not such a terrible assignment since they had Willie Mays as their star center fielder. But Kahn had had other tussles with editors. He had grown to admire Jackie Robinson, not only because he was electrifying on the field but also because he fought baseball's color barriers—a fight that journalism was reluctant to publicize. "Many marvelous aspects illuminated baseball writing in the 1950s," Kahn wrote in *The Era*, "but sensitivity to the conditions of blacks was not among them." Kahn wanted to write stories that went beyond the ball field. His moment came when Robinson and teammate Joe Black, also African-American, were barred from the team's hotel in St. Louis. The *Tribune*'s copydesk rejected his story with simple advice: write baseball, not race relations. Kahn turned to *Sport* magazine and *Our Sports*, a small magazine for blacks, to write about bigotry. The censorship "was a constant problem," Kahn recalled. "They're killing my stuff and I gotta look Jackie in the eye and be my own person."

The final strike against the *Trib* came when Kahn got into a dispute with Giants manager Leo Durocher, who Kahn described as "cheap and obscene and suspicious and wholly magnificent." The fiery Durocher managed the Dodgers from 1939 to 1946 and the Giants from 1948 to 1955. He was fond of using journalists for his own ends. Trying to motivate his ballplayers, he would plant comments with reporters—as he did with Kahn in the spring of 1955, the year after the Giants won a world championship. When his words appeared in the *Tribune*, making some players furious, Durocher denied having uttered them. He then cut off Kahn from any information about the team; the *Tribune* asked Kahn to retract the statements. He would not because they were true. But the *Tribune* refused to back Kahn up. As painful as it was to admit, Kahn said, "I was telling myself, 'Gotta get outta here.'" He resigned. The *Tribune* had taught him "exactness and erudition," but now Kahn wanted more—a principled journalism in which reporters were not pawns and where they could leave the field of dreams to write about America's nightmares. For this he would need to turn to magazines. When Ed Fitzgerald at *Sport* told Kahn that with two articles a month he could match his *Trib* salary, he departed, however mournfully. "To cover these people and events was a young man's dream," Kahn wrote, and leaving was not easy. Of course part of him never left newspapering. Today Kahn still mentally rewrites reporters' lead paragraphs; he complains about what is on page one; he eschews the comma police but cares where the commas are placed. When the Yankees lost to Miami in the 2003 World Series, he told me what follow-up stories made sense, as if he was still a beat reporter. In his 1992 book, *Games We Used to Play*, he wrote, "Once you have been a newspaperman, part of you remains a newspaperman." But that changed in 1956. He began to write for *Sport* and became sports editor at *Newsweek*, then a distant second to *Time* as a weekly newsmagazine. The position was "freighted with obscurity," Kahn said. Nonetheless, the next chapter of his fifty-year journey in writing had begun. And he would make the most of it.

Roger Kahn was remarkably productive between 1956 when he left the *Herald Tribune* and 1972, the year *Boys of Summer* was published. In 1961 he edited a book of articles written by his friend John Lardner, writer Ring Lardner's son with whom he worked at *Newsweek*. A year later he wrote a children's baseball book, and then in 1968 and 1970 he produced two long books of reportage. He also wrote nearly one hundred magazine articles in, among others, *The Nation, Sport, Sports Illustrated*, and the *Saturday Evening Post*, where he became editor at large in 1963. Kahn was eager to shed his image as the young fellow who covered the Brooklyn Dodgers. "I was interested in other things. I wasn't labeled as I am now," he told me. When Kahn, thirty-three, met with Robert Frost, eighty-five, as he prepared a *Post* article on the poet, they had this exchange: "So you're a sportswriter," Frost said as they stood on a hill in Vermont. Kahn answered, "Yes, but I write a few other things as well." "Of course," the old man answered. "Nearly everybody has to lead two lives." So, Kahn fiddled with things other than sports. He ghostwrote an autobiography of the actor Mickey Rooney and wrote profiles of Doris Day and Jackie Cooper. He briefly toyed with staying in Hollywood. "The money was great," he said, but "writers were pretty much treated like dirt. So I came back east." At the *Saturday Evening Post* he had the freedom to write about Lyndon Johnson, Barry Goldwater, and Jascha Heifetz, the greatest violinist of the twentieth century. In 1968 his first big book, *The Passionate People: What It Means to be a Jew in America*, was published. His blend of character sketches and history received mixed response. One critic called it a "fascinating combination of flavor and fact," while another said it was filled with "vulgarity and distortion." It brought Kahn, who is Jewish, letters of protest. Two years later he wrote *The Battle for Morningside Heights: Why Students Rebel*, which reported on the events leading up to the 1968 rebellion of Columbia University students. Since Kahn lived near the Morningside Heights campus of Columbia, he was easily able to interview students, professors, police, and neighbors. Kahn's impressive reporting—one reviewer noted his "fine eye for the humor and irony in the midst of turmoil"—won praise. Senator Eugene McCarthy, in the Foreword, called it "the finest book written on the issue of student unrest." Although a few reviewers faulted his political analysis, Kahn was more upset that the book was a commercial failure. Nonetheless, he did not have trouble finding an audience for his sports articles as he successfully mined his years as a reporter with long articles on Jackie Robinson and Willie Mays, for example. But he also wrote about the most famous athletes in America—Hank Aaron, Stan Musial, Kareem Abdul Jabbar, Mickey Mantle, and Roger Maris. Eventually five of his magazine pieces won awards as the best articles in the country.

Since magazine articles are often expanded feature-style stories, the transition to magazine writing was easy for Kahn. The *Trib* had prepared him. As we sat one day in his living room he explained that in a newspaper story he might describe the subject's face, but in a magazine piece he could also detail the couch, the rug, and pictures on the wall in the room where the subject sat. "You can draw the picture sharper," he said. But his magazine pieces differed in another significant way: Kahn emerged as a character—albeit a minor one—as he visited athletes out of the arena of their triumphs. "I wish I could figure a way," he once thought while at the *Trib*, "to get beyond the ball games and get the real story into the paper." Now he could. In magazine articles he retold the pain of Jackie Robinson's assault on the color line. He watched Yankees pitcher Whitey Ford chase his children in his Queens, New York, house, Chicago second baseman Nellie Fox hunt in Pennsylvania, and a contentious Hank Aaron sip coffee in Philadelphia. When he wrote about third baseman Eddie Mathews of the Milwaukee Braves, Kahn was more concerned with how the future Hall of Famer is coping with emerging stardom than with his batting stance. Similarly, with Roger Maris, it was the media feeding frenzy that drove the Yankee slugger to the brink of nervous breakdown that interested Kahn. In doing all this Roger Kahn was preparing, perhaps unknowingly, for the biggest reporting and writing assignment of his life.

"A Word or Two" That Made Kahn Famous

When the *Saturday Evening Post* folded in 1969, Kahn looked for another magazine, saying, "I had to support my family," then consisting of his wife and three children. He was also paying alimony from a divorce. But a project that had kicked around in his head for two decades was nagging at Kahn. While still working at the *Herald Tribune*, "I had begun to dream, like newspapermen everywhere," Kahn writes in *Memories of Summer*, "of holing up in a cabin with a typewriter and perhaps a pretty girl and emerging months later with a bearded chin and a finished epic." He recalled a scene from Shakespeare when Othello has killed Desdemona out of a jealous rage. Othello says, "Soft you, a word or two before you go." Kahn felt he had a word or two to say—about his growing up a Dodgers fan, about a father and son going to the ballpark, and about the players he had met on the Dodgers. "I thought they were quite wonderful people," he said. "I wanted to memorialize them, and my own experience. And my father all in one." His friend and editor at the *Post*, Otto Alva Friedrich, wondered if the book made sense. "Do you want to write about second basemen your whole life?" he asked Kahn, then forty-three. "Well the answer was no," Kahn said, "but it is a two-part answer. If the second baseman is Jackie Robinson, then I am not writing about second basemen." In fact, baseball is a minor part of the *Boys of Summer*. Certainly the Dodgers' repeated attempts to beat the Yankees is central to the book's early chapters, but the book is really about, as Kahn puts it, "what happens when life goes on, when the cheering has stopped, and these men can't play major league baseball anymore."

Kahn got into his tan Citroen station wagon and drove across the country to visit "the boys." He was apprehensive. "If they were old, I was old," he recalls thinking. Moreover, he said, "I didn't know what to

expect." Some of what he found shocked him. Billy Cox, the third baseman, was in Pennsylvania, surrounded by racists. Roy Campanella, the
catcher, was paralyzed from a car accident, but he was not sour. "He had
grown tremendously, and I was moved," Kahn said. Jackie Robinson's
diabetes and high blood pressure had taken a toll on his health; his son
was battling drugs and would soon die. Center fielder Duke Snider was
trying to grow avocados in California. Clem Labine, a pitcher, cried
when he told Kahn about his son who had lost a leg in the Vietnam War.
Kahn had once seen Labine cry when he lost a World Series game.
"Now Clem wept again," Kahn recalled. Carl Erskine, another pitcher,
was devoting much of his life to helping disabled children. Erskine had
a son with Down's syndrome. And then there was Pee Wee Reese, the
team captain from Arkansas who could not easily talk about himself.
Reese was Kahn's best friend on the Dodgers. "There was more an
iconic sense with Jackie," Kahn recalled. "With Pee Wee it was more
relaxed." On the first day Pee Wee took out a Cutty Sark whiskey when
Kahn arrived. They drank, they threw around a football, and the next
day they talked of many things. He asked each player: "If you close your
eyes, can you see Ebbets Field?" Sometimes there was almost a sob as
Kahn transported the ballplayers—and eventually his readers—back to
the 1950s. Indeed, one reviewer said, what makes the book "a classic"
is Kahn's use of "mature nostalgia—a fine balancing of a fond and reas-
suring view of the past with a realistic appraisal of its faults." The past
was a father and son bonding over baseball, and talented men in their
prime hitting homers, stealing bases, throwing baseballs like only young
men can. But the 1950s was also the overt racism that bedeviled Robinson and America; it was Kahn's father dying, at fifty-two, from a heart
attack; it was the Dodgers shocking Brooklyn and breaking Kahn's heart
by moving to Los Angeles.

After three years of research and interviews, Kahn now tried to capture in writing all that was Brooklyn of another era. The book's title
had come to mind years earlier when, while living in Manhattan, he
went to hear poet Dylan Thomas, famous for his flamboyantly theatrical readings. With a voice like a church organ, Thomas bellowed the
opening line of a poem: "I see the boys of summer in their ruin." The
title was the easy part; the writing more difficult. But the ballplayers

inadvertently helped him. One night, after attending a dinner to honor the Dodgers' former first baseman Gil Hodges, Kahn went out for drinks at Toots Shor's Restaurant in Manhattan with Erskine. "I don't know if I can finish this book," he told Erskine. "It is such an emotionally difficult book." But Erskine told Kahn: "The whole team is counting on you, Roger. Gil is counting on you, Pee Wee is counting on you." The next day Kahn got down to work. "Knute Rockne never made a better speech," Kahn says today, smiling.

The book was an immediate success when it was published in the spring of 1972. The first printing—twelve thousand copies—sold out in days. Harper, his publisher, bought thirty thousand copies from the Book of the Month Club to keep stores stocked while more printings were prepared. Johnny Carson asked Kahn to appear on his nationally televised "Tonight" show. Dick Cavett devoted an entire ninety-minute program on ABC to the book. "For the rest of the summer I could not get ten minutes alone," Kahn recalled. As author David Halberstam observed, *The Boys of Summer* was "the one we all shoot for . . . the work that showed us that a sports book could be about a lot more than just sports." Of course, Kahn did not invent the genre. In 1959 Jim Brosnan, a former major-league pitcher, wrote *The Long Season*, a mildly irreverent behind-the-scenes look at life in the majors. And former Yankees pitcher Jim Bouton's bestselling *Ball Four* (1964) focused on ballplayers' drinking and sexual habits and on their salary grievances. Kahn, however, thinks his book owes more to the baseball novels of Bernard Malamud (*The Natural*, 1952) and Mark Harris (*Bang the Drum Slowly*, 1956). But in the end, *The Boys of Summer* is not about sports, Kahn feels, but about "time and what time does to all of us. *King Lear* is on the same subject, and my work differs from *Lear* in that it isn't as good." But it was good enough to win rave reviews. "It is not just another book about baseball or a boy growing up to like baseball," *Newsweek*'s reviewer wrote, "but a book about pain and defeat and endurance, about how men, anywhere, must live."

The book succeeded for three reasons. First, the time was ripe for a writer to leave the arena and capture players in the rest of their lives, as Kahn had been doing in magazines for a decade. "You can read a season of sports pages from 1951 without learning anything of the interplay of the fading patriarch (DiMaggio) and the bucolic wunderkind (Mantle)," complains Kahn, who recalls what reporters were told: "Write only about the games. Emotion—indeed, humanity—was irrelevant." *Boys* helped change that. By 1977, when Kahn was writing a column for *Time*, he could assert: "Contemporary sports reporting offers dramatis persona, dialogue, sex and sometimes even baseball." Second, America was in the midst of a terrible war and an even worse clash of cultures when *Boys* appeared. The nation was ready to look back at the serene 1950s, a longing that climaxed in 1980 with the election of Ronald Reagan, who embraced the seeming values of a past era. And lastly, the book is elegantly written. Novelist James Michener described it as "a work of high moral purpose and great poetic accomplishment," perhaps "the finest American book on sports." In assaying the work of Kahn, two scholars wrote: "*The Boys of Summer* helped to spur a renaissance in sports-book publishing during the 1970s and 1980s and helped baseball reestablish its place in American popular culture." No small accomplishment.

Triumph, Tragedy, Terrific New Books

Roger Kahn has faced television cameras for twenty-five years, answering the same questions over and over. Inevitably, no matter what his latest book is about, the questions come around to *The Boys of Summer*. "Sometimes," Kahn told me when I interviewed him for a television program, "I feel like Conan Doyle, who used to say, 'I have written other things than Sherlock Holmes.'" Kahn was smiling, but clearly he has reason to be dismayed if people do not realize that his work goes well beyond his 1972 classic. Sometimes, he says, "People come up to me and say, 'I read your book,' and if I'm feeling contentious I'll say, 'Which one?' Or they'll say that *Boys* was great for a first book. But I'd already written two books that I was proud of. It goes on and I just live with it." Of course, Kahn did more than live with it. He made the most of it. *The Boys of Summer* made Kahn famous, emboldened him as a writer, and gave him new options. "When I finished it I still thought I would have to go to work for a magazine to keep the kids eating," he said. Not so. Kahn could now have his cake and eat it too—he began to write more than ever for magazines as well as pursue book projects. He wrote a column for *Esquire* from 1969 to 1975 when it was helping carve out the "new journalism." Then in 1976–77 Kahn wrote a sports column for *Time*, the nation's largest newsmagazine. The *Time* column exacted a measure of revenge for Kahn. When John Lardner died in 1959, Kahn expected to replace the *Newsweek* columnist, but he was ignored by *Time*'s main competitor. When he finally did get to write a column, however, Kahn felt penned in by space constraints, observing: "They're always eight hundred words. You write a letter to a friend and it's eight hundred words." Soon after he left *Time*, he turned down a column offer from the *New York Times* because books were what drove him. And after *Boys* the books came at a steady pace.

A 1973 anthology, *How the Weather Was*, came first, showcasing Kahn's magazine work. In 1976 *Sports Illustrated* gave him a dream assignment: spend a summer watching baseball wherever he wanted. The result, *A Season in the Sun*, finds Kahn visiting Dodgers owner Walter O'Malley in Los Angeles; watching Little League baseball in Puerto Rico; and going to church in Portland, Oregon, with Artie Wilson, a black ballplayer who never got a shot at the majors but who longed, even in old age, to coach for a team. The Wilson story continued Kahn's career-long outrage at how major-league baseball has treated people of color. "The integrating of this country," Kahn insists, "begins with Jackie Robinson, not Rosa Parks." Kahn's passion for racial justice is difficult to explain. He did not have a particularly religious upbringing. He did suffer minor anti-Semitic slights growing up, and he believed the column snub from *Newsweek* was because he was a Jew. This made him more sympathetic to the Dodgers' players of color. Kahn explains his passion for Jackie Robinson simply: "It was only right. It was only fair to let him play." Robinson telephoned Kahn soon after *Boys of Summer* became a bestseller. "You son of a bitch," he said. "Why am I a son of a bitch, Robinson?" Kahn replied. "Your damn book has my telephone ringing all the time. I get no peace," the fifty-three-year-old Robinson said. "Some of them called me an Uncle Tom for working for white bosses. Now they're finding out I wasn't an Uncle Tom after all because of your damn book." When Robinson died soon after

Boys was published, Kahn repeatedly wrote—and told on the lecture circuit—Robinson's inspiring story. "I was pleased that my book had made him current again in the last summer that he would know," he says. In 1987 Kahn entered the eye of the storm when, on a nationally televised news program commemorating Robinson, he prompted Al Campanis, a Dodgers executive, to say that blacks lacked the "necessities" to be major-league managers. Although given the chance, Campanis refused to retract his statement. Incensed, Kahn fired at Campanis, "Oh, I get it, Al. Blacks have the ability to work in the cotton fields, but not to manage a baseball team." Campanis was promptly fired, but Kahn had raised pointedly the question of racism in sports. As for *A Season in the Sun*, it was a critical and sales success. Writing in the *New York Times*, Donald Hall found the book "thick with the old virtues."

Journalists always dream of writing great fiction. Some—like Stephen Crane and Ernest Hemingway—actually succeed. In the wake of his nonfiction success, Kahn wrote two novels in the late 1970s. His most serious stab at fiction came in 1979 when in *But Not to Keep* he took up divorce and child custody, a painful subject for Kahn, who has been married four times and has three children. His first marriage of thirteen years ended in 1963; his second marriage in 1974. "It's the novel I really wanted to do," he says, and it garnered favorable reviews. The title is taken from a Robert Frost poem about a World War I soldier who comes home, injured, but then returns to war. His wife did not get to keep him. Kahn's book is about weekend visits by a child of divorce. One critic saw "anxious, self-dramatizing filler," but another saw a "sensitive, honest, credible" first novel. Writing about divorce was painful, Kahn concedes, but "nothing is going to be any harder than writing about Pee Wee dying or Jackie's kid dying." A second novel about baseball, *The Seventh Game*, came in 1982, focusing on an aging pitcher, forty-one-year-old John Lee Longboat, whose entire life comes down to one pitch in the seventh game of the World Series. (Longboat's opponent hits a home run, by the way, and his team loses, while Longboat leaves his lover and stays true to his wife.) The novel can be ribald at times, and it is a throwback to earlier models of baseball fiction. The critics were less than kind. "It became apparent that the American public was not waiting for my novel," Kahn says without a trace of bitterness.

And so he turned back—with little regret—to what he knew best: baseball. "This is my instrument, my violin," Kahn says. "If I try to do something else like play the flute, it may not come out as good. I don't tire at all of the game because I'm a fan of people and can always find good people to root for and write about." More important, says Kahn, "Baseball is a reasonably good metaphor for what is going on around us. It works for me to do a baseball setting and then go and do larger things." In the next seven years Kahn wrote four books—a gauzy collection of anecdotes about Joe DiMaggio and Marilyn Monroe; a controversial book on baseball's all-time hit leader, Pete Rose, begun before he went to prison for tax evasion; a history of pitchers and pitching; and a memorable account of the summer of 1983, when Kahn owned a minor-league baseball team, the Utica Blue Sox. In *Good Enough to Dream* sportswriter Kahn becomes a full-fledged character. A friend thought Kahn should try managing a team and then write about it, but Kahn opted to own one instead. The resulting book chronicles a magical summer with a charming cast of youthful players, a gritty manager, and Kahn's sixteen-year-old daughter, who worked for the Blue Sox. Hollywood could not have provided a better script. The Sox win the New York–Penn League championship with a grand late-season finale. As novelist George V. Higgins commented: "This is the way stories are supposed to be. Especially stories about baseball . . . people struggling against adversity . . . people conquering weaknesses . . . dedication and courage . . . and they should have splendid writers on the scene." Wrote Christopher Lehmann-Haupt in the *New York Times*: "Except for the lack of a nostalgic dimension . . . one could call it as good a book as *The Boys of Summer*; and since this reader was never much of a Brooklyn fan, he's willing to call it a better book than the one about the Dodgers." *Good Enough to Dream* was named the best baseball book of 1985.

The joy of baseball soon turned to torment, however, when Kahn's twenty-two-year-old son, Roger Laurence, committed suicide in July of 1987. Kahn was in the middle of his next project: a ghostwritten account of the life of the Cincinnati Reds' Pete Rose, who had broken Ty Cobb's all-time hit record the previous season and was ready to retire. For the first time in his professional life Kahn could not write. Not that writing had ever been easy. "When you get to the end of a book, you are so tired intellectually, so tired emotionally and maybe physically, that you may think, oh, I can't go through that again," Kahn says. "It's a woman in labor. You've just given birth and it hurts like hell." His son's death was worse. He played tennis and moped before finally resuming work. He had ghostwritten before, early in his career, writing articles for Jackie Robinson and Hall of Fame pitcher Early Wynn, and then a book for actor Mickey Rooney. This was different. Kahn was now too famous to simply fade into the background. Thus, the book's dominant voice had to be Kahn's, with Rose providing recollections and vignettes. The project turned into a nightmare. When he was almost finished writing, Kahn learned that Rose was under federal investigation. Rose and his attorneys clammed up, cutting off Kahn. After that, Rose and his fiduciaries flat-out lied. Still, he produced the book, which included his own painstaking investigation of baseball's case against Rose ("persuasive in spots" but "overall . . . an unconvincing mix of allegation and distortion," Kahn concluded). By the time the book appeared, Rose had been banned from baseball and was sentenced to prison. "The best thing about [the book's] reception," Kahn wrote sardonically in the *Los Angeles Times*, "was that nobody sent me a letter bomb."

The Rose book, however, made something else clear about Kahn: while he is known largely as a literary journalist, he can also be a hardnosed reporter. He put aside storytelling to scrutinize the allegations made against Rose, calling it "the hardest reporting job of my life." For *Boys of Summer* he dug into old newspaper archives to find the facts. In *The Era: 1947–1957, When the Yankees, the Giants, and the Dodgers Ruled the World* (1993), Kahn turned historian, placing New York baseball of the post–World War II and Eisenhower eras in a cultural context. The book, which is only ostensibly about baseball, earned Kahn his first Pulitzer Prize nomination. *The Era* also whetted Kahn's appetite for a non-baseball book that had been kicking around in his head ever since he went a mock round of boxing with Jack Dempsey in the former world heavyweight champion's Manhattan restaurant. Dempsey, champ from 1919 to 1926, was a pioneer of modern boxing and one of the toughest men ever to enter the ring. "I was looking at my old notes," Kahn recalled, "and I saw all this stuff on Dempsey," who Kahn had interviewed many times. The 1920s are mostly associated with Babe Ruth, but two other sports figures—Dempsey and tennis player Bill Tilden—were also icons of the Jazz Age. And off he went into book number sixteen, the life and times of Dempsey, in which Kahn the historian mastered another era of American sport and the wild 1920s. Con men, gangsters, prostitutes, and starlets inhabit his Prohibition-era story, as do sportswriters Grantland Rice, Ring Lardner, and Damon Runyon. The result is Kahn's favorite book, *A Flame of Pure Fire: Jack Dempsey and the Roaring '20s*. "This is quite simply Kahn's finest work since he made *The Boys of Summer* part of the language," wrote Ron Fimrite of *Sports Illustrated*.

I first met Roger Kahn after the Dempsey book was completed and as *October Men* was awaiting publication. I first saw him speak in public in the fall of 2001 when I invited him to address journalism classes at SUNY at New Paltz. I was nervous. I did not know if my students could relate to this writer who was more than fifty years their senior. As I prepped the students I became more fearful. They could not tell me who Robert Frost was, nor did they really understand the significance of Jackie Robinson. *The Boys of Summer* was published fifteen years before they were even born. Mentioning Ebbets Field brought blank stares, even from my Brooklyn students. We crowded into a ninth-floor lounge with a spectacular view that overlooked the Shawangunk Mountains. I introduced Kahn as the best and most well-known sports writer in America—sure to bring argument, but close enough to the truth that I could get away with it.

After adjusting his hearing aid, Kahn stood in front of a small wooden lectern. Without hesitation, he launched into a discussion of a controversy that was swirling around retired Dodger pitcher Sandy Koufax. Was he gay? Did a new biography of the Hall of Fame left-hander ignore this possibility? Do publishers today have the guts to explore the question? Is the question even relevant? Kahn had the students' attention. Soon he was telling a story about the infamous dugout fight between Reggie Jackson and Billy Martin in 1977, which led him directly to *October Men*, his eighteenth book, which was due out in a few months. The students peppered him with baseball questions. Did he like the designated hitter rule? Why didn't he ever write about the Mets? What did he think of escalating baseball salaries? Kahn, who expected questions on writing, answered dutifully, but he kept coming back to what he always comes back to—social history. He deftly managed to slide into a Jackie Robinson story. The room was hushed, just as it would be at the Unison Arts Center months later. Many years ago, Kahn said, he was preparing to go to a ceremony in Boston to honor Robinson. Kahn was the keynote speaker. Before he left home he asked his son, Gordon, now a successful architect, what he should say. Gordon had met Robinson at his Connecticut home when Gordon was very young. Hearing that the youngster was interested in architecture, Robinson gave him a tour of his rambling stone house. "Just tell them," Gordon said, "that Robinson was kind to a young boy many years ago, and that the boy still remembers that kindness." I stepped in as Kahn finished the story to the quiet audience. He was choked up. The students were surprised. Their professors don't usually cry in class. One student, Sean Endress, who is not a sports fan, wrote to me later that Kahn made him realize the "importance of personal anecdotes and storytelling in sustaining human connections." Endress was surprised at all the nodding and smiling faces as Kahn mentioned Casey Stengel, Pete Rose, and the Brooklyn Dodgers. Kahn's "layering of stories evoked [in me] nostalgia and a longing to be part of something bigger than myself," noted Endress, who likened Kahn to "a wise old tribesman bestowing folk legends upon a new generation." The "old tribesman" shrugged and smiled when I showed him Endress's comments. I had to look to the last line in his book *A Season in the Sun* to find an appropriate Kahn response. He wrote: "If I have sustained one overwhelming objective across my eight decades, it has been to create writing that achieves beauty." Read the collection of articles and book chapters that follows and you are bound to agree.

Rob Miraldi

Stone Ridge, New York

PART I

GROWING UP AND BEING YOUNG

CHAPTER 1

A FATHER, A SON, AND BASEBALL IN BROOKLYN

Ebbets Field in Brooklyn was, as Kahn has called it, "the shrine," a ballpark and a civic rallying point for Brooklyn residents until the Dodgers moved to Los Angeles in 1957. More important, however, it was the place where fathers and sons bonded for generations. Kahn recalls and captures an impending visit to the ballpark with his father, Gordon Jacques, in this excerpt from his 1997 memoir, Memories of Summer.

I saw my first World Series game in 1920, seven years before I was born. The viewing instrument was my father, who relished baseball and had so vivid a memory that friends called him, somewhat laboriously it now seems to me, The Walking Encyclopedia.

We were indeed walking along Prospect Avenue, a quiet Brooklyn street, under sycamore trees with peeling, patchy bark, and fruit clusters abrim with itching powder. Far back from the bluestone sidewalk, large homes sprawled behind shields of hydrangea bushes and spiked, iron fences—immobile vigilantes in a neighborhood without crime.

My mother had banished us into the springtime for violating a rule: no ball playing in the house. All mothers in that generation said no ball playing in the house. All mothers also said, "Take off those sneakers. Take them off at once! Don't you know that sneakers are bad for your feet?"

My father had decided to show me how to spin a breaking ball, and winding up in a long hallway—I wore Buster Brown oxfords, not sneakers—I turned out to have more wrist snap than control. The gray rubber ball slipped off my fingers and slammed into one wall, ricocheted into the other, and went crashing along the hardwood floor. All that machine-gun racket summoned my mother from her book, which I believe was *Leaves of Grass*. A covey of Brooklyn mothers was rediscovering Walt Whitman that season, and homes like ours resounded with the poet's sometimes mournful tread. *Grass*, I knew, because my mother recited the lines, is the beautiful uncut hair of graves.

Outside I was not certain if my father had decided on a destination. One particular dream seemed too extravagant. More immediately, I had no idea what conversational paths my father, the walking encyclopedia, would navigate this sunlit afternoon.

Ginkgo trees. That was his topic on the previous Saturday. Ginkgo trees grew in Brooklyn, but did not originate there. They were found first in eastern China. They had vanished from the forests but remained on the grounds of temples. These odd trees, with fan-shaped leaves, right here on Prospect Place, probably had religious significance in old Cathay, during the time of Marco Polo, and what did I think about that?

Nothing, really, except that ginkgo was a funny-sounding name. I was seven years old. It was nice to walk with Dad, and I wanted to make an effort to show that I shared his interest in natural wonders.

"If you put a grizzly bear and a Bengal tiger in the same cage at the Prospect Park Zoo, and they got into a fight, which one would win, the grizzly bear or the Bengal tiger?"

My father was short, green-eyed, bald, mustached, powerful, and he smiled and looked into the distance. "Nature," he said, "is red in tooth and claw." Then he began to tell me about the sycamores.

I seem to remember a great deal about the trees of Brooklyn, but I merely tolerated the arboreal lectures, if a seven-year-old can be said to tolerate a parent, in the hope that my father would veer away from botany. He played third base for City College, covering, he said, "a dime, or on a good day a quarter." The coach valued him for his bat, I suppose. Whenever I watched my father play weekend baseball, he walloped long drives over and beyond left center field that thrilled and awed me. At some point, when I was very young, I decided that there was nothing I wanted to do in life as much as I wanted to hit long, high drives over and beyond left center field, like my father. Through six decades—births and deaths, bonanzas and busts, wars, divorce, and even the absurdity of major-league labor strikes—that part of me has never changed.

Squealing with the steel wheels rolling on steel tracks, the Nostrand Avenue trolley rattled across our path. Unlike the trolleys in Manhattan that rode over submerged electrical lines, Brooklyn trolley cars drew power from an overhead cable. A sort of crane rose from the top of the Brooklyn trolleys, maintaining contact with the high cable unless the trolley swung around a turn too rapidly. Then the crane broke away from the high cable, losing contact in a crackle of sparks. The motorman had to dismount and reposition the crane, a delicate process, often conducted over a background of "godammit," and worse.

"Wee Willie Keeler drove a trolley car," my father said. We were crossing Nostrand in the wake of the trolley. "Little bit of a fellow, Keeler, but he almost always hit .300. If you put a gray derby upside down on the green grass in right field, Keeler could slap a line drive into the hat. Quite a batsman, but when he was finished he had to go to work as a trolley motorman."

My heart leaped up. This was not going to be another ginkgo tree perambulation. This walk would shine with baseball talk. My father's strides became urgent. Periodically, I had to shift from walk to canter matching his lurching pace. I would happily have sustained a full gallop to talk baseball with my father. That part of me never changed either, for as long as he was on the earth. There was nobody I enjoyed talking baseball with as much as this green-eyed, strong-armed, gentle, fierce, mustached, long-ball hitting, walking encyclopedia who was my father.

Touches of sad far-off days still linger. Diffident and soft-spoken men approached my father on our walks and offered him boxes of pencils for a dime. His green eyes softened and he found the dime, but he never accepted the pencils. Every Sunday the *New York Times* published a sepia picture section called the rotogravure, after a particular printing process, and from time to time momentous photographs appeared: Benito

Mussolini, the jet-jawed "Sawdust Caesar"; pipe-smoking, avuncular, oddly ominous Joseph Stalin; a sort of landscape-smoke rising from a Chinese village after Japanese soldiers had ravaged the houses and the people. The Depression reigned and the dictators were rising.

One day a deferential bald-headed man came to the door selling paper flowers cleverly folded in brightly colored little pots. He told my father that he had been a businessman in Germany and that he had opposed the Nazis and one day the Brownshirts came and broke his shop windows and struck him with clubs and terrorized his wife. My father bought a dozen of the little pots with paper flowers. It was natural to miss your homeland, my father said to the refugee flower salesman, but his decision to leave Nazi Germany might in the end turn out to be a good one. America was the land of opportunity.

The salesman said, in a confessional tone, "But I am Jewish."

My father blinked. "Even so," he said, "this is the land of opportunity."

I mention such matters to suggest aspects of the world in which my father and I lived when I was seven. I listened as hard as I could to geopolitical conversations, but my ability to contribute was nonexistent, except for certain questions.

"Why didn't you take the poor man's pencils, Dad?"

"Because now he can sell them to someone who really needs them."

"What are Brownshirts?"

"Hooligans. German hooligans. A bad lot."

I wanted to do more than ask questions. I wanted to understand the world around me and to be respected as a person capable of understanding. My father understood everything. That was why people called him The Walking Encyclopedia. I wanted to be like my father. I wanted to enter the world of men. Baseball became my magic portal.

A game of catch is a complicated communication. The father has the stronger arm, the surer hands. The child has the enthusiasm, a passionate hope that his ballplaying will improve, and something immediate to find out. The first time a baseball bounces against your shin, or pops out of your glove into your cheekbone, you learn the presiding reality of the sport. The ball is hard. After that, you make a decision.

Is the pain the ball inflicts worth the pleasure of playing the game? Pain and pleasure, the stuff of love and life, runs strong in baseball.

I don't remember consciously deciding to play ball, but I knew boys who made decisions *not* to play. "Baseball is boring," one said. I sensed that it was not boredom at all, but fright, dominating hard-ball terror, that led him to choose kick-the-can, or stoop tag, or other city games where pain did not lurk disguised as a one-hop grounder.

In childhood I suffered on Ferris wheels, particularly in the jiggling cars that swung on rails high over Coney Island and threatened to launch you into the Atlantic. Large Airedales alarmed me. But I was not afraid of a baseball. The passion to play dominated my spirit, that and the distinct but overlapping passion to win the good opinion of my father. He hit grounders at me in a dozen sandlots, ten thousand grounders in dusty, city fields. The governing discipline was severe. To subdue a grounder you have to watch the ball, watch it from the bat, watch it skim and bounce, watch it right into your glove. But that exposes your face and a baseball can glance off a pebble and zoom into your teeth, like a micro version of one of today's smart bombs. You see it suddenly, mouth-high, and feel the ball at the same instant. The baseball feels like a concrete punch. After a few of these blows, you may want to lift your face as a grounder approaches. Except . . . except . . . that way you lose sight of the ball. You'll miss it then, sure as the ball is round. You have to keep your glove low and you have to look the zipping baseball into your glove, or else you'll hear the teasing cry: "You played every bounce right except the last one." You need equal measures of concentration and courage. When I stayed with a nasty grounder—and my father saw me stay with its final, hostile hop—I felt I had achieved something worthy of pride.

The fly ball was another kind of dragon. A child's first tendency is to run at a ball in the air; the heartless baseball then sails over his head. Although this causes no physical pain, it can raise another cry, "How come you're standing over *here*, when the ball bounced over *there*?" The psyche grimaces.

My father began fly-ball drills with soft, arcing tosses, gradually increasing height and range. Then he took a bat and tapped gentle fungos, explaining with great formality that "fungo" is one English word whose origin not even Noah Webster knew. When a baseball carries long, you want to turn. You should not run backwards; that is both awkward and slow. You spot the ball and turn and run to the point where it will descend. If you can determine where it will descend. That is a tricky business, and one of the wonders of major-league ball is the way outfielders run down 350-foot drives and make the play seem easy. I possessed no native gift for judging fly balls, but when I did succeed in running down a long one and taking it over my shoulder, my father beamed and said, "Good catch." The praise spoke banners; I worked harder to win those words, "Good catch," than I ever worked at homework or piano lessons. My mother noticed and she never forgot nor, until almost the end of a long life, did she ever entirely forgive my father, myself, or baseball.

We crossed Franklin Avenue and my father abruptly turned left, stirring in me a thrill of hope. "The records say that Keeler batted .432 in the 1890s," he said, "but the game was played differently then. The ball was dead. Batters poked instead of swinging from the heels. Just about the only way you hit a home run was when one of the outfielders fell down."

"Running backwards," I said, "instead of turning and taking the ball over your shoulder can make you fall down in the outfield."

"Conceivably," my father said. He pressed his lips together to suppress a grin, and I could see that he was pleased. "The most solid Brooklyn hitter in the modern game was Zack Wheat, who came from Missouri. He's a motorcycle cop in the Midwest these days. He was a terrific left-hand-hitting outfielder who had a singular trait. Waiting for the pitch, Buck—we called Zack Wheat 'Buck'—waggled his back leg. Then he'd wallop a line drive off the right-field wall."

Zack Wheat was Buck Wheat. How bountiful is the trove of baseball nicknames.

We passed St. John's Place and Lincoln Place, walking alongside four-story apartments, tenements really, with street-level shops selling fish and stationery and toys. At length we reached Eastern Parkway, a broad avenue with six lanes of traffic and two access roads, set behind pedestrian pathways and green benches and rows of newly pruned sycamores. This distinctive boulevard was patterned after the Champs Elysees, including at its font, Grand Army Plaza, an imposing monument for the Union war dead, modeled on the Arc de Triomphe.

"Brooklyn had a pitcher once," my father said, "a left-hander named Nap Rucker. Nap stood for Napoleon. He threw the slowest slowball in the world."

"If his pitches were so slow, why didn't everybody hit them? If he threw that slowly, I could have hit him, right?"

"Wrong. Nap Rucker had a deceptive windup. He made the batters think he was rearing back for a fastball. Then, after all that motion, he threw the slow one. Everybody missed the slowball because they had been completely and utterly fooled. Missed the slowball or popped it up."

I needed half an Eastern Parkway block to assimilate that. Pitching was more than throwing fast and accurately. You were also trying to confuse the hitters. You made it look as though you were going to throw fast and then you threw a slowball. You could make it look as though you were going to throw slow and fire the fastball. I got the idea. I didn't actually have a fastball when I was seven years old, but I believed one would appear in time through an unusual mix—practice and spontaneous generation. Then I'd like to try that deception stuff, fooling the hitters with crafty slow ones, and blowing them out of town with my unborn fastball.

"Dazzy Vance in his prime had a different trick," my father said. "For seven years he was the best strikeout pitcher in the league. Vance wore a long undershirt and he took a scissors and cut slits in the right sleeve. It ran clear down to the wrist. When Vance pitched, the long sleeve flapped. It was a white sleeve and the hitters had one heck of a time seeing that white baseball coming out of that white sleeve. Before they knew it, the fastball was in the catcher's mitt. Strike three."

"He's out," I said.

We reached the busy intersection of Eastern Parkway and Bedford Avenue, a street that ran almost the entire length of Brooklyn, from the cramped treeless blocks of Williamsburg into affluent Flatbush, before coming to its end near the fishing boats that docked at Sheepshead Bay. "If the Dodgers had all these good players," I said. I paused to savor the ballplayers' names: Wee Willie Keeler. Zack Wheat. Buck Wheat. Nap Rucker. Dazzy Vance.

"If the Dodgers had all these good players, why is it that Brooklyn never wins the World Series, like the Giants and the Yankees?"

My father slowed his stride. "That's quite a long story," he said.

I had asked a defining question about an era. *Cartago delenda est.* Carthage must be destroyed. As I would later learn in a tower classroom at Erasmus Hall, Cato's repeated declaration defined an era in Rome. Why can't the Dodgers win the World Series? That question spoke to the core of early- and mid-twentieth-century life in Brooklyn.

Brooklyn was settled in 1636 by adventurous Dutch farmers, whose descendants named their academy after the Reformation scholar, Desiderius Erasmus. The English seized Brooklyn in 1664 and Brooklyn was the site, in August 1776, of the Battle of Long Island, a vital defensive action in one of George Washington's strategic retreats.

By 1890, the population exceeded 835,000 and Brooklyn had become a boomtown, storing grain, milling coffee, and manufacturing barrels, shoes, machine tools, chemicals, and paints. Then on January 1, 1898, a date of limited infamy, the leaders of Brooklyn forgot the legacy of Washington and surrendered their independence. Brooklyn became a borough, nothing more, in New York City. Ridicule followed. Brooklynites were said to talk funny, or in the patois tawk funny. They pronounced "earl" as "oil." They pronounced "oil" as "earl." And how, down by the Gowanus Canal, did people say, "The Earl just changed his oil?"

The humor was relentlessly denigrating, and largely unfair. You heard the so-called Brooklyn accent in spades, strident spades, mouthed in Hell's Kitchen, on the west side of Manhattan. The real Brooklyn was a place of wooded parks and white sand beaches, neighborhoods, libraries, and decidedly preppy schools. The perceived Brooklyn was a group of stumpy characters, tawkin' funny and trowin' nickel cigars into an open manhole. At best, some said, Brooklyn was Manhattan's bedroom. Brooklynites were born, lived, slept, made love, and died in the figurative shadow cast by the towers of Manhattan. The denigration nurtured paranoia in the Brooklyn psyche. Presently, the focus for a grand assortment of paranoid anxieties became a baseball team peopled by athletes as splendid as Zack Wheat and Dazzy Vance, that still, somehow, *how long, oh, Lord, how long,* could never win the World Series.

My father turned left at Bedford Avenue. Anticipation gave me a clutch in the throat.

"Could we?"

"If you don't tell your mother."

"I promise. Why can't I tell her?"

"She doesn't want you being spoiled."

"Who's pitching?"

"Mungo."

I knew a bit about the mighty right-hander with the name from an ancient Mongol court. Mungo. Van Lingle Mungo. I loved to roll that name along my tongue. With his huge kick and his mighty fastball, Mungo could strike out anybody, anybody at all, Mel Ott or "Ducky Wucky" Medwick. Strike out anybody at all, if he didn't walk him.

"Boston is starting Fred Frankhouse. His specialty is the old round-house curve. We have an interesting matchup—a big strong fastball pitcher against a man with a sweeping roundhouse curve."

We were walking downhill. The street was paved with cobblestones. I could see, from my walking trot, the roof of Ebbets Field and, atop the roof, the flags, the many-colored flags, the flapping flags that meant Ball Game Today.

CHAPTER 2

COMING OF AGE

With tongue in cheek and a novelist's eye for detail and characterization, Kahn goes to New Jersey to observe a Bar Mitzvah, as a thirteen-year-old reaches the age of religious duty and responsibility but has to put up with the comical and boorish behavior of relatives. This chapter from The Passionate People *in 1968 brought Kahn some angry mail.*

There are no poets in this enormous room; no poets, painters, or novelists. The closest one comes to a literary critic is brushing the downy, thrice-braceleted arm of a full-busted lady whose defense of Sam Levinson's *Everything but Money* was published in the letters column of a Sunday newspaper book supplement. We are in the great banquet hall of Temple Beth-El (Place of God) standing beneath one of a matched pair of crystal chandeliers so delicate that each year Temple Beth-El administrators fly in two artisans from Switzerland to clean them. We are attending the Bar Mitzvah reception of Michael Farberman, aged thirteen, who lives in a homogeneous, heavily Jewish suburb of New York. Mike is a brown-haired, medium bright, freckled, pleasant, and increasingly weary young man.

In the tradition of roughly seven centuries, boys are initiated into "the full practice of Jewish faith" at the age of thirteen by becoming Bar Mitzvah. The term mixes Aramaic (Bar) and Hebrew. It means Son of the Commandment. A Jewish boy who becomes Bar Mitzvah accepts the full responsibilities of following the commandments of his God. Early this October Saturday, Michael, his younger sister Lanie, and his parents Max and Barbara Farberman drove to Temple Beth-El for the regular 10 A.M. Sabbath service. Although Jews who interpret certain religious codes rigorously do not drive on a Sabbath, Rabbi Martin Blochman of Temple Beth-El has decreed that "the exigencies of transportation in the suburbs make Sabbath driving to Temple permissible. Frivolous driving, however, should be avoided as far as possible."

The Farbermans rode in their Oldsmobile Toronado, midnight blue, with four on the floor. Max Farberman is founder and president of The Fly-Ban Screen Door Company, a business he began fourteen years ago when the storm window company, for which he worked as a salesman, went bankrupt. Designing most of the doors himself and selling all of them himself in the beginning, Max Farberman has built Fly-Ban into a corporation with a $930,000 annual gross. A poor boy once, raised without formal religious training, Mr. Farberman now donates $1,250 every year to Temple Beth-El. "I hope eventually to make it even more," he says, "the good Lord and the stock market willing."

The temple is six years old. It was designed by a firm specializing in contemporary synagogue architecture and presents a busy front to the four-lane islanded parkway that runs close by. The basic material, buff brick, is supplemented with panels of stone, stained glass, and wood. "Jewish baroque," one of the younger congregants calls it. Inside, in the foyer, Max Farberman's name appears on a large bronze plaque that lists twenty-five leading contributors to the original building fund. Glass cases stand against the foyer walls. Two display religious objects, ranging from a massive bronze menorah to tiny wooden spice boxes used in a ritual that marks the end of the Sabbath. A discreet sign reminds: "All these objects available for purchase through the Temple Sisterhood, for benefit of Temple Fund." A third englassed case displays books. Here, above Herbert Gold's *Father* and Molly Goldberg's *Jewish Cookbook*, rests an aged, gold-lettered Haggadah—a book of instructions for the Passover meal. The illuminated manuscript is not for sale.

Michael and his family paused in the foyer for ten minutes this morning to greet relatives. Seventeen were there. They came from four separate suburbs and New York City itself and they represented six different congregations. As they shouted greetings to one another Michael stood silently against the case offering the bronze menorah. He felt partly confused and partly frightened. Barbara, his mother, went from relative to relative, with embraces. "Darling," she cried. "Oh, Ben. It's simply marvelous, Nancy. How thrilling of you to come. It will make Michael very happy." Aunt Nancy Farberman, sturdy but not plump, spotted Michael and charged. "Well, well, well," she called, "the Bar Mitzvah boy!"

Michael hunched his shoulders and cringed. Nancy pinched his right cheek and said, "So, my little Mike, whom I knew as a baby and wheeled in his carriage. So. You are a man. Huh? A mensch." "Hope so, Aunt Nancy," Michael said, and began studying the bronze menorah.

As always, Rabbi Blochman opened the Sabbath service with prayers in English and in Hebrew. All the congregation joined the rabbi in chanting. Michael's Bar Mitzvah was a minor part of the Sabbath service but he had to sit on the platform alongside Rabbi Blochman's pulpit where everyone at temple could see him. His lips moved constantly. He was repeating over and over to himself the Hebrew words that he would have to say. The rabbi proceeded briskly. More prayers and singing. Then the rabbi read from the Torah.

When the rabbi had almost concluded, he nodded at Michael, who marched to his place beside the pulpit. Michael inhaled hard twice, gulping air so close to the microphone that a gasping sound issued from eight concealed loudspeakers in the synagogue. The whispering of congregants rushed up to Michael as a threat. Loudly, then, to still the sound; flatly, in the accents of New York; fluttering, in the inconstant octaves of puberty, Michael spoke the great Jewish benediction: "*Baruch ata Adonai. Elohenu melech ha-olam asher . . .*"

He had not silenced them with his Hebrew. The whispers still rose. Michael glumly turned to the pages from the Haftorah.

"*Eliahu ha-navi,*" Michael began. *Elisha the Prophet.* He read the rest in English. As Rabbi Blochman put it, Michael's eighteen months of

Hebrew lessons "didn't take," and the rabbi thought it would be best for everyone if "young Mike" read the Haftorah in translation. The point, the essence of Bar Mitzvah, was for the boy to participate in the fullness of Jewish practice, whatever the language, the rabbi said. Jewish practice had meant not only Hebrew but at different times Portuguese, Spanish, even German. "So why not English?" Rabbi Blochman said.

Michael's voice was surer now, but staccato and still flat. He was concluding: *Then she went in and fell at his feet, and bowed herself to the ground, and took up her son, and went out.*

He grinned. He couldn't help himself. He had participated. It was over. He was Bar Mitzvah.

With practiced paternalism Rabbi Blochman clutched both of Michael's shoulders. Karl Wasserman, M.D., president of the Temple Beth-El Men's Club, strode to the pulpit and presented a large black Bible, embossed in gold letters, *Michael Eli Farberman*. Michael, now a Bar Mitzvah, sat down and Rabbi Blochman began a sermon on "the art of growing old with grace and faith." To one of the women, whispering in a front pew, "It sounds like having an affair with a couple of aging Quakers."

All that was earlier. Now, in the temple ballroom, it is six o'clock and the gentle weather has held, and all of Michael's family is there, twenty-two persons, except for Aunt Paula, who has phlebitis. The mixed clan of Farbermans and Steinbergs, a professional photographer named Katzman, five musicians including bandleader Buddy Arrow, eight waitresses in red-and-black blouses and skirts, four busboys in tuxedo pants, three cooks, two chefs, a salad man, the personal catering supervisor of Harry Aaron's Kosher Katerers, Inc., two bartenders costumed to match the waitresses, Rabbi and Mrs. Stanley A. Blochman, 120 carefully chosen guests, are gathered in the enormous ballroom of Temple Beth-El to help Michael celebrate his own Bar Mitzvah. Michael feels better than he did in the morning. The worst of it, the Hebrew, is behind him.

Brown-haired, freckled Mike stands somewhat stiffly between his parents, contending with an army of mercenaries, arrayed in a reception line. He is proud of his new charcoal sports jacket and its silver-colored buttons. The line stretches farther than he can see.

The men, when they approach, clutch Michael's hand. The women hug him. With most of the handshakes Michael is given an envelope containing a check. Michael says thank you and grins and says thank you again. After a little while, he begins to have trouble remembering the names of the grown-ups, even of the grown-ups he likes. He places each envelope in a side pocket of the new charcoal jacket. Before a quarter of the line has passed, the pockets bulge. The jacket assumes a hippy, wealthy look.

Katzman the cameraman and his portable lights piece out faces in the greeting line without tolerance. The movie camera whirs. The hot lights blaze. Some of the guests are annoyed but one plump, florid man stares into the camera and winks. Then he taps his wife and orders, "Hey, Belle, I want you should look, too."

"Look? Me look?" says Belle. She is blonde as straw. She could be thirty-seven or fifty-five. "Why should I look, Sam?" Belle says. "You know I take a terrible picture."

Two bars are manned. The real one is doing a moderate business with premade martinis and the caterer's private brand of eighty-proof Scotch. The women prefer sours, and blended whiskey and ginger ale. Adjacent is a smaller bar, under a little sign reading: "The Bar's Bar." Lemonade, a purple punch, and pink Shirley Temple cocktails are served to Michael's contemporaries, boys and girls.

The room fills quickly with prosperous, enthusiastic people, buzzing and boisterous. A crowd gathers around Michael's Uncle Sandy Farberman, who is a vice president of The Fly-Ban Screen Door Company and likes to tell jokes.

"So the ambassador has to go on a secret mission to Geneva," Uncle Sandy is saying, "and on the way he gets lost in the Alps. It could happen, if he used the CIA as guides." This is the pre-joke joke. It demands a snicker.

"So a rescue party goes out to look for the ambassador, calling 'Goldberg, Goldberg, Goldberg, Red Cross!'

"So finally near the top of the highest mountain in Switzerland they hear a faint answering holler." Uncle Sandy cups his hands to ready his mountain call. Then he softly cries his punch line: " 'I g-a-a-ve at the office!' "

Uncle Sanford had meant to be a comedian. He played dates at small clubs on Ocean Avenue in Brooklyn and he spent a summer as an emcee in the Catskill Mountains, but in the end it hadn't worked out. The big break, as he puts it, never came. So he sold screen doors. What could he do? Was it so terrible? For tonight at least Uncle Sandy is an emcee again, at the Bar Mitzvah reception of his nephew, Michael.

Barbara Farberman, brunette, hard-eyed, wide-mouthed but pretty, has escaped from the receiving station. She breaks into the little circle and stands beside Sanford. "I think now, Sanford," Barbara says.

"Yeh, yeh, Babs," Uncle Sanford says. He drapes an arm around her, urging her toward him, and looks deep into the hard mysterious eyes. "If you weren't my sister-in-law," he says.

Barbara leans toward him rigidly. His hand slides toward her bottom. "Please," Barbara says, sharply. "Now." She claps a hand on his, which is just below her waist. She spins away.

"Okay, okay, why not now?" Uncle Sanford says. He turns and walks to a microphone standing near the head table.

"Ladies and gentlemen," Uncle Sanford says, "and I even include all goyim in that remark, ladies and gentlemen." An amplified voice is authority. The ballroom quiets. "I know there is still some Scotch not drunk but my hostess and yours, the beautiful Mrs. Barbara Farberman, has asked me to make the following announcement of great gustatorial—whatsa matter? You didn't know I went to college—importance."

Uncle Sanford steps back from the microphone and bellows: "Places everybody! Places!" The guests surge toward where the food will be.

This is the critical moment for Barbara Farberman. Arranging the seating plan was her ordeal, her Hebrew lesson. Actually, she wanted fifteen or twenty tables but her husband Max made her settle for twelve. "It'll go to fifteen hundred even that way," he told her. So, aside from the head table, she had twelve others to work with. Eleven really. One was taken up by children. "Considering our circle," she told Max, "eleven tables doesn't give me very much. It isn't as if we were only starting out. We happen to have a certain position in the community."

He was adamant. He could be a regular mule about money, as if they didn't have plenty, as if they were poor. So she had to work with only eleven tables. Well, that made correct groupings even more important.

The seating was more difficult than selecting the invitations. For those she took the trouble to go to Cartier's in New York. You could make a mistake in Cartier's? Not likely. Not likely at all.

In the ballroom of Temple Beth-El, the guests find their table numbers printed inside the glossy programs supplied by Aaron's Kosher Katerers. Barbara tries to see how things are working out. Doctor Moskowitz sits down before his wife. They must have had a fight. Why tonight? Why isn't she nicer to him? No, he's smiling; it is going to be all right. It would have been terrible if they'd picked tonight to fight.

The head table, placed on a raised platform, is reserved for Michael's immediate family and Rabbi and Mrs. Blochman. Almost all the other tables are full; the room is loud with creak of chairs, clang of silverware, and voices. Then Uncle Sanford barks a command into the microphone: "Everybody rise." Slowly, before a standing audience, the Farbermans themselves start toward the head table. Someone applauds. Someone else says, "Ssh!" The time for applause will come later.

Michael walks behind his father, head down. He has given his father all the envelopes. His pockets are empty now, but the new charcoal jacket and Michael's hair are rumpled beyond redemption.

Uncle Sanford still has the microphone. "As they used to tell them at the end of the last mile," he says, "Be-e-e-e seated."

Dinner begins with an appetizer of chopped chicken livers, scooped into balls and deposited within folds of lettuce. The dish is heavy, nourishing, and, to most tastes, delicious. Chicken soup follows, steaming and fatty, with knadloch, a ball of matzoh dough, carefully allotted one to each guest.

At the Moskowitz table, an accountant says, "If we ate this every day, you'd be out of business, soon, huh Doctor?" It is an old Jewish fable that chicken soup cures all ills from a sore throat to athlete's foot. Moskowitz refuses to be amused. He does not like to hear medicine called a business. The socializers do that; they and the beatniks. "Call me at the office if you have questions," he snaps.

"Doctor works so hard," Mrs. Moskowitz announces.

"Well, I hope you make Internal Revenue very happy," says the accountant. He freezes his face into a smile.

At another table, Jerry Gaines, who owns The Big J, Television and Appliance Discounts, lifts the knadloch from the soup and examines it as it steams before his eyes. "This is like one of Grandma's," Jerry says. "Remember, Heshy? They were so rubbery, I hit 'em three sewers back on Crown Street." The distance between "sewers"—manhole covers—was used to measure batting power in stickball, a game of baseball with a broomstick that New York children played before automobiles commandeered their streets.

Rock Cornish game hen is the main dish. Aaron's serves it with kasha (groats) and stuffed derma, cow's entrails surrounding a heavy meal. The waitresses in their red-and-black costumes are efficient. One or two are even cute. The meal is going very smoothly. Nothing has been served cold. Everything is at least passable. The hen is outstanding. The ballroom is quieter now; at table after table, eating replaces active conversation.

Twenty minutes later, the catering consultant walks to the microphone in front of Uncle Sanford's place at the head table. He gets a confirming nod from Barbara Farberman and proclaims—it is more a shout of triumph—"Ladies and gentlemen: Dessert!"

Busboys rush to their clearing. The ballroom lights dim. In formation, the eight waitresses wearing red and black parade from the Temple Beth-El kitchen bearing aloft and ablaze flaming cherry tarts—the *spécialité de la maison* for Harry Aaron's Kosher Katerers, Inc. A ripple of applause, proper now, begins. Flames from the cognac surrounding the tarts lick high in the half-dark room. With the girls marching in perfect formation, it is spectacular. The applause grows. Even Doctor Moskowitz, feeling better after the first three courses, joins in. "Barbara!" he shouts, "Barbara!" He stands up at Table Two to catch Mrs. Farberman's eye. "Barbara!" he calls. "Le flambé, c'est magnifique."

"Merci, merci!" Barbara Farberman cries.

"Irving, sit down," says Mrs. Moskowitz.

As if *cerises flambé* were not enough, Harry Aaron's Kosher Katerers, Inc., has brought forth from the earth at no extra cost a mocha layer cake for the head table. It bears thirteen candles. When the cake appears, with the lights still dim, Uncle Sanford recaptures the microphone. . . . Strongly, resonantly, he says: "And now, the man—and I don't mean boy—whose day this is. It's all yours, Mike. You're a grand little guy."

Michael Farberman, the forgotten, stands. Applause spurts, stops and spurts again. Michael's hair is no longer rumpled. For all the excitement, Barbara Farberman has seen to that. The dim light conceals two shiny chicken soup spots on Michael's lapels. His hands are trembling.

Uncle Sanford hands Michael a matchbook and says into the microphone, "You're old enough to play with these now." Michael grins and lights a match, which promptly dies. He lights another, angling the match to feed the flame, and moves it stiffly to the thirteenth candle in the center of the mocha cake. He does not burn himself. The candlewick catches. Buddy Arrow stamps his foot, the band breaks into "Sunrise, Sunset" from *Fiddler on the Roof*.

After coffee, Michael makes his speech. It is well past nine o'clock and Barbara Farberman has let him drink an entire cup of coffee. It is so late, she says; the boy has had to do so much; it is amazing that he can keep his eyes open at all, although, Barbara points out, he certainly has had plenty of preparation. Nobody can accuse her of letting Michael go to his Bar Mitzvah unprepared.

Writing the speech challenged Michael. He was frightened until he came to realize that he would have a chance to explain some of his feelings to grown-ups. He wanted to do that so much that the fright became less dominant. There were a number of things that he felt he had to say but after several conversations at dinner, he understood that his mother felt that there were a number of things he *should* say. And they were not all the same. And Rabbi Blochman had further suggestions. And his own father simply said over and over: "It's your talk, Mike. Nobody else can make it for you. It's your talk."

Finally, tentatively, Michael told his dilemma to David Bar Oman, a blue-eyed Israeli engaged by Mrs. Farberman so that Michael could learn his Hebrew from someone who himself spoke it as a child.

"What are your disagreements?" Mr. Bar Oman wanted to know.

"Well, like, Mom says, I should be sure to mention her father, but I don't think I should because I never knew him."

"You have the right," Mr. Bar Oman said.

"But I don't want her to get sore at me," Michael said.

"It is your day, not hers," Mr. Bar Oman said. "Besides, if the speech is excellent, she won't be angry. She'll be proud."

"I don't know," Michael said.

"I'll help you with it," said Mr. Bar Oman, "at no charge."

Now tired, but excited by the day and fired by the memory of the hours with Mr. Bar Oman, who unfortunately was not invited, Michael rises to address the assemblage of well-fed, chattering adults. "Thanks," he says, above the buzzing, "are truly all that I have to offer to everyone here in this room."

"Closer, kid," says Uncle Sanford. "Move in on the mike."

"Mort!" a woman's voice shrills, louder than Michael's. "Quiet! The child is trying to speak."

"Is this okay, Uncle Sandy?" Michael says.

"A quarter-step in."

"Okay?" Michael says.

"Yeah," Uncle Sanford says.

"Shut up, Mort!" cries the shrill woman.

"Thanks," Michael says, "are truly all that I have to offer to everyone here in this room.

"I thank my parents for looking after me with love, even though I may have given them—Dad, anyway—a few gray hairs. I thank them for sending me to Hebrew school, even though on many days, I, like so many my age, protested I would rather play basketball. . . .

"I also thank," he says, "my younger sister Lanie for her love, even though I know that on many occasions, she has wished that she was my older sister." He grins quickly at Lanie. He waits for laughs. Mr. Bar Oman told him that the audience would break into laughter. It does not. There are not even chuckles. Lanie looks embarrassed.

Michael inhales and says, "I . . ."

"Closer," commands Uncle Sanford.

"Thanks," Michael says. "I especially want to thank my grandmother, Dora," Michael says. "I only wish the Lord had seen fit to spare my grandpa, Solomon Farberman, for this day, so that he could see me as I now am, Bar Mitzvah." Michael looks straight ahead so that his mother cannot catch his eye. He will only mention grandparents he has known.

"In the Torah this morning," he says, now glancing toward the notes Mr. Bar Oman helped prepare, "we read how the father of all our people was called on to sacrifice his own son. Although I am so fortunate in my life that I have not had to make great sacrifices—again, I thank my own father—I know that I am a Jew. Even as my fellow people did in Europe so recently, I would be willing to make any sacrifice that is necessary for my heritage. As I understand it, that heritage is one of peace and learning."

The buzzing is almost still. Not everyone is listening, but no one makes loud sounds any longer. The reference to the Holocaust brought quiet.

"In the Haftorah this morning," Michael says, "I read how the prophet Elijah revived a dead boy with the warmth of his body. . . . So it is with Judaism. Tyrants come and try to destroy it, but the warmth of our heritage—peace and learning—and our belief in a firm but just God, will always revive the Jewish people, as it is doing everywhere today." Michael pauses. Mr. Bar Oman had worked hardest with him at this section. It was most important, Mr. Bar Oman said.

"I will always remember this day. I will always remember my Jewish heritage and my belief. I only hope," Michael Farberman says, concluding the first speech of his thirteen years, "that I am worthy of all these wonderful things that have come to me."

A few minutes later dancing begins. Buddy Arrow's band plays on for hours; the band plays and the dancers dance long after Michael Farberman, the Bar Mitzvah, has ridden home in the midnight-blue Toronado and clambered safely to the heights of sleep.

CHAPTER 3

AND THEN
THERE IS SEX

Johnny Longboat, the hero of Kahn's second novel, The Seventh
Game, *published in 1982, becomes a Hall of Fame–bound pitcher
who gets to showcase his stuff in the climactic game of the World
Series. He is also entangled in a messy love affair while still married.
But growing up in Oklahoma he experienced a first innocent but
erotic sexual encounter.*

At Cordell High School, classmates called Helen Arnett "The Book-
worm," which was not like being reputed a bookworm at Milton
Academy, near Harvard, or at the High School of Music and Art in New
York City. Helen read books in clusters, and when Mr. McCurtin, the
florid bald teacher of "Mainstreams in American Literature," assigned
Arrowsmith, Helen went on and read *Main Street*, *Babbitt*, and
Dodsworth as well. Then she read *Winesburg, Ohio*. Fascinated by small
towns and the people in them, she proceeded to *Spoon River Anthology*.
Now, in *Look Homeward, Angel*, she was entering the town of Altamont,
and comparing the state of Catawba and the Gant family with persons
and places in southwestern Oklahoma. Bookish for Cordell High, pretty
Helen Arnett, who was sixteen, had not read a line of Dickens, Balzac,
Henry James, or Thomas Hardy.

Some other girls at Cordell said Helen carried books to impress Mr.
McCurtin or certain boys, or even her private tennis teacher, Alva Teagarden. But that wasn't why she was bookish, Helen believed. She

wanted to explore the world beyond the windy Oklahoma flatness, but Mother disliked travel and her father, Dr. Robin Arnett, a dentist, disliked leaving his practice and never went anywhere, except to Mercedes, Texas, where he shot buck. So to Helen the wonder of Zenith City and Winesburg was that she was transported from the fields of cotton and alfalfa. Later, when the twitting persisted, she did carry books for effect. She felt that she was a step or two higher than the others. Her father did not pump ethyl at Waynoka Gas and Diesel. He was a dentist. If her manner bothered other girls, the children of field hands, very well, let them be bothered. Although her slim body made her a fine gymnast, Helen refused to try out for Cordell's cheerleading squad. Instead she took her private tennis lessons on the cracked cement court at Rush Springs Golf and Country Club. The golf pro, Alva Teagarden, doubled as tennis teacher, and when he worked on Helen's serve Alva positioned her right arm with great care. As he did that, Alva always brushed her right breast. Men had different ways of being pleasing and pleasing themselves. With Mr. McCurtin it was talks about Thomas Wolfe; with Alva it was a broad, caressing hand.

"What do you think is in there?" Helen pointed to the windmill shed blown bare of shingles.

"Animal nests, probably," Johnny Longboat said.

The others had gone. Randy Lugert shouted that Helen had to leave with him, but Helen gazed through her round eyeglasses and said she would just as soon bike home by herself as ride with somebody who fell down trying to hit a fastball thrown by a kid.

"You know I'm not a kid," John Longboat said.

"Let's go see what's inside," Helen said. She fastened a button on her white-and-yellow blouse.

"Snakes,'" Johnny said. "Could be sidewinders."

Helen yelped softly. "Then maybe we better not go inside," she said.

"I'll go ahead and scout them out," John said. The warped wood door gave slowly to Johnny's forearms. He kicked about. "No snakes," he called. Then he and Helen stood inside the shed. Half-light broke through the doorway and the floor was straw, and there was a little cot on the right side. Johnny kicked the straw and announced, "No squirrels been here lately, either."

Helen placed the Modern Library copy of *Look Homeward, Angel* on the cot and ran her hands along Johnny's right arm. "So strong," she said.

"A good thing, too," Johnny said, "because I'm going to be a big-league pitcher."

"That means you leave Oklahoma," Helen said.

It surprised him that she accepted his hope as certainty. Didn't Helen know how hard it was to be a big-league pitcher? Didn't she know that in forty-eight states and in the Caribbean, there were ten thousand who wanted to pitch in the major leagues?

"There're no big-league teams west of St. Louis," Johnny said. "There're teams in Philadelphia and Chicago and New York."

"I'd like to go there," Helen Arnett said.

"Where?"

"All of them. All those places."

"I'll be going to all those places when I'm a big-league pitcher," Johnny said. "Dad says I just have to grow some and take care of my arm. When the wind gets bad, you can feel it inside the trailer, and I wrap my arm in a sweater 'fore I sleep." Under Helen Arnett's stroking, his arm tingled.

"I'd also like to go to London, England," Helen said, "and Paris, France." She removed her eyeglasses and placed them on *Look Homeward, Angel*. It was light enough to see a soft look in her gray-blue eyes. "That's what I'd like to do *most*," she said. "Travel."

"I'd like the most to be a big-league pitcher."

Helen unbuttoned John's cuff and rolled his sleeve and kissed his upper arm. "What would you like to do most right now?" she said.

She's asking me, John thought. I'm not asking her. "For you to take off your pretty blouse and things," he said.

Helen yelped the way she had when Johnny mentioned snakes. "That wouldn't be right," she said.

"Why not?"

"Because it's not as if you were my boyfriend."

"I am for now," Johnny said.

Helen turned her back and unbuttoned her blouse and took it off and unsnapped her brassiere and spun around.

"They're small," John said. Helen cried out and covered her breasts with her hands. "You've looked at too many cows," she said. Then she said, "You shouldn't talk to me like that, if you're my boyfriend."

"They're not too small," John said. "Take your hands away. Small and nice and just right, is what they are." It surprised him that a few dark hairs grew about each nipple. He reached and touched a breast and Helen threw her arms around his neck. Her wrists were thin and delicate. He let her pull him onto the cot, where they lay next to Helen's spectacles and *Look Homeward, Angel*.

"Doesn't your thing hurt?" Helen said. "Does it hurt when your thing is hard and pressing against your jeans?"

It was like Dad said about the way you behaved when you pitched. You listened more than you talked. That kept you ahead.

"It doesn't hurt none, Helen," Johnny said.

"But if you took it out, wouldn't you feel more comfortable?"

"Might."

She opened his jeans and stroked his penis evenly with both her hands. John made no sound, but shuddered as he ejaculated.

"Oh," Helen cried. "Oh. You're a very strong young man, Johnny."

"My rocket sure went off," he said. His breath came back at once. "Now let me see your bush. You know. Your private hair." He ran his hands up the inside of her thighs, remembering to be gentle, and Helen Arnett moaned and shook her head and said, "Wait."

"Why?"

"I can't let you see my parts."

"Why not?" Johnny had risen. He adjusted his jeans and looked down at Helen. Her lips were tight against her teeth.

"Girls get excited, too," Helen Arnett said. "That's why I moaned. If I let you see my parts, we might both get so excited something bad would happen."

"Pregnant," John said. "I'll bike over to Waynoka Gas real fast. In the bathroom, they got this machine. You put a quarter in and out comes a pack of things. They're three for a quarter."

"Contraceptives," Helen said.

"What?"

"Those rubber things are called contraceptives. It's better to use the specific word than to say 'thing.'"

"I'll remember that, Helen. I really will."

Beyond the doorway, twilight threatened. "It's too late, Johnny," Helen said. "And I relieved you, didn't I? You don't hurt."

"Nope."

"Tomorrow, then. You have some money from your pitching. You have time to get the contraceptives early. Buy the best brand."

"'Kay." He was starting to lose his breath.

"Will it be the first time for you?" She was holding him gently by the upper arms. She looked naked although she still wore a yellow half slip and white underpants.

"Yep."

"We'll be together, then," Helen said. "We'll be together for a long time."

"I want to be together with you for a long time," Johnny said.

"Even when you're a famous big-league pitcher?"

"Even when I'm a famous big leaguer, if I make it. If you'll help me make it. Especially when I'm a famous big-league pitcher."

"We'll see all the great cities then," Helen Arnett said. Her eyes went wet. "London, Paris, Detroit."

"Cleveland and Pittsburgh, too," Johnny Longboat promised.

CHAPTER 4

THE DREAMS
OF THE YOUNG

For one summer, the writer turned owner. Kahn purchased a minor-league baseball team, the Utica (New York) Blue Sox, and then wrote about a dramatic, touching, and learning summer—for both author and players—in Good Enough to Dream *(1985). This "kangaroo court" scene finds the team meting out punishment for bad behavior, including against Kahn's impish daughter.*

O ur third meeting site, which we kept strictly stag, was the team bus.

We began with a school bus for short trips and a coach only for overnights, until we started to win. Then Tim Birnie relented and said we could always ride a coach when he had one available for the same price as a school bus. (Victory hath its privileges.) The difference was that the coach offered reclining seats, air-conditioning, and a toilet, a significant amenity when the team played particularly well and I bought the ballplayers a few cases of beer. We rolled back and forth to Auburn, site of that gray-walled maximum security prison, and Geneva, which offered Hobart College. Since we were defeating everybody, the rides were pleasant and, once we left the drab ribbon that is the thruway, reasonably scenic. Rolling country. Small farms. Metal-topped silos. Red barns.

Rocky Coyle, the outfielder nicknamed Mister Magoo, took to calling out the stars of each game and demanding applause. Rocky would order a golf clap (quiet), a tennis clap (louder), or a concert clap (rhythmic, in the manner of European audiences urging an encore). Eventually, someone ordered a Magoo clap for Rocky. To execute a Magoo clap, the hands come close together but miss. The applause is silent.

Gattis had a parlor trick that he played on many bus-ride nights. Place six beer cups on the floor. The manager has to look away during this process. Invert them and conceal a coin under one. Gattis would then turn, kneel, work his right hand back and forth over the inverted cups, and invariably select the one hiding the coin. We suspected Moss or Joe Picchioni, our first-base coach, of flashing a signal.

"Naw," Gattis said. "It's kind of magnetism from the coin toward my brain. You know I've got this metal plate in my skull. Metal seeks out metal."

Perfectly absurd. But we never caught a signal. And Gattis never missed.

Moss organized the most elaborate bus-ride merriment. Following Finnegan's Wake on July 2, the Sox worked their way back into first place and made the first extended trip, to Jamestown and Batavia in the western part of the state. When we swept Jamestown, a Montreal farm team, we moved a game ahead of Little Falls. The bus trip to Batavia next day turned into a kangaroo court.

Moss structured the proceedings in his thorough way. Somewhere he found a black cape which he gave to Dan Gazzilli, who was to preside as judge. He prepared a written list of charges. He appointed Robin Dreizler, our backup catcher, as clerk. Moss himself would run the prosecutions. Defense attorneys could be selected by defendants from the balance of the team. Or one could elect to defend himself.

Bailiff Rocky Coyle stood up as the bus rode north on Route 60, past summer-green farms and hills, and spoke into the driver's microphone.

"The Utica Blue Sox' first kangaroo court"— there never was another—"will come to order. No talking. Judge Daniel Gazzilli presiding. All rise, please."

Everybody stood, and then sat down.

"The prosecuting attorney will now read the cases. Anyone accused must stand trial. He will be granted five minutes for himself or his defense counsel."

Moss rose. The bus rolled smoothly. It was not hard to keep your footing. He spoke in carefully austere tones.

"Case Number One. The Blue Sox versus Shawn Barton for wearing his stirrups as high as his knees and for continually talking to himself in a psychopathic manner."

Laughter. Barton grinned and blushed.

"Case Number Two. The Blue Sox versus Daryl Pitts and Larry Lee for wearing knee pads at their ankles during batting practice.

"Case Number Three. The Blue Sox versus Ralph Sheffield for continually throwing equipment, notably after striking out, and for swearing at children alongside the first-base dugout.

"Case Number Four. The Blue Sox versus the pitchers for not carrying the trainer's gear.

"Case Number Five will be the Blue Sox versus Alissa Kahn, in absentia, a minor who must be represented by her father, for sipping beer and smoking a carton of cigarettes a day.

"Case Number Six is the Blue Sox versus Michael Zalewski for not abiding by his contract with the court. The court has determined that, to be employed as traveling secretary and statistician, your physical body must be maintained within twenty years of your chronological age. The prosecution further charges, Mike, that your body is that of a sixty-five-year-old woman. It is also alleged that your body is hazardous to your health."

"Wait a minute," Zalewski screamed.

"Silence," ordered Judge Gazzilli.

Unruffled and unsmiling, Moss proceeded. "We cite a case from 1982, when Zulu, convicted on various charges, failed to complete his sentence of brushing his teeth for seven consecutive days. He brushed them once, that being after French-kissing his dog during a wet dream." Our prosecutor/designated hitter sat down with just the smallest suggestion of a smile.

Shawn Barton engaged Wild Willie Finnegan as his mouthpiece. "My client," Finnegan began, "wears his stirrups high to show our fans that his sanis [white undersocks] are clean. I say that's good for the ball club. As for talking to himself, he's in better company than he would be talkin' to some other members of this club who I won't mention. The defense rests."

Debate. Vote. Barton was acquitted. This prompted Pitts and Lee, next on the docket, to reengage Finnegan as counsel. Willie simply pointed out that knee pads at the ankle might not look tidy but they were protection against foul balls hit straight down. "There's no way," he said, "a fair-minded club like the Blue Sox can convict two good ballplayers for protecting themselves. What are you gonna do next, take away their cups?" Another acquittal.

Sheffield insisted on defending himself. "I can either do that," he said, "or give you guys my famous Richard Pryor imitation."

The Blue Sox hooted. Someone called, "Fuck Richard Pryor. You gonna set yourself on fire, Sheff?"

Ralph made a mistake and he grew contentious. "Now *you're* cursing," he said. "I didn't swear at little children. I was swearing at myself for striking out."

"Little children heard your swear words," Moss said.

"They ought to be watching the game," Sheffield said.

He was convicted quickly and sentenced to help the pitchers carry gear.

"You want a hundred-and-fifty-pound man to carry out two hundred pounds of bats?" Sheffield said.

"Quiet," Gazzilli ordered, "or I'll cite you for contempt."

Outside a tractor-trailer swept past us. Inside the bus everyone— except Joe Braun, the driver—had been transported to a fairy-tale kangaroo world.

Jimmy Tompkins, wearing mirrored sunglasses, strolled to the front of the bus and made an elaborate defense on behalf of the pitchers. "Every day," he said, "we have a starter and possible four or five relievers. Now anyone who knows basic kinesiology recognizes that it can hurt an arm to extend it and carry heavy equipment. We have men here like Mike Zamba, John Seitz, Roy Moretti, who continually go out and pitch well. For our defense, then, we state: if we're carrying the team, why should we carry the equipment too?"

Ten pitchers stood up and applauded. All the position players jeered. Moss called Joe Picchioni, who quickly penciled a pseudomedical sketch to show how lifting gear builds triceps and the pectorals. "Carrying equipment can increase fastball velocity five to maybe ten miles an hour," he concluded.

"Now," Moss said. "on the issue of carrying the club, will Don Jacoby please rise? Ah, thank you, sir. How many hits did you get last night [in a 7–1 victory over Jamestown]?"

"Five," Jacoby said.

"In how many at bats, sir?"

"Five."

"That's five for five, Mr. Jacoby. Would you feel you carried the club?"

"I ain't gonna say that," Jacoby snapped. "In your face, Moss."

"I believe the answer to my question should have been yes and I ask the court to so record it. Jacoby carried the club last night. Others have on other nights."

A long deliberation followed. Moss announced the decision. "The pitchers are found guilty and hereby sentenced to carry all the equipment, and carry Ralph Sheffield, for the remainder of the trip."

Moss cleared his throat and proceeded. "We come now to the Blue Sox versus Alissa Kahn, represented by her father, for sipping beer and smoking a carton of cigarettes a day. Will you kindly stand, Mr. Kahn?"

I stood.

"Remove your Blue Sox cap," Moss said. "You are in court. You may proceed."

I took the microphone. "I don't think any of you men has a daughter yet, but believe me, when you do she'll be a light of your life. When I first thought of bringing Alissa here, I was not concerned with smoking or drinking. I just knew she'd be around twenty-five horny bastards."

The players loosed a cresting wave of laughter.

"As a father I concentrated on the area of chastity. Now we have, at the mercy of the court, a redheaded sixteen-year-old girl."

"Sixteen?" shouted Brian Robinson. "She told me she was eighteen."

That broke up the bus (and the club president). When I recovered, I said, "I'm not going to burden you with denials. But think of her youth and remember these lines from the Bard: 'The quality of mercy is not strained/It droppeth as the gentle rain from heaven.' Not only myself but Shakespeare speaks for Alissa. If you can sentence her despite that, you have hearts of stone."

"Through?" Moss said.

"Yep."

Barry took the microphone and said, "William Shakespeare is not on trial here. Alissa Kahn is on trial." She was convicted and sentenced to go out with a young, ungainly batboy, a sentence she later reversed when she appealed and cut down her smoking.

The Zalewski case was resolved quickly. He was sentenced to sleep with Bob Veale's little black dog, Smokey, but not to molest the animal sexually.

Finnegan came forward. "Last night our manager, Jim Gattis, walked into the motel restaurant with his uniform on. At the beginning of the year he ordered all of us not to hang around the concession stands in uniform.

"What's good for the players is also good for the manager. I say we give Jimmy a stiff punishment."

The deliberations came alive with pleasure. The players could get back at their stern and volatile manager. Rocky Coyle announced the sentence. "From now on Gattis cannot mention that game in Auburn [of June 24] which we lost 6–5, which we admit we should have won. He can't bring that ball game up for the balance of the season."

The bus pressed northward toward Batavia, site of a factory which manufactured a cloth guaranteed to clean your automobile as thoroughly as a car wash. Advertisements for this product began: "Does your car get *shameful* dirty?" That would be Batavia (and two more early victories) but, amid the laughter and the fellowship, we might as well have been rolling east toward Eden.

CHAPTER 5

RESTLESS YOUTH: THE COLUMBIA UPRISING

By the late 1960s America was boiling over about the Vietnam War, racial injustice, and the clashing of values between the "silent majority" of Richard Nixon and the long-haired, bell-bottomed, politically left generation typified by student Mark Rudd. The clash was never more evident than at Columbia University, where protests turned violent. Kahn spent nearly a year in research to re-create The Battle for Morningside Heights *(1970).*

A most interesting description of Mark Rudd was written by Dan Bell, Doctor Daniel Bell, editor of *The Radical Right*, Ph.D. (Columbia), L.H.D. (Grinnell), Litt.D. (Case Western Reserve), once ranking professor in the Columbia Department of Sociology, recently moved to Harvard, and thirty years ago an ambitious City College undergraduate. To Bell, Mark Rudd is "hulking and slack-faced." Rudd's jaw is not merely prominent, it is "prognathic." The "blue-gray eyes are so translucent that his gaze seems hypnotic." Finally, Professor Bell points out, "Rudd's father [was] born Rudnitsky." It is a tribute to Mark Rudd's ability to shake academicians to their ganglia that one of the best of them is driven to assert that Rudd is a Jew.

The Columbia revolutionist is a curiously appealing young man, except when he is possessed by vulgarity or hostility or arrogance. He speaks earnestly and forcefully about a new order. He wants to see mankind freed from toil. How? He is not certain, and he does not take suggestions well. When someone corrects Rudd, the teeth clench and the jaw really does become prognathic. His rhetoric grows simple. "Aw, fuck off."

People at Columbia enjoy making catalogs of Rudd's weaknesses. They are ample and he is twenty-two years old. His philosophy is derivative, emotional, and sometimes puerile. His speaking voice is high and often monotonous. He has no clear image of the future. He is bright and clever, rather than brilliant, not deep at all. He is irresponsible and ruthless. But against these failures of intellect, morality, and technique, Mark Rudd possesses an overwhelming strength. He knows how to make his opposition cringe.

When the faculty wanted to mediate his revolution, Rudd found himself sitting across a desk from a professor who was urging "reason." Abruptly, Rudd removed his boots, and put his socks in the professor's face. On another occasion, he addressed a supposedly congenial faculty group. It was there that he cried that mediatory talks were "bullshit." Professors were startled. Rudd keeps people off balance. He enjoys rattling them, the way good fighters do, and like a good fighter, he trusts very few.

The Columbia revolt was not Mark Rudd's doing, any more than it was the doing of [Columbia President] Grayson Kirk or Lyndon Johnson or Ho Chi Minh. But Rudd influenced it mightily, and if one wishes to understand the events of Columbia, one must pay attention to Mark Rudd, a charismatic, not always pleasant young man. The country, as Rudd sees it—and his father sees it as well—is surfeited with affluence. Jacob Rudd, a lieutenant colonel in the U.S. Army Reserve, owns a real estate brokerage firm in the north Jersey suburb of Maplewood. "My concern," concedes Jacob Rudd, "has always been making a living. Mark doesn't have to worry about that."

The absolute freedom from economic terrors provided Rudd with time to rebel. His parents speak fondly of his disinterest in material things, of his ability to be happy sleeping in the woods. It was not, however, the sleep of a hobo. Rudd, in the woods, always had a good house and warm bed awaiting his whim.

The situation is not unique. Thousands, perhaps millions of young people who have been raised in comfort develop a need to rebel against the conditions of their upbringing. Typically, they are aware between the ages of seventeen and thirty. Frequently they are the children of recent immigrant groups. They are, in short, the offspring of a generation that had to drive very hard for success. As the Maplewood Syndrome seizes them, they fight against what their parents built. They attack the success and the society that lauds it. Some enact rebellion by embracing the Castro experience, or Stalinism, or by trying to embrace hostile blacks. Occasionally, the Maplewood Syndrome vanishes with maturity. But the situation does not lend itself to simplification, not the condition and certainly not the times.

In Maplewood and Bel Air, and Shaker Heights and Dobbs Ferry and Boxford and even dull, wasp Bloomfield Hills, we are rounding out three decades of a spiraling prosperity that has remade the nature of the country. The managerial-technical-professional class numbers more than ten million families. It is a class with businesses to leave to children. Or law practices. Or money in Xerox. Or investment land in East Hampton. Or cash. All one has to do to come into money is to survive.

The removal of a requisite struggle to succeed disturbs the American pattern. It would in any era. If Lincoln had been born to wealth and power, would he have ended up a wealthy clubman, the disappointing father of his beloved Tad? Possibly so. In this particular time, the death of struggle is catastrophic. It has taken place against the increasingly desperate struggle of black America against poverty. The sensitive child of the suburb sees this: no blacks live in his street. Some come to work but only as menials. He reads that blacks are hungry and that black children are bitten by rats. Intuitively he sympathizes with blacks and wonders why they are denied. An early symptom of the Maplewood Syndrome is the early awareness of the unfairness of things.

If the suburban child decides to investigate the traditional treatment of blacks in the United States, he finds, as Eugene McCarthy put it, that we practice colonialism. When the young suburbanite recognizes the colonialism, in opposition to endemic affluence, he becomes upset. He wants to say he is sorry that blacks suffer, and that he didn't make them suffer, and that he admires them. Suffering lends the appearance of nobility. The suburbanite admires the noble blacks and tries to join them. He fails, and admires them more. ("I've never really been that comfortable with blacks," Mark Rudd concedes. . . .)

Mark was the second son born to the Rudds. His older brother, David, is a lawyer. His mother, Bertha, says that Mark was a good boy, well disciplined and mannerly. He grew up blond and plump and busy. He liked jazz and short-wave radios and the Boy Scouts. He was popular at Columbia High School in Maplewood, a model suburban school. Four out of five graduates enter college. Even then, as he posted good grades in English and history and mathematics, Rudd began to believe that something was wrong in Maplewood and beyond. His grandmother owned a candy store in the Central Ward of Newark, a section going black and getting poorer. (The ward eventually exploded into a riot.) It is a short drive from Maplewood to Newark, not more than half an hour, and Mark was stunned by what he saw in grandmother's neighborhood. Children begging. Tattered clothes. Blacks without shoes. In the rotting Central Ward, a discontent seized Rudd.

Despite his fine grades and good extracurricular record in high school, he was rejected by Harvard. But Columbia was happy to get Rudd, and I suppose it tells us something of the nature of the revolutionary that he wanted to attend an Ivy League school. No free college, open to all, for Rudd. If not Harvard, then Columbia, the gem of the establishment.

On the sprawling, confusing campus, reaching to the very lip of Harlem, Rudd, the child of parents who struggled, found himself an instant Ivy Leaguer. In his indoctrination, he was bluntly told, "The mission of Columbia College is to train a small number of the most promising minds in each generation." It was not a message that he found appealing, but he did his work well enough. He grappled with Contemporary Civilization, a two-year program at Columbia, which sets out to "make the students deal, as graduate students do, with original writings of the major thinkers since the fifteenth century and to form and express opinions." He sweated through Humanities, another two-year sequence. . . . Today *Paradise Lost*; next week *Tristram Shandy*. Rudd's more meaningful education was taking place outside the lecture halls.

Like most other frosh, he found Columbia enormous and impersonal. Like many others, he thought, with the sureness of eighteen years, that much classroom work was useless, irrelevant. Here, it seemed to him, the blacks were being oppressed, the American nation was being transformed into a neo-fascist military state, and the professors lectured from notes about things that didn't matter, just as they'd been doing for the past dreary decades. It wasn't right, Rudd concluded, with some justification. If Columbia people refused to establish relations with Harlemites, except as duke to serfs, at least Columbia ought to recognize the present. It is perfectly fair to assert that Columbia had a hand in the creation of this rebel. Her weaknesses helped push him to the left.

While Rudd was wondering why so few blacks attended the college, why so few full professors taught freshmen, and whether he would have to go to Vietnam, he attached himself to a number of upperclassmen. One, Michael Neumann, was [philosopher Herbert] Marcuse's stepson. Through him, Rudd learned of *One Dimensional Man*. As one philosophy professor suggests, "Marcuse's work is not only wonderful because of itself; it's also a framework in which you can find explanations for your own hang-ups, in fact for almost anybody's hang-ups." Rudd took comfort from Marcuse's argument that American society was irrational. It isn't just men, then, is what Rudd thought. He also swallowed another hypothesis: revolutions are not accidents; they are created by an act of will, the will to revolution.

Rudd joined the radical Students for a Democratic Society and as a sophomore was put in charge of organizing dormitory support for SDS. He spoke up often at meetings and developed a reputation as a skillful debater, a fair humorist, and an intractable hard-liner. But in Rudd's junior year, moderates elected Ted Kaptchuk as president, and Rudd, the activist, found himself an outsider within the SDS.

Columbia SDS consisted only of one hundred or so young people, and a repetitive topic at meetings was "how can we broaden our base." Kaptchuk favored discussion and explanation of "what the state of the country is and what the issues really are." Rudd favored demonstrations. Kaptchuk was a "verbalist," he charged, while the time was crying out for action. The best way to "radicalize" the student body, he believed, was to demonstrate again and again against Columbia's connection with the American war machine.

That winter, in 1968, Rudd flew to Cuba with a group of other students. Rudd's view of the Cuban government confirmed his existing beliefs. He saw the Malacon, the handsome boulevard that winds above the sea and where, in other days, fine manors served as brothels for American tourists. He saw the Miramar, a section of ornate homes, some built of marble. They once housed the rich and servants; now many had been turned into living quarters for workers. He talked to young Cuban revolutionaries. They delighted him. They had thrown out a military dictator, Batista, who was supported by strong elements in the United States. The trip strengthened Rudd's resolve to make a revolution and encouraged his belief that one could succeed. There does not seem to be any evidence to support the theory that the Columbia debacle traces from Cuba. Rudd was a hard-liner before he saw Havana. And there is absolutely no evidence to support a right-wing theory that Cuban money helped finance the rebellion. What money the Columbia rebels needed came from the sale of pamphlets and articles and from the pockets of middle-class parents. Castro (and Mao and even Brezhnev) may have cheered. They did not have to invest.

Back on campus in March 1968, members of the SDS were impatient with the cautious stewardship of Ted Kaptchuk. Another election was coming. Rudd campaigned on a promise of action and, in March, became president of the Columbia chapter of the SDS.

As president and leader, Rudd was motivated by two forces. The desire to remake unjust America was sincere. So was his developing ambition. During the following months, action followed action so swiftly that the Columbia left was like a runaway. There was no telling where it would go or when it would stop. Rudd did not really control the movement, but he was adroit at setting forces in motion. He sought confrontations and found them. He did not know how the confrontations would end, nor did he seem to be concerned. What disturbed him most was someone's suggestion: "If this movement peters out, Mark, you're through."

He developed a taste for power and importance. He liked to put down professors and to dominate meetings and to see his name in headlines, although the last soon lost appeal. The press, in reporting, tended to patronize him. He resolved that shrewdly. He stopped granting interviews, and began to write himself. He was able to sell one article to a national magazine and another to a book publisher.

His leadership was imperfect. He made mistakes and antagonized potential friends, and was forever changing his mind. But it was the most vital student leadership the Columbia campus had ever seen. That is a bulky pill to administer to Columbia graduates, from the leftists of the '30s to the jocks, the muscular conservatives, of today. But it is true.

Mark Rudd at twenty-two is a successful lecturer, the chairman of one branch of the SDS, and a college dropout. To regain admission to Columbia he would have to eat crow, and of course he will not. Despite difficulties, he remains a leader, *the* leader. The unity of the left at Columbia dissolved almost as it was created. The liberal left, put off by Rudd's intransigence, split with him in June 1968. The extreme left, the radicals who want to fight in the streets, to join with the workmen, quickly found Rudd to be bourgeois. But to many of the radical students, Rudd is almost heroic.

"Look," one of the captains of one of the multitudinous subcommittees within the Columbia SDS has said. "It's hard to get Mark. He's busy. He's got so many things to do. But when I do get a few minutes with him, it's worth it. He's so goddamn alive." Some women of the left find him overwhelming. A male radical celebrates this by referring to him as Mark Studd.

I talked with him a few times and listened to him on other occasions. He is busy, self-occupied, vain, and careless with facts. He says that more students supported him than supported the administration. The best surveys showed that many students supported his objectives and very few, only 19 percent, endorsed his tactics. He says that the *New York Times* is a tool of Columbia and attacks A. M. Rosenthal, "the managing editor." The first statement is excessive and the second is wrong: when Rudd spoke, Clifton Daniel was managing editor; Abe Rosenthal was his assistant.

He is a big boy, with square, rather high shoulders, and a stoop. When he listens, he cocks his head forward, nodding quickly, impatiently. He answers rapidly and thoughtlessly. One day he says that there were no issues at Columbia. "I made them all up." Another day he says, "The issues were symbolic." On a third day, "Every fucking issue was real." He means what he says, as he says it, but he cannot contain his need to be dramatic, his need to surprise, to shock, to call attention to himself. It might be difficult to take him seriously, except for what he has accomplished. And that is serious beyond questions. He knows it and he means to do more. He was the right man in the right place at the right moment once. He would like to continue to play that role for the rest of his days.

CHAPTER 6

KAREEM ARRIVES

By the time he retired in 1989, nearly two decades after this article was written, Kareem Abdul Jabbar, formerly Lew Alcindor, led the National Basketball Association in nine categories, including points scored (38,387), seasons played (20), most valuable player awards (6), minutes played (57,446), games played (1,560), and blocked shots (3,189). Kahn caught up with the emerging twenty-three-year-old superstar during his rookie season in 1970, when he averaged 28.8 points per game and 14.5 rebounds.

The motel was called Quality Court, which meant this was no Plaza Suite, and the black man lying under the brown blanket seemed endless, and you had to wonder what was going to happen when he stood up. Would there be room for all of him under that low plasterboard ceiling?

"I have a hyperactive mind," the black man said. He threw his head from one side to another, as though in pain. "I have to clear my mind to play basketball, see? I can't have it all cluttered, man. That's why I look relaxed, but I'm not relaxed." He paused. His moments are full of silences. Then, "I'm all worked up, man, deep down inside."

The tall and troubled black was Ferdinand Lewis Alcindor, Jr. It had been difficult to get an appointment to see him. His employers at the Milwaukee Bucks appeared cowed, as well they might. The personage of Lew Alcindor may be more consequential than the Milwaukee basketball franchise. Certain press reports described Alcindor as mercenary, rude, possibly anti-white. Finally, he had an unnerving recent record of aggressiveness toward opponents: one broken jaw, one knock-out, and one foiled attack in a few months. You go into this kind of interview carefully, preparing all the questions, gauging your subject, wondering about your own jaw.

That was how it had been, but now it wasn't that way at all. Now I was sitting in this dreary room in St. Louis with a bright, sensitive, aesthetic young man, wondering if he was going to bump his head and wondering, too, about the rest of us and the society that had made him both millionaire and nigger.

Alcindor gazed at the wall. It was four o'clock in the afternoon of a game; the drapes were drawn, and the only light came from a reading lamp on the night table. He was lying on his side, the great legs bent under the brown blanket, and the upper part of his body supported by an elbow. His body was curled so that he could lie with his head on the pillow and stare at the wall.

"How do you see your role in the black movement?" He blinked. No other sign or motion.

"When Jackie Robinson broke in," I said, "it was enough, it was significant, for him to get base hits. That was enough."

Only his mouth moving, Alcindor said, "Because white people thought he wasn't good enough to do it."

"But it isn't enough anymore. Black intellectuals don't want black athletes for leaders. They feel there've been enough famous blacks in sports and jazz."

Alcindor made a spasmodic nod. "I know that," he said. He lunged from the bed and began to stride. He bent slightly at the waist. There was room between his head and the ceiling, but he had better not jump.

"I'm figuring it out," Alcindor said, pacing, towering. "It's fragmented, man. Some go to church. Some go to school. Some do nothing. Some want revolt."

The black community at large. That was what he had decided to talk about. "Where do you stand?" I said.

"Try to get change as quickly and painlessly as possible." Alcindor returned to the bed. "Try to stand for something positive. Be something positive."

"What about violence?"

The body shifted under the blanket. Alcindor resumed considering the wall.

"What about violence on the basketball court?"

"You want to know what happened in Seattle. Someone hit me a couple times. Bob Rule got a finger in my eye. Man, I went for Rule. And I spit. And a kid, some big-mouthed teenager, I gave him a shove. And I want to stand for something positive, and I managed to have everyone in the whole arena dislike me. I was a protagonist." Alcindor shook his head. I thought he might spring up again. "These things you want me to talk about," he said. "They're hard to put into words." He smiled and scowled, as though in a private dialogue. I wondered if violence was something he disliked.

"Lew. When you went for Bob Rule, did you mean to hurt him or just give him a shove?"

Alcindor turned and looked directly at me and said, quite evenly, "When I went for Rule there was murder in my heart."

It is not going to add up. Of that you can be assured. In a society that does not add up, the Lew Alcindor phenomenon, frozen in full flow, which is what we are trying to do, is not going to provide one of those comfortable *Reader's Digest* pieces with smooth beginning, anesthetic middle, tidy end. The Alcindor phenomenon is a mix of rough edges and incompleteness and immaturity and wisdom and misinterpretations and rages and regrets. It makes Ray Patterson, president of the Bucks, discuss dimensions of maturity; and John Erickson, the general manager, speak of uneven development; and Larry Costello, the coach, long for days that may never have been, when professional basketball players concerned themselves only with professional basketball.

These things are important, but important, too, is what Guy Rodgers had to say. "Lew is a very nice guy, with a fine sense of humor, a terrific person."

We were sitting over steak in a Milwaukee restaurant late at night. Rodgers, at thirty-four, had played a brilliant game against Los Angeles, and his young wife, Lita, had just learned that their seven-month-old baby, who has an eye disorder, was not going to need an operation. It was a cheerful time.

"Lew is your teammate," I said. "Suppose you didn't think much of him? What would you tell me then?"

Rodgers was wearing steel-framed spectacles and an ascot. "You didn't know me in Philadelphia," he told me.

"I was wondering," Lita said, "why we're having dinner with him, if the story he's doing is about Lew."

Rodgers winced slightly.

"I wanted to have this dinner," Rodgers said, "because there are a couple of things people ought to get straight.

"Ask anyone who really knew me in Philadelphia, and they'll tell you I'm a pretty honest guy. If I didn't like Lew, maybe I wouldn't knock him to you, but you can bet we wouldn't be having dinner right now. What I'm trying to say is that this is a special kind of kid, and I played with Wilt in the beginning and I've been in this league for a long time. Believe me, this kid is a rare human being."

That is something to remember as we work our way across the jagged edges. Alcindor, at twenty-two, has won the warmth and admiration and friendship of a fine old professional.

I had heard of Alcindor a long time ago, a gifted black from Inwood, which is a hilly section of Manhattan, far north of Harlem, with trees and grass and integration, to which vanguards of the black middle class escaped during the 1950s. He was Roman Catholic, or his parents were, and he burst upon us, a gloriously gifted young giant, at Power Memorial Academy, a Catholic prep, accompanied always by a white man, his coach, Jack Donohue. The coach hid Alcindor from the press and seemed to be his closest adviser, and right or wrong, the word was that Jack Donohue was going to hang on to Alcindor's Achilles tendons and follow him a to college job. The recruiting of Alcindor—he could have gone anywhere—produced at least one charge that Donohue was writing himself into the letter of intent. But then, to general surprise, Alcindor fled to UCLA, far from his old schoolyard, far from Donohue, and far from his parents, who had moved to Queens.

The Alcindor era was the finest in UCLA basketball annals. The Bruins pivoting around him were chronic national champions. After that the only question was where he would play professionally and for how much. He was fortunate to graduate at a time when two leagues were battling. The Milwaukee Bucks, for the NBA, and the New York Nets, for the American Basketball Association, made offers. Alcindor settled on Milwaukee, a lovely city in many ways and in many ways a backwater, for a supposed $1.4 million. That is roughly $200,000 per foot, and also, when you consider it, possibly more than the owners of a new and rather modest NBA franchise carry in a checking account. Then Alcindor began playing, with enough potential to draw this from Bob Cousy: "Alcindor is the only man I've seen with the possibility of combining Bill Russell's mental concentration with Wilt Chamberlain's physical dominance."

Later Alcindor crashed into print, selling three installments' worth of memoirs to *Sports Illustrated* for a reported $200,000, or about a dollar a word. The memoir paired Alcindor with a talented, busy author named Jack Olsen, and offered us this quite early:

> *I'm going to tell you my life story . . . and if you think that it takes a lot of conceit for a 22-year-old basketball player to tell his life story, then that's your hang-up. The way things are in America today—and have been for 200 years—the story of any black man has meaning, even if he's a shoeshine "boy" or porter or your friendly neighborhood Uncle Tom.*

That was the tone. The story described how being called "nigger" had wounded Alcindor; friendly neighborhood coach Donohue had told him once, "You're acting just like a nigger." It presented background and outlook and anecdote, but always with a kind of insolence, which, I would learn, was not entirely fair. It is a weakness of the genre, the collaborative form, never to be wholly true to either party. Two egos are working and sometimes clashing. When one man is white and the other black, the conflict becomes more complex, and when both are working to provide a black life for a magazine that caters to affluent whites, the impure art form must be discolored. What we have is not pure Alcindor and not pure Olsen. Instead we have a hybrid: Olsendor.

On the telephone John Erickson would not comment on the stories. "As general manager," he said, "it's my job to be concerned about Lew on the court. I make it a point not to interfere with other matters. He had every right to do those stories, and he has every right to see or not see whom he pleases. . . ."

I telephoned a newspaperman who had been covering Alcindor. "He can be very difficult," the newspaperman reported. "Says very little. Gets into fights. Not always cooperative."

After two more calls to the Bucks, one to the commissioner of the NBA, and two to a California stockbroker who was supposed to be Alcindor's confidant, I mounted the jet to Milwaukee. There was not going to be any trouble seeing him, I was assured. And sure enough, when I went to the Milwaukee Arena there he was, in a sweat suit of forest green and white, practicing layup shots—swish, swish, slam. The Bucks were going to play the Cincinnati Royals, who offer Oscar Robertson and an interesting supporting cast, with Connie Dierking, a somewhat fleshy six-ten, playing center.

Alcindor seemed listless during the warm-up. His face was expressionless. Often he stood by himself. There was no enthusiasm to his moves, no adventure. He does not go out of his way to stuff shots, and several times I had to remind myself of Cousy's quote and of another observer's remark: Alcindor possessed so much ability that he is a basketball third force all by himself.

Alcindor won the tap, but the Royals stole the ball. Robertson dribbled, jumped, and scored. Then the Bucks drove. Alcindor, moving slowly, trailed everyone else. A shot missed. The Royals stormed. There were two fast passes. Suddenly Johnny Green laid up an easy shot. Where was Alcindor?

Two minutes into the game, Lew put in a pretty hook, spinning toward the center from a post on the left. Quickly Tom Van Arsdale hit a jump shot, and Robertson drove, faked, fed to Dierking, who sank a layup. Alcindor looked confused. At the end of the quarter, Cincinnati led, 33–20. Rodgers stirred the Bucks in the opening minutes of the next period, but Dierking hit from the circle, then with a hook, then with a running layup. Alcindor still trailed plays, got himself boxed out, seemed out of things. Halfway through the second quarter, he was out of things. Larry Costello sat him down in favor of Dick Cunningham.

Alcindor returned for the second half, and the Royals, more or less ignoring his presence, ran five straight baskets. Connie Dierking was dominating underneath. He scored at the rate of a basket a minute until, four minutes into the half, Costello yanked Alcindor again. The Royals walked in that night 129–104.

It is difficult to describe this late November performance except in terms of negatives. Alcindor did not often get position for rebounds, and when he did, he would not fight for the ball. The statistician credited him with five rebounds for the first half, when the issue was in doubt, while Rodgers, more than a foot shorter, grabbed six. Overall, Alcindor took thirteen shots, several from underneath, and sank five. He scored just thirteen points. He was not a third force or any force at all. He was a cipher.

The Bucks' dressing room is closed for a time after each game, but on the other side, Coach Cousy was smiling and relaxed and smoking a large cigar. "It isn't fair to comment on Alcindor's play tonight," Cousy said, making a comment. "He's a rookie and he's having troubles. It's hardest for rookies at center. But everything I said about his potential still goes."

The Bucks dress in cramped quarters. . . . I wandered toward Alcindor, who was dressing quickly, silently. He was neither friendly nor hostile. He was civil. "How's four thirty tomorrow?" he said.

"Fine."

I returned to Costello, who was becoming more upset. The performance was disturbing him slowly but surely, like a bad clam. "I don't understand some of these guys," he said. "Here they play a terrible game like this, and now they're taking off, going their separate ways. It wasn't that way when I was playing." Costello gulped a soft drink from the bottle. He has a flat, pleasant, tough Irish face. "If we played one like this, we'd want to sit around for a long time and talk, talk among ourselves." At that moment, not twenty feet away, Alcindor slipped out of the dressing room alone. . . .

The situation was charged in a community with an unhappy recent sports history. Milwaukee tried to support professional basketball in the early 1950s—Ben Kerner's Hawks. The community failed, and the Hawks moved on to St. Louis, where they prospered until hockey swept down the Mississippi.

Enter the Bucks, organized by a Milwaukee syndicate. . . . They did not break great a year ago. The Bucks won twenty-seven games, finished last in the East, and the NBA guide spelled their name Milwua-kee. At about this time, when the rustlings of spring 1969 stirred, the downbeat Milwaukee trail and the upbeat road of Lew Alcindor inter-sected. The NBA operated with a draft, and since Milwaukee and Phoenix, last in each division, were expansion teams, Commissioner Walter Kennedy drew cards to see who would have the first pick, then the call. The card came up Phoenix. The call was heads. The coin came up tails. Milwaukee had won.

In Encino, a San Fernando Valley city where Alcindor had holed up with a friend, Lew was aware that a fortune awaited. But he was con-scious too that blacks were once peddled from the slaver's block. He didn't want that; it had been humiliating. Paul Robeson used to sing: "No more auction block for me." "There won't be any bidding for me," Alcindor decided. "Each team (Milwaukee and the New York Nets of the American Basketball Association) can make one offer. Then I'll pick the one I like."

Everyone . . . promised that the Milwaukee offer would be kept secret. The figure of $1.4 million comes from an excellent source, but that source can provide no detailed breakdown. "Probably it will be spread at about $300,000 a year." Suffice it, then, that Alcindor appears to have been paid three and a half times what Joe Namath appeared to have been paid to become a professional athlete.

Lew talked to Milwaukee on a Monday and to the New York Nets on a Tuesday. He decided quickly for the Bucks. "All things being equal, it would have been easier to play in New York, but things were not equal."

When his decision became known, an ABA spokesman made the doomsday bid. To play for the Nets, Alcindor could have a $500,000 cash bonus, five years each at $200,000 salary, an annuity of $62,500 a year for twenty years starting at age forty-one, 10 percent of a proposed ABA television contract, and 5 percent of the Nets franchise. Alcindor declined. "I told each of them," he said, "to make one offer. I'm stick-ing to that. I'm going to Milwaukee."

On April 3, Alcindor affixed his Ferdinand Lewis to a Bucks con-tract. . . . John Erickson said he was thrilled, not only because of Alcin-dor's skill but "because of the quality of the person. He carried on his contract talks with the greatest trust and integrity I've been a part of."

Larry Costello said he expected to play Lew at both a high and a low post. "Lew has the talent to shoot from outside," he said, "but since he's seven-four, I'd rather have him under the basket."

Officially Alcindor was, and is, seven feet one and three-eighths inches. Had Costello let something slip? One more mystery. Erickson moved to the microphone and said smoothly, "Lew appears to have grown today because he has entered the business world."

Alcindor then answered a few dozen questions courteously and for the most part well. Yes, the ABA actually had made that $3.25 million offer, but only after it appeared in the newspapers. Yes, he thought the ABA had demeaned itself. Yes, he did look forward to dunking again because it would be good playing basketball the way it was meant to be played. Yes, he had a boyhood idol, Jackie Robinson. Yes, he'd had some bad experiences with the press, but 85 percent of the experiences were good. No, he couldn't describe his impressions of Milwaukee. He hadn't really seen it yet. The Milwaukee press was delighted, and after touching base with his parents in New York, he flew back to California, a dignified, literate, and now wealthy man who had only "a few inconsequential courses" to complete for his degree and who had earned a little time for quiet breathing.

Trouble shattered the quiet in June. Playing what is described as a pickup game at a Los Angeles high school, presumably for fun, Alcindor suddenly lost control of himself. According to one witness, Alcindor's team was taking the ball out of bounds when "Lew turned and threw a punch and walked off the court and left the gym." There is enormous leverage in those lank arms: Alcindor's punch struck the jaw of one Dennis Grey, six-eight and 215 pounds. The jaw was fractured, and surgeons . . . had to wire it together.

Grey was under contract to the Los Angeles Stars of the ABA. A teammate, Warren Davis, said, "There was the usual shoving that occurs when guys are tired, but Dennis couldn't understand why Lew hit him." Grey consulted a lawyer and presently sued Alcindor for $750,000. "Frankly," said Grey's lawyer, Paul Caruso, "the injury may have ruined Dennis's basketball career."

The suit was still pending when Alcindor joined the Bucks, and despite a sprained ankle, he worked out impressively. The Bucks were not simply a changed team. They were a new team, capable on any night of defeating anyone. They would not be last, and although they would not win, they were certain of reaching the NBA playoffs. Lew could drive and dribble as no big man before him. He had a remarkable eye. He had speed and quickness, which are different things, and grace and intelligence, and he was tough.

On October 31 the Bucks defeated the Philadelphia 76ers for the first time, and that night Alcindor's temper burst again. It was rough under the boards. Darrall Imhoff, who is shorter than Alcindor but just as heavy, had been shoving and elbowing underneath. Suddenly, in the second quarter, Alcindor swung his right elbow full force into the back of Imhoff's neck. Imhoff fell forward onto all fours, the way fighters sometimes do, and stayed there on knees and elbows, too dazed to move. Alcindor walked to midcourt. He placed both hands on his hips and watched impassively. Imhoff could not play again until the second half.

The Philadelphia crowd began to hoot. When Alcindor fouled out late in the game, he responded smartly to the boos. He gave a "V" sign—victory and peace. The boos continued. Alcindor clenched a fist and held it high. Black Power.

"I have no comment," he said in the dressing room.

A Philadelphia sportswriter said, "Could it be that you wanted to hit Imhoff, but not around the head?"

"I have no comment," Alcindor repeated.

But Luke Jackson, six-nine and 240, had a comment from the other side. "That was dirty," he said. "Deliberate and malicious. If I'd had an opening later, I would have nailed him."

Trouble with the Milwaukee press flowered the next month. In Milwaukee nearly everyone reads the *Journal*, a fine, fat afternoon and Sunday paper. Each weekend the *Journal* carries a slick, nicely written magazine section called *Insight*. Because Alcindor was important autumn news, George Lockwood, who edits *Insight*, assigned a writer named Evans Kirkby to prepare a feature. The story was cast as a visit, a rather easygoing account of a reporter's adventures and impressions as he calls on a celebrity. Conversation gives a "visit" thrust; the subject, ideally, is voluble.

Whatever Alcindor's natural inclinations, he had already made his $20,000 arrangement with *Sports Illustrated*. For the money he had to promise not only his life story but also exclusivity. In effect, until the *S.I.* series appeared, he could grant interviews only if they were dull.

Trying to be true to his word to the national magazine, Alcindor antagonized the man from the local paper. "My first attempt to meet Alcindor," Kirkby began, "had been a social and professional failure." He found the rookie "aloof in speech and habit." Alcindor was brusque and late. "When the photographer said he thought he had what he wanted," Kirkby wrote, "Alcindor turned, a West Pointer doing an about-face, and strode off to change his clothes. He did not say good-bye." Kirkby called his article "A Short Visit with Lew Alcindor." It's a fact that getting a bad press feeds itself. If one experience is sour, why try to make the next sweet? Damn 'em all.

In Detroit, Alcindor walked into a press conference arranged for him by the Pistons and, according to *Detroit Free Press* columnist Joe Falls, "Never have I seen such a discourteous display." By Falls's account, Alcindor refused to answer questions or made one-word answers or simply grunted. "Farewell, Alcindorella," Falls began an ensuing column. Alcindor, he added, "is one of the smallest men I have ever met."

Finally, at about the time I was asking Erickson about arranging an appointment, came the Seattle blowup. The Bucks held a three-point lead before thirteen thousand at the Seattle Center Coliseum, with fifteen seconds to play. Alcindor held the ball near a foul line, looking to pass. Then Bob Rule tied him up. The referee called a jump. In abrupt fury Alcindor lunged at Rule. All four teammates grabbed him. The Bucks called time.

When action resumed, Alcindor lost the jump. Three seconds later he fouled Lucius Allen, an old UCLA teammate, as Allen took a short shot. Costello gazed in agony. The ball dipped into the basket and spun out. No three-point play. Still, Allen would have three chances to make two free throws.

That was Alcindor's sixth foul, and as he walked off, fans jeered. He responded by spitting on the court. Allen made only one of three, the Bucks won by two points, and as they started toward the dressing room, a teenager ran toward Alcindor, shouting, "You big bum." One sweep of the giant arm and the teenager was knocked to the floor.

So there we were, a few days later, in the motel room in St. Louis, Alcindor and I trying to understand what was happening.

"It gets me," he said from under the brown blanket, "the way people say now you've got the money, you've got contentment. The money makes for a stability, but there are pressures, man. Out there you're a vector for all the hostility in the stands. It all comes and they're shouting that I'm not hustling and that I stink and I'm a bum. Maybe there are some bad calls; the refs miss some or call something they shouldn't. And all that's happening, you know, and you're trying to be positive and you know if you let all this upset you, you can lose your mind. Sometimes I think about what Wilt said in the beginning. Turn on. Tune in. Get out."

He talked about his background after that. He has traced his family back to the Caribbean through a great aunt, and he has heard of a forebear who stood almost six-ten. "I don't know how well he moved. They say he had flat feet. The name Alcindor is originally Moorish," he said.

"I know *al* means 'the.' What about the rest?"

"The firebird," he said. "You know, the bird that rises from its own ashes. That's what Alcindor means."

His father, a trombone player, attended Juilliard, one of the finest classical music schools on earth, but because classical music organizations retain frightful prejudices, he had to go to work for the New York subway. Imagine years spent studying Brahms and Berlioz and Beethoven, great longings expressed in exquisite sound, and then, because of the color of your skin, having to listen every day to the subway's atonal, grinding roar.

Growing, Alcindor went from six-three to six-eleven in two and a half years, between the seventh and the ninth grade. He was a good all-round athlete, swimming, running track, playing baseball, and he says he did not mind the tremendous rate of growth, although for a while his knees hurt constantly. He always wanted to win in whatever he did; he took pride in winning.

"What about your temper?" I said. "Has that always been a problem?"

He sat up in the bed. "It was when I was very small, until about the sixth grade. Then I got it under control, and I thought I had it under control until this year."

Bob Rule is black; Alcindor has gone after blacks and whites with impartiality. Still I wondered about the fan in Seattle.

"There was nothing racial there," Alcindor said. "I just didn't like what he said. I shouldn't have spit and I should have ignored the kid."

"Do you get much racial needling? Does that trigger things?"

He shook his head. "I don't hear any of that; just once in a while in the mail I get a letter that calls me a no-good nigger."

We talked about Jackie Robinson, and how Jack had heard "nigger" almost daily in the beginning, and how Eddie Stanky once held up a pair of shoes in the St. Louis dugout and screamed at Robinson, "Hey, porter. Shine these."

Alcindor seemed surprised. "Stanky did that? What did Robinson do?"

"He took it; he had to take it. Maybe he stole an extra base."

We considered the press. Alcindor insisted that he would never give up his right to privacy. It was very difficult in Milwaukee. "I like to walk, and I could walk in California, but in Milwaukee as soon as I step outside I get mobbed." He had been interviewed while at UCLA, but that was nothing like what was going on now, when the press wanted him all the time, it seemed.

"You better get used to it," I said. He turned and gazed.

"You're going to play for a while, maybe fifteen years. Well, you better be ready for fifteen years of interviewing. That's part of what all the money is for."

"I don't have to give up my privacy," Alcindor said. "I'm not peddling that."

I remembered Roger Maris and the year of his sixty-one home runs; troops of journalists attached themselves to the Yankees and put questions to him day after day. [See Chapter 9, on Roger Maris.] The same faces asking the same questions. Alcindor grimaced. "He got good questions," I said, "and stupid questions and rude questions. He handled all the questions pretty well."

"What bothers me," Alcindor said, "are stupid questions. Somebody asks a stupid question, man, I think why are you taking up my time?"

Sometimes a seemingly stupid question is a reporter's way of starting a subject talking. (Other times, to be sure, it is simply a stupid question.) But what seemed to me to be the point for Alcindor was that he accept the questions with grace. Like jump shots, they are a part of his professional life.

He mentioned feeling good about his past. He had left the Catholic Church to become an orthodox Muslim because that was his true heritage. The book that had influenced him the most was *The Autobiography of Malcolm X*. He speaks a number of languages, including Yoruba, a West Nigerian dialect. At length in the motel, he seemed to enjoy talking; seemed happy to be able to describe himself and his heritage; seemed relieved to be able to say that yes, the press versus personal privacy was a problem; seemed unburdened to review the story events of Seattle and to concede that he, proud Lew Alcindor, had been wrong. His movements became less spasmodic.

I rose to go. Alcindor stood and from his great height extended a hand. "Good luck, tonight," I told him.

"I'll need it," Alcindor said. Then, quite warmly, "If you think we ought to talk some more, I'm available. Just get me the word."

We were a short walk from the restaurant Stan Musial runs. The Bucks were going to play Atlanta that night in the St. Louis Arena. Ben Kerner had arranged the game, which would benefit a local charity and honor a number of old stars from the St. Louis Hawks. I went to the arena on foot, the better to think, and passing Musial's, the contrast was almost too pat. Stan had answered questions with grace and charmed the press (and kept his private life private) with the same ease he displayed when he clubbed a curve. Now here was Alcindor, to whom everything, except perhaps the $1.4 million, was coming so hard.

Traffic was filling the St. Louis street. There was going to be a crowd at the arena. I had been here often for hockey, but tonight was basketball, and as cars turned by me toward the parking lot, more Negroes were coming than I had ever seen come here to watch the Blues.

It was foolish then to contrast Alcindor with Musial. Alcindor, to you and me, may be one of the great athletes of the era; to himself he is one of the significant black athletes. He carries all that heritage within him, a sense of black aristocracy and black dignity and how the Moors were warriors and how his uprooted family was supposedly free, in a society that condemned a Juilliard man to work in subways.

Then it was game time.

Milwaukee won, 130–115. "We were collapsing on Alcindor all night," complained Richie Guerin, the Hawks' coach, "but we were collapsing stupid." Alcindor had confused or panicked the Hawks. That changed the game. He finished with thirty-three points, six assists, and thirteen rebounds, but the numbers don't tell it. He dominated. "How do you feel?" I said in the dressing room.

"Redemption time," he said, and grinned.

The next night, back in Milwaukee, Lew played another splendid game, but my eye was caught by Rodgers, who in a few spurts moved the ball beautifully and drilled passes through openings that had not seemed to exist. That was the evening Rodgers and I were to go out. I stopped at Alcindor's locker and told him how much I'd liked Rodgers's passing. "I liked it, too," Alcindor said. He looked relaxed. "Hey," he said. "Rodgers could get the ball to Jimmy Hoffa, and he's in jail."

It was my turn to grin and thank him. He was doing one of the kinder things an athlete can do for a writer: he was throwing me a line.

What surely can we take from these few days in the life of Lew Alcindor? Something about the man and something about the times in which we live.

The pressure is enormous. He generates a good deal himself with inner drives, but much of it hangs ominously, there, always there, never dissipating. He is potentially the black athlete of this era, as Jackie Robinson was the black athlete of another. His role is not more difficult than Robinson's—after all, the Klan is not threatening to shoot Alcindor for what he did to the Atlanta team. But it may be more complex. The black movement has become more complex.

He is no racist; most of his closest advisers are white. Nor is he militant in the sense that Stokely Carmichael is. But he is more militant than, say, Willie Mays, and this goes hard with some.

He accepts advice from others on income spreading and such; one suspects that the lawyers who read the *Sports Illustrated* contract for him advised him badly. Starting in a new city $1.4 million ahead, what should have come first was new relationships, not additional cash. By allowing one magazine to dictate his relationships to all magazines and newspapers and television stations, the lawyers did him no favor. He could have demanded less restrictive terms from *Sports Illustrated* or simply put off composing his autobiography until he reached the advanced age of twenty-three. By then, working relationships in Milwaukee and around the league would have been established. He feels enough pressure this first year on the basketball court without a sideshow of fencing with the press.

But he is a great athlete and a strong man and to me a winning person. At twenty-two this proud, intense black has magnificent moments and dreadful ones, which, if memory serves, is what being twenty-two is like. It is going to be a pleasure to watch his poise and understanding grow—almost as much of a pleasure as it will be to watch him play basketball as no one ever has for the next ten or fifteen years.

PART II

LIVING YOUR LIFE

CHAPTER 7

THE BABE: FATHER
OF THE HOME RUN

*"The greater the hero, the more prevalent the fictions." So wrote
Kahn in this 1959* Esquire *article as he prepared to see what the
"Bambino" was like off the field when he was not hitting 714 home
runs in Yankee Stadium. The article shows that many years before
Kahn visited the old Brooklyn Dodgers players in preparation for
writing* The Boys of Summer, *he was as interested in athletes off the
field as on.*

In his time and in his way, George Herman Ruth was a holy sinner.
He was a man of measureless lust, selfishness, and appetites, but he
was also a man undyingly faithful, in a manner, to both his public and
to his game. Tradition, which always distorts, had remolded Babe Ruth
almost as extensively in a decade as it has remolded Abraham Lincoln
in a century. Just eleven years after Ruth's death and twenty-four years
after his last disastrous season, only the image of holiness remains.

Ruth died on August 16, 1948. After the funeral service, as a great
crowd stood in reverent silence, pallbearers, many of them Ruth's own
teammates, carried the casket into the fierce heat of the summer day.

"Lord," whispered Joe Dugan, the Yankee third baseman during
Ruth's prime. "I'd give my right arm for an ice-cold beer."

Waite Hoyt, the former pitcher, grunted under the burden of the
coffin and turned slightly. "Joe," he murmured, "so would the Babe."

The middle-aged men, who spent their youth playing side by side with Ruth, remember. They remember more clearly than the writers who traveled with him or the fans who watched him; even more clearly, perhaps, than the women—the adopted daughters and the wife who loved him most. For they knew him in the camaraderie of strong, successful men, where no man passed verdict on the other but where everyone knew "Jidge" Ruth was at once the strongest and most successful.

There is a curious derivative of Gresham's Law that applies to American heroes. Just as good money drives out bad in economics, so heroic fancy drives out heroic fact and, in the case of heroes, we are often left standing in a forest of chopped-down cherry trees wondering what our man was actually like. The greater the hero, the more prevalent the fictions. Since Ruth was the most popular of all baseball heroes, movie companies, careless writers, and glib storytellers busied themselves with the obfuscation of fact.

But to begin with, everything you have ever heard about Ruth on a baseball field is probably the truth or close to it. Ruth could hit a baseball higher, farther, and more dramatically than anyone else. His record of 60 home runs in one season is unquestionably the classic of all sports standards. His career totals of 714 home runs and 2,056 bases on balls are still far beyond mortal challenge. His great swing, even when he struck out, was more awesome than the stroke of a lesser man which happened to produce a home run.

He does seem always to have made the right play in the outfield. He did have superlative baseball instincts. He did bring all players' salaries up behind his own and, more assuredly than anything else, he was the savior baseball had to find after the Chicago White Sox dumped the 1919 World Series. All these are part of the legend and all ring true.

But once the stories of Ruth move off the diamond, fact fades away and dies. He liked children, but his life was not a priestly dedication to healing sick boys. He liked jokes, but his humor at best was coarse. He was devoutly religious, but only sporadically, when suddenly he felt compelled to make up for lost time in church. He may not have been an utter social boor, but he was something less than tactful, something less than gracious, something very much less than sensitive.

Once when he accidentally spiked a Yankee named Ray Morehart, he apologized profusely, then said to a veteran, "Hey, when did that guy join the club? Last week?" Morehart had been with the club for months. Ruth hadn't noticed. To him everyone under thirty-five was "Kid" and everyone older was "Doc." He was absorbed in himself and his talent and although he was generous with audiences to fans, these were never anything more than audiences. Fans came to Ruth. Celebrities came to Ruth. The world came to Ruth. Ruth went to no one, unless summoned.

What was he like? Bennie Bengough, the old catcher, remembers that in his own rookie year of 1923, Ruth, the veteran, made a point each payday of displaying his paycheck from the Yankees. "Hey, kid," he'd say to Bengough. "Hey, Barney Google. How'd you like to have this, kid?" Each two-week check was for $2,000, which Bengough says was more than he got all year. "But," Bengough adds, "he didn't show it in a boasting way. More like it was his idea of fun."

Dugan was already established as a star when the Yankees acquired him from the Boston Red Sox that season. On the day Dugan joined the club, Ruth dumped a batch of mail in his lap. "Open these for me, will ya, kid?" Ruth said. "Keep the ones with checks and the ones from broads. Throw out the others." It was just before game time and Ruth, following his custom, was late. He undressed quickly while Dugan went through one pile of mail and Whitey Witt, the center fielder, went through another.

"Here's a wire from Ziegfeld," Witt said. "He'll give you fifteen hundred bucks a week to go in a show next winter." Ruth crumpled the wire and threw it away. "I ain't an actor," he said.

"Cripes," said Mike McNally, a reserve infielder, "make it while you can. For fifteen hundred a week, learn to act."

"Yeah," Ruth said, putting on his spikes. "Yeah."

"If you go in a show," McNally said, "and I come into town to see you, can you get me a couple of 'Annie Oakleys'?"

"If I go in a show, I'll get you guys all the broads you want."

Babe Ruth, a huge, ignorant, sentimental emperor, was the product of a childhood so bleak that it was almost no childhood at all. Then, in his early manhood he found himself earning considerably more money and possessing far more popularity than the president of the United States. He was not humble in his change of fortune. He knew that he was the biggest name in baseball and whatever his skill brought him, he not only accepted, but demanded it.

Once when he visited France, accompanied by his wife and daughter, he surprised Americans who knew him well by announcing, "Paris ain't much of a town." Parisian crowds had failed to recognize him. The American embassy there, receiving a letter addressed to George Herman Ruth, took an advertisement in the Paris *Herald Tribune* listing Ruth's name along with many others found on unclaimed mail. "How do you like them guys?" Ruth said in anger and in pain. "Taking an ad in the paper to find out where the hell I am! That could never happen in New York."

It never could have. Ruth lived for fifty-three years, but his special time was the fifteen seasons he played for the New York Yankees. In the '20s the country teemed with sports figures whose names meant immediate idolatry: Tilden and Grange, Rockne and Dempsey, Ty Cobb and Bobby Jones and John McGraw. No one gathered and awed so many crowds for so many years as the man the whole nation called "The Babe."

On the field, Ruth's shape was unique. It was thick through the shoulders, prodigious at the belly, and set on comically thin legs. He was pigeon-toed and he ran with delicate, mincing steps that all but concealed his speed. Off the field the man had other marks. He chewed cigars and wore camel's hair polo coats and affected a light brown cap. His face was broad and wide, dominated by a vast, flat nose and an overhanging brow. His voice was hoarse and loud. As he moved, center stage moved with him.

Ruth appeared on the American scene through the unlikely gateway of Baltimore, Maryland, where he was born in 1895, one of the number of children with which the union of Kate Schanberg and G. H. Ruth, Sr., was blessed. In later years Ruth invariably claimed that his father owned a saloon and that he had been born a few flights above the bar. This is open to serious question. Photographs of Ruth's birthplace show no ground-floor saloon, only the inevitable Baltimore white stoopfront. Undoubtedly, the elder Ruth was familiar with Baltimore saloons, but whether as entrepreneur or client remains uncertain.

Like W. C. Fields, Babe Ruth never tasted liquor before he was six. He also chewed tobacco and appears to have stolen whatever loose change his parents left about the house. "I was a bad kid," Ruth himself said afterward. In 1902, when he was only seven, Ruth was placed in St. Mary's Industrial School as an incorrigible. He was not, of course, an orphan, as legend insists. He was the unmanageable child of parents who were not passionately dedicated to parenthood.

St. Mary's, a pile of masonry as solemn as a prison, was fenced off from the outside world and run by the Roman Catholic Order of Xavieran Brothers. There, under the guidance of Brother Matthias, a gentle man six and a half feet tall, Ruth was taught to read and to write, schooled in the crafts of tailoring and shirtmaking and, in his spare hours, he played baseball. No one ever had to teach him baseball. Ruth was the ultimate natural. At nineteen St. Mary's released him to the Baltimore Orioles, who were then in the International League, and, staggered by a $600-a-year contract, Ruth went forth into the world. He was a babe; the nickname came quickly and logically.

Within two seasons he was starring as pitcher and pinch hitter for the Red Sox. In eight matches with Walter Johnson, the finest of modern American League pitchers, Ruth won six, three by scores of 1–0 and once when his homer provided the only run. In World Series competition he pitched twenty-nine consecutive scoreless innings, a record that stands. Ruth was a superb left-hander. He chose to move into the outfield for Boston in 1919 only because his pinch-hitting was so effective that he felt he could earn more playing every day.

In 1920 the Yankees, then as now owned by millionaires, purchased Ruth for $100,000. Colonel Jake Ruppert, one of the owners, had to take out a $370,000 mortgage on Fenway Park, the Red Sox' field, as the second provision of what was the biggest of all baseball deals up to that time. Dividends were prompt. In his first season with the Yankees, Ruth hit fifty-four home runs, almost double the old record and an achievement beyond belief to fans accustomed to home run champions with totals of ten or twelve. Abruptly, Ruth was the wonder of baseball. The fans recognized it and so did Ruth.

This, then, was his stage: an incredulous, idolizing America, gaping through the '20s, all the while congratulating itself on its own maturity.

Here were the supporting players: Jumping Joe Dugan, out of Holy Cross, intelligent, quiet, gifted. Could take a drink. Waite Hoyt, high school graduate who later attended a school for undertakers. Acerbic, witty, skilled. Could take a drink. Miller Huggins, manager. Diminutive old baseball pro. Acid, tough, and unamused by jokes about his size. Could take a drink, but preferred his players not to. Bob Meusel. Tall, silent. Could take a drink. Whitey Witt. Short, garrulous. Could take a drink. Assorted other players, courtesans, lords, ladies, and presidents.

This is what he did: Led the American League in homers every year but one in the decade. Led the Yankees into seven World Series. Drew a salary that went in rapid stages to $52,000 to $70,000 to $80,000. Provided the gate appeal that built Yankee Stadium. Rebuilt the game, which had been scientific, into an extension of his own slugging style.

And this is how he played his role: One day in 1924 (forty-six homers for the Babe) Herb Pennock, a genteel pitcher, was asked to attend a party sponsored by a prominent family near Wilmington, Delaware. "Hug," Pennock said, "they want some Yankees; I need a dozen autographed balls and three players, Ruth, Dugan, and Meusel."

"Okay," Huggins said, "but remember. We got a game in Philly tomorrow."

Ruth was the hit of the party. Yes, he said, baseball had come easy to him. The swing? Well, he'd liked the way Shoeless Joe Jackson used to swing and maybe he kinda copied Jackson's wrist action. That guy swung good. Later, after hours of drinking and baseball talk, Ruth grew bemused and set out for a brunette, who, it developed, was one of the maids.

"Babe," said a boxing promoter from Philadelphia, "you got to get outta here."

"Not without that broad," Ruth said.

"Come on," said the boxing man, "I'll get you broads in Philly better than her."

"You sure?" Ruth said.

In Philadelphia the boxing man took Ruth to a building in which he was absolutely certain they would find girls. Hours later, as dawn came up over eastern Philadelphia, the boxing man suggested that Ruth leave. Ruth was sitting in an easy chair, a girl on each knee. He held an open bottle of champagne upside down over his head. "I ain't gonna be leaving for a while yet," Ruth said.

At Shibe Park that afternoon, Ruth, who may not have slept, announced, "I feel real good."

"You don't look real good," said Fred Merkle, a National League veteran who was finishing his career with the Yankees.

"I'll hit one," Ruth said. "Bet?" Merkle said.

"A hundred," Ruth said.

"Wait a minute," Merkle said. "This is an easy ballpark."

"All right," Ruth said. "I'll give you two-to-one."

On his first time at bat, Ruth walloped an outside pitch into the left-field stands and won his bet. Then he lined a triple to right, crashed a triple over Al Simmons's head in center, and pulled a homer over the right-field wall. He had gone four-for-four, with two triples and two homers, without benefit of bed rest.

One day in 1928 (fifty-four homers and $70,000), it came up rain in Yankee Stadium and Ruth, who had spent the morning waiting for the rain to stop, grew bored. "What are we gonna do?" he asked Hoyt. "Let's get drunk."

"Not me," Hoyt said. "I pitch tomorrow."

"Joe?" Ruth said to Dugan.

"Let's go out to the track," Dugan said.

Ruth bet $500 across the board, a total of $1,500, on a steeplechase horse that had caught his fancy. The horse fell at the first jump. "You Irish so-and-so," he roared at Dugan. "You shanty buzzard. We couda been drunk for six weeks on the dough I dropped." Before the afternoon ended, Ruth recouped. "Come on, Joe," he said. "You had a helluvan idea. I'm gonna throw a party, soon as we get back."

To George Herman Ruth, women, money, and liquor were equally important. They were necessities he took for granted. In his first full year with the Red Sox, he married a Nova Scotia girl named Helen Woodring, but a few years later they separated. The first Mrs. Ruth died in a fire in 1929. Ruth then married a former actress named Claire Hodgson, whom he called Clara and to whom, despite her continual efforts to tame him, he remained deeply attached. Still, Ruth was more than a two-woman man.

"Every spring," says one old Yankee, "he used to hand me a big laugh. We'd play in one town after another in the South and whenever the train pulled out of the station, there'd be a half-dozen girls waving good-bye to him. 'Good-bye,' the big guy would say real sweet. 'See you next year, girls.'"

One year it caught up with him. He collapsed on the field, all doubled over, and the club had to put out a story that he'd eaten a dozen hot dogs and drank a couple dozen bottles of soda pop. He was real sick and it made a lot of headlines. "The bellyache heard round the world," the writers called it. Well, Ruth hadn't been drinking that much pop and it wasn't even a bellyache.

Until Whitey Witt left the club after the 1925 season, he roomed with Dugan and the two had a standing invitation to join Ruth in his suite early any evening. It was always the same. Cases of good bootleg liquor were piled in the bathroom and a keg of beer stood in the tub. When the phone rang, Witt was expected to answer.

"Tell her to come up," Ruth would shout. "Tell her I'm glad to see her."

By midnight, Ruth would have made his selection from the available entries. "Good night," he'd tell Dugan and Witt, who would then leave in a swirl of rejected applicants.

In the course of this existence, money was a casual thing, except during the late winter, when Ruth negotiated his contract with Ruppert. Overall, Ruth earned $1,076,474 from baseball. No one, least of all Ruth, ever calculated what he earned from ghostwritten articles, personal appearances, and endorsements. The generally accepted figure is $1,000,000 and it must stand.

One April, when he was earning $70,000 a year, Ruth found himself without funds to pay his income tax bill, which in those laissez-faire days was $1,500. Hoyt and Dugan each put up $750 and Ruth paid the tax.

A month later Ruth approached with a bankroll. "I wanna, give you six percent," he said. "You guys figure it out."

"Six percent," Hoyt said, shocked.

"What do you think we are," Dugan said, "taking interest from a teammate?"

It was some time before the two convinced Ruth that the loan was a favor, not a business transaction. Later, on a western trip, Dugan found himself strapped before a dinner date in Cleveland. Ruth was talking to tourists in the hotel lobby, and Dugan walked up quietly and said, "Jidge, I am empty-handed."

Without looking and without interrupting his conversation, Ruth pressed a bill into Dugan's palm. Dugan pocketed it, also without looking and, when the check was presented in the restaurant, he handed the borrowed bill to the waiter.

"You kidding, mister?" said the waiter, who looked.

"What?"

"I can't change it. Come on, gimme a twenty."

Dugan examined the money. It was a five-hundred-dollar bill. As soon as the Yankees returned to New York, he gave Ruth a $500 check.

"What the hell is this?" Ruth asked.

"The dough you lent me in Cleveland," Dugan said.

"Cripes," Ruth said, "I thought I blew it."

Ruth apparently never voted in an election until 1944, when, moved by opposition to a fourth term for Mr. Roosevelt, he registered, took a literacy test, and passed. But without benefit of voting, he was actively interested in the 1928 campaign of Al Smith, who, like Ruth was a Roman Catholic. Ruth organized a political-action group called "Yankees for Smith," which was effective in a limited way.

During the early stages of the 1928 race, Herbert Hoover, as all presidential candidates, became an ardent baseball fan. During one of his trips to Griffith Stadium, he decided a picture with Ruth might be in order. One of the Yankees overheard a Washington official discussing the plans and tipped off Ruth, who then remained in the clubhouse until game time. "I ain't gonna pose with him," Ruth said. "I'm for Smith."

Actually Ruth had already acquired some experience not only with presidential candidates, but with presidents. Once when Calvin Coolidge went to a ball game, the Yankees were lined up for formal introductions. "How do you do, Mr. President," said Hoyt. "Good day, sir," said Pennock.

Coolidge was walking slowly, shaking hands with each of the players, and Ruth, as he waited, took off his cap and wiped his forehead with a handkerchief.

"Mr. Ruth," the president said. "Hot as hell, ain't it, Prez?" Mr. Ruth said.

People were always trying to reform him. Miller Huggins tried, first gently, then severely and ultimately with a $5,000 fine for breaking training. Ruth responded by holding Huggins at arms' length off the rear car of a speeding train. Christy Walsh, Ruth's agent and one of his many ghostwriters, ultimately did convince Ruth that the $80,000 income would not long endure. Trust funds set up by Walsh and an attorney helped Ruth live out his years in comfort. Mrs. Claire Ruth succeeded somewhat in slowing her husband's pace, but significantly, at the end of his active baseball career, it was the old wild instinct that betrayed him.

After the 1934 season, in which Ruth's salary had dropped to $35,000, he realized that he was no longer a full-time player. Ruppert released him, and Ruth joined the Boston Braves as part-time outfielder and full-time vice president and assistant manager. The last two titles were meaningless. Judge Emil Fuchs, who owned the Braves, wanted Ruth to hit home runs. When Ruth failed—he was batting .181 in June—Fuchs dropped him as a player. The other two jobs promptly disappeared. The specific was a party in New York. "I'm slumping," Ruth told Fuchs, "and a slumping ballplayer ought to get away from the ballpark. I want some time off." The French liner *Normandie*, then the largest ship afloat, was docking in New York, and Ruth had been invited to a welcoming brawl.

"Stay with the team," Fuchs ordered.

"I'm going to the party," Ruth said.

When Ruth went, Fuchs announced that team morale had been impaired and that Ruth, clearly, was neither managerial nor executive material.

The later years were not bright. Ruth wanted to manage in the majors, and the Yankees offered him their farm team in Newark, New Jersey. "You can't take care of yourself," Ruppert said. "How can I be sure you can take care of my best players? Newark, Ruth, or nothing."

"Nothing," Ruth said.

In 1938 Larry MacPhail hired him as a Dodger coach in midseason. That winter Leo Durocher, whose only talent in Ruth's view was a sharp tongue, was appointed Brooklyn manager. Ruth resigned and was out of baseball forever.

He lived in a large apartment on Riverside Drive, high above the Hudson River, and each year he threw a big birthday party for himself. He occupied his days with golf, fishing, and watching baseball. Once he spoke at the Baseball Writers' dinner in New York. "I gave twenty-two years of my life to big-league baseball," he said, "and I'm ready to give twenty-five more." Nearly a thousand baseball men heard him. No one offered him a job.

Was it simply Ruth's intemperance that kept him out of baseball? Or was it the mass resentment of club owners against a man whose personal impact pushed baseball salaries up as his own income soared?

The reason is less important than the fact. Baseball turned away from the man who, more than anyone else, made it big business. Yet till the end, outside the game, Ruth the man and Ruth the legend grew. Anywhere he wandered he was The Babe, unique, unrivaled, unchallenged. What made him happy was that children knew him. He loved children genuinely, as well might a man who had no childhood of his own. Nor any sons.

Cancer struck him in 1946 and he faced death, for two agonizing years, with utter disbelief. Dugan saw him when Ruth was confined to a wheelchair. "Joe," Ruth said, his voice cut to a whisper by the cancer. "Joe," he said, caught in the final horror of truth, "I'm gone, Joe. I'm gone." Dugan clutched his old friend's hand and the two men wept. A few days later Ruth was dead.

"To understand him," says Dugan, who probably knew "Jidge" better than any man alive, "you had to understand this: He wasn't human. He was an animal. No man could have done the things he did and been a ballplayer. Cobb? Could he pitch? Speaker? The rest? I saw them. I was there. There never was anybody close. When you figure the things he did and the way he lived and the way he played, you got to figure he was more than animal even. There never was anyone like him. He was a god."

CHAPTER 8

THE HOMER HEARD ROUND THE WORLD

Before Bucky Dent hit an October 1978 home run to help the Yankees beat the Boston Red Sox—described in Kahn's 2003 book October Men—*the most famous home run in baseball history came from the bat of one Bobby Thomson as the New York Giants overcame the Brooklyn Dodgers in the final game of a playoff for the 1951 National League pennant. The homer was detailed in Kahn's* The Era *(1993) and in* Sport *magazine, where Kahn published much of his early journalism.*

Some days—they come rarely—are charged with public events so unexpected, so shocking, so far beyond the limits of belief, that the events are not really public at all. Their impact thrusts them into the private lives of millions of people, who forever after remember these events in personal terms.

Pearl Harbor day was like that. There was the day President Roosevelt died. Such impinging days are not always tragic; one, in particular, was joyous and heroic for many people, though tragic for some. It was the day, in the most exciting of all baseball seasons, when Bobby Thomson hit his home run. . . .

The night before nearly everyone slept well. Bobby Thomson was troubled because he had struck out with the bases full, but after a steak dinner and a few beers, he relaxed. Ralph Branca fell asleep quickly. He had pitched on Sunday, the last day of the regular season, and on Monday in the first game of the playoff. Tomorrow, October 3, 1951, would be Wednesday, and Branca did not expect that he would be called on to pitch again so soon.

Sal Maglie, who knew he was to start for the New York Giants, spent a comfortable night in his room at the Concourse Plaza Hotel. For all his intensity, Maglie had learned to control his nerves. So, to a degree, had Don Newcombe, who was to start for the Brooklyn Dodgers. "I can always sleep," Newcombe said, a little proudly. "I don't need to take pills like some guys do the night before they pitch."

Charley Dressen, who managed the Dodgers, went out to an Italian restaurant called Rocco's and ate a dinner of clams, mussels, lobsters, and spaghetti with hot sauce. A few people asked him how he felt about tomorrow's game, and Dressen told them he wasn't worried. "Our ball club is ready," he said.

One man who did feel restlessness was Andy Pafko, the Dodgers' new left fielder. The Dodgers had traded for Pafko at midseason, in a move the newspapers called pennant insurance, and Pafko, reading the papers, was impressed. Now he felt that the pennant was almost his personal responsibility. Lying in his room at the Hotel St. George in Brooklyn, he thought of his wife, Ellen, in Chicago. He had sent her a ticket to New York so she could watch him play with the Dodgers in the World Series. Next year there would be time to find an apartment together in Brooklyn, but for the moment Andy Pafko was alone. Perhaps it was loneliness as much as pressure that depressed him.

Although New York City was bright with the quickening pace of autumn, none of the ballplayers went out on the town. Everywhere, harboring their energies, they went to bed at about eleven o'clock, and soon, everywhere, they slept.

These were two tough and gifted baseball teams. The Dodgers had been built around such sluggers as Duke Snider and Gil Hodges, and in Jackie Robinson they had the finest competitor in baseball. For months that year the Dodgers won big and won often. On the night of August 11 they had been in first place, a full thirteen games ahead of the Giants, who were their closest competitors.

Under Leo Durocher the Giants were combative, strong in pitching and opportunism, concentrated in themselves. Bobby Thomson, like the other Giants, knew none of the Dodgers socially; the teams did not fraternize. He thought that Gil Hodges was a pleasant man but that the rest of the Dodgers were unpleasant. This was a sermon Durocher had preached ceaselessly in the last months of the season until finally the ballplayers came unquestionably to believe their manager.

Durocher's Giants, jelling slowly, spent some of May in last place. It was only when Willie Mays was called up from Minneapolis and Thomson became the regular third baseman that the team began to show fire. Then, from August 11 on, the Giants blazed, winning thirty-seven games and losing only seven under demanding, unrelenting pressure.

The Dodgers, playing .500 ball as some of their sluggers slumped, were nonetheless unreachable by all the traditions of baseball. But the Giants, establishing a new tradition, caught the unreachable, forced them into them into a playoff, and won the first game, 3–1, defeating Ralph Branca at Ebbets Field. Then Clem Labine, a Dodger rookie, shut out the Giants at the Polo Grounds. The score was 10–0, but the game was close for some time and seemed to turn when Thomson, with bases full, struck out on a three-and-two pitch, a jumping curve that hooked wide of the plate.

No one expected the deciding game of the playoff to be easy, but no one, not Thomson, or Branca, or Durocher, or Dressen, felt any dramatic foreshadowing of what was ahead. The game would be tense, but they'd all been tense lately. That was all. It was against this background of tension, which the players accepted as a part of life, that everyone slept the night before.

Robert B. Thomson, brown-haired, tall, and swift, said good-bye to his mother a little before 10 A.M. and drove his blue Mercury to the Staten Island Ferry. The Thomsons lived on Flagg Place in New Dorp, once an independent village, now a community within the borough of Richmond. As he drove, Thomson thought about the game. "If I can just get three-for-four," he mused, "then the old Jints will be all right." The thought comforted him. He'd been hitting well, and three-for-four seemed a reasonable goal.

Ralph T. Branca, black-haired, tall, and heavy-limbed, said good-bye to his mother in suburban Mount Vernon, New York, the town where he had grown up, and drove off in his new Oldsmobile. He felt a little stiff from all his recent pitching. It would take him a long time to warm up, should Dressen need him in relief.

It was a gray day, darkened with the threat of rain. The temperature was warm enough—in the high sixties—but the crowd, waiting for the gates of the Polo Grounds bleachers to open, was smaller than the one which had waited in bright sunshine the day before.

Most of the players arrived by car, but Andrew Pafko came by subway, an hour's ride from downtown Brooklyn. "I'll beat the crowd," he decided, "so there's no sense wasting money on a cab." The crowd, it was to develop, was scarcely worth beating: 34,320, some 15,000 under standing-room capacity.

As a ballpark, the Polo Grounds was unique: oddly shaped and with clubhouses 600 feet from the dugouts. It was, actually, a football horseshoe and as such made strange demands upon pitchers. The foul line in right field ran only 250 feet until it reached the lower deck of the grandstands. The left-field line ran slightly longer, but in left a scoreboard was fixed to the facade of the upper deck, a facade that extended several yards closer to the plate than did the lower stands. A short fly, drifting down toward a fielder, could become a home run merely by grazing that projecting scoreboard.

Both walls fell away sharply, and the fence in center field was 485 feet out. The pitching rule was simply to make the batter hit to center, where distance didn't matter. The outfielding rule was to crowd the middle. The right and left fielders conceded drives down the line and tried to prevent hits from carrying into the deep alleys in left and right center. At the Polo Grounds, outfielders stood in a tightly bunched row, all seemingly about the same distance from home plate.

Back of center field stood an ugly green building which contained the clubhouses, a dining room for the press, and an apartment for Horace Stoneham, the Giants' owner. Since both Durocher and Dressen believed in intensive managing, each team was gathered for a meeting in that green building shortly before noon. The announced purpose was to review hitters, although the two teams had played each other twenty-four times previously that season and there was nothing fresh or new to say about anyone.

During batting practice Branca was standing near the cage with Pee Wee Reese and Jackie Robinson. "You guys get butterflies?" a reporter asked.

"No matter how long you been playing, you still get butterflies before the big ones," Reese said. Robinson laughed and Branca nodded solemnly. Ralph's long face, in repose, was sad or, perhaps, deadpan. One never knew whether he was troubled by what was around him or whether he was about to laugh.

The game began badly for the Giants. Sal Maglie, who had won twenty-three games and beaten the Dodgers five times that season, walked Reese and Duke Snider in the first inning. Jackie Robinson came up and lined Maglie's first pitch safely into left field for a single. Reese scored, and the Dodgers were ahead 1–0.

Newcombe was fast but not untouchable, and in the second inning Whitey Lockman reached him for a single. Thomson followed with a sharp drive to left, his first hit, and briefly the Giants seemed to be rallying. But very briefly. Running with his head down, Thomson charged past first base and had almost reached second before he noticed that Lockman had stopped there. Thomson was tagged out in a rundown, an embarrassing end to the threat.

When the day grew darker and the lights were turned on as the third inning began, the ballpark buzzed with countless versions of a joke: "Well, now maybe Thomson will be able to see what he's doing."

During the fifth Thomson doubled, his second hit, and Branca began to throw. Newcombe pitched out of the inning easily, but Branca threw a little longer. He wasn't snapping curves or firing fastballs. He was just working to loosen his arm, shoulder, and back.

Branca threw again during the sixth inning, and when Monte Irvin doubled to left in the seventh, Branca began to throw hard. He felt loose by then. His fastball was alive. Carl Erskine, warming up next to him, was bouncing his curve, but Branca had good control and good stuff.

With Irvin at second, Lockman pushed a bunt in front of the plate, and Rube Walker, the Dodger catcher, grabbed the ball and threw to

Billy Cox at third. Irvin beat the throw, and now Thomson came to bat with the tying run at third base late in a 1–0 ball game.

Bearing down, Newcombe threw only strikes. After two, Thomson fouled one: a fastball. Then he hit another fastball deep into center field, and Irvin scored easily after the catch. As the eighth inning began, the score was 1–1.

"I got nothing left, nothing," Newcombe announced as he walked into the Dodger dugout. Jackie Robinson and Roy Campanella, who was not playing that day because he had pulled a thigh muscle, took Newcombe aside.

"My arm's tight," Newcombe said.

"Obscenity," Robinson replied. "You go out there and pitch until your obscene arm falls off."

"Roomie," Campanella said, "you ain't gonna quit on us now. You gonna hum that pea for us, roomie." While the two built a fire under Newcombe, other Dodgers were making the inning miserable for both Maglie and Thomson. Reese and Snider opened with singles to right; and when Maglie threw a curve in the dirt and past Wes Westrum, Reese scored and Snider sped to third. Then Maglie walked Robinson, and the Dodgers, ahead 2–1, once again had runners at first and third.

Pafko pulled a bounding ball up the third-base line and Thomson, breaking nicely, reached backhand for it. The play required a delicate touch; the ball glanced off the heel of Thomson's glove and skidded away from him. Snider scored, making it 3–1 Brooklyn, and Pafko was credited with a single. Then Billy Cox followed with a fierce one-hopper, again to Thomson's sector.

One thought—"Get in front of it"—crossed Thomson's mind. He did, lunging recklessly. There were other times at third when Thomson had thought of hard smashes coming up and hitting him in the face. This time he didn't. He thought only of blocking the ball with his glove, his arm, his chest. But the ball bounced high and carried over his shoulder into left field. The Dodgers had their third run and a 4–1 lead.

Newcombe blazed through the eighth, his arm no longer tight, and Larry Jansen retired the Dodgers in the ninth. "Come on," Durocher shouted as the last of the ninth began. "We can still get 'em. Come on."

Newcombe threw two quick strikes to Alvin Dark. "Got to get my bat on the ball," Dark thought. "Just get my bat on it."

Newcombe threw again, and Dark rapped a bounder into the hole in the right side of the infield. Both Hodges and Robinson broke for the ball and Newcombe ran to cover first base. Hodges, straining, touched the ball with the tip of his mitt and deflected it away from Robinson. Perhaps if he had not touched it Robinson could have made the play. As it was, Dark reached first on a single.

It was then that Dressen made a curious decision. He let Hodges hold the bag on Dark as though Dark as base runner were important. Actually, of course, Dark could have stolen second, third, and home without affecting the game. The Giants needed three runs to tie, not one, and the Dodgers needed only outs.

Don Mueller, up next, quickly bounced a single through the right side—close to Hodges's normal fielding depth—and the Giants had runners at first and third. All around the Polo Grounds people stood up, but not to leave.

With Monte Irvin coming to bat, Dressen walked to the mound. Branca and Erskine were throwing in the bullpen, and Clyde Sukeforth, the bullpen coach, had told Dressen that Branca was fast and loose. But on the way to the mound the Dodger manager thought about catching, not pitching.

Campanella had a way with Newcombe. He knew how to needle the big pitcher to fury, and this fury added speed to Newcombe's fastball. Walking to the mound, Dressen wondered about replacing Rube Walker with Campanella. There was only one drawback. Foul territory at the Polo Grounds was extensive. A rodeo, billed as colossal, was once staged entirely in the foul area there. Campanella, with his bad leg, could catch, but he could not run after foul pops. Dressen thought of Hodges and Cox, both sure-handed, both agile. They could cover for Campanella to some extent. But there was all that area directly behind home plate where no one would be able to help Campy at all. Dressen thought of a foul pop landing safely, and he thought of the newspapers the next day. The second-guessing would be fierce, and he didn't want that. No, Dressen decided, it wouldn't be worth that. He chatted with Newcombe for a moment and went back to the dugout. When Irvin fouled out to Hodges, Dressen decided that he had done the right thing.

Then Newcombe threw an outside fastball to Whitey Lockman, and Lockman doubled to left. Dark scored, making it 4–2, but Mueller, in easily at third, slid badly and twisted his ankle. He could neither rise nor walk. Clint Hartung went in to run for him, and action was suspended while Mueller, on a stretcher, was carried to the distant Giant clubhouse.

"Branca's ready," Clyde Sukeforth told Charley Dressen on the intercom that ran from dugout to bullpen.

"Okay," Dressen said. "I want him."

Branca felt strong and loose as he started his long walk in from the bullpen. At that moment he had only one thought. Thomson was the next batter, and he wanted to get ahead of Thomson. Branca never pitched in rigid patterns. He adjusted himself to changing situations, and his thought now was simply to get his first pitch over the plate with something on it.

Coming into the infield, he remembered the pregame conversation with the newspaperman. "Any butterflies?" he said to Robinson and Reese. They grinned, but not very widely.

At the mound, Dressen handed Branca the ball and said: "Get him out." Without another word the manager turned and walked back to the dugout.

Watching Branca take his eight warmup pitches, Thomson thought of his own goal. He had two hits. Another now would give him his three-for-four. It would also tie the score.

"Boy," Durocher said to Thomson, "if you ever hit one, hit one now." Thomson nodded but said nothing. Then he stepped up to the plate.

Branca's first pitch was a fastball, hip-high over the inside corner. "Should have swung at that," Thomson told himself, backing out of the box.

"I got my strike," thought Branca. Now it was time to come up and in with a fastball. Now it was time for a bad pitch that might tempt Thomson to waste a swing. If he went for the bad ball, chances were he'd miss. If he took it, Branca would still be ready to come back with a curve, low and away. Branca was moving the ball around, a basic point when pitching to good hitters.

The pitch came in high and tight, just where Branca had wanted it. Thomson swung hard and the ball sailed out toward left.

"Get down, get down," screamed Billy Cox as the line drive carried high over his head.

"I got a chance at it," thought Andy Pafko, bolting back toward the wall.

Then the ball was gone, under the overhanging scoreboard, over the high wall, gone deep into the seats in lower left. For seconds, which seemed like minutes, the crowd sat dumb. Then came the roar. It was a roar matched all across the country, wherever people sat at radio or television sets, a roar of delight, a roar of horror, but mostly a roar of utter shock! It was a moment when all the country roared and when an office worker in a tall building in Wall Street, hearing a cry rise all about her, wondered if war had been declared.

As the ball sailed into the stands, Thomson danced around the bases, skipping and leaping. The Giants crowded from their dugout to home plate. Ed Stanky, the second baseman, ran to Durocher, jumped on the manager's back, wrestled him to the ground, and hugged him.

In left, Pafko stood stunned. Then he started to walk slowly toward the clubhouse, telling himself over and over: "It can't be." Most of the Dodgers were walking before Thomson reached second base, but Jackie Robinson held his ground. He wanted to make sure that Thomson touched all bases before conceding that the Giants had won, 5–4, before conceding that the pennant race was over.

Clyde Sukeforth gathered gear in the bullpen, and nearby Carl Erskine turned to Clem Labine. "That's the first time I've ever seen a big fat wallet go flying into the seats," Erskine said.

As Thomson touched home plate, the Giants lifted him to their shoulders. Then, inexplicably, they lowered him, and everyone ran for the clubhouse. Champagne was waiting. "Gee whiz," Thomson said. "Gee whiz!"

Wes Westrum and Clint Hartung grabbed Ed Stanky, who liked to boast that he had never been drunk, and pinned him to a rubbing table.

Westrum poured champagne into Stanky's mouth. "You're gonna get drunk now," he shouted. Westrum turned to the rubbing table, where Mueller lay, ice packs at his ankle. "Hey, Don," he shouted, and emptied a magnum over the injured leg.

"Isn't this the damndest thing you ever saw?" Durocher said.

"Gee whiz," Thomson said. "Gee whiz."

"How the hell did you go into second with Lockman there?" coach Fred Fitzsimmons said to Thomson. "But the hell with that," he added, and kissed Thomson damply.

"Congratulations," Charley Dressen said to Durocher. "I told you we'd finish one-two. Well, we did, and I'm number two."

"Gee whiz," Thomson said.

In the Dodger dressing room, Branca wept a little, showered slowly, and, after submitting to some questioning, asked reporters to leave him alone. Then he went to the Oldsmobile, where his fiancée, blonde Ann Mulvey, was waiting with Father Frank Rowley of Fordham.

"Why me?" Branca said inside the car. "I don't smoke. I don't drink. I don't run around. Baseball is my whole life. Why me?"

"God chose you," the priest said, "because He knew you had faith and strength enough to bear this cross."

Branca nodded and felt a little better.

Thomson went from the ballpark to a CBS studio, where he appeared on Perry Como's regular Wednesday night television show. Everywhere he went he was cheered, and always three thoughts ran through his mind. The old Jints had won. He had pushed his runs-batted-in total up over one hundred. He had got his three-for-four.

When Thomson reached the house in New Dorp, his older brother, Jim, was waiting for him. "Do you know what you've done?" Jim said, all intensity and earnestness.

Only then, some six hours after the event, did Bobby Thomson realize that his home run was something that other people would remember for all the rest of his days.

CHAPTER 9

ROGER MARIS: THE ORDEAL OF HIS SUCCESS

When Roger Maris chased Babe Ruth's home run record in 1961, he was hounded by reporters and given a mixed response from fans unhappy that he was outpacing their idol, Mickey Mantle. Kahn trailed Maris that season, and came up with this sympathetic portrait of a quiet hero under fire. When he ran into Kahn in spring training the next year, Maris told him: "Of all the horseshit that got written, yours was the best." Maris died of cancer in 1985 at the age of fifty-one.

Someone has described Roger Maris as "the most typical ballplayer in the world." That summary is glib and incomplete, but it serves as a starter. Beyond anything else, Maris is a professional baseball player. His speech, his mannerisms, his attitudes, derive from the curious society that is a ball club. But into this society he has brought an integrity that is entirely his own, a combative kind of integrity that is unusual in baseball, as it would be unusual anywhere. It is the integrity, and his desperate effort to retain it, that has made the ordeal of Roger Maris compelling and disturbing to behold.

Maris is handsome in an unconventional way. The most arresting feature is his mouth. The points of the upper lip curl toward his nose, creating the effect of a Cupid's bow. When one of the blur of photographers covering him orders, "Come on, a nice smile," the response is quick. Then, as soon as the picture is taken, the smile vanishes. It goes to

Cheshire. This knack—the forced unforced smile—is common among chorus girls but not among ballplayers, who, after all, are not in the smiling business. It is the only public relations device that Maris has mastered.

When Maris is angry or annoyed or upset, the mouth changes into a grim slash in a hard face. His nose is somewhat pointed, his cheekbones Slavic high, and the expression under the crew-cut brown hair can become menacing. Since Maris's speech is splattered with expletives, some form an unfortunate first impression. They see a hard-looking, tough-talking man and assume that is all there is to see.

Maris's build bespeaks sports. He was an outstanding right halfback at Shanley High School in Fargo, North Dakota, and he might have played football at Oklahoma "except during the entrance exams I decided not to." He is a strong six-footer of 197 pounds, with muscles that flow rather than bulge. He would be hard to stop on the two-yard line.

At bat he is unobtrusive until he hits the ball. He walks to the plate briskly, pumps his thirty-three-ounce bat once or twice, and is ready. He has none of the idiosyncrasies—[Stan] Musial's hip wiggle, [Rocky] Colavito's shoulder shake—by which fans identify famous sluggers. Nor does he, like Ruth and Mantle, hit home runs 500 feet. By his own estimate, "If I hit it just right, it goes about 450 feet, but they don't give you two homers for hitting one 800 feet, do they?" His swing is controlled, compact. He uppercuts slightly, and his special talent is pulling the ball. Maris can pull any pitch in the strike zone. Only one of his homers has gone to the left of center field.

His personality is unfinished; it is easy to forget that he has just turned twenty-seven and only recently become a star. He may change now, as his life changes, as his world grows larger than a diamond, but at the moment he is impetuous, inclined to gripe harmlessly, and, literally, truthful to a fault.

Recently a reporter preparing an article for high school students asked, "Who's your favorite male singer?"

"Frank Sinatra," Maris said.

"Female singer?"

"I don't have a favorite female singer."

"Well," the reporter said, "would it be all right if I wrote Doris Day?"

"How could you write Doris Day when I tell you I don't have a favorite?" Maris said, mystified by the ways of journalists.

In Chicago someone asked if he really wanted to break Ruth's record. "Damn right," Maris said, neglecting to pay fealty to the Babe.

"What I mean is," the reporter said, "Ruth was a great man."

"Maybe I'm not a great man," Maris said, "but I damn well want to break the record."

This is an era of image makers and small lies, and such candor is rare and apparently confusing. Newspapers have been crowded with headlines beginning "MARIS BLASTS . . .", which is a bad phrase. He doesn't blast, he answers questions. Fans, some rooting for Ruth's memory, others responding to the headlines, have booed Maris. "Hey, Maris," someone shouted in Chicago, "the only thing you got in common with Ruth is a belly." In Baltimore fans called, "You'll choke up on your glove."

Every day Maris has been surrounded before and after games by ten or fifteen newspapermen. Necessarily, many questions are repeated. Some of Maris's answers are misinterpreted. Occasionally taste vanishes.

"Do you play around on the road?" a writer from *Time* magazine asked.

"I'm a married man," Maris said.

"I'm married myself," the writer said, "but I play around on the road."

"That's your business," Maris said.

A reporter from Texas asked if Maris would rather bat .300 or hit sixty home runs. A reporter in Detroit wanted to know if a right-hander's curve broke in on him. ("I would suppose so," Maris said with controlled sarcasm, "seeing that I bat left.") But aside from such extremes, most of the questions have not been either very good or very bad. What they have been is multitudinous.

Under this pressure, which is both the same as and distinct from the actual pursuit of Ruth, Maris has made four mistakes. A wire service carried a story in late August quoting Maris as saying that he didn't care about the record, that all he wanted was the money sixty-one homers meant. "I don't think I said that," Maris says, "and I know I didn't say it like it came out." Then, in the space of ten September days, he criticized the fans at Yankee Stadium and the calls of umpire Hank Soar and finally, hurt and angry, refused to meet the press after a double-header in Detroit.

"An unfortunate image," comments Hank Greenberg, who as Cleveland general manager signed Maris for a $15,000 bonus in 1952. "I know him, and he's just a boy. They get him talking, and he says things you don't say to reporters. The year I hit fifty-eight [1938] drunks called me Jew bastard and kike, and I'd come in and sound off about the fans. Then the next day I'd meet a kid, all pop-eyed to be shaking my hand, and I'd know I'd been wrong. But the writers protected me then. Why aren't the writers protecting Maris now?"

Even if they chose to, reporters could not "protect" Maris because Maris is being covered more intensely than any figure in sports history. Not Ruth or Dempsey or Tilden or Jones was ever subjected to such interviewing and shadowing for so sustained a period. No one can protect Maris; he must protect himself. But to do this he would have to duck questions and tell half-truths, and both are contrary to his nature.

Maris talks softly and clearly, but he is not a phrase maker. He is not profound. He is a physical man trying to adjust to a complex psychological situation. This day he is wearing a tomato-colored polo shirt, and he is smoking one of the cigarettes he is paid to endorse.

He is asked what word he would use to describe all the attention he has received. He thinks for a moment and says, "Irritating. I enjoy bull sessions with the guys [reporters]. But this is different, the questions day after day, the big story. I say a guy [umpire Hank Soar] missed a few. I've always said it. Now it's in the papers, and it comes out like I'm asking for favors. I'm saying"—anger colors his voice—"call a strike a strike and call a ball a ball, but in the papers it appears like I'm looking for favors."

About the people he meets?

"Mostly they're inconsiderate. The fans, they really get on me. Rip me, my family, everything. I like to eat in the Stage [a delicatessen in New York], and it's got so bad I can't eat there. I can't get a mouthful of food down without someone bothering me. They even ask for autographs at Mass."

Now he is talking more easily, going from topic to topic, like this:

Babe Ruth: "Why can't they understand? I don't want to be Babe Ruth. He was a great ballplayer. I'm not trying to replace him. The record is there, and damn right I want to break it, but that isn't replacing Babe Ruth."

Money: "I want enough for me and my family, but I don't really care that much for money. I want security, but if I really cared about money I'd move to New York this winter, wouldn't I? That's where the real money is, isn't it? But I'm not moving to New York."

Fame: "It's good and it's bad. It's good being famous, but I can't do the things I like anymore. Like bulling with the writers. I like to go out in public and be recognized a little. Hell, I'm proud to be a ballplayer. But I don't like being busted in on all the time and now, when I go out, I'm busted in on all the time."

Cheers: "I don't tip my cap. I'd be kind of embarrassed to. I figure the fans who cheer me know I appreciate it."

His current plight: "I'm on my own all the way and I'm the same me I was, and Mickey is, too. Once in a while, maybe, it makes me go into a shell, but most of the time"—pride stirs in his voice—"I'm exactly the same as I was."

When the Yankees arrived in Minneapolis late in August, Maris had fifty-one homers and Mantle forty-six. Both were comfortably ahead of Ruth's record pace, and both had to share uncomfortable amounts of attention.

A chartered bus appeared in front of the Hotel Radisson well in advance of each game to carry the Yankees to Memorial Stadium. The downtown area of Minneapolis is compact, and the bus served as a signal to hundreds of Minneapolitans. As soon as it appeared, they herded into the hotel lobby. "Seen Rog?" they asked. "Where's Mick?" Enterprising children posted a watch on the eighth floor, where many of the Yankees were quartered. When Maris or Mantle approached the elevator, a child scout would sprint down eight flights and shout to the lobby, "Here they come." The second day, tipped off by a bellman, Maris and

Mantle began leaving the elevator on the second floor and taking a back stairway to the street.

Nothing much happened the first night in Minneapolis, except that Camilo Pascual of the Minnesota Twins became the father of a son and pitched a four-hit shutout. But a day later Mantle hit his forty-seventh, lifting a slow curve over the left-field fence, and the following day he hit number forty-eight in the fourth inning. Maris did nothing.

The Yankees flew to New York, where they settled the pennant race by sweeping a three-game series from Detroit. They beat Don Mossi 1–0 in the first game on Bill Skowron's single in the ninth inning. Maris and Mantle were hitless but still attracted the largest crowds in the clubhouse.

"Mossi had good stuff," Mantle said of his own effort.

"When you're going lousy, you're lousy," Maris said of his.

The next day Maris hit two home runs, numbers fifty-two and fifty-three, but Mantle pulled a muscle checking a swing. "I'll take you out," Houk told Mantle on the bench. "I'll help," Mantle said. "I'll bunt, I'll field, I'll get on." Mantle stayed in the lineup, and a day later he hit two, his forty-ninth and fiftieth. The Tigers never recovered, and now, with the Yankees certain to win the pennant, fans, reporters, and photographers turned all their attention to Maris and Mantle. Newspapers started guessing games, with cash prizes for those who forecast how many homers the two would hit. A stripper playing a burlesque circuit adopted the name Mickey Maris. A Japanese sports editor sent eighteen questions to the Associated Press in New York, requesting that Maris and Mantle answer all.

After hearing five, Maris said to the AP reporter, "This is driving me nuts."

"That's my next question," the reporter shouted. "They want to know how you're reacting to all this."

During the following week at Yankee Stadium, Maris hit number fifty-four, a fierce liner to right center off Tom Cheney of Washington; fifty-five, a high drive into the bleachers off Dick Stigman of Cleveland; and fifty-six, another drive into the bleachers, off Mudcat Grant, another Indian. Mantle also hit three, and this week, which ended on

September 10, was the last in which Mantle fully shared the pre- and postgame pressures.

As a young ballplayer, Mantle had been almost mute in the presence of interviewers. "Yup" was a long answer; "maybe" was an oration. But over the years he developed a noncommittal glibness and a fair touch with a light line. "When I hit forty-eight," he told a group one day, "I said to Rog, 'I got my man. The pressure's off.'" (The year Ruth hit sixty, Lou Gehrig hit forty-seven.) Such comments kept Mantle's press relations reasonably relaxed, but Maris, three years younger than Mantle, ten years younger as a star, had to labor. Maris insists that such laborings had no effect on his play, but others close to him are not so sure. Two days before the Yankee home stand ended, a reporter asked Maris about the fans behind him in right field. "Terrible," Maris said. "Maybe the worst in the league." He recounted remarks that had been shouted at him and, under consistent prodding, ran down the stadium customers for ten or fifteen minutes. The next day, after reading the papers, he said to me, "That's it. I been trying to be a good guy to the writers, but I quit. You heard me talking. Did I sound like the papers made it look?"

"No."

"Well, from now on I'll tell the writers what pitch I hit, but no more big spiels."

"Because one or two reporters roughed you, are you going to take it out on everybody?"

Maris looked uncomfortable. "Listen," he said, "I like a lot of the writers. But even so, they are number two. Number one is myself, I got to look out for myself. If it hurts someone else, damn it, I'm sorry, but I got to look out for myself more than I have."

Maris hit no homers in the doubleheader that concluded the home stand and afterward committed the only truly graceless act of his ordeal. "Well?" a reporter said to Maris, whose locker adjoins Elston Howard's.

"He hit a homer, not me," Maris said, gesturing toward Howard. "Mr. Howard, tell these gentlemen how you did it."

"If I had fifty-five homers, I'd be glad to tell the gentlemen," Howard said pleasantly. "Fifty-six," Maris snapped at his teammate. "What are you trying to do? Shortchange me?" Then he marched into the players' lounge to watch television.

A fringe of Hurricane Carla arrived in Chicago on Tuesday the twelfth, shortly after the Yankees. The game had to be called in the bottom of the sixth, when a downpour hit Comiskey Park. Maris had come to bat four times and hit no homers. Reporters asked if he'd had good pitches to hit.

"I didn't get too many strikes," Maris said. "But they were called strikes. Soar had me swinging in self-defense."

The next day's newspapers headlined that casual, typical ballplayer's gripe. Maris was shocked. Until that moment he had not fully realized the impact his sentences now carried. He had not fully realized the price one pays for being a hero. He was disturbed, upset, withdrawn. Tortured would be too strong a word, but only slightly. He showed his hurt by saying little; his mouth appeared permanently set in its hard line. He hit no home runs in Chicago, and when the Yankees moved on to Detroit he hit none in a doubleheader.

That was the night he declined to meet the press. His brother, Rudy, a mechanical engineer, had driven from his home in Cincinnati to see the games, and later Roger and Rudy sat in the trainer's room, from which reporters are barred. "Get him out," a reporter told Bob Fishel, the Yankees' publicity director.

Fishel talked briefly to Maris. "He says he's not coming out," Fishel announced. "He says he's been ripped in every city he's been in, and he's not coming out."

Eventually Maris reconsidered, relaxed, and emerged.

"Any complaints about the umpiring tonight?" a Detroit newspaperman asked.

"Nope," Maris said, "and you got me wrong. I don't complain about umpiring."

When the reporters left, Mantle walked over to Maris. "Mick, it's driving me nuts, I'm telling you," Maris said.

"And I'm telling you, you got to get used to it," Mantle said.

The next night Maris hit number fifty-seven, and a day later, after missing a home run by a foot, he won the game for the Yankees in the twelfth inning with number fifty-eight, a drive into the upper deck in right center field.

As the ball carried high and far, the Yankee dugout erupted in excitement. "Attaboy, Rog!" the most sophisticated players in the major leagues shouted, and "Yea" and "Attababy."

"It was one of the warmest things I've seen all year," said Bob Cerv, the outfielder. "We all know how tough it's been for Rog, and I guess we all decided right then, all at once, that we wanted him to know how much we were for him."

The team went to Baltimore by train. Maris had hit and lost a homer there on July 17, when rain stopped a game in the fifth inning. He had hit no other homers in the Orioles' park. If he was going to catch Ruth in 154 games, he would have to hit two there in two games.

He hit none the first night, dragging through a doubleheader. Now, in addition to hoots from the stands, he was getting hoots by mail (two dozen letters) and wire (six telegrams). "A lot of people in this country must think it's a crime to have anyone break Ruth's record," he said.

The second night, in the Yankees' 154th game, Mantle, who had long since left center stage, vanished into the wings with a cold.

No one who saw game 154, who beheld Maris's response to the challenge, is likely to forget it. His play was as brave and as moving and as thrilling as a baseball player's can be. There were more reporters and photographers around him now than ever before. Newsmen swelled the Yankee party, which normally numbers forty-five, to seventy-one. This was the town where Babe Ruth was born, and the crowd had not come to cheer Maris.

The first time up, Maris shot a line drive to Earl Robinson in right field. He had overpowered Milt Pappas's pitch, but he had not gotten under the ball quite enough. An eighth of an inch on the bat was all that kept the drive from sailing higher and farther.

In the third inning Maris took a ball, a breaking pitch inside, swung and missed, took another ball, and then hit number fifty-nine, a 390-foot line drive that maybe broke a seat in the bleachers. Three more at bats and one home run to tie.

When he came up again, Dick Hall was pitching. Maris took two strikes and cracked a liner, deep but foul, to right. Then he struck out. When Maris came to bat again in the seventh inning, the players in the Yankee bullpen, behind the fence in right center, rose and walked to the fence. "Come on, Roger, baby, hit it to me," shouted Jim Coates. "If I have to go fifteen rows into the stands, I'll catch that number sixty for you."

"You know," said Whitey Ford, "I'm really nervous."

Maris took a strike, then whaled a tremendous drive to right field. Again he had overpowered the ball and again he had hit a foul. Then he lifted a long fly to right center. There was that eighth of an inch again. An eighth of an inch lower on the bat, and the long fly might have been a home run—the home run.

Hoyt Wilhelm was pitching in the ninth. He threw Maris a low knuckleball, and Maris, checking his swing, fouled it back. Wilhelm threw another knuckler, and Maris moved his body but not his bat. The knuckler, veering abruptly, hit the bat, and the ball rolled back to Wilhelm, who tagged Maris near first base.

"I'm just sorry I didn't go out with a real good swing," Maris said. "But that Wilhelm." He shook his head. He had overpowered pitches in four of his five times at bat and had gotten only one home run. "Like they say," he said, "you got to be lucky."

Robert Reitz, an unemployed Baltimorean, retrieved number fifty-nine and announced that the ball was worth $2,500. "I'd like to have it," said Maris, "but I'm not looking to get rid of that kind of money."

The Yankees won the 154th game, 4–2, and with it clinched the American League pennant. Maris wore a gray sweater at the victory party, and someone remarked that in gray and with his crew cut, he looked like a West Point football player. One remembered then how young he is, and how he believes in honesty, as youth does.

"The big thing with you," I said to him, "is you tell the truth and don't go phony."

"That's all I know," Roger Maris said. "That's the only way I know how to be. That's the way I'm gonna stay."

CHAPTER 10

HENRY AARON: A SUCCESS STORY

When Henry Aaron finished his baseball career in 1976 he had surpassed Babe Ruth as the major-league home run hitter with 755. But when Kahn caught up with "Hammerin' Hank" in 1959, the talk was not about Aaron's home run prowess, but about whether he would be the next hitter to top the almost impossible .400 mark. (He never did; his highest average was .359 in 1959.) Kahn found Aaron elusive—and a bit cantankerous.

During one of the Milwaukee Braves' swings around the National League circuit last May, Henry Aaron arrived in Philadelphia with a .468 batting average and a curious complaint. "I ain't seen a movie all trip," Aaron remarked with considerable longing as he stood outside the Hotel Warwick. "I'm a big movie man. I sure miss those movies."

There are all sorts of perils attached to hitting .468. A man could be mugged on any side street by a gang of pitchers. He could go hitless for a day and drop twenty points. Or he could find his path to the movies constantly blocked by brigades of sportswriters, photographers, radio interviewers, television cameramen, and small boys.

"I'm telling you," Aaron said, as he walked toward a restaurant for breakfast. "I got to get me some privacy."

At twenty-five, Hank Aaron is unquestionably a mature hitter. (The chances are he was a mature hitter at twelve.) But he wasn't quite prepared last spring for the tremendous publicity demands that descended on him as he lowered the boom on the National League's pitchers.

"I mostly like to talk to writers I know," he said, between bites of toast. "That way it's better 'cause they ain't going to hurt me. This trip, there've been so many writers I don't know all asking the same questions, like I could tell 'em all something different." Aaron shook his head, and it was clear that he was only partly resigned to being famous as the best hitter in baseball.

There really isn't much question about that any more. Both Ted Williams and Stan Musial are entering the twilight. For reasons not fully apparent, neither Mickey Mantle nor Willie Mays seems capable of replacing them as men who, over weeks and months and years, will consistently pound pitchers to distraction. That leaves Aaron, young, strong, and serious, as the logical choice to be baseball's best hitter for the next decade. Rogers Hornsby, a man not given to raves, believes that Aaron has a reasonable chance to hit .400 at least once before he is through. "With those wrists," Hornsby says, "he can be fooled a little and still hit the hell out of the ball."

The most remarkable thing about Hank Aaron, as an enemy of the pitchers, is that he has come this far this fast on the strength of his natural skill. If he ever acquires the professional touch of Musial and Williams, he could conceivably become the finest of modern batsmen. Of course such a touch conceivably could just get in his way. . . .

Henry Aaron's special technique is to swing at the ball and whack the daylights out of it. He tries to anticipate, as all hitters do, and those stories that he doesn't know whom he is batting against are absurd. He is, in fact, a smart hitter who thinks hardest about the pitchers who bother him most. But Hank has not yet approached the degree of batting sophistication represented by Williams and Musial. He has only approached them in results.

"How many walks has Aaron got?" Mickey Mantle asked one night in June, when talk in the Yankee dugout drifted to Aaron's implausible average. "Five, I'll bet." Actually, Aaron had walked only thirteen times in his first forty games, which is a ridiculously low total for a hot hitter. Aaron does not work pitchers for walks, which offends purists.

But, in a team sense, Aaron's natural style brings its own rewards. With the tying run at second, Williams may walk on a pitch just below the knees. Aaron may choose to swing, and if he is on a good streak, it's a reasonable bet that the score will be tied. Over a year, it's probably a good team risk, but over the same year this tendency pulls Aaron's individual batting average down. To both Musial and Williams, walks are a measure of effectiveness. Aaron accepts them with bad grace. "I'd rather hit," he says.

From this, the purists go one step further and conclude that since Aaron doesn't work pitchers for walks, he doesn't work pitchers at all. "He doesn't swing at his pitch, he swings at their pitch," complains one veteran star, who would be embarrassed if his name were used.

Finally, there is photographic evidence that Aaron swings off his front foot. This is considered a major offense in baseball since it indicates that the batter shifts his weight before the bat meets the ball.

What would happen to Aaron's average if he tried to add Williams's science, Musial's technique, went for more walks, worked pitchers more thoroughly, and shifted his weight a split second later? No one knows, and what is more important no one will soon find out. "A manager," says [manager] Fred Haney, "would have to be crazy to bother a hitter like that. You look at his average and you leave him alone."

As of now, Henry remains a natural man. He stands calmly between pitches, well back from the plate, slightly slouched as he swishes his bat. There is none of the tension about him that most hitters radiate. Robin Roberts once said jokingly, "How can you fool Aaron? He falls asleep between pitches."

But as the pitcher rears back there is a transformation. Henry cocks his bat, and at the last possible instant, he strides forward decisively. Power flows up from his hips, through his sinewy arms, and down to those incredible wrists. The bat flashes, and then, when he connects, the ball rides a rising line that is curiously his own. The ball simply carries, not as high as Mantle's best drives, but straight and long, in the arc of a perfect low-iron golf shot.

Two years ago during the World Series, Aaron hit a line drive into the left-field bullpen at Yankee Stadium. Hitters had reached the bullpen before, but usually with soaring wallops that gave everyone time to stop and wonder. Aaron's liner, close to 450 feet, reached a knot of relief pitchers quicker than Mel Allen can say, "There's activity in the bullpen."

Until this season, Aaron scattered his rising liners. He had almost as much power to right field as he did to left, and sometimes it seemed that his greatest power was to right center. As this season began, he suddenly started to pull everything. "I don't think he's got more than two or three hits to right," [teammate] Ed Mathews said in late May. "I don't know why," Aaron said. "I'm still swinging like I always did. It just seems I'm getting the bat around quicker."

Since most people agree that Aaron is a natural, and let it go at that, it is extremely difficult to get expert analysis of his success or the secret behind the rising line drives.

Often serious questions draw fanciful replies. "How do I pitch him?" Don Newcombe says. "I wish I could throw the ball under the plate." Often they draw the statement, "Don't give him the same pitch twice." This means there is no pattern for Aaron; the pitcher must ad-lib his way along.

Once Bobby Bragan, when he was managing the Pittsburgh Pirates, ordered right-hander Vern Law to throw Aaron a knuckleball on the first pitch. "Let's see what he can do with that to start," Bragan said, although Law customarily gets ahead of a hitter before going to the knuckler.

Aaron hit the first pitch over the fence. "What's the use?" Bragan said. "No matter what you throw that guy will hit it."

Fred Haney insists that he wasn't startled by Aaron's remarkable early pace this season. "I've seen him hit like that for stretches before," Haney says, "only not that early in the season. He does it early and everyone's amazed. He's done it in July and August lots of times since I've been here and nobody was much surprised."

But the evidence, as the season wore on, was that Aaron had improved considerably. After all, until this year he was a .330 hitter with good power. If he finishes up under .350, his average will be, to some extent, disappointing.

The one man with a concrete theory on Aaron's improvement can speak freely since he is no longer a player. "It's the knockdown rule that's helping him," [former Giants pitcher] Sal Maglie says [about the rule which imposes a $50 fine on a pitcher who intentionally throws at a batter's head]. "The only way I could handle Aaron," Maglie says, "was to get his face in the dirt. Then he'd be edgy and I could work on him. Not always, but sometimes. It was the only way I could pitch to him."

I mentioned Maglie's point to Aaron one afternoon. "You're starting this conversation all wrong," Henry said.

"It's a legitimate point."

"I never talk about knockdowns," Henry said.

"Well, are they throwing at you less?"

"I never talk about it," Henry repeated.

"Never?"

"Never."

Looking back on the deep silence that followed, I can only conclude that Henry was right. I did start the conversation all wrong.

But quite likely, Maglie has a point. For one thing, Sal knows more about the care and treatment of high inside fastballs than anyone this side of Early Wynn. Then, too, about twenty minutes later, when Aaron and I were talking about the weather in Milwaukee, Hank got back to the Maglie thesis in a way. "The reason I didn't talk much before," he said, "was because of the way you began. You shouldn't ever ask about knockdowns. Somebody once wrote something I didn't say about a knockdown, so I just never say nothing about them any more." The world is full of potential journalism professors, and one must take them as he finds them. Aaron, as always, meant well.

But assuming that Maglie is right—which no one on the Braves will assume for publication—Aaron's chances of hitting .400 this year, or some year, are immeasurably brightened. If concentrating on Aaron's only weakness, which is his skull, is out, then most pitchers have no alternative but to work on his strength, which is the strike zone.

Will this make Hank a .400 hitter? "It could," says Rogers Hornsby, who hit .400 three times within four seasons. "Those wrists . . ."

Fred Haney played with both Ty Cobb and Harry Heilmann, each of whom batted .400 when Haney was an infielder for the Detroit Tigers. "Cobb," he said, "was everything, a superb ballplayer. Aaron is more like him than like Heilmann in that when he smells a hit he gets down the line like hell. I'm not comparing Aaron with Cobb except on this point. But no matter whether you slug like Heilmann or play every angle like Cobb, you still have to be lucky to hit .400. . . ."

Aaron himself shunned questions on his chances of batting .400 as consistently as he shunned questions on the knockdown. He told one New York newspaperman that baseball could be cruel and that he hoped that his sons, unless they are enormously talented, seek careers outside of baseball. "Don't get me wrong," Aaron said. "When you make it big, it's great, but this can be a hard life for most of the guys. Not to me, but I'm thinking of a lot of my friends. They're in the majors, then back in the minors; they worry about it. They make six, seven thousand dollars. It costs a ballplayer more than that to live."

Delighted with such candor, the newspaperman said, "Can you hit .400?"

"I don't like to talk about that," Aaron said.

To a Philadelphia columnist, Aaron, in a fresh burst of candor, confessed that he preferred seafood to steak. (To most of Aaron's colleagues, this is radical nonconformity.) "I eat seafood seven days a week, if I can," Aaron said. "Especially shrimp salad. I like to catch fish and cook 'em. I shop around Milwaukee for good fish, but it's not like it was back in Mobile."

The columnist then tried to sneak in the .400 question sideways. "What is your hitting goal?" he asked.

"I want two more hits so I'll have one thousand," Aaron said. "Then I'll only be two thousand behind Musial."

Aaron's face is solemn, his voice is soft, and he uses both to work occasional drolleries. Once he arrived at Bradenton, Florida, for the first day of spring training, put on a gray road uniform, swished a borrowed bat a few times, and then hit the first three batting practice pitches out of the park. "Ol' Hank," he said, stepping out of the cage, "is ready." Ol' Hank was then twenty-two.

When he was summoned for a draft board physical in Milwaukee, he reached the induction center at dawn, as ordered, and surveyed the crowd of young men who had arrived still earlier. "With all these fellers," he said to Donald Davidson, the Braves' publicity man, "what they need me down here for?"

During a World Series game, Yogi Berra of the Yankees pointed out that Aaron wasn't holding his bat properly. "You don't have the label up," Berra said.

"I ain't up here to read," Aaron answered.

This is pleasant humor, but by baseball standards it is somewhat subtle and so it is subject to misinterpretation. Both misinterpretation and overstatement of humor account for Aaron's suspicion of strange sportswriters much more than does his fear of inflammatory misquotation.

When Hank played for Jacksonville in 1952, he liked to pretend that he was a simple country boy who didn't know the names of the opposing players, much less what opposing pitchers might throw him. Mobile, his hometown, is hardly the backwoods, and Aaron's early success with the curveballs came partly from the fact that he knew when to expect a curve. But Hank, a Negro pioneer in the Sally League, was dead set on avoiding trouble. Probably he reasoned that if he had to play the role of happy-go-lucky Negro, he'd play it. Hadn't Jackie Robinson played the role of silent man in his first years?

Then, in the majors, Aaron sometimes hit upon the same sort of gag. When he went four-for-four against Robin Roberts, he later remarked that he didn't know who Roberts was. When Ford Frick fined him for reporting early one spring, an anecdote got out that Aaron had never heard of Frick. Both stories had the same minstrel-show punch line: "Who dat?"

There aren't any minstrel shows any more because our taste in humor has been refined. Happily, the integration issue has reminded us that jokes poking fun at Negroes are humorless, just as Adolf Hitler earlier demonstrated to the horror of all civilized peoples that there was nothing funny in jokes about Jews.

When the Ford Frick story hit the newspapers, Jackie Robinson was furious. "I don't believe Aaron said it," Robinson insisted, "and if he did say it, they shouldn't have printed it. That's the worst story of the year." Jackie, a fierce, proud, educated Negro, did not elaborate. He didn't have to.

At the time, Aaron himself made no comment on the story, and when we were talking in Philadelphia this year, I asked him about it. "It never happened," he said, looking straight across the breakfast table. "Never."

He paused, stumbled as he started a sentence, stopped, and then started again. "What kind of story you gonna write?"

"It's hard to say until I write it."

"Listen," he said, "if you hear a lot of silly things, ask me about 'em before you write. I know what happened and what didn't."

"Well, your batting average has to be a big part of it, Hank, and that isn't silly."

"I mean," Aaron said, "a guy once wrote something about me and it wasn't much. There was a lot of dumb stuff. Like every time I said I, he spelled it 'Ah.'" Aaron paused again, groping. "I mean this isn't gonna be one of those Uncle Tom stories, is it?"

"No. . . ."

If it weren't for [racist and heckling] fans, "Uncle Tom" stories might not bother Aaron so much. But such people exist, and now, as a premier batsman, Henry is free to set the record straight, where a few years ago, as a mere rookie, he felt he wasn't. In time, more and more will be written strictly about Aaron's batting, and more people will come to understand that his drollery is something other than racial humor. As these things happen, we can expect Aaron to become less suspicious of strangers. Ed Mathews can now charm anybody but a pitcher, yet even Eddie had a period of adjusting to the demands fame placed on his personality.

Already, Aaron seems to be developing the direct, laconic eloquence so many fine athletes acquire. Earlier this season, a stranger shoved a pad under his nose and asked him for an autograph. "I don't read the sports pages much," the man said, "but aren't you Hank Aaron?"

"I'm Aaron," Henry said, signing.

"Well, don't be modest," the man said. "After all, you're hitting four-hundred-and-something."

"If I was hitting .200," the ballplayer said, "I'd still tell you I was Aaron."

When Hank first joined the Braves in 1954, he was capable of no such sophistication, perhaps because he possessed no such confidence. But since the advance reports were bright and the stories out of Jacksonville seemed to indicate a latter-day Satchel Paige, Aaron was inter-viewed with fair regularity right from the beginning.

I tried once after learning that the Braves had misspelled Aaron's name above his first big-league locker. Large and clear, the letters read: A-R-O-N.

"How do you like it up here?" I asked, some time after the error had been corrected.

"Good," Aaron said.

"You look like a hitter."

"I'm swinging," Aaron said.

"What's different about the pitching?"

"I ain't been around long enough to know."

"Anything funny ever happen to you in baseball?"

"Sure," Aaron said. "There's lots of funny things."

"Such as?"

"Well, I can't remember any offhand," Aaron said.

He had to be marked down then for what he was—a rookie exciting only when he had a bat in his hands.

Just three years later, Aaron had become considerably more fluent. "I guess what's coming sometimes until I get two strikes," Aaron told a reporter who asked him to talk about hitting. "After that I'm not look-ing for anything. I don't guess with two strikes."

"What's on your mind when you hit?"

"I try to keep my mind clear," Henry said. "I don't want to think of nothing but the baseball. Except for one thing. I try to remember not to swing too hard. I hit a homer, I wanna hit another and I start swing-ing too hard. My eyes fly up in the air. I stop looking at the ball. That's a big thing, telling myself not to swing too hard."

By the time he started making headlines this year, Aaron was fully capable of a long, facile conversation on baseball, if he felt inclined to take the trouble.

"I try to get comfortable up there," he said, "and I figure I'll hit what they're gonna throw." This is an ideal approach. Instead of reasoning, as many batters do, "I'll hit if I get my pitch," Aaron was walking up to the plate, saying to the pitchers, in effect, "Throw what you want. I'll hit your pitch."

"What about the bat?" I asked. There was a story once that Henry's knowledge of bats was confined to the realization that bats can be long or short and that long bats are best to hit outside pitching.

"I use something like a [Del] Crandall model," he said, "with a real thin handle. It goes thirty-five ounces, thick on the end and thin at the handle. I like the thin handle 'cause I can whip with it better."

"What about your wrists?"

"They're just the way they are naturally," he said. "I never did any special exercises, nothing like that. There was some story that I got 'em strong working on an ice wagon. I worked on an ice wagon a little when I was a kid, but mostly I just mowed lawns. That work won't make weak wrists strong. They just are the way they are."

"Is that where you think the power comes from?"

"Power comes from timing," Aaron said. "It's more timing than anything else. You hit a ball just right, you don't need a real wild swing. The ball will go. You don't have to be real big. Time it right and you'll hit it far enough."

In his apprentice days, Aaron played third base, second base, and shortstop, but with the Braves he has tried to stay in the outfield, even though he has looked competent at second in the few major-league games he has played there. Since Aaron's lithe form moves so smoothly, it is easy to forget that he is an excellent defensive outfielder, either in right or in center. He has caught a few liners bare-handed, and once, when a drive popped out of his glove, he demonstrated the speed of his hands with a move most of the Braves remember clearly.

After a long run, Aaron speared a line drive, which then slipped from his glove and struck a knee. With Aaron running all out, the ball popped off the knee and into the air ahead of him. The right hand flashed out and Aaron had his putout. With more lenient scoring, he might also have been given an assist. "The kind of play," one of the Braves suggests, with mild malice, "that if Willie Mays had made, everybody in the country would have heard about. With Hank, you just got to see him every day to know what a good fielder he is. Nobody makes a big thing out of it."

"It's that loping gait of his," Fred Haney says. "He doesn't look like he's really hustling out there. Then you notice Hank always seems to get up to a fly ball when there's any chance in the world of making the play."

Like the innate perfection of his swing, the baseball beginnings of Aaron are hard to explain with precision. Sports editors in Mobile have pretty well given up trying to get a consistent portrait of Aaron as a young man. "Every time we start the thing," one of them says, "we find a couple of things that don't add up. No one has ever been able to put the whole thing together." What does add up most clearly is that Aaron fell in love with baseball at the age of eleven, and that after that nothing else mattered much as he grew up in the midst of a poor family in the deep South.

Herbert and Esteller Aaron, Henry's parents, moved to Mobile thirty-six years ago from the small farming town of Camden, Alabama, and their first son, Herbert, Jr., was born two years later. In all, the Aarons have seven children, four of them boys, and Hank was the second child.

"There was always enough money for what we needed," Hank remembers, "but it was week to week, you understand. It was always one week to the next waiting for the pay."

Herbert and Esteller Aaron insist that they are just as proud of Tommy, who is an eighteen-year-old prospect in the Milwaukee chain, as they are of Hank, but this is probably the enforced impartiality parents learn to assume. The family lived at 2012 South Wilkerson Street when Hank was born, but within two years they moved to 2010 Edwards Street, where they now live in a frame house which has been remodeled with financial help from Hank. Herbert Aaron works as a boilermaker's assistant at the Alabama Drydock and Shipbuilding Company.

Both the Aarons are sturdy and cheerful and, as they sit on a sectional sofa near the TV set in their home, discussing the exploits of their son Henry, their faces split in smiles of delight. "He was a quiet boy," Esteller remembers. "He never made many friends and he just loved to play baseball. Every time there was a game anywhere and he could join in, he'd be there. He liked to play shortstop the best. He most always played there when he was here."

At the age of eleven, Henry's interest in baseball changed radically. Before that he played football and basketball with about as much enthusiasm, but at eleven baseball became his game and his life. "If he wasn't playing the game," his mother says, "he was reading about it. He was reading every newspaper and magazine about baseball he could find. All the time he was around the house he was reading."

Every time a major-league team stopped off for a game in Hartwell Field, on the way north from a spring training camp, Henry sat in the stands. "He just seemed to sit there," Mrs. Aaron says, "and watch the players. He didn't talk to anyone, but he seemed to be fascinated by seeing people like Jackie Robinson go to the plate."

Sometimes, Aaron would say to his mother, "Some day, I'll be out there. Some day I'll make the big leagues." By the time he was fourteen, he was telling all the family and Connie Gilles, his one close friend, "I'm a good player. I know I am. I'll make it. I'll make it all the way to the top."

Henry went to Toulminville Grammar School, Central High School, and Allen Institute, a private school in Mobile. "He was well-liked by his teachers," Mrs. Aaron says. "He never gave them any trouble and he studied very hard. He liked school, but I think he liked it mostly because it gave him a chance to play on a ball team."

Aaron's actual grades appear to be lost to history. "Records weren't kept very carefully then," one school official says. "We'd look for them," someone else says, mysteriously, "but they'd be too hard to find." Henry did not graduate from Central High, but he may have received a diploma from Allen Institute.

At Central High, Henry played softball; there was no baseball team. Edwin Foster, his coach, remembers him as vividly as one might expect. "Hank was with us two years, 1950 and '51," Foster says, "and he was kingpin when he was with the team. We lost only three games in the two seasons he was with us. He was a great player."

Foster used Aaron as a catcher and as a third baseman. When he moved Hank to third, the boy he replaced, Sonny Hill, complained. "I'm good at third," he told Foster.

"Sure, you're good," the coach said, "but you're not as good as Hank." Presumably, later events have soothed Sonny Hill's pride. "Hank always seemed so unconcerned when he played," Foster says. "You wouldn't think he was as good as he was because of that. But he had wonderful eyes and he hit and made all the plays you wanted. I'm not really surprised at the way he's moved up. He could sure hit hard when he was with me, and I wouldn't be surprised if his average went even higher."

At the age of sixteen, Henry was playing a sandlot game in Mobile when Sid Pollet offered him a contract with the Indianapolis Clowns, a Negro team. Aaron signed and became the Clowns' shortstop. By 1952, major-league scouts were attending Negro games regularly, and before long both the Giants and the Braves were interested in Aaron's contract. The price was firm: $2,500 down and $7,500 more a month later, or no Aaron. If Aaron didn't make good in thirty days, he could be returned to the Clowns. The $2,500 was nonrefundable. It was a good, safe arrangement for the Clowns.

The Braves had first crack at him, and one day when the Clowns were playing in Buffalo, New York, they were told either to sign Aaron by 7 P.M. that night or to forget him. At 7:01, he would be sold to the Giants. It drizzled that day and the field at Buffalo grew more and more soggy, but scout Dewey Griggs endured the weather to watch his quarry. At 6:57, he called John Quinn, who was then the general manager of the Braves.

"What do you think?" Quinn said. "Can he play short?"

"To tell you the truth," Griggs said, "the field was so wet I couldn't figure out whether he's a shortstop or not. But he's worth $2,500 just for his swing."

At 6:59, give or take a few seconds, the Braves bought Aaron's contract, a decision which was to keep the National League balanced for years. Had the Giants been able to buy him, San Francisco would now possess the admirable entry of Aaron and Mays. Or, perhaps, New York would, for it is difficult to imagine a team built around Aaron and Mays ever having to jump its franchise.

After a .336 season at Eau Claire in the Northern League, Henry moved up to the Sally League and Jacksonville. There, in a single season, he won the attention of all baseball. He led the league in batting, runs batted in, hits, runs, and doubles. He was nineteen years old.

"The South can be kinda easier than the North," he says. "There you know where you can go and where you can't. In the North sometimes you find out you can't go where you thought you could." Still, there was considerable pressure on Aaron that season, and he responded in the manner he has come to regret.

At midseason, manager Ben Geraghty, who now runs the Braves' Louisville farm team, decided to change the team's signs. A day later Geraghty gave Aaron the signal to take a pitch and Henry responded by hitting a home run.

"Why didn't you take it like I signaled?" Geraghty asked mildly afterwards.

"I thought that was the hit sign you was giving me," Aaron said.

"That was the old hit sign," Geraghty said.

"Damn," Aaron said, "I only got around to learning it yesterday."

For the rest of the season, Geraghty says, he gave Aaron no more signs. Henry just went up and hit away.

On the bus trips the Jacksonville Braves made, Henry invariably went to sleep. "Nothing ever bothered him," Geraghty says. "He was the most relaxed kid I've ever seen." By sleeping and playing dumb, Henry stayed out of trouble, but the combination produced the unfortunate image that he is still trying to live down.

"I have to admit now," Geraghty concedes, "that I was never quite sure when he was pulling my leg. You know, he's got that deadpan. I guess a lot of us thought he was serious when he was kidding."

Appreciation of Aaron's sense of humor lagged considerably behind appreciation of his batting. In a spring training game five years ago, when he was still on a minor-league roster, Aaron came to bat against Curt Simmons, the Philadelphia left-hander who had one of the best fastballs in the National League.

"What did you think of Simmons?" a reporter asked him later.

"Oh, was that Simmons?" Aaron said. "He didn't show me much."

The quick conclusion that Aaron was either an absurdly cocky rookie or a naive country boy was too quick. Remember Aaron sitting at ball games in Hartwell Field in Mobile, watching each major leaguer in turn, staring out at big-timers in a bush-league ballpark with utter concentration, feeling the longing to make it big stir strong with him. Think of Aaron at home in the house on Edwards Street poring through newspaper box scores, studying baseball magazines. Then ask yourself if in 1954, Hank Aaron could have failed to recognize Curt Simmons or Robin Roberts or even a second-line major-league ballplayer. The problem in 1954 was that no one then knew the preparation Aaron had given himself for the majors. No one realized the single-mindedness and dedication that had gone into developing such advanced skills so quickly.

People know now. . . .

The discovery that Aaron was ready for the majors was entirely accidental. The accident was Bobby Thomson's broken leg. After a disastrous season in 1952, the Braves left Boston, to the yawns of the populace, and abruptly jumped from seventh to third. Still, Quinn realized, the team needed further strengthening, and he dealt Johnny Antonelli, the left-hander, to the Giants for Thomson in a deal which also involved lesser talents. In Ed Mathews, the Braves had a left-handed long-ball hitter, but there was no comparable right-handed batter. Thomson was acquired to balance the order and provide extra long-ball strength.

That was the spring after Aaron's great year at Jacksonville, but the feeling in the Braves' office was that Henry could do with a season at Toledo before being exposed to big-league pitching. Henry was invited to train with the Braves, but his name was placed on the Toledo roster.

Again Aaron, always working toward the majors, had been giving himself special grooming. He had played winter ball in Puerto Rico under Mickey Owen. He had kept his batting eye sharp and, through Owen's help, he had mastered the art of hitting to right. When Thomson snapped his ankle during an exhibition game, the Braves suddenly found themselves without Antonelli and without a right-handed power hitter. Aaron, after a hot winter in the Caribbean, was having a hot spring. At twenty, Hank Aaron made the Braves.

As a rookie he hit .280, but it was a .280 with a difference. There are .280 hitters who get that way by batting .450 against the worst pitchers in the league and batting very little against anyone else. Then there are the tough .280 hitters like Tommy Henrich and Pee Wee Reese, who in their time got many of their most important hits against many of baseball's most important pitchers. That was how Aaron started in the big leagues.

The Dodgers, everybody reasoned, were the team to beat, and Aaron loved the Dodger pitching. The Giants were the team that won, but Henry played no favorites. He hit Giant pitching, too. It is puzzling now to recall that he failed to become rookie of the year. Wally Moon won over him in a close vote. He might have caught Moon, but in a double-header late that season, he lashed five straight hits, and on the fifth, a triple, he slid into third base and fractured an ankle. That finished his season, but it meant only that 1955, not 1954, was to be the year in which he established his stardom.

In 1955, he batted .314 and hit twenty-six home runs. During the season, the Dodgers made a small trade which brought them a pitcher from another club. Carl Erskine and a few other Dodger veterans immediately surrounded the newcomer. "How are you guys pitching to Hank Aaron?" the Dodger pitchers all wanted to know.

The answer was no salvation. "Not good."

When the Braves finally got around to winning a pennant in 1957, Aaron hit forty-four home runs and won the decisive game with a homer against the St. Louis Cardinals. In the clubhouse afterwards, Henry dropped his mask of lethargy, perhaps for the first time during his baseball career.

"What did you think the moment you hit the home run," one reporter asked.

"First thing I thought about was Bobby Thomson's homer," Aaron said, referring to the preposterously dramatic wallop Thomson made in the 1951 playoff which won the pennant for the Giants. "That's always been my idea of the most important homer. Now I got one myself. For me to get the hit myself. Am I excited!" Aaron grinned, and then the solemn mask slipped back.

"I'm excited for the first time in my life," he said.

But in truth Aaron had been excited about baseball for more than half his life. Like most ballplayers who are acclaimed as naturals, he became a natural through years of unnaturally hard work.

Recently, when someone asked him what he looked for when he went to hit, Aaron answered with typical brevity. "The baseball," he said.

It was a line that was pleasantly dry, like good Milwaukee beer, but there is considerably more to the story of Aaron than that. At twenty-five he is already living a dream that was born only ten or fifteen years before in a poor neighborhood in Mobile. "Pretty soon," Henry says, "I'd like to get me a farm. Not one of those twenty-five-acre jobs, but something big, like the ones [teammates] Warren Spahn and Joe Adcock have."

Something big goes hand in hand with being at the top, and Aaron has arrived there faster than even he could have expected. He has become the premier hitter of his day, and now he asks only a little of the respect that is due a premier hitter. He likes his small jokes because they come more easily than discussions of skinned sandlots on the hot summer afternoons in Mobile, but he resents stories that show him as a joker.

As he continues to hit, the offending stories will surely be buried in the past. Within the next few years, as Henry continues to swing, baseball fans everywhere will come to realize that beneath the surface drollery, Aaron is just about as comical as Murderers' Row.

CHAPTER 11

THE GREAT
CORK CRIME

When Chicago Cubs home run hitter Sammy Sosa (539 homers in fifteen seasons) was caught putting cork in his bat, a violation of baseball's rules, Kahn, ever the baseball historian, reached back into the game's past to give fans a frame in which to understand the incident. This short commentary appeared on the editorial page of the Los Angeles Times, *where Kahn has written frequently in the past few years.*

The first and somewhat primitive reaction to the great and ongoing Sammy Sosa corked-bat affair is harsh laughter. The principal in this episode is not an ethicist. He is a thick-necked professional athlete playing a children's game for millions and millions of dollars.

Like other sporting characters going back more than a century, when Sammy Sosa hauled his corked bat up to home plate he was saying, in effect, "Don't bother me with rules, baby. I'm here to win." (I know Sosa said it was all a mistake. That is his right, as it is mine and yours not to accept his explanation.) But before we pass judgment, we should remember that cheating in baseball is about as old as the game itself.

In *Pitching in a Pinch*, Christy Mathewson, the stellar old New York Giant pitcher, tells an intriguing tale of baseball dishonesty dating from 1899. That season, Mathewson reports, the Philadelphia Phillies stationed an observer in the clubhouse beyond center field. He was armed with binoculars, so he could see the opposing catcher's signs, and with a Western Union "bug" to transmit electrical impulses. A wire ran under the playing field all the way to the third-base coach's box. There, the Phils coach stationed a shoe over a designated spot and picked up vibrations. One buzz, fastball. Two buzzes, curve. Line drives followed.

"One day after a rainstorm," Mathewson recalled, "there was a big puddle in the Philadelphia box, but the coach, Cupid Childs, stood with one foot in the puddle although the water came up to his shoe laces. Between innings visiting players, already suspicious, began pawing in the dirt and water and found a square chunk of wood with a buzzer on the under side." Up came a wire, which led the ballplayers clear through the outfield to the clubhouse 450 feet away. There the sign stealer, one Morgan Murphy, looked up from his field glasses and said, "I guess you've got the goods."

Mathewson remembered that "the newspapermen got a big laugh, but the National Commission [which then supervised baseball] intimated that any team using such tactics would be subjected to a heavy fine and possible expulsion from the league."

Buzzers vanished, but sign stealing with binoculars is said to have persisted at least through 1951. In that year, according to a later Giant, catcher Sal Yvars, an operative in center field tipped off Bobby Thomson that the Dodger pitcher, Ralph Branca, was about to throw a fastball. Thomson homered, the Giants won the pennant, and a significant portion of old Brooklyn wept.

Other episodes of big-league cheating rush to mind. Before the advent of resin bags, pitchers dried their hands in the dirt around the pitcher's mound. One manager had his ground crew sow soap flakes in most of the dirt. The home pitcher knew just where the undoctored earth was. Visitors came up with soapy fingers.

Want to slow down a speedy visiting team? Overwater the base paths. Damp dirt slows down everyone. Have some great bunters on your side? Manicure the earth so the foul lines slope inward. That will keep many a good but borderline bunt in fair territory. Whenever Hank Aaron slid safely into second after hitting a double, Jackie Robinson leaned on him and shoved infield dirt into his shoes. "Maybe cost him a half step," Robinson told me years later through an innocent smile. (Aaron could have called time and cleaned his shoes, but he was too proud to do so.)

Much of this stuff is amusing. A ball game is, after all, only a ball game, less critical to our future than nuclear proliferation, and we should be wary about taking it or ourselves too seriously. Yet after the laughter, something about Sosa's corked bat lingers on and ceases to be funny.

Just because you can cheat in baseball obviously doesn't mean you should. I retain from childhood some idealized concepts of a major leaguer that include such elements as honesty and integrity. Cheating at the bat by one of the great home run hitters of our era is, to put this quietly, disillusioning.

Sosa had appeared to be a model modern ballplayer, hardworking in the field as well as at bat, appreciative of his fans and appropriately proud of his Latino heritage. Now sadly I find myself echoing the words of the boy who found out that Shoeless Joe Jackson had taken gamblers' money to help throw the 1919 World Series. "Say it ain't so." Jackson's response then is about the only one appropriate for Sosa today. Shoeless Joe wept.

X-rays of seventy-six other Sosa bats show no evidence of cork. But pending a complete inquiry, I have to list Sosa now with another great ballplayer who wouldn't follow rules: Pete Rose. Let's hope the lords of baseball deliberate with great care as they seek a punishment that fits the great cork crime.

PART III

WILLIE, MICKEY, DUKE: THE NEW YORK CENTER FIELDERS

CHAPTER 12

THE "SAY HEY KID" UP CLOSE

Roger Kahn barely hesitated when an interviewer asked him who was the greatest ballplayer he had ever seen. "Willie Howard Mays of Fairfield, Alabama," he answered. "The greatest total player—run, hit, field, throw, steal—and the most joyous player. I've never seen anybody whose love for playing baseball exploded from the ballpark, and everybody felt it." What follows here is Kahn's view of Mays as seen in a 1969 Sport *magazine article. Mays retired in 1973 after twenty-two seasons and 660 home runs.*

He is sitting on the three-legged stool they give to ballplayers and milkmaids, and he looks enormous and supple and strong. He has a massive flat chest and bulging arms and shoulders and the kind of muscled stomach I remember from comic-book drawings of Tarzan. Still, he is thirty-eight years old.

"What do you do to stay in shape, Will?" I say.

"Nothin' special," Willie Mays says. "I walk a lot and I play golf now, 'stead of pool. And I don't eat too much and I never did drink, except three times, when we won pennants." A smile briefly lights the handsome brown face.

"Well, you look like you can go on forever."

"I won't lie to you," Mays says. "It gets to be work. Sometimes when I get tired and with all that pressure, it gets to be work. I knew when I was sixteen years old, I never did want to work for a living." Again the smile.

"You want to manage?"

"Yeah. I think I'd like to."

"What about handling pitchers? Could you do that?"

"You're a manager," Willie says, "man, you get to hire help."

It is eleven o'clock the morning after a night game, and Willie will play this afternoon. The team is not going well, and last night in the ninth inning, with the count three and two, he guessed curve. Then Ron Taylor of the Mets threw a fastball by him. Willie is not playing for fun today, but from a sense of obligation. He has come out early so we can talk in an empty locker room, and the conversation sweeps across a broad range. We go back a way together and when Willie trusts you, he is warm and open and droll and humorously sly. Together, we consider divorce and alimony and child-raising and financial security and how time, the subtle thief of youth, steals from you, me, and even Willie Mays.

A spring, fifteen years ago, comes back in a rush and I see again the wide pellucid sky, the baked hills wanting grass, and the desert winds blowing whirls of sand. I hadn't wanted to come to Phoenix. I hadn't wanted to cover the Giants. For two previous years I'd been assigned to the Dodgers. This nurtured a condition, described in a general way by the late nonpareil of sports editors, Stanley Woodward. "Baseball writers," Woodward observed, "always develop a great attachment for the Brooklyn ballclub if long exposed to it. We found it advisable to shift Brooklyn writers frequently. If we hadn't, we would have found that we had on our hands a member of the Brooklyn ballclub rather than a newspaper reporter. You watch a Brooklyn writer for symptoms, and, before they become virulent, you must shift him to the Yankees or to tennis or golf." Woodward was gone from the *Herald Tribune* by 1954. I was shifted, under protest, to the Giants.

The ride from New York to Phoenix was interminable. We had to change trains in Chicago, wasting time, and somewhere near Liberal, Kansas, we stopped dead for ten or twelve hours in a snowstorm.

Perhaps fifty hours after we had left New York, the train pulled into Phoenix and we stepped out into a cool and cloudless morning. Louis Effrat of the *Times* alighted with me, and looked about the station. A few Indians were sleeping. In the distance lay brown hills. "Three thousand miles," Effrat shouted. "I leave my wife, my daughter, my home, and travel three thousand miles." He inhaled before bellowing, "For what?" He was making a joke, but that was the way I felt.

My outlook did not improve immediately. The Giant manager, Honest Leo Durocher, offered me tidbits on his swelling romance with a post-virginal actress, but was more devious when asked about the club. The ballplayers were decent enough, but I didn't know them, or they me, and I was starting from scratch, building up confidences and new sources. And aside from that, the team bored me. I was used to the explosive Dodger atmosphere, with Jackie Robinson holding forth and Charlie Dressen orating and Roy Campanella philosophizing. The Giants seemed somber as vestrymen.

While I struggled and wrote a story a day, plus an extra for Sunday, Willie Howard Mays, Jr., was struggling with an Army team at Fort Eustis, Virginia, hitting, as he later put it, ".470, or something like that." They were all waiting for him. The Giants had won in 1951 with Mays. Without him in 1952 and '53, they lost. Each day in the pressroom, one of the regular Giant writers or one of the officials would tell anecdotes in which Willie was always superman. In exasperation, I sat down and wrote a story for the Sunday paper that began, "Willie Mays is 10 feet 9 inches tall. His arms reach from 156th Street to 154th. . . . He has caught everything, hit everything, done everything a centerfielder can possibly do."

"Look," I told Charles Feeney, the Giant vice president, amid the amber torrents of the Phoenix press bar. "There are a couple of other center fielders, too. Ever hear of Mickey Mantle or Duke Snider?"

Mr. Feeney erupted in song. "In six more days," he choired, to the tune of "Old Black Joe," "we're gonna have Willie Mays." He may have sung it "going to." He is a Dartmouth man. Each day Feeney warbled, amending the lyrics cleverly enough, say changing the word "six" to the word "five." The song, like the sandy wind, became a bane.

M Day, as I came to call it, dawned like most other days, with a big bright sky. Durocher had scheduled an intra-squad game and was elaborately underplaying things. The post-virginal movie star was gone, making him somewhat irascible.

"Nothing unusual," Leo announced in the lobby of the Hotel Adams early M Day. "Just a little intra-squad game, boys, that's all." Then he walked off, barely able to keep his footing for his swagger.

The Phoenix ballpark was typical medium minor league. Old stands extended partway down each foul line. A wood fence ringed the out-field. The players, Monte Irvin, Whitey Lockman, Alvin Dark, were in uniform and, as always in spring, it seemed odd to see great major lea-guers in a minor-league setting.

Willie was coming by plane, we all knew that, and in Phoenix you can see great distances. Whenever an airplane appeared, one of the writers or Giant officials leapt up with a cry, "Willie's plane." Two Piper Cubs, four Beechcrafts, and one World War I Spad were positively iden-tified as the transcontinental Constellation bearing Mays.

"Feeney," I said, "this is ridiculous."

This time he chose the key of C-sharp minor.

> *"In no more days,*
> *"We're going to have Willie Mays!"*

The athletes were still playing catch, the intra-squad game had not started, when a trim figure in slacks and a dark open-collared shirt appeared in the dugout. He was blinking at the sunlight, mostly because he had not been to sleep, and seemed to be trying to hide, to be as unobtrusive as possible. "There's Willie," someone cried in ecstasy, and the sportswriters swarmed.

Mays stood next to Irvin, probably the closest friend he has had among ballplayers in a curiously lonely life. Irvin was very poised, very strong, very sensible.

"Hey, Willie," someone shouted, "what you got in that bag?" He had dropped off his large suitcase, but clung to a smaller one.

"Not much," Willie said. "A couple things."

"What?"

"Just my glove and my jock."

Durocher hugged him repeatedly for joy and for the news photog-raphers. Monte, who felt like hugging him, shook his hand.

"He's shaking hands with the pennant," Barney Kremenko, one of the baseball writers, proclaimed.

"Hi, roomy," Irvin said.

"Hey, Monte."

Irvin smiled. "Roomy," he said, "how's your game?"

Willie shook his head. "What you mean my game, Monte? You talking about pool?"

"No, Willie," Irvin said. "I'm talking about your game, about baseball."

"Oh yeah," Willie said, as if surprised there should be a question. "My baseball. I'm ready any time."

A few minutes later, when the intra-squad game began, Mays remained on the bench. Durocher, with his sure sense of drama and his always brilliant sense of handling Willie, was letting the elements cook. The game proceeded without much excitement. The most interesting thing at the Phoenix ballpark was watching Number 24, striding back and forth, looking at Durocher, asking with his eyes, and being ignored.

Halfway through the game, he was sent in to hit. Willie sprang from the dugout. He ran to the batter's box. He took a tremendous swing at the first pitch. His form was flawed. There was a little lunge in the swing. But I don't believe I have ever seen anyone swing harder. Three swings, and mighty Willie had struck out.

"The thing about Snider," I told Kremenko in the press box, "is that his butt doesn't fly out of there when he swings."

"Now, listen," Kremenko began, as though I had assailed the family honor. And I suppose I had.

The first unusual thing that Willie did was snatch a sinking liner off the grass. The ball came out to center field low and hard, and Willie charged it better than anyone else could have and dove and made a graceful somersault and caught the ball. "Nothing!" Kremenko shouted. "For Willie that's absolutely nothing."

The next time he came to bat, I resolved to look for specific flaws in his form. I was doing that when he hit a fastball 420 feet and out of the park. An inning later, and with a man on first, someone hit a tremendous drive over Willie's head. He turned and fled and caught the ball and threw it 300 feet and doubled the runner. Pandemonium. The camp was alive. The team was alive. And Willie had gone through the delays of a discharge, then sat up all night in a plane. I conceded to Kremenko that given a little rest, he might show me something.

Then I sat down and wrote an account that began, "This is not going to be a plausible story, but then no one ever accused Willie Mays of being a plausible ballplayer. This story is only the implausible truth." It ran quite long and I had no idea whether the *Tribune* copydesk would eviscerate it, until a day later when a wire came from Red Smith in Florida. Red was the columnist in the *Tribune*, a thoughtful man, and his telegram, a personal gesture, was the first indication I'd had in a month that my stuff was getting printed and was syntactical.

That night Feeney, selecting the rather cheerful key of D major, honored me with the final version of his aria.

> *"Gone are the days,*
> *"When we didn't have Willie Mays."*

After Willie's debut and Red's wire, I was genuinely surprised to hear how much Feeney's voice had improved.

Willie conquered me. I had not come to praise him and sycophancy annoys me, but he brought to the game the outstanding collection of skills in our time and the deepest enthusiasm to play I've seen. He was the ultimate combination of the professional full of talent and the amateur, a word that traces to the Latin *amator*, lover, and suggests one who brings a passion to what he does.

They used to play pepper games, Leo and Willie, sometimes with Monte Irvin as the straight man. Willie has what his father, Kitty-Kat Mays, described as oversized hands, and Durocher was one of the finest defensive shortstops. They'd stand quite close and Leo would hit hard smashes at Willie's toes, or knees, wherever. Mays's reflexes were such that he could field a hard line drive at ten or fifteen feet. And he liked to do it. He threw, and Leo slugged, and Willie lunged, and threw, and Leo slugged again. Once in a while Willie bobbled a ball. Then he owed Durocher a Coke. Durocher made great shows of cheating Willie. One morning he hit a hard smash on one hop, well to Willie's right, and Willie knocked the ball down with a prodigious lunge.

"Coke," Leo roared. "That's six you owe."

"Ain' no Coke for that," Willie said. His voice piped high and plaintive. "That's a base hit."

"Six Cokes you owe," Leo insisted.

"Monte," Willie pleaded at Irvin. "What you say, roomy?"

"Six cokes," Irvin said, solemnly. Willie's mobile face slumped into a pout. "I'm getting the short end," the expression said, "but I'll get you guys anyway."

Sometimes Irvin hit, and then there was added by-play. Not only did Durocher and Mays stab smashes, they worked to rattle each other. Durocher seized a line drive, wound up to throw to Irvin, and with a blur of elbows and hands tossed the ball to Mays at his left. Leo has the skills and inclinations of a juggler. Willie caught the toss, faked toward Irvin, and there was the ball floating down toward Leo. Durocher reached and Mays slapped a glove into his belly.

"Ooof," Leo grunted. Willie spun off, staggering through his own laughter. It wasn't long before people started coming to the ballpark long before the game, just to watch the pepper. The clowning would have done honor to Chaplin.

Willie ran and threw and hit and made his astounding catches, and slowly that spring I began to get to know him. I was the youngest of the baseball writers, and that helped. We had little conversations after the workouts and the exhibition games, and he always became very solemn and gave me serious answers. "Who suggested," I asked one day, "that you catch fly balls that way?" The technique is famous now: glove up, near the belt buckle.

"Nobody," Willie said. "I just start it one day. I get my throw away quicker."

"Nobody taught you?"

Willie's eyes, which sometimes dance, grew grave. "Nobody can teach you nothing," he said. "You got to learn for yourself."

On another afternoon we were talking and Ruben Gomez, a pitcher from Puerto Rico, came up and said, "Willie. That man in New York. I forget the name. I sign a paper for him."

Willie mentioned a New York agent.

"That's him," Gomez said.

"You sign a paper," Willie said, "and you worried because you haven't got your money."

Gomez nodded.

"Well, don't worry," Willie said. "Long as you sure you signed. It may come soon, or it may come late, but long as you sign something, you'll get money." He looked at me. "Ain' that right?" I thought of leases, installment contracts, and overdue bank loans, but I said, "Yes." Maybe it would always be that way for Willie, spring and youth and plenty of cash and laughter. But it wasn't, not even that spring.

Along with the Cleveland Indians, a team wealthy with pitchers, the Giants flew to Las Vegas for an exhibition game late in March. The Giant management did not want the ballplayers spending a night in Las Vegas. The Stoneham regime is paternalistic, and the idea of a troop of young ballplayers abroad among the gamblers and the bosoms of Vegas was disturbing. The team would play its game with the Indians. The players would be guests for dinner at one of the big hotels. They would watch a show and seek as much trouble as they could find up until 11 P.M. Then a bus would take them to the airport for a flight to Los Angeles, where two other exhibitions were scheduled. We wouldn't get much rest. It was a gray, raw afternoon in Vegas, and Bob Feller pitched for the Indians. Sal Maglie opposed him. My scorebook is lost, but I believe the Giants won by one run. Afterwards we wrote our stories and took a bus to the hotel that invited us all. We ate well, and I caught up with Willie in the hotel theater, where Robert Merrill, the baritone, was to sing. As I joined Willie's table, Merrill began "Vesti la Giubba," the famous aria from *Pagliacci* in which Canio, the clown, sings of having to make people laugh, although his own heart is breaking.

Merrill gave it full voice and all his passions. When he was done, Willie turned to me amid the cheering. "You know," he said, "that's a nice song."

An hour later, he was in a gambling room. He was standing quietly amid a group of people close to a dice table. Monte Irvin and Whitey Lockman were fighting a ten-cent one-armed bandit. Sal Maglie, looking like Il Patrone of Cosa Nostra, was losing a steady fifty cents a game at blackjack. I walked over to Willie. "How you doing?"

"Oh," Willie said, "I'm just learnin' the game." We both grinned.

I moved on. A stocky, gruff man grabbed me by the arm. "Hey," he said. "Wait a minute."

I shook my arm free.

"That guy a friend of yours?" said the man. He pointed to Mays.

"I know him."

"Well, get him the hell away from the dice tables."

"What?"

"You heard me. We don't want him mixing with the white guests."

"Do you know who he is?"

"Yeah, I know who he is, and get that nigger away from the white guests."

If there was a good answer, except for the obvious short answer, I didn't come up with it. Very quickly. I was appalled, unnerved, angry. What unnerved me was the small significant bulge on the man's left hip.

"Do you know that boy just got out of the Army?" I said.

"That don't mean nothing. I was in the Army myself."

"You bastards invited him down to your hotel."

"Who you calling a bastard?"

We were shouting and Gary Schumacher, the Giants' publicity director, suddenly loomed large and put a hand on my shoulder. "What's the trouble?" Gary said.

"This guy," the tough began.

"I asked him," Gary said, nodding at me.

I had a sensible moment. "No trouble, Guv," I said to Gary. I took my wallet out of a hip pocket and withdrew the press card. "This joker has just given me one helluva story for the Sunday *New York Herald Tribune*."

The hood retreated. I walked over to Irvin and told him what was happening. Lockman listened briefly and then, taking the conversation to be personal, stepped back. "Maybe Willie and I'll get on the bus," Irvin said. It was his way to avoid confrontations, but he was also worried lest Willie be shocked or hurt.

Now a hotel vice president appeared, with a girl, hard-faced but trimly built. He asked if "my assistant and I can buy you a drink, Mr. Kahn."

We went to the bar, and the man explained that he had nothing against a Negro like Irvin or Mays playing one-armed bandits. It was just that the dice table was a somewhat different thing. As far as he, the vice president, was concerned, Negroes were as good as anybody, but he had to concern himself with customers. That was business.

"We're really in the South here," said the brunette.

"I thought the South was Alabama, Georgia, Texas."

"That's it," the brunette said. "We get a lot of customers from Texas." She glanced at the bartender, and I had another drink. "We're really a very liberal place," the girl said, "even though we are in the South. We not only book Lena Horne to sing here, but when she does, we let her live on the grounds. We're the only hotel that's liberal." She leaned toward me, a hard handsome woman, working.

"Why did you invite him if you were going to crap on him?" I said, and got up and joined Monte and Willie in the bus.

Later Irvin asked me not to write the story. He said he didn't know if it was a good idea to make Willie, at twenty-one, the center of a racial storm. That was Monte's way and the Giants' way and Willie's way, and you had to respect it, even if dissenting. I never did write the story until now.

In the visitor's locker at Shea Stadium fifteen years later, the headline on a folded newspaper cries out: "CITY COLLEGE TORN BY BLACK AND WHITE STRIFE." The times are different, and I have heard a prominent Negro criticize Mays as self-centered. It was the job of every black to work for a free society, he said. To the militant—a Stokely Carmichael or a Rap Brown—Willie is the embodiment of the well-fed declawed Tom.

"They want me to go out on some campus?" Willie says. "Why should I lie? I don't know nothin' about campuses. I never went to college. I wanted to play ball."

"Well, what about the whole black movement."

"I help," Willie says. "I help in my way." His face becomes very serious. "I think I show some people some things. I do it my way." He is a good fellow, serious and responsible, never in trouble, never drunk, never in jail.

"Do you speak out?"

"Like what?"

"On schools, or full employment, or whatever?" He eyes me evenly. "I don't think I should. I don't know the full value of these things. I'm not the guy to get on the soapbox." He pauses, then announces with great assurance and pride, "I'm a ballplayer."

In the autumn of '54, after Willie led the Giants to the pennant and a sweep over the Indians in the World Series, our paths crossed again. I was putting together a book featuring articles by all-star ballplayers on the qualities that make one an all-star. I sent questionnaires to many like Ted Kluszewski and Bob Lemon. I telephoned Stan Musial. I went to see Willie in the flesh. He had made his classic World Series catch, running, running, running, until he was 460 feet out and grabbing Vic Wertz's liner over his head. He had taken Manhattan, the Bronx, and Staten Island, too, and was in demand. At the Giants someone gave me the name of his agent.

After hearing what I could pay, the agent said Willie would let me have three to four minutes on a slow Tuesday afternoon, but while we talked he might have to sign four endorsements, accept six speaking engagements, get his shoes shined, and telephone for a date. His business was being handled brusquely, although not, we were to learn, very well.

A few seconds before the appointed minute I appeared in the agent's office. Willie was in an anteroom, only signing endorsements. When I appeared he waved and smiled, relieved to see a familiar face. "Hey," he said, "Roger Kahn, is that you? I didn't know that was you. What you want to talk to me about?"

I explained.

"You writin' a book?" Willie said. "That's real good, you writin' a book."

Disturbed by gratuitous friendliness the agent vanished, and Willie held forth on playing center field. "The first thing," he said, "is you got to love the game. Otherwise you'll never learn to play good. Then, you know, don't drink, and get your sleep. Eight hours. You sleep more, you get to be lazy.

"Now in Trenton, where I played when I first signed, I was nowhere near as good as I am now, but I have my way to learn things. People tell me, 'Willie do like this, like that,' but that ain't the way."

He sat in a swivel chair, which he had tilted back. His considerable feet were on a desk. "Well, how do you learn?" I said.

"Some things maybe when you're real little, you got to be told. But mostly you got to be doing it yourself. Like once I was a pitcher and now I'm in the outfield. Watch me after I get off a good throw. I look sort of like a pitcher who has thrown.

"You got to be thinking, 'What am I doing wrong?' And then you look at the other two outfielders and think, 'What are they doing wrong?' And you're thinking and thinking and trying not to make the same mistake three times, or four at the most, and you're also thinking what you'll do if the ball comes to you. Understand?"

"Pretty much."

"You don't want to be surprised," Willie said with finality.

But on what Branch Rickey called the best catch in baseball history, Mays was indeed surprised. The Giants were playing in Pittsburgh, where center field runs 457 feet deep, a good stage for Willie. Rocky Nelson, a left-handed hitter, smashed a tremendous line drive, and Willie, calculating at a glance, turned and sprinted for the wall. Nelson had hit the ball so hard that there was a hook to it. While Willie ran, the ball drifted slightly to the right.

At precisely the right instant, Willie looked. He had gotten back deep enough, a mini-miracle, but now the ball was to his right and sinking fast. He might have been able to reach across his body and glove the ball. Or he might not. We will never know. He simply stuck out his bare right hand and seized the liner at the level of his knees. Then he slowed and turned, his face a great, wide grin.

"Silent treatment," Durocher ordered in the dugout. "Nobody say nothing to him."

Willie touched his cap to acknowledge the crowd and ran down the three steps into the Forbes Field dugout. Everyone avoided Willie's eyes. Durocher was checking the lineup card. Bobby Thomson was pulling anthracite from his spikes. Hank Thompson was taking a very long drink. The silence was suffocating.

"Hey, Leo," Willie piped. "You don't have to say 'Nice play, Willie.' I know that was a nice play."

A minute later a note from Rickey arrived. "That," Rickey wrote, "was the finest catch I have ever seen and the finest catch I ever hope to see."

I finished the story by Willie with a comment that he offered in the agent's office. "You got to learn for yourself," he said, "and you got to do it in your own way and you got to become much improved. If you love the game enough you can do it." It reads right after all the years, and true, but even as I was finishing I understood that no book was likely to help a young man play center field like Willie Mays.

In Shea, we start talking about the old times. "New York was a good town for center fielders," I say, "when you were here with Mantle and Snider."

"Yeah," he says, "Mick and I broke in together, but he had a real bad body. Legs."

"How do you feel being the only one left?"

"Proud. Proud that I'm still playing."

"Lonely?"

"There's more new faces, but . . ." He turns his palms up and shrugs. "That doesn't bother me none. I worry, though," he says. "I get worried now that I can't do the job. 'Course I always was a worrier. I get the ball out, but I can't get it out as often as I used to."

"About old friends," I say.

"You know," Willie says. "I don't have many friends. People I know, people to say, 'Hi, Willie,' there's a million of them. My friends, I could count them on a few fingers."

I went calling in 1956, four days after Willie had taken a wife. Because he is handsome and country slick, and also because he is famous and well-paid, he does not lack for feminine attention. Joe Black, the Dodger relief pitcher, told me Willie was getting married. We played winter basketball together, and after one workout Joe said he hoped Willie knew what he was getting into.

"I'm sure of that," I said.

"I mean I hope he doesn't get hurt."

"What's the girl like?" I said.

"The girl," Joe said, "is older than Willie and has been married twice before."

A number of people counseled Willie against getting married, but he doesn't like to be told how to run his life, and each bit of counsel was a shove toward the altar. Then, in February, he gathered Marghuerite Wendelle, stuffed her into his Lincoln, and set off for Elkton, Maryland, where one can marry in haste. On the way, he picked up a $15 fine, for driving seventy in a sixty-mile zone.

He set up housekeeping in a tidy brick home not far from LaGuardia Airport. East Elmhurst was one of the early colonies open to the black middle class, and I remember the white taxi driver looking at the clean streets and detached houses in surprise. "Colored people live here?" he said.

Mrs. Mays received me with a cool hand, tipped with pointed fingernails. She was a beautiful woman, who stared hard and knowing when she said hello. It was midday, but Willie hadn't come downstairs. "Just go on up," Marghuerite Mays said. "I have to go out to the beauty parlor."

I found Willie sitting in an enormous bed, gazing at morning television, a series starring Jackie Cooper and a talking dog. Willie was wearing tailored ivory pajamas. "Sit down," he said, indicating a chair. "What you doing now? How come you don't come around? You okay?"

I had left the newspaper business and gone to work as a sportswriter for a newsmagazine. The salary was better and the researchers were pretty, but the magazine approached sports in an earnest, sodden way. One of the supervising editors had been a small-town sportswriter once and then become a sportswriter on the newsmagazine. The change of fortune downed poorly. He alternately tried to relate great events to his own experiences, perhaps covering a playoff game between Bridgeport and Pittsfield, or he demanded scientific analyses of the events and men. A great story on Mays, he told me, would explain in complete technical detail how Willie played center field.

In the bridal bedroom, I told Willie I was fine. I was wondering how to swing the conversation into a technical analysis. I asked what had made him decide to marry.

"Well," Willie said, "I figured that's it's time for me to be settling down. I'm twenty-four years old."

"You figure being married will affect your play?"

"I dunno," Willie said. "How am I supposed to know? I hit fifty-one home runs last year. Man, if you come to me last spring and tell me I was gonna do that, I woulda told you you were crazy." Willie shook his head and sat straight up. "Man," he said. "That's a lot of home runs."

On top of the TV set rested three trophies. The largest was a yard-high wooden base for bright gilt figurines of ballplayers running, batting, and throwing. It bore a shiny plaque which read: "To Willie Mays, the most valuable player in baseball."

"What are you hoping to do this year?"

"I dunno," Willie said. He frowned. "Why you askin' questions like that?" he said.

I stopped, and after a while we were talking about marriage. "You hear some people say they worried 'bout me and Marghuerite," Willie said. "Same people last summer was saying I was gonna marry this girl and that girl. But they was wrong then, like they're wrong now." He thumped his heart, under the ivory pajamas. "I'm the only guy knows what's in here."

They didn't know what to make of my story at the newsmagazine. They cut out chunks of it, and devoted equal space to the picture of a 2-to-5 favorite winning a horse race. Willie's love song was not news-magazine style.

The marriage went. I like to think they both tried. They adopted a son and named him Michael, but some years later they were divorced. "Foundered on the rocks off the Cape of Paradise" is how the actor Mickey Rooney likes to put it, but there is nothing funny about the failure of a marriage or having to move out from under the roof where lives your only son.

In Shea before the game against the Mets, Willie is talking about the boy. "He's with me, you know," Willie says.

"How come?"

"He was with Marghuerite, but when he started gettin' older I guess he missed me, and we kind of worked something out.

"Michael is ten years old," Willie says, "and there's a lady who keeps house and she looks after him when I'm away. A real nice boy. I send him to a private school, where they teach him, but they're not too hard with him."

I think of the ironworker's son with a boy in private school.

"I've made a deal with him," Willie says. "He needs a college degree in times like these, and the deal is I send him to good schools, put it all there for him, and after that it's up to him to take it."

"You think he will?"

"He's a real good boy."

Two men have come into the Mets' clubhouse to see Willie. Paul Sutton is a patent attorney and David Stern is a vice president of Sports Satellite Corporation. Willie hopes that these men and a Salt Lake businessman named Ernie Psarras will build his fortune up to seven figures. For now Willie is concerned about filling the house he is building on an acre, in Atherton, down peninsula from San Francisco. He stands to greet Sutton and Stern and says, "Hey, what about the furniture?"

"We're seeing about it," David Stern says.

"Man," Willie says. "I got to stay on you guys."

"Willie doesn't like to pay retail," Stern explains.

"I don't like to pay," Willie says, and he laughs.

Larry Jansen, a coach who pitched for the old Giants, approaches and asks Willie about a doctor or a dentist. Willie gives him a telephone number. Willie owns the keys to the kingdom in New York.

When the Giants moved to San Francisco after the 1957 season, I lost touch with Willie. I read he was having problems. He moved into a white neighborhood, and a Californian threw a soda bottle through his living room window in protest. It was a good thing for the Californian that Willie didn't grab the bottle and throw it back. With that arm, he would have cut the man in half. Later, at least as we got word in New York, some San Francisco fans felt disappointed in Willie. They didn't appreciate him as we had; a number said they preferred Orlando Cepeda.

I was paying less attention to sports and writing more about other things, but I knew Willie was not disgracing himself. He kept appearing in All-Star Games and driving homers into the high wind over Candlestick Park. But I wondered if the years and the franchise shift and the divorce had dampened the native ebullience.

It was 1964. Forces that would explode into Black Revolution were gathering, and an editor asked me to spend a few months in Harlem, "a part of New York that white New Yorkers don't know."

"I don't know it," I said.

"You've been there," the editor said.

"Sure. Whenever I took a taxi to the Polo Grounds, I'd ride right through."

This time I got out of the taxi. I went from place to place on foot, trying to grasp the bar of music, the despair, the life and death, the sour poverty, the unquenchable hope of a black ghetto. It was different than living in a press box.

To shake off the grey ghetto despair, a man can stand a drink, and one evening I walked into Small's Paradise, with my new blonde wife on my arm. Across the bar a major leaguer was drinking hard, although he had a girl with him. She was quite young, a soft off-tan, and wore an enormous round black hat. The athlete and I raised glasses to each other's ladies. Suddenly Willie walked in.

It was a cold day in January, but his stride was bouncy. Willie wore a beautifully tailored topcoat of herringbone charcoal. He has unusual peripheral vision, and he covered the bar with a glance. Then he bounced over with a smile.

"Buy you a Coke?" I said.

Willie shook his head. "How are you? You okay? Everything all right? What you doing around here? Who's that girl over there with . . ." And he mentioned the other major leaguer's name.

"I don't know."

"You sure you okay, now?" Willie said.

"Fine." I introduced him to my wife.

Willie put an elbow on the bar and placed a hand against his brow and fixed his gaze at the girl. "Who is that chick, man?" he said.

None of us knows what happened next. Willie was around the bar quickly, greeting the other ballplayer, talking very fast to the girl. Then he bounced out of the bar, calling, "See ya, man." Five minutes later the other major leaguer was drunker and the pretty girl in the big round hat was gone. "That," said the blonde on my arm, "has to be the smoothest move I've seen."

You don't judge a man's vigor only by the way he pursues fly balls.

Back at Shea, Willie is asking if he'd given me enough to write an article, and I tell him I think so.

I find his father sitting in the dugout. Kitty-Kat Mays has his son's big grin and says sure, he'd like to talk about the boy. Kitty-Kat is smaller than Willie. He has a round belly. He was a semipro around Fairfield, near Birmingham, Alabama.

"I was down there, Mr. Mays, when Bull Connor was the police commissioner."

"Things are a lot different now," Kitty-Kat says.

"You still live there?"

"No. I'm up here. I've got a good job."

The man knows baseball, and I ask when it first struck him that his son was going to be a superlative ballplayer. Kitty-Kat screws up his face, and I can see that he is going backward in time. He says, "Well, you know we lived right across from a ball field, and when Willie was eight he had to play with older kids."

"I mean even before that."

"Soon as he started walking," Kitty-Kat says, "he's about a year old, I bought him a big round ball. He'd hold that big round ball and then he'd bounce it and he'd chase it, and if he ever couldn't get that ball, he'd cry."

"I knew he'd be a good one, with those oversized hands." Mr. Mays extends his own palms. "I was pretty good, but my hands are regular size. Willie gets those big hands from his mother."

Willie emerges, taps his father's shoulder, and goes out for batting practice. He does not take a regular turn in rotation. He hits for three or four minutes, then sits down. That way is a little gentler on the legs.

He doesn't dominate the series. The Mets do. In one game Ron Swoboda hits a 430-foot home run to left center field. Willie sprints back, the way he can, but this is not the Polo Grounds. He has to pull up short. He is standing at the fence when the ball sails out. In his time, and in his park, he would have flagged it.

Later, he crashes one single to left so hard that a runner at second couldn't score, and then he says he wished he'd hit it harder. He hits a long double to left that just misses carrying into the bullpen for a home run. He leads off the ninth inning of a close game with a liner to left that hangs just long enough to be caught. The Giants lose three straight and, in the way of losing teams, they look flat.

When we say goodbye in the clubhouse, Willie seems more annoyed than depressed. The last game ends with the intense frustration of a Giant pitcher fidgeting, scrambling, and walking in the winning run. "What can you do?" Willie says. "You got to play harder tomorrow."

For an aging ballplayer, he seems at peace with himself. He went through money wildly in the early days, borrowing from the team, spending August money by April. "You're really okay financially?" I say.

"Oh, yes," Willie says. "Very good." His face was serious. "I ought to be, I've been working a long time."

Back in the Arizona spring we wore string western ties and we worried about flying DC-3s and we ate in a restaurant where a man dressed like a medieval knight rode a charger and pointed with his spear to show you where to park. Who would have thought then that the Giants would leave New York, and that my old newspaper would fold, and that in another spring, my hair showing grey, I would sit in a strange ballpark and ask Willie Mays about legs, fatherhood, investments, and fatigue?

Driving home, while Willie flew to Montreal, that spring kept coming back. I saw in flashes a hit he made in Tucson, a throw he loosed in Beaumont, how Leo made him laugh, and I could hear how the laughter sounded. The racists were appalled that year. A Cleveland coach snapped at me for praising Mays, and one writer insisted on betting me $20 Willie wouldn't hit .280. We made it, Willie and I, by sixty-five percentage points.

All this crossed my mind without sadness. Once Willie was a boy of overwhelming enthusiasm. He has become a man of vigorous pride. I don't say that Willie today is as exciting as Willie in '54, but what he does now is immeasurably harder. Playing center field at thirty-eight was beyond the powers of Willie's boyhood idol, DiMaggio, or his contemporary rival, Mantle. Willie stands up to time defiantly and with dignity, and one is fortunate to write baseball in his generation.

I guess I'll look him up again next trip.

CHAPTER 13

THE MICK ON AND OFF THE FIELD

After hitting 536 home runs, Mickey Mantle retired to his Texas home in 1968. He was in his third year of retirement, reading scrapbooks, dreaming of the cheers, and still limping from his baseball injuries when Kahn visited the legendary Yankees center fielder. This article was written for Kahn's long-running Esquire *magazine column. While preparing a chapter on Mantle for* Memories of Summer, *Kahn returned to see him many years later when the slugger was mired in alcohol woes. Mantle died of liver cancer in 1995.*

It all passes so swiftly for Mickey Mantle, the vaulting home runs, cheers like thunder, and the dark devil's wine of fame, that he cannot believe it is done. But it will not come again, even in dreams. "At night," he says, "my knees can hurt so bad it wakes me up. But first I dream. I'm playing in the stadium and I can't make it. My leg is gone. I'm in to hit and I can't take my good swing. I strike out and that's when it wakes me. Then I know it's really over."

He is thirty-nine now and so enormously powerful that he can drive a golf ball four hundred yards. But baseball begins with a man's legs, and Mickey Mantle's right knee is grotesque. Four injuries and two operations have left the joint without supportive structure. It flexes outward as well as in. Bone grinding on bone, and there is nothing more that surgery can do. "A flail knee," doctors say, and make analogies to a floppy rag doll. So, still sandy-haired, still young, but no longer able to play ball, Mantle sits in Dallas, living hard, dabbling at business, working at golf, cheerful, to be sure, but missing major-league baseball more than he ever thought he would.

"I loved it," he says, his voice throbbing. "Nobody could have loved playing ball as much as me, when I wasn't hurt. I must have fifty scrapbooks. People sent 'em to me. Sometimes after breakfast, when the boys get off to school, I sit by myself and take a scrapbook and just turn the pages. The hair comes up on the back of my neck. And I remember how it was and how I used to think that it would always be that way."

For two decades Mickey Charles Mantle of Commerce, Oklahoma, Yankee Stadium, New York, and Dallas, Texas, bestrode the world of baseball. He could throw and he could run down fly balls. Someone with a stopwatch timed him from batter's box to first base in 3.1 seconds. No ballplayer has yet matched that speed. He drove home runs for shattering distances: 450 feet, 500, 565. With one swing he could make a ballpark seem too small. Sometimes when Mantle connected, the big number 7 stirring as he whipped his bat around, it seemed that a grown man was playing in a park designed for Little Leaguers.

Center field at Yankee Stadium stretches toward monuments and flagpoles and a high bleacher wall, 461 feet from home plate. People talk about prodigious outs stroked there by Hank Greenberg and Joe DiMaggio. But one summer night not so very long ago, Mantle stepped up and swung, and everyone watching knew this drive would not be caught. It climbed farther and higher than seemed possible, carrying into a bench halfway up the bleachers. Briefly the crowd sat silent. You couldn't hit a baseball that far. Then came a swelling roar. "Make it an even five hundred feet," called a newspaperman, one hand to his face in amazement, "give or take a couple of miles."

I don't remember whether Mantle hit that home run batting right-handed or left-handed. He hit the 565-footer batting right-handed in Washington. Batting left-handed, he hit a line drive that was still rising when it hit the roof of the third-floor tier, 108 feet high in right field at the stadium. "The guys I played with," he says, "figure that was my best shot."

Mantle is not very big—about five eleven and 185 pounds at his playing prime—but there is not mystery to all that power. In the great years, his frame was fashioned of thick, supple muscle. For all his strength, there was no stiffness, no weight lifter's rigidity. "The body of a god," said Gerry Coleman, a teammate. "Only Mantle's legs are mortal."

He ran as if pursued. He cocked each swing for distance, and when he missed, the exertion drew a grunt. Watching him one could see a man driving himself harder than human sinew could endure, until at last, too soon, the body yielded. Mantle disagrees with that view. He traces his physical problems to a single injury suffered in 1951. Whatever, with the exertion and the power and the pain, there was no sense of ease to Mickey Mantle.

He did not court the press. Even when relaxed, he tends to limit himself to short comments and dry one-liners. Interviews discomfort him, and in time he developed a special response to questions he did not want to answer. It was a baleful, withering look. Scorn all the more startling on the open country face. As he saw it, his job began and ended on the field. For fun he'd run with Whitey Ford or Billy Martin. Answering all those reporters—What did you hit, Mick? Where was the pitch?—was bullshit. Where was the pitch, Mick? Hell, in the upper stands in left.

Elvin "Mutt" Mantle, an Oklahoma lead miner, trained his oldest son to be a ballplayer. As Mickey remembers it, he began learning baseball in 1937 when he was five years old. It was a familiar American scene, the father pitching relentlessly in the hope that the son might someday hit well enough to make the major leagues and carry the family out of a depleting existence. Not one boy in ten thousand is signed to a professional contract; no more than one in twenty-five professionals is good enough to play in the major leagues. "But I got an idea," Mutt Mantle said. "A time is coming when ballplayers will be platooned. A boy who can switch-hit will have a real advantage."

When a right-handed batter faces a right-handed pitcher, the ball seems to be coming toward his ear. Then, as the batter fights a reflex to duck, the curve breaks down and across the plate. The batter sets himself and digs his heel spikes into the ground. Now the pitcher throws a fastball at the chin. In this frightening game, the pitcher holds the wild cards. But when a left-handed batter stands in against the right-hander, the balance turns. The ball seems to be coming from the outside. "You see it real good out there," hitters say. A curve breaking inwards can be a fine pitch, but the illusion of impending concussion is lost. Everybody hits better from the opposite side, left against right and vice versa. The switch-hitter always bats that way.

Against both percentages and logic, Mutt Mantle's ambitious dream came true. The Yankees signed Mickey at seventeen. Two years later, when Mickey became a major leaguer, Casey Stengel was introducing platoons in Yankee Stadium, just as Mutt had foretold in Oklahoma fourteen years before.

Cancer invaded the Mantles' happiness. The Yankees won the pennant in Mickey's rookie season, but by World Series time, October 1951, Mutt lay in a New York hospital, dying at thirty-nine. In the fifth inning of the second Series game, Willie Mays lifted a looping fly to right center field. Mickey sprinted toward the ball; he had a chance to make a backhand catch. "I got it," called Joe DiMaggio from center. Mantle braked. His right spikes cut through turf and slammed against a hard rubber tube, part of the sprinkler system. His leg jammed and he fell heavily. As the ball was dropping out of DiMaggio's reach, Mantle lay in motionless agony, knee ligaments terribly torn.

He was bedridden now like Mutt, and by the time the father died, a somber identification had occurred. Mantle believed that an early cancer awaited him. When players discussed pensions at a clubhouse meeting once, he said, "That's for you guys to worry about. I won't be around." When someone made the remark that cancer was not purely hereditary, Mantle said, "Sure. And it killed my uncle, too."

His career mixed glory and pain. He was the hinge on which the Yankees wheeled to eight pennants in a decade. In 1956 he led the league in batting, runs batted in, and home runs. In 1957 he batted .356. In 1961 he hit fifty-four home runs. Through all these seasons injuries nagged him. With the bad right knee, he was forever straining muscles. As he was running to first in 1962, a right hamstring tore. He pitched forward and crashed heavily on the left knee, the good knee. It was not a good knee after that. A year later he broke a foot. Throwing hard, he chipped a bone fragment in his shoulder. He kept playing, but the bone sliver worked its way into sinew, giving him a chronic sore arm. By 1965 Mantle, then thirty-three, could not play every day or hit .300. The Yankees have not since won a pennant.

He liked good living, but off the field he shied at crowds. The New York pace excited him. But country stayed strong in Mantle. "I don't want no fuss," he said, "no big deal." If Babe Ruth's image shows an ultimate libertine, and Leo Durocher is the corner crapshooter, Mantle by contrast has been a shadowy bucolic.

Last summer Jim Bouton's unfortunate *Ball Four* pried into the Mantle mystique. Bouton drew Mantle as a voyeur, as a grouch who disliked autographing baseballs, and as a hedonist whose training habits were less Spartan than, say, Jim Bouton's.

With his mustachioed ghost, Leonard Shecter, Bouton wrote: "I ached with Mantle when he had one of his numerous and extremely painful injuries." And to show the full measure of their hurt, Bouton-Shecter added, "I often wondered, though, if he might have healed quicker if he'd been sleeping more and loosening up with the boys at the bar less."

"What did you think of Jim Bouton's book?" someone asked.

Mantle stared. Then he said, "Jim who?"

Dallas was warm and windy, and Mantle said he was going to play some golf and make a talk, and why didn't he start by showing me where he lived. He wore blue slacks and a blue shirt when he picked me up at a motel. He was slightly heavier than when he played, but still boyish. He hadn't read Bouton's book, he said, just a chunk in some magazine. "Anybody," he said, "who's been on the road can write a book with sex in it. You could, I could. But I wouldn't do it. Why do you suppose the sons of bitches picked on me?"

"It was a commercial effort," I said, "and you're box office."

"Roger Maris hated Bouton. He always wanted to belt the bastard. Is the book rough on Maris?"

"He's hardly in it."

"The other guy, Shecter, was an agitator. I didn't speak to him for the last four years at the stadium. I'd just give him the stare. Do you think maybe the son of a bitch was trying to get even?"

"Yes."

"Do you think maybe that book ought to read: by Shecter, edited by Bouton?"

"For lots of it, sure."

"Only thing that really bothered me was the stuff about autographs. New York was my town, but for all those years I couldn't walk a block without getting stopped. I wouldn't sign? Hell, I've signed maybe a million." Mantle shook his head. "Well, come in and have a cup of coffee."

Mantle lives in a rambling buff ranch house, set on a cul-de-sac on the north side of Dallas. His wife, Merlyn, has decorated the den into a shrine. One wall shows twelve framed magazine covers of Mantle batting, running, smiling, glaring. Another is crowded with pictures of the Mantles and famous men, Babe Ruth and Bobby Kennedy. Locked behind glass are the jewels of a great career: the silver bat he won as batting champion; his last glove, bronzed like baby shoes; three plaques celebrating the seasons in which he was most valuable player in the American League; a baseball signed by Mays, Mantle, Ed Mathews, Henry Aaron, and Ted Williams, an aristocracy in which everyone has hit five hundred home runs. Mantle stood in the den, shifting his weight from side to side.

Preston Trail Golf Club, limited to 250 members, no pool, no tennis, spreads over rolling acreage twenty miles north of Dallas. Under the clear wide sky, city towers shape a fringe of horizon. "Good weather here," Mantle said, "but sometimes it turns. It's warm and then wind shifts—a norther they call it—and the sky gets blue as a marble and you have to hurry to the clubhouse. It gets cold." He walked out to practice putting, and Gene Shields, the house professional, described Mantle's game. "Swing is a little flat, like all ball players, but he's the longest hitter around. Our tenth hole runs four hundred and ninety-five yards, and last October, with a little wind, he drove it within seventy yards of the green. Ed Hoffman saw it, and no matter how you figure that, he drove, counting roll and all, four hundred and twenty-five yards."

Mantle played in a fivesome of serious, laconic Texas golfers, who bet as they rode along in golf carts. Mantle's cart made the best time. He whipped up knolls and spun around turns, the first to reach each tee. "You know the old rule," he said. "He who have fastest cart never have to play bad lie."

The wind gusted, eased, and gusted, disturbing the precision of everyone's game. Mantle smacked enormous, low drives, and his chatter was easy and professional. Landing behind a tree, he said, "Well, I can make a fine golf shot from here." On the eighth hole, hitting in a quartering wind, he drove an astounding three hundred yards. He waited impatiently for the others to make their second shots, then found his ball dead center in the fairway. "You sometimes give up distance for accuracy," he said.

As he roared toward the clubhouse in the cart, someone drove up, bellowing, "Mantle, Mantle. Goddamnit. Gimme your spare putter."

"Another club in the water?"

"Never mind. Just gimme your spare putter."

Mantle obliged with a small grin. "I got some clubs in the water myself."

The wind hoisted scores, and Mantle's eighty-two was good enough to win his bets. "Double J.D. and Seven-up," he ordered in the locker room and insisted on taking the check. His limp was worse. "With the cart it's not so bad," he said, "but without it, I can just about make eighteen holes. That's all the leg has left."

He spoke at a banquet in Fort Worth that night. "They say I was a hitter," he began, "but I struck out around seventeen hundred times. Then I walked around eighteen hundred. Figure that out and it comes to five years I came up to the plate and never hit the ball." Three other major leaguers sat on the dais. Mantle was the star. Afterward he had to sign programs and baseballs for forty minutes.

We went to a Dallas club for a nightcap, and at one point rock musicians made it difficult to talk. "The question," Mantle said, "is not, is the piccolo player a son of a bitch? The question is, is the son of a bitch a piccolo player?"

"You want to manage?" I asked when it was quiet.

"If they got a major-league team in Dallas. I had good managers. Casey gave me my chance. Ralph Houk kept saying as Mantle goes, so go the Yankees. He's the leader. Like that. It gave me confidence. I wouldn't want to manage outside of Dallas. I wouldn't want all that time on the road."

"What's tomorrow?"

"More gold. Talk with my lawyer, Roy True. We got things going. The employment agency with Namath. Some other things. I stay in touch."

"You bored?"

"Hell no. I enjoy what I'm doing. I miss baseball, but I like to play golf. There's nothing bored about me, nothing sad. My health's good, 'cept for the knee. I'm not worried any more than anybody else."

He grabbed for the tab and said, "You got enough to write?" and when I nodded he started out of the club toward his car, still looking like a kid from Oklahoma but limping from the agony that baseball has left him, along with scrapbooks and memories that give him chills.

CHAPTER 14

THE DUKE IN
A NEW PASTURE

When The Boys of Summer *was published in 1972 it climbed onto the bestseller list—and Kahn became an instant celebrity. It was a book only Kahn could have written: the boy from Brooklyn who got to know the Dodgers while covering them as a reporter for the* New York Herald Tribune. *And then, after years of writing magazine articles (and four books), Kahn decided to track down the old Dodgers players to see how civilian life and mortality were treating them. He caught up with the "Duke of Flatbush" in California, where the Hall of Famer who hit 407 home runs had retired to raise avocados.*

D uring my last trip with the team, I finished the story of an easy victory in Milwaukee, stowed my typewriter in a bare room at the Hotel Schroeder, and, rather than consider prints of strawberries, I walked across Wisconsin Avenue to a bar called Holiday House. Inside, Duke Snider gestured for me to join him.

Across drinks, Snider was serious, soft-voiced, opinionated, and quietly insistent that each opinion was correct. The more intense he became, the more softly he spoke. "Did ya write a good story?" he asked in a low tone. "What'll you drink?"

"Medium. It was a medium game. Scotch, thanks."

"I'm buying," Snider said. "Bring him a double Scotch and soda."

"Something bothering you, Duke?"

"Something? Everything."

"You're hitting .335."

"I know." The long face fell into a pout. "But it's this whole damn life. You know what I'm gonna do? Get some good acreage. I know a place south of Los Angeles. I'm gonna move there and raise avocados."

"You're kidding."

"I'm not kidding. I dreamed of being a big leaguer once, but that's not it for me any more. Last fall in the World Series, I'm out there. Big bat. Seventy thousand watching. Great catch. You know what I'm dreaming then? About being a farmer."

"There's the money."

"That's right, and if it wasn't for the money I'd be just as happy if I never played a game of ball again." He was twenty-six years old.

"Duke, if you mean what you're saying and you're willing to put your name to it, we can both make a little money just by printing it."

"I mean it," Snider said. "You go write it, just so's it comes out I'm explaining, not complaining."

I put off the story for years. Then Gordon Manning, the penultimate managing editor of *Collier's*, called me for lunch and asked if I had any article ideas. "We'll give you enough for the Jaguar you always wanted, or the down payment anyway," he said.

When I mentioned the old conversation with Snider, the editor glowed faintly and made a fair offer for each of us. A week later he handed me a round-trip ticket to Los Angeles and an expense check of $500.

"I'll only be a day or two," I said.

"Spend it all. Keep the Duke happy."

The Sniders owned a small white house on a quiet street in Compton, which lies just south of the Los Angeles city line. Duke was grossing $50,000 a year, but his house could have belonged to someone earning a fifth as much. The rooms were compact. The children slept in bunks. "We aren't getting anything fancier until we're sure it's for keeps," said Beverly Snider, a trim, forceful woman. "Baseball isn't all that secure." Duke was large, long-striding, somewhat jowly. Beverly was petite, unlined, determined. As I set up a recorder and Duke groped for the sources of his disenchantment, Beverly wandered in and out of the small living room monitoring.

A few fans threw marbles at him when he chased fly balls, Duke said. The endless travel bothered him. The press could be cruel. "It isn't any one thing, but when they all come at the same time, when you get off a train after a couple of hours' sleep and a manager snipes at you before the game, and the fans throw stuff during the game, and the writers second-guess you after, you begin to wonder about baseball as a trade."

"Could you think of one particular bad day?"

"No," Duke said, "but lots of bad times. Like once when Charlie [Dressen] was managing, a bunch of us went to see *The Caine Mutiny* in Philly. Well, in the movie Captain Queeg blew up over a quart of strawberries. The next damn day Charlie blew up over an order of creamed cauliflower. The Warwick Hotel was expensive and someone had a good meal and added creamed cauliflower à la carte for an extra seventy-five cents. That night it was drizzling and we got stuck in the clubhouse and Charlie opened up. 'You damn wise guys. You got nothing better to do than order creamed cauliflower, seventy-five cents extra?' He kept repeating it and it wasn't raining that much and around the fifth time I said, 'Hey, Charlie. What say we go out on the field?'

"'What you trying to do?' he hollers. 'Run this ball club?'

"'Hell, no. I just want to loosen up.'

"'You'll loosen up when I tell you to loosen up. Now about this creamed cauliflower, you listening, Snider?'

"'Look,' I yelled. 'I didn't even eat at the hotel on the club. I ate in a restaurant with my own money. Why don't you deduct the seventy-five cents for the cauliflower from the six bucks meal money I didn't use?'"

Remembering, Duke made a little laugh. "And then he reamed me."

We walked out of the white house in Compton to a clothing store where Duke said he would sell sports jackets during Christmas week. We stopped in a bar, and he drank Seven Crown and Seven-Up. When he tried to take the bill, I explained about the $500 expense check.

"Keep the money," he said. "Bev and me don't need entertaining."

"Well, I have it. Why don't we go to a club tonight on Sunset Strip?"

"It's Saturday," Snider said. "We couldn't get in anywhere good."

"Can I use your name for the reservation?"

"Sure, but that won't help. They don't know me here. I'm not a coast-league ballplayer."

We reached Ciro's at eight thirty. "Mr. Snidair," cried a maitre d', in great excitement, "we didn't think it was really you. People call all the time and use famous names. What a pleasure." Busboys began chattering and pointing. The maitre d' led us toward the stage and placed us at a table, second-row center.

"I don't know," I said, "if I should have tipped, or if movie guys have all the first rows tied up."

"I'm just surprised they know me," Duke said.

Beverly considered a menu and cried, "Look at these prices."

"I don't see any creamed cauliflower," Duke said.

Eartha Kitt's act at Ciro's built to a climactic number in which she stripped to black brassiere and underpants, while singing variations of a lyric:

> *I'm getting nothing for Christmas,*
> *That's why little Eartha is sad.*
> *I'm getting nothing for Christmas*
> *'Cause I didn't want to be bad.*

At the final chorus she leaped into the arms of a Latin, who suddenly appeared at one wing and carried her off, presumably to ecstasy and other Christmas gifts.

"Well," said Beverly Snider, as the lights came up. "Well!" Duke gazed toward a wall. "Certainly not the sort of thing," Beverly said, "one could recommend to one's friends."

"Depends on the friends," I said. *Collier's* paid our check. We departed in silence.

In the spring of 1956 *Collier's* published the article, Snider and myself sharing the byline. The piece stands as accurate, reasonably balanced, and mild compared to the commercial sports iconoclasm of the 1970s. Snider described some of his disillusion, said he hoped to play through 1962 and then looked forward to retirement. He imagined a California

Elysium, with avocados bursting from every tree. For all its bluster, the story was genial, no more mature than either author, harmless.

But the sporting press hurried to flagellate us for unorthodoxy. At least fifty newspaper articles described Snider as an ingrate. Red Smith composed an arch column in which Snider was said to have grabbed my lapel and wept. Stanley Woodward, rescued from Miami, was working for the *Newark Evening News*. He wrote that I had sat in a little room, invented the article, and gone forth to find a ballplayer, any ballplayer, to lend a name and share the profits.

"Son of a bitch," I told him afterward. "You were wrong."

"Not wrong," Woodward said. "Entertaining and short of libel. And that's my definition of a good column."

Only John Lardner, who was writing for *Newsweek*, took us seriously. He was a tall, bespectacled, profound man, infinitely gentle to his friends, and typically he found depth in the article beyond what Snider and I had conceived.

"You see," Lardner said at the long bar of the Artist and Writers Restaurant, "Duke thought if his dream came true he would be a different person. He's not unhappy about the dream. He's unhappy that he is still the same man. Happens to a lot of us. We get somewhere we wanted and find we're still ourselves." Lardner had revealed more than he intended. He said quickly, "Needles has the staying power to win the Belmont."

"I don't like to bet horses," I said. "You really think the dream is killing Snider?" Lardner gazed at me with kind, despairing eyes.

I telephoned Gordon Manning and said that we ought to do something for Duke. "You could write an editorial, for example. He's getting murdered."

"He should have thought about reaction before he did the piece," Manning said.

"I didn't think about it. He certainly couldn't have."

"But you each have the down payment on a Jaguar," Manning said. He was closing another issue, he said. If I had any other story ideas, would I let him know?

Snider played for more seasons than anyone else [on the Brooklyn Dodgers of the early 1950s]—curiously, none of the team had an exceptionally extended career—but in the 1959 World Series he strained a knee. After that he had to cramp his swing. In 1963 the Dodgers shipped him to the Mets, where he was a sentimental favorite and batted .243, a hundred points below his best standard. A year later the Giants signed him to pinch-hit. He batted .210, and a few months after his thirty-eighth birthday he retired. He had hit 407 home runs, more than any Dodger, more than all but about a dozen men in baseball history. And he had found forty rolling acres outside the village of Fallbrook, California, and bought his farm.

To reach Fallbrook, you drive south from Los Angeles down Highway 1, out of yellow haze into an open country of tan beaches and golden fields. You pass San Juan Capistrano, the Marine base at Camp Pendleton, and then you turn into a smaller road toward handsome uplands and a crossroad village called Bonsail. There you follow a two-lane blacktop winding among citrus trees. Two miles before Fallbrook, a narrow road cuts toward Green Canyon, and a few minutes down Green Canyon Road, in a pleasant ranch house looking toward Mount Palomar, one finds the Duke of Fallbrook. The setting is attractive but not overwhelming. Eight years out of baseball, Duke Snider has had to sell the large home, the avocado trees, the farm.

He seemed cheerful, almost unchanged. He had put on weight at the jowls, but he always did tend to go puffy. His hair, gray in 1953, was black. He had performed on television for a hair darkener, and the contract required him to keep using dye. Beverly, still trim, made soup for lunch, and Duke asked if I wanted to see the town and the countryside. He walked his two acres lovingly, showing me a small pool and dwarf lemon trees. A few avocados stood on a slope where he had installed sprinklers. "Bev and I like to grow things," he said. We got into a car and drove slowly over rolling dun ridges, green where irrigation touched them. "See that?" Snider said, pointing to a rambling Spanish-style manor on the shoulder of a hill. "That was our house. And that all over there—those rows of avocados was the farm."

"I'm sorry it didn't work out."

"Aaah," Snider said. "I made a bad guess. Look at those things. I owned them all." Avocados grow short, stumpy, and gnarled. Against a memory of eastern maples, they are not handsome, but Duke considered the stumpy rows tenderly. "They were bearing fine," he said. "Then we decided to do a little more, invest in a bowling alley near Camp Pendleton. The Marine families would be permanent customers. Vietnam happened. The families were broken up. The recruits want more action than a night of bowling. So I had to get out of the business.

"By the time I did, I'd lost a lot. There went the farm. But Buzzy's taken care of me. I broadcast for his San Diego club and do some coaching."

"Back on the damn road."

"It's not that bad," Snider said, "but you know what bothers me? This house there"—he pointed at his lost manor—"is set so high we could get TV stations from L.A. and San Diego both. Now where we are, down Green Canyon, we only get San Diego." A breeze stirred through the avocado fields. "Come on," Duke said. "Let's get a brew."

We drove into Fallbrook, a low, sprawling town, and as we walked into the bar, men called greetings. Snider introduced me, and one of the men said, "Keep your money in your pocket. You come all the way from New York, we won't let you buy."

"Thanks."

"But if you come all the way from New York, how can you speak English? I didn't know they spoke English in New York." Others nodded. "How do you like it out here?" the man asked.

"It's great," I said, quoting Fred Allen, 1938, "if you're an orange."

"Hey," said the man, "that's all right." He was wearing work pants and a khaki jacket. "You know we let Duke in our softball game once."

Snider nodded. "They told me it was fast pitch, but everything I hit went foul. Fast pitch to these guys, but I pulled everything inside first base."

They took softball seriously, said the man in khaki, as someone bought a second round. They played through the summer in informal leagues, building to "a kind of world series." A year before, the Fallbrook team had reached the series against a team from an Indian reservation. The Indians went ahead, three games to nothing. The Fallbrook team sent for the Duke.

"Right," Snider said, "and I said I'd help if I could use a hardball bat."

"I don't remember what he used, but we put him at shortstop, and from losing three games to nothing, we won the series four games to three."

"He still hits good," someone said.

"Different league," the Duke said. "My round." And he bought the beers with a flourish.

As we drove home, he reminisced. "My dad, Ward, come out west from Ohio. He used to see Cincinnati play. He kept putting the bat on my left shoulder when I was little because he knew the right-field fences were closer. Pete Rozelle and I were forwards on the same basketball team in Compton, and he wrote for the newspaper, the *Tartar Shield*. My wife was with him the day he went ice skating and fell and lost his two front teeth. I could throw a football seventy yards. Pete says I coulda been a T quarterback. But I liked baseball. The Dodgers give me seven hundred and fifty dollars to sign and I took a train acrost the country to Bear Mountain, where they were training. I was seventeen and I never owned a topcoat."

"Did you buy one?"

"No. I stayed indoors a lot." Snider smiled at his own joke. "That was '44 and I got in an exhibition game at West Point and Glenn Davis was in the outfield for Army. I was the professional, but I got a thrill being on the same field with the amateur.

"I made it to Brooklyn in '47. In the first game Jackie Robinson played, I pinch-hit for Dixie Walker. Base hit to right. I sent the clippings to my mother, and I wrote that it wasn't only a colored person's first game in the big leagues, it was also her son's.

"I really made it after 1951. You know I struck out eight times in five games during the 1949 Series. I don't remember it bothering me much in '50, but in the last month of 1951 I kept thinking I was gonna face those Yankee pitchers again. I went in a terrible slump. I'm no psychologist, but I know that was in the back of my mind. I didn't hit, and then we lost the playoff. The next year, you were there, I got straightened away and that Series I hit four home runs.

"I could always go back good in the outfield, and when I went to my left, Furillo and I had this trick. If we thought we might collide, I'd take a step in and try to catch the ball high and Furillo would take a step back and try to backhand it low. Not much got through us all those years, and we never did run into each other."

When we reached his house, I said maybe we ought to go out for dinner again. "If we can find where Eartha Kitt's playing."

"You remember," Beverly said. "Well, there isn't any of that kind of thing in Fallbrook, but there is a fine restaurant called Valley Forge."

"An old Marine sergeant is behind the bar," Duke said, "and if you wear a tie, he clips it. I'll call ahead and fix it so he won't cut yours."

The sergeant, a massive man with a great waxed mustache, waved as we entered, winked to indicate that my tie was safe, and made drinks. "Did you see *The Graduate*?" Beverly said.

I nodded.

"You work hard for your money. Why give it to a dirty movie like that?"

"It wasn't much good, but I wouldn't call it dirty."

"Well, I sing in the Methodist choir," Beverly said, "and a lot of us don't see any reason for putting sex on a movie screen."

"Sex exists, Bev."

"I know it does, and it's very beautiful and *very* private."

Duke seemed to be considering the oak floor. "I've always meant to tell you two that I was sorry about the reaction to the *Collier's* story," I said.

"Fergit it," Duke said. "Like Rickey put it, don't worry what they say about you, as long as they say something. Boy, I sure got my ink.

"And most of that story still goes. Except after I got done playing, I come to realize that baseball was what I knew, all I knew. When we had losses, and I had to get back, it wasn't like before. I'm older. I don't mind things so damn much."

"He misses the old team," Beverly said. "Everyone was so close."

"Heck, once in Pittsburgh," Duke said, "after a day game we went to watch the Kentucky Derby at the men's bar of the Schenley Hotel. There was nineteen of the twenty-five ballplayers in that bar. Lots of times after a game, there might be fifteen of us go to the same place. I credit Rickey, from the way he was working to bring us together. Hey, who you seen?"

I told him and mentioned [Andy] Pafko's remark that Duke was so fine a ballplayer he deserved a steak. Snider nodded. That seemed fair.

We went to eat. Brooklyn or Fallbrook, his swagger endured. Over the sirloins I told Beverly Pee Wee Reese's favorite Snider story. Four players rode a car pool from Bay Ridge to the Polo Grounds in 1951, and on Reese's night to drive a motorcycle patrolman stopped them. Approaching, the policeman burst out, "Pee Wee. It's you. Why you driving so fast?"

"Big series with the Giants, officer. Kind of nervous."

"Don't listen to that, officer," Snider said. "He deserves a ticket."

"Hiya, Duke," the cop said. "Gee, fellers. What a thrill for me. Good luck, and take it easy, will ya, Pee Wee?"

Snider drove the next night, and within a mile of the same spot another policeman sounded a short siren burst from *Die Walkure*. Then he took Snider's license and started writing.

"Say, officer. That Edwin Donald Snider is *Duke* Snider. I'm the Dodger center fielder."

Without looking up the policeman said, "I hate baseball." He handed Snider a ticket for speeding.

Beverly smiled faintly. Duke nodded. "That's about right, and I woulda had to pay it, too, if John Cashmore, the borough president of Brooklyn, hadn't fixed it for me." And buoyant and boyish though fifty was approaching and the farm was gone, Duke resumed his attack on the steak.

PART IV

DAMN GOOD HITTERS AND PITCHERS

CHAPTER 15

EDDIE MATHEWS, THE MAN ON THIRD

Over his seventeen-year major-league career, Eddie Mathews hit 512 home runs, played in three World Series, and drove in one hundred or more runs five times playing for the Braves in Boston, Milwaukee, and Atlanta. Along with Hank Aaron, he made up one of the most fearsome power-hitting combos in history. In this 1958 article, the year after his Braves beat the Yankees in the World Series, Kahn visited the Hall of Fame third baseman as he tried to master "the business of being a big-league idol in all its bewildering complexity."

When Ed Mathews considers the most difficult thing that he had to do in baseball, he grins and shrugs and mouths a simple phrase. "You have to learn to get along with people," he says.

Ed Mathews is a ballplayer, and a good one, eloquent at bat and now fluent with a glove. If he were an actor, schooled in talking about himself, he might stand up, beating his arms, and speak of how he came to terms with life. If he were a psychologist, schooled in talking about others, he might lean against a couch and discuss personality integration. But Mathews is a ballplayer. So he grins and says you have to get along with people, and even though he means a great deal more, he lets it go at that and grins again.

To baseball writers, who stand around a batting cage swinging pencils, the most difficult thing in major-league baseball seems obvious. The game is impossible to play. The pitches move too swiftly to hit, the fly balls sail too high to judge, the ground balls bounce too hard to field, and the line drives go into orbit. But for Mathews, the infinitely difficult process of becoming a major leaguer was achieved naturally and almost easily. His swing, level and devastating, was always there. As soon as he learned to take pitches outside the strike zone, he was a slugger. Fielding required practice, but after a time Mathews stopped throwing left hooks at grounders and began grabbing them. After two years in the majors, he was an excellent third baseman.

The rest should have been simple. All Mathews had to do was keep swinging, keep fielding, smile at the citizens of Milwaukee, answer newspapermen cheerily, and select a good broker to handle the money. But, of course, the rest was not simple at all. Ed Mathews, who understood the curveball, was mystified by the art of public relations.

In 1954, when he was to Milwaukee what Winston Churchill used to be to London, Ed married a pretty Wisconsin girl named Virjean Lauby. Before the ceremony, two reporters, a photographer, and a television crew arrived at the county clerk's office in Marshfield, a Milwaukee suburb, to cover the wedding.

"You fellows better get out of here," Harry Zaidins, Mathews's lawyer, told the newsmen. "Eddie won't stand for it."

"Publicity is Eddie's bread and butter," said Gerard Paradowski, a deputy clerk. "The man lives by ink and, besides, he's getting married in a public place." A compromise was reached when the photographer and TV men agreed to leave and the reporter agreed to stay. As the wedding party swept into the office, Mathews sniffed once, scowled, and said,

"Who's that?"

"I'm from the *Milwaukee Journal*," the reporter said.

Mathews marched on the newspaperman. "If this wasn't my wedding day, buddy," he said, quietly, "I'd bust your adjectival neck."

"Give Eddie a break," said somebody in the wedding party. "He's all excited."

The reporter gave Mathews a break. He wrote that Mathews was married "in a dark blue suit with a white fleck."

A few months earlier, Ed had spent an evening sipping beer and talking baseball with his friend and roommate, Bob Buhl. Quite innocently, the evening passed, and when Mathews climbed into his light blue convertible, it was well past 2 A.M. On the way home, he drove through a red light, which a police sergeant named Howard Haag was guarding in the line of duty.

Haag sped after Mathews, who then quickened his homeward pace. A few blocks later, with Haag gaining slowly, Mathews ducked into a side street and turned out his lights. Haag followed, Mathews turned on his lights, and when Haag threw his police spotlight on the convertible, Mathews stopped.

"Are you Eddie Mathews?" Haag asked.

"Yes," Mathews confessed shyly. "I am."

"Well, Eddie," the sergeant said, "you've just done a damned foolish thing."

When the case reached court three days later, a reporter and a photographer were waiting. "Right this way," a bailiff told Mathews. "Right up to the judge's bench."

Mathews pointed a finger at the photographer. "You take one picture," he said, "and I'll break your arm."

"I'm taking your picture," the photographer said, ducking behind the bailiff.

"I'll break your arm," Mathews repeated, for emphasis.

"Here," said Justice Edgar A. Bark, a pacifist. "There'll be none of that in my court."

The trial, which lasted five minutes, ran Mathews $50 for reckless driving and $4.15 for court costs.

"Sorry," Judge Bark said, when it was over. "Now, I wonder if you'd mind signing this autograph book. I'm planning a little surprise for my daughter."

Mathews signed. As he left the courtroom, the photographer took a halfdozen pictures.

It is never notably wise to antagonize newspapermen who are gainfully employed. No matter how much a reporter may hate his job, he will strike back with surprising initiative when someone insults him. Walter O'Malley, who insulted New York newspapermen, now gets a worse press in Manhattan than any man since Adolf Hitler. Ed Mathews, who did not realize that his home runs had made him a public figure, got a restrained press in Milwaukee which would have been rougher if the editors had not decided that insulting Mathews would not sell papers.

But no determined reporter can be stopped permanently by an editor's decision. The Milwaukee baseball writers in a secret ballot elected Mathews the worst tipper and the worst dressed man on the Braves. Then they made the results of the secret ballot public. "That burns me up," Mathews said. "Wonderful," said a reporter.

Then, some years after he had became a major leaguer, Ed Mathews realized that as long as he hit home runs, reporters and photographers were going to be part of his life. The change came to life most pleasantly last autumn when the Braves were winning the World Series from the Yankees.

Mathews, you may remember, did not start hitting until the last three games. But from the beginning of the Series, he fielded as though he were a late-inning defensive replacement, feeding the family on fancy stops. He went into the hole, he backhanded wallops down the line, he charged bunts, and generally put on the finest fall showing at third since Billy Cox, the acrobat disguised as an infielder, hung up his cavernous glove. And Cox never saw the day he could hit with Mathews.

After the second game, reporters and photographers crowded around Ed in the Braves' dressing room. It is not an easy thing, a Series press conference. Newspapermen who have not seen a game all year appear, and their questions may be pointless or antagonistic. The reporters line up in rows and there is bellowing.

"Hey, Eddie," said a reporter in the first row, whispering to keep his question a scoop, "what are you in there for, your glove?" Mathews grinned. His face, dark and handsome in repose, lights up when he smiles. "Guess so," Mathews said, and chuckled.

"What did he say?" shouted a man in the back row.

"He said 'guess so,'" the front row reporter called, still concealing his question.

"I'll tell you," Mathews said, speaking loudly and clearly. "My fielding ought to be better if practice means anything. I've worked on it long enough."

"That right?" said a reporter in the second row.

"Quiet," said a man in the third row. "Shut up and let the guy talk."

"I'm letting him talk," the man in the second row said.

Mathews kept on the topic. "Hell, I remember when I was playing in the minors," he said, "I sometimes used to wish I'd boot the grounders. That way I knew the guy would only get to first base. If I picked the ball up, I figured I'd throw it away and the guy would end up on second."

Everybody laughed.

"How did you practice?" a reporter asked.

"I fielded grounders," Mathews said. "There isn't any other way. I'd go out there and I'd have them hit to me for hours until I was aching all over. You do that every day for a couple of years, you'll learn how to play third base, if you live. . . ."

"What about the hitting, Eddie?" came a voice.

"It isn't there," Mathews said.

"You figure it will be tomorrow?"

Now, there was a magnificent question, worthy of a sullen reply.

"I hope so," Mathews said, pleasantly. "I don't think there's anything much wrong. My timing is all right. It's just, well, it's just that I haven't been hitting."

"What's he say?" asked the third row. "What's he say?"

"He says he ain't hitting," said the second.

"I had to come all the way down here to find that out?" the third row complained.

Mathews was tired, and the pressure of the Series still weighed heavily on him. "All you fellows have enough?" he said. "Need anything more?"

"That's fine, thanks, Eddie," a reporter said, and the massed press moved on to the next victim.

"See you fellows in Milwaukee," Mathews said. Then, perhaps twenty minutes after the game had ended, be began to take the dirty uniform from his back and peel down for the shower he had wanted as soon as the game ended. By any standard, it was an impressive performance, and to those reporters who remembered Mathews as he had been, it was more surprising than anything he did on the field all Series, including the backhand stop he made for the last out in the last game.

When most ballplayers finish baseball, they have mastered the technique of talking to groups with enough charm to hold attention. Watching Mathews's inordinate charm now, the wonder is that he ever had any difficulty. But first consider the speed with which fame was thrust upon him and consider the position of the ballplayer.

Actresses, politicians, and successful novelists all are protected from the press by middlemen. They are told what they can safely tell reporters, and they are told what they should keep to themselves. You don't just interview Marilyn Monroe. You call her agent, who calls her press agent, who asks what you want to discuss. Then afterwards the press agent feeds you Scotch until he thinks you've forgotten what you did discuss, which is one reason why reporters rarely quote actresses as saying: "I'll break your arm, buddy." The movie stars say it often enough, but the press agents drown them out.

In major-league baseball, each ball club hires a press agent and keeps him busy with promotional plans, speaking dates, statistics, and preparing a yearbook. Baseball publicity men rarely have much time to spend with the players. Further, most players resist front-office orders, preferring to take what guff they must from one source, the manager. Since the manager's job depends on developing good, but not necessarily well-adjusted, ballplayers, the result is often haphazard. Rookies are not briefed on how to handle all the new demands on their time, and they learn public relations only after painful experience.

For the rookie who does not hit, the problem is academic. There may be a few simple questions during spring training, and then, as the curveballs start breaking more sharply, silence falls. Nobody asks the weak hitter to speak at a father-and-son banquet on the night that he wants to play bridge. No reporter involves the losing pitcher in a three-hour discussion on the slider that didn't slide.

Ed Mathews could hit from the beginning. He smacked twenty-five homers in Boston as a rookie of twenty. When the Braves moved to Milwaukee the following year, he hit forty-seven and everyone wanted to shower *gemuttichkeit* on this graceful, handsome boy, who, the papers said, was going to be the next Babe Ruth.

"Mathews," Stan Musial remarked, "has the greatest future of any player in the game. I've never known any man to improve so much in a single season."

"Mathews," Ralph Kiner said, "has the power to rank with Williams, Mize, and DiMaggio."

"Mathews," Eddie Stanky said, "has the best chance of anyone around to break Babe Ruth's record."

During the 1954 season there were three full-length articles in major magazines on Mathews, and the titles did not undersell the subject. "The Wrists That Made Milwaukee Famous," announced *Collier's*. "The Inside Dope on Home-Run Mathews—the Idol of Milwaukee," the *Saturday Evening Post* headlined. "The Milwaukee Blaster," blared *Look*.

All these stories meant demands on Mathews's time, above the regular demands of Milwaukee baseball writers, and each served to make the man more famous, which, in turn, meant even more demands upon him.

If he walked down a street in Milwaukee, a crowd gathered and tagged along. One Sunday night when the Braves returned from Chicago after winning a doubleheader from the Cubs, some three hundred bobby-soxers met them at the Milwaukee station. Within fifteen minutes all of the players but Mathews had broken away. Eddie had to stay and sign autographs for more than an hour. After each game at County Stadium, a mob of Milwaukee fans ambushed Mathews. "Sign mine, sign mine, sign mine," a twelve-year-old girl shrieked into his ear one afternoon.

"Stop that," Mathews said. "Didn't your mother teach you any manners?"

"Oooh, Eddie," said the girl delightedly.

"I'm sorry," Mathews said. "Give me your book. I'll sign it."

Older girls presented a different problem. Mathews was single, strong, and prosperous. "The women will drive you crazy," he told a friend at the time. "Unless I leave a no-call order at the Wisconsin Hotel, they wake me up at any hour and ask me to come down and join them in the bar, or invite themselves up to visit me. I never knew women were as nuts as they are."

Merchants in Milwaukee crammed store windows with Eddie Mathews displays. Mathews's fan mail averaged more than fifty letters a day. Donald Davidson, the Braves' publicity man, took to ordering picture postcards of Mathews in lots of 2,500. A Milwaukee dentist, in trouble as he tried to drill a small boy's molar, saved the situation when he asked, "Sonny, don't you want an Eddie Mathews filling?"

In any town, a handsome young slugger would be popular, but Milwaukee was more than any town. If Mathews had accepted every invitation to speak, every request to sign an autograph, every attempt to loop him into a promotion, he would have had to stop playing baseball. There simply wouldn't have been time.

Beyond this, too, there were rumors. If Eddie sipped a beer, rumor made it a double martini. If he dated a girl, rumor created a romance. Here Mathews stood, at twenty-three, a major-league star, doing what he had always wanted to do, and yet it wasn't working out as he had dreamed it would. The homers came from his dream book, but who sent all these people to break in on his privacy, these strangers to steal his leisure hours? And couldn't he ever get away from the reporters?

When Mathews talks about the early years now, he seems almost to be laughing at himself. One recent afternoon in Philadelphia, an agent who had been sent to discuss the old Ed Mathews with the new Ed Mathews found only maturity and poise. Eddie had not been hitting for a few games, and the thought occurred that he might not want to talk at all.

Mathews smiled. "I'll even talk about hitting," he said, "but I probably won't give you the right answers."

The session, which had begun in the lobby of the Hotel Warwick, was adjourned to a restaurant called "1614" a block and a half away. The 1614 is an informal place, popular with ballplayers visiting Philadelphia because it is close to the hotel and reasonable and not jammed with fans who interrupt dinner to ask how to hit the outside screwball. One room is a bar, the walls covered with photographs of ballplayers. The other room is a restaurant.

Mathews took a table in the restaurant and ordered shrimp cocktail and steak. A girl leaving the restaurant noticed Mathews and walked by slowly, staring. "Damn," Mathews said, "some of them are crazy. I'm a married man with two kids."

Mathews's hairline has receded somewhat, but so, after all, has Marlon Brando's hairline. Eddie is still a highly attractive man.

"My wife, Virjean," he said, "has been the best thing that ever happened. That's what really settled me down and got everything squared away for me."

"You seem," the agent suggested, "a good deal happier than you were a few years ago."

"I guess I am," Mathews said.

When the shrimp arrived, the agent recalled what it had once been like to interview Mathews. "You'd say hello, or maybe nod," he said, "but you didn't look as though you'd ever say anything else."

"There were a lot of reporters," Mathews said, "and most of them were pretty nice to me. I don't think I was uncooperative, but I just didn't go for this attention. I mean, the last thing in the world I could do, even now, is go into a room full of people and say, 'I'm Ed Mathews.'"

He thought for a minute about the press. "What offended me when I was single," he said, "were the personal questions they used to shoot at me. 'Who are you dating? How's your love life?' Things like that."

The steak came up medium rare. "I used to figure," Mathews said, cutting, "that if I could go about my business and nobody knew who I was, that would be fine. Just play the ball game and then live like you always did. I used to go back home to Santa Barbara (California) in the winter and not see any ballplayers. But when I got married, Virjean and I settled down in Marshfield. That's right outside of Milwaukee."

"You gave away a lot of climate," the agent said.

"It made sense," Mathews said. "Virjean is from around there, and my job is in Milwaukee, and there are more things I can do in business there. I'm in a construction business now. Not big like Early Wynn, but it's something. I can set myself up better for when I'm through if I live in Milwaukee. You don't get to keep much money. There are federal taxes and state taxes, and playing ball you aren't gonna end up rich."

After the meal, Mathews reached for the bill.

"I'll take it," the agent said, thinking of his expense account.

"No," Mathews said.

"It's all right. I'll get it back."

"No," Mathews said. "I mean, I don't want you to think the reason I've been talking to you at dinner was that you'd pay for the meal."

"That's not what I'm thinking," the agent said.

"Well, okay," Mathews said, "if you're sure you'll get it back."

In the cab out to Connie Mack Stadium, Mathews began to talk about the vulnerability of public figures. "You see kids," he said, "they get careless, they don't know. Why, a ballplayer is wide open. Anything he does, anything he says, can get him in trouble. Look at [Ted] Williams. Boy, you have to be careful."

Mathews had thought most of the problem through. "One thing I can't figure is these scandal magazines," he said. "The stuff they run about famous people. They even run stuff about ballplayers. Is that stuff true?"

"Probably not," the agent said.

"Well, then why don't they get sued?" Mathews asked.

"How can you sue," the agent said, "if somebody writes you beat up your wife? Sure, you'll collect, but before the case is over, there'll be a dozen more headlines. It isn't worth it. Just walk away and forget it."

"Boy," Mathews said, "a ballplayer is wide open."

He stared out of the taxi window at the drab tenements along the way to the ballpark. Scandal and rumor were not items on which Ed Mathews was coached as he learned how to be a ballplayer.

There is, perhaps, no way to teach a boy that becoming a ballplayer involves a way of life. For every man like Pee Wee Reese or Stan Musial, who seems to know instinctively just how to conduct himself on the day he first sees a major-league camp, there are a dozen who are baffled. Some, like Mathews, withdraw within themselves. Some, frightened, insist "the majors don't look so tough."

Ed Mathews was brought up in a situation where he had some hint of what a baseball life would be, but he had no advance hint of Milwaukee. No one did. So when his life became totally ringed by baseball fans and bobby-soxers, he was surprised. . . .

Mathews's father, the late Edwin Lee Mathews, Sr., was a friendly and well-spoken man who worked as a Western Union telegrapher until tuberculosis struck him down. One of the senior Mathews's first assignments was telegraphing stories from Marlin Springs, Texas, where the Giants trained. Over the years, he worked baseball press boxes around the country, and when his only son was very young and showed signs of possessing good coordination, the elder Mathews encouraged him to swing a bat. When Ed was four, his family moved from his birthplace, Texarkana, Texas, to Santa Barbara. It was there, under the warm California sun, that his baseball training began.

As a telegrapher, the father had seen great ballplayers, and often he told his son about them. "Maybe I took a little storyteller's license," Mathews, senior, once remarked, "but I really wanted to get the kid enthused. When he was a little guy, we used to go out to the school grounds at La Cumbre Junior High and round up some neighborhood kids. The main idea was to let Eddie swing that bat and hit. Even then I could see he was a natural."

Many of the other boys of six and seven backed up when a pitch came close. Ed stood his ground, swung hard and hit the ball enormous distances. Often a group of men would gather just to watch Ed hit. . . .

Mathews signed [with the Braves] in 1949, hit the majors three years later, and had his forty-seven-home-run season just four years after his high school graduation day. . . .Now, less than four seasons later, the shirt fits, soft and comfortable. Bob Buhl, the fine right-hander who rooms with Mathews, says he has noticed a considerable change. "I've roomed with him for five years," Buhl says, "and I know Eddie pretty well. He's really learned how to relax. He sleeps a lot. It's sort of that he's gotten settled. He knows what to expect and he knows how to handle it. He's gotten a lot more confident."

Mathews, hitting forty-seven home runs at the age of twenty-two, did it with a swing, not with confidence. For almost as long as he can remember, he has admired Ted Williams, but that year he told a friend, "When I saw Williams in the spring, I sure would have liked to talk hitting with him, but I didn't think he'd want to bother with a kid like me."

Mathews could hit that well, while still thinking of himself as a kid, for only one reason. He is extremely close to being a natural. He stands at the plate, his feet wide apart, his front foot pointing toward right center, the bat held high and motionless. He does not crouch. Then, as the pitch comes in, he takes a six-inch stride and, when the ball seems almost to have passed him, the bat stirs, whipped by his thick wrists. Like Williams and Hank Aaron, Mathews is a wrist hitter. His forearms are enormous and as a result he can wait until the last fraction of a second before deciding whether to swing. At bat, he follows one simple rule. "I guess fastball," he says. "Then if it's a curve or a change, I can adjust. But, if you guess curve and it's a fastball, you've had it. By the time you adjust, the catcher is throwing the ball back to the mound."

From the day he first picked up a bat, Mathews possessed something approximating his current swing. "He's had a lot of good coaches," Mathews senior once said, "but there's one thing I wouldn't let any of them touch. That was the kid's swing. It was perfect; everyone left it alone. . . ."

During Mathews's first year with the Braves, his one batting weakness came to light. He swung at fastballs high, tight, and out of the strike zone. Major-league pitchers, of course, maintain an underground. Should Stan Musial miss two outside curveballs at the Coliseum, word will go out on the underground before Stan pops the next curve off the end of his bat and over the screen.

As soon as Mathews missed a few high, tight fastballs, the news got out and, swinging at hundreds of high, tight fastballs that season, he struck out 115 times. He hit twenty-five homers and there were repeated references to the new Ruth, but still Mathews could not develop real confidence. How confident can a man be, missing a bad pitch for a third strike?

That winter, when a reporter asked about the sophomore jinx, Mathews scowled. "Why should I worry about that?" he said. "I wasn't so hot last year."

Someone else asked if he had been mobbed for commercial endorsements. "Who'd mob me?" Mathews said. "I haven't done anything yet."

Braves Field in 1952 was a solitary place. Reporters showed up, along with ballplayers and umpires. But the fans deserted. It was a good place to read and, since it was quiet, anyone could hear what the infielders chirped to the pitcher, or what the managers said to the umpires. It was a curious version of big-league baseball: some good games, but no people.

From Braves Field, Mathews and the Braves switched to County Stadium, where people glutted the market. "Which one is second base?" they'd say, or "Why doesn't the first baseman play on first base?" They brought saxophones and made noise, and brought cowbells and made more noise, and, although they cheered foul balls, they were the most dedicated mob of fans modern baseball has yet seen.

Coincidentally, Mathews stopped swinging at the bad fastballs that year. By July, when the Milwaukee fans had discovered that a home run was more valuable than a foul, they found that right there in County Stadium, they had the hottest home-run hitter in baseball. Girls began squealing when Mathews came to bat, the way girls once squealed at Frank Sinatra. Ed, who had solved the problem of his fielding and had solved the problem of the high, inside fastball, now had to solve the problem of being public property.

It would be simple if you could point to a single day, or a single incident, and say, "Here. Right at this point. This is where Ed Mathews mastered public relations." But there was no single point at which it happened.

"I'd say," says one of Mathews's closest friends on the Braves, "that it was about the beginning of 1956. He'd married, settled down, and done some thinking. You can't play on this club and try to keep to yourself. The people won't stand for it. I figure Eddie thought about this a lot, and maybe he and Virjean talked about it, and slowly, over a couple of years, the thing hit home." Here Mathews's friend smiles. "Can you think of a more pleasant guy around now?" he asks.

Because Mathews is big and strong and can play baseball so easily, he always seemed to be a man who should have been glib but wasn't. Why wasn't he? There were mixed opinions.

"Well," said one baseball man, "the best reason I can give you is that he's stupid." This was a considerable canard.

"He's all wrapped up in himself," another man suggested. This was more valid, but an oversimplification. Of course, he was wrapped up in himself. Everyone who met Ed Mathews wanted to talk about one thing—Ed Mathews. The questions were always about himself, the speeches were supposed to be about himself, and so, if his thoughts turned inward, this was natural. For most people, conversation is give and take, with ideas passing back and forth. For Mathews in Milwaukee, conversation was entirely one-sided. "Come on," people said, "tell me all there is to tell about you."

I think it is a mark of Mathews's intelligence and sensitivity that he has come to grips with his abnormal existence as quickly as he has. Mickey Mantle, given a similar buildup but far less put upon by local fans, still is fighting the battle Mathews has won. Ted Williams, after twenty years, has lost it.

Mathews, mature at twenty-seven, can now make friends with his personality as surely as he makes friends with his bat. He lives and travels quietly, but when a reasonable demand is made upon him, he disrupts his schedule to meet it.

It is fairly apparent now that Mathews is not likely ever to break Babe Ruth's record. The Milwaukee ballpark is big, the ball does not travel well there, and it's been two or three years since anyone mentioned Mathews and Ruth's record seriously. But it's also been two or three years since Mathews has threatened to break anyone's arm. He has mastered the business of being a big-league idol in all its bewildering complexity, and he had to do it all by himself. At a time when politicians crowd the game, it is a comfort to have Eddie Mathews around. Watching him play, watching him talk to fans, you forget for a little while that his game has become a business.

CHAPTER 16

WHITEY, THE CHAIRMAN OF THE BOARD

He was nicknamed "the Chairman of the Board," probably because he was always able to close the deal—winning 236 games, compiling the best earned run average of any pitcher of the twentieth century, and adding ten World Series wins on his way to the Hall of Fame. Kahn met with the Queens, New York, native in 1958 while Ford was chasing his children around the house.

An article of faith among the forlorn millions who spend their summers rooting against the New York Yankees holds that the champions are the most overpublicized collection of platoons since the Light Brigade. The point is wrong, of course. People who root against the Yankees make careers out of being wrong. But they are persistent.

"This guy can't hit the high fast one," they tell you, just before Mickey Mantle drives a high fastball 445 feet for three bases.

"This fellow's just a gorilla, all muscles and no skill," they say, as Bill Skowron steps in and slaps an outside curve to right, scoring Mantle.

It goes on like this for nine innings, pretty nearly every summer day.

"Winning pitcher Ford," the public address announcer says, when matters have run their course.

"Who?" says the anti-Yankee man.

"Ford. Whitey Ford."

"Oh," says the anti-Yankee man. "Oh, yeah, Ford. Boy, how do you figure Mantle getting all that publicity?"

Here again the man who stands against the Yankees is following his star. He is asking a question which is entirely wrong. Mantle has earned his publicity because he is consistently the longest hitter in the major leagues. A proper question deals with something else. How do you figure Whitey Ford getting so little publicity?

This much is true of the conditions which all good Yankees have to bear: Along with regular audits of their income tax returns (everyone in that bracket is audited), they must adjust to living in a spotlight. Sometimes a Yankee, played at selected times by Casey Stengel, shunted into the World Series each October, can seem to be a little better than he is. Edward Charles Ford of the 34th Avenue, Astoria, Fords, is the one Yankee who is even better than he seems.

Since he joined the champions in 1950, Whitey Ford has built himself a more imposing reputation among other ballplayers than he has among fans. It is a rather perplexing development because Ford is not only a remarkable pitcher but also an intriguing young man.

In the beginning, he moved right in with Allie Reynolds, Vic Raschi, and Ed Lopat and won nine games in half a season. "It's not much different than the minors," he confessed, while helping the Yankees to the 1950 pennant. Now, with Reynolds, Raschi, and Lopat gone, Ford remains, continually helping the Yankees to pennants, beating the White Sox or the Indians or any other club that is attempting to disrupt the old order of finish. Even last season when his left elbow went bad, he was consistent. The pain didn't start until the Yankees had transformed their season into an extended World Series warm-up.

What does a pitcher need to get publicity? Aside from ability, a special gimmick, perhaps, such as, for instance, Carl Hubbell's screwball, Preacher Roe's spitball, or Early Wynn's literary flair. Ford has a gimmick. His pickoff move to first base, or to second or third, delights everyone but the base runners.

Some special color off the field, in the manner of Dizzy Dean? Ford is a charter member of the Martin-Mantle-Ford social triangle, a group colorful enough to have made George Weiss see red.

A chance to play with a winner and gain national attention? Ford has had almost no chance to play with a loser.

Viewed objectively, the facts on Ford add up to a figure worthy of the homage of Yankee fans, and coincidentally meriting the same voodoo rites practiced on images of Mantle and Berra in the badlands beyond the Hudson River. But the evidence, as our vast string of bureaus has gathered it, indicates something else. Yankee fans take Ford for granted at the ballpark, just as they accept surly ushers and overpriced, warm beer. Outlanders fail to hate Ford, as they once hated Reynolds and Red Ruffing and Joe Page. . . .

Whitey is a detached, professional workman who gets his outs on grounders rather than strikeouts, so possibly when he beats your team, 1–0, it doesn't seem to be quite as bad as when Reynolds beat your team, 1–0. But, if anything, it's rougher on the players. They get a little piece of every pitch and a good piece of none. The professionals were talking about it one day late last summer near the batting cage at the Stadium.

"If I had to pick one pitcher to win a game for me," said Enos Slaughter, "I'd want Ford."

"I remember when he first came up," said Phil Rizzuto. "He was just as cocky then as he is now. Somebody would get a hit off Lopat and Whitey would say, 'Hey, Ed, I'll show you how to get that guy out.'"

"You gotta give him credit," said Rocky Colavito, of the Indians, who was standing on the other side of the cage. "He's a helluva pitcher. He's one of the smartest pitchers in our league. He keeps you thinking all the time. Me, he throws mostly curves, but he can mix 'em up real good. Sometimes when I expect the curve, I get the fastball."

A few days later Early Wynn, pitcher-writer-photographer for the Chicago White Sox, was discussing the same topic. "The most important thing that makes Ford a helluva good pitcher," Wynn said, "is that he doesn't give you the same pitch all the time when he's behind you. There are guys who only throw the fastball when they're behind, say, three and one. Other guys have to go to the curve. Ford, when he's behind you, can go to a fastball or a curve or a slider or a change."

Wynn considered, then went on. "His best pitch is the curve. That's his ace in the hole. But even that isn't just one pitch. I mean, I can throw it at different speeds to different spots. If the hitter guesses curve, that's only about half of it. He's also got to guess which curve."

Then Wynn turned to Ford's specific equipment. "His best curve," he said, "breaks sharp and moves quick. His fastball isn't the fastest in the league, but it isn't the slowest, either. He's not as fast as [Billy] Pierce, but it sneaks up there pretty good. He's just one helluva good pitcher who knows what he's doing all the time."

Casey Stengel's special book on his own ballplayers falls into three general categories. There are men Stengel prefers not to talk about either in English or in his native language. Then there are athletes Stengel will discuss under the pressure of questioning. Finally, there are a handful of players whom Stengel discusses in enraptured monologues that start themselves, continue without any encouragement, and run from batting practice clear into the first inning. Ford fits into the last category.

One night when the bench was empty and twilight crept softly past the rapid-transit station in back of center field, the great man sat in the dugout and interviewed himself on Ford.

"What makes him such a great pitcher?" Casey began.

"Well," Stengel said, "there are three things which he does which can help the club and himself, which are picking a man off first, picking a man off second, and picking a man off third." The Professor stopped to inhale, crossed his legs, and then split his personality again.

"What help is it to pick a man off first?" Casey asked.

"It's help in three ways," Stengel shot back. "The man on first gotta think about staying close to the base, which makes it difficult for him to think about stealing second. The man don't get a jump, so when you're making the double play he can't knock you down at second base. He don't have no chance to get to third on a single, which makes it impossible for him to score when his man hits a fly ball." Stengel sat forward, waiting for the next question.

"What help is it to pick the man off second?" Casey asked, glowering.

"Well, the man can't go running down the baseline, because he's gotta think about protecting himself in case he throws to second," Stengel said. "He can't think about stealing third, which don't happen too much anyway. Sometimes he's gonna have trouble scoring on a hit and you're gonna catch him at the plate, if you got an outfielder that's throwing good."

Casey nodded, satisfied, then sprang the last part of the question. "What help is it to pick a man off third, which he's done sometimes up here in the big time?"

"The man gotta stay near the bag," Stengel said without hesitation, "and he's gotta worry about what he's gonna do when he's pitching. Where is he gonna throw?"

"He don't get a jump on ground balls, and maybe he's gonna stay on the base," Stengel said, "and you're gonna get the three outs and he's still gonna stay on the base and he doesn't score a run."

Lightning flashed behind the Bronx County Courthouse, and suddenly Casey and Stengel were one again. A reporter appeared in the runway and the manager turned. "That's three ways which he helps you," he said. "Besides, he throws three good pitches—a fast one, a curve, a slider, and a change, which can all be good ones."

"That's four pitches," the reporter said.

"He keeps thinking out there," Stengel said, "and he doesn't get frightened and he'll give you a good job all the time. Sometimes he gets mad when you take him out, but you know he wants to win, and he don't hurt you at the bat neither. He can hit .200, which is good for a pitcher, and I got some guys who aren't pitchers which don't hit much more than that, so I figure he don't hurt me none, which is why he is a good pitcher and he helps me a lot."

"Who are you talking about?" the reporter said. Stengel shrugged and walked to the water cooler.

Where Whitey Ford's skills and gimmicks have failed to make him a premium box office attraction, his association with Billy Martin and Mickey Mantle should have succeeded. Here were three Yankees who seemed to have at least some of the habits of Babe Ruth. They lived big, they ate in fashionable restaurants, and they seemed always to be feuding with the front office.

Martin, with medium baseball skills, became a national symbol of the dead-end kid in high society. Broadway columnists used his name on slow days. Stengel told stories about his insolence. For a while Martin ran as an entry with pretty girls.

Mantle, with his tremendous talent and his rustic background, symbolized something else. Here was the small-town boy, clean-cut, honorable, and gentle, braving the wickedness of the big city. If someone mentioned that Mantle had been seen at the fashionable and expensive Harwyn Club, someone else always mentioned that it must have been Martin who made the reservations. Nobody mentioned Ford.

There is one general theory about this. Ford does not possess Mantle's vast baseball talent and his background is not quite as rugged as Martin's. Columnists and gossips concentrated on extremes, and Ford, the man in the middle, was left alone. But there is more to the matter than that. No ballplayer courts publicity about his private life. A man who sips a beer with a major leaguer will probably elaborate when he tells his friends. The one beer may become two or six, and, through the alchemy of hero worship, it may even become a beaker of martinis.

To defend himself, a ballplayer does well to choose his company. (Ford has always sipped most of his beers in his old neighborhood with boyhood friends.) Then a ballplayer should ignore rumor, rather than publicize it with a fierce denial as Billy Martin sometimes has done. (Ford ignores personal questions. At most he offers unquotable replies.)

There was not much publicity given Ford's private life when he rode high with Mantle and Martin because Whitey is a shrewd and sensible young man, schooled in a tough New York neighborhood, who understands the power of "no comment." When, for example, Martin's Copacabana birthday party turned boisterous and Hank Bauer got himself accused of slugging a citizen, Ford was there but he was in the background. He made no public statement, and as a result, the public quickly forgot that Whitey had been there at all.

There was very little about pitching or public relations Whitey Ford had to learn when he joined the Yankees. He was then what he is now: tough, confident, and quiet. When you spend a day with him, it is frequently possible to forget how he makes his living. Although he is a considerable student of his trade, he makes no fetish of studying it. He is a man with a job he knows he can do well. Off-days bore him, but cash continues to hold his interest.

Ford has moved from Astoria to the comfortable suburban village of Glen Cove on the North Shore of Long Island. We worked our way past miles of picture windows one morning near the close of last season until, peering across a wide, neat lawn, we saw the comfortable split-level house where Whitey is raising his family.

Joan Ford, an attractive, dark-haired girl, answered the knock on the door. "Whitey didn't tell me you were coming," she said. "He's asleep, but you can come on in and wait." She was wrapped in a robe. It was 9:40, still early for ballplayers in this era of night games. The Fords' living room and dining room form an L that is tastefully furnished with modern pieces. A bookshelf lines one wall of the living room. In it are children's books and a large collection of popular novels chosen for the Fords by the Book of the Month Club.

As we sagged into an orange brown couch, six children immediately laid siege. Sally Ann, six, Ed, five, and Tommy, four, were Ford's; the others were nephews. . . . Tommy held up a baseball. "I'm a righty," he said. Ed, Jr., displayed two right-hand model Whitey Ford gloves. "They're no good for Tommy 'cause he's a lefty," he said. It was confusing.

A black French poodle bounded in, carrying a rubber ball between his teeth. "Hi, Casey," one of the children said. "His name is Casey." Ole Case offered us the ball, and we grabbed it and tossed it to his left. He leaped, caught it in midair, and came back for more. Casey made five excellent catches before he became overenthusiastic and bit the ball in half.

Finally Whitey entered, clad in striped pajamas. He is bigger than he appears from the grandstands, thick through the chest and shoulders. "Sorry," he said. "I forgot to tell Joan you were coming." Then he turned to the junior legion. "Okay, kids," he said. "Let's get dressed." The children vanished, and Ford went into the kitchen for breakfast. He was dressed and sipping coffee when the children reappeared.

"Fix my bike, Daddy," Tommy said.

"Play hoop with me," Eddie said.

"Look at me, Uncle Whitey," Kevin said, aiming a plastic rifle.

Ford went into the garage to look at Tommy's bike. "The chain's broken, Tommy," he said. "Where's the little piece that goes right here?"

"I don't know, Daddy."

"Where did it break?"

"Up there," Tommy said, pointing toward a distant end of the block.

"I'll have to get a new part from the shop where we got the bike," Ford said. "I'll fix it when I get home from work."

"I want it now," Tommy said, and started to cry.

Ford shook his head and climbed into the front seat of a beige Oldsmobile. Sally Slattery, Mrs. Ford's sister, and her husband, Tom, got into the backseat. Whitey was going to drop them in Astoria on his way in to Yankee Stadium. "Dealer's car," Ford said. "He's fixing mine up, so he gave me this. It's got air-conditioning."

Ford drove to Northern Boulevard, a main artery on Long Island, guiding his borrowed car carefully. "I'm thinking about moving to New Jersey," he said. "Probably Tenafly. It's too long a drive from Glen Cove to the Stadium every day. I can usually make it in an hour, but on Friday after a day game, it takes me three."

No one seemed inclined to discuss baseball. We tried a question on Ford's special technique of pitching at Municipal Stadium in Cleveland.

"Yeah," he said, "I throw different out there. Just during night games. See, they're on the same time as New York, but it gets dark about a half hour later and they start the games at the same time. There's more sorta dusk, twilight. So I throw a lot of curves in the beginning. They're harder to see at dusk. For four innings, I throw mostly curves. Then it's dark. It doesn't make any difference after that."

Ford turned onto a parkway and stayed on it until he came to the exit for Astoria. There, in his old surroundings, he offered an enthusiastic running commentary. "See that garage?" he said. "That used to be a ball field. Now Donahue's (a bar and restaurant) is right down the block. That's where Tom works. And the other way is the Ivy Room, where my father works. I used to live down that street, and Joan lived around the corner."

Ford dropped the Slatterys at the intersection of 34th Avenue and 41st Street. It is an area of old buildings. After Ford stopped, an elderly woman leaned out of a third-floor apartment. "Hey, Whitey," she called. "You working hard? How's it going, boy?" This was Tom Slattery's mother, Bela.

"You just getting up?" Ford shouted back, grinning.

"Want a cup of tea?"

"You make the worst tea in town," Ford said, broadly.

Ford got back in the car and began to wind back toward the parkway. "Do you get much kick out of baseball?" we asked.

"No," Ford said, quickly. "I get bored sitting around for four, five days between starts. I'd rather be an outfielder and play every day."

Ford's voice, touched with a strong New York accent, often sounds flat, but now he was speaking with some measure of intensity. "Of course, I probably wouldn't have made the big leagues as an outfielder," he said, "but the way things are, baseball is just a job. The routine on the road is so dull. After a night game I get up at ten thirty and eat breakfast. Maybe I go to a show then and eat a late lunch around four. Then I go to the ballpark and sit on the bench most of the time. After the game, I'll have dinner and maybe a couple of beers. Then back to bed. It's dull."

"But things like studying hitters, don't they take up a lot of time?"

"Not that much," Ford said. "Now that Martin's gone, I pal around mostly with Mickey. Darrell Johnson, too. But it ain't the same as it used to be."

At Yankee Stadium, Ford pointed to a parking lot. "I used to play ball there when I was a kid," he said. "I was an office boy for Equitable Life, and I used to come up here to play ball. That's when I enjoyed playing. I played all the time every weekend."

Ford parked near a door marked "Executive Offices," and a mob of boys closed in on the car. "Same kids all the time," Ford said. "They must trade autographs. Two Fords for a Mantle." He opened the door and worked his way slowly through the boys, signing until he reached the door.

The baseball boredom that Ford feels is an entirely natural thing. Any routine, even pitching for the Yankees, becomes somewhat tedious once a man finally masters the attendant problems. Ford mastered them with very little struggle. But in the man's boredom, I think, lies part of the explanation for his anonymity. He doesn't enthuse, and as a result the people about him must generate all their own enthusiasm. For Stengel, still fascinated by baseball, this is a simple thing. He watches Ford work, compares the thought with the execution, and raves. But to people less schooled in the game and less preoccupied with it, the problem is different. Ford's non-excitement seems to be contagious.

There are some athletes who generate a presence simply and naturally spontaneously. Fred Corcoran, who is Ted Williams's agent, likes to talk about the effect a visit from Williams has on the Corcoran household. "Everybody starts getting excited a couple of hours before the guy gets there," Corcoran says. When Williams arrives, the excitement grows higher. It was impossible to be close to Jackie Robinson without feeling a certain tension. Sal Maglie on the mound seemed to radiate dark thoughts. Willie Mays can make catching a fly ball seem like high adventure.

You cannot simply say that good ballplayers are exciting or that bad ballplayers are dull, for there comes a point when presence is independent of ability. Some athletes possess it, others do not, and no one understands precisely why Ford, working brilliantly at his job, seems to impress people as a man working at a job. Allie Reynolds, doing the same thing, or simply strutting in from the bullpen, made people tingle.

Inside the clubhouse, Ford dressed quickly, signed baseballs for a few minutes, and then went to the outfield, where he ran with the rest of the pitching staff. When the Kansas City Athletics took batting practice, Ford moved to the dugout and watched. . . .

A few minutes before the game, Ford went inside and plunged his left arm into a whirlpool bath. When he came out, the game had just started and Honest Antonino Rocca, the wrestler, was walking up the hallway that leads from the Yankee dugout.

"I got some new pills for you, Whitey," Rocca said. "These are special ones. Vitamins. I just started using them myself. Real good. I'll send them to you."

"Thanks," Ford said. "Maybe I'll see you after the game."

"I'll sit in left field," Rocca said. "I'll take off my shirt, maybe get arrested." He laughed.

"A great guy," Ford said, after Rocca moved on. "Speaks seven languages. He puts me on diets, especially during spring training. He recommends lots of fish and chicken. No fried foods. Not much steak. Lay off the beer for a month and cut down on smoking. I feel real good then." Ford walked toward the dugout, where he expected to be bored for the next two and a half hours. The Athletics scored seven unearned runs in the first inning and won 11–5. On the bench, Ford was neither upset nor excited. There was no reason for him to be. The pennant race had ended two months before.

Nearly everyone who grew up with Ed Ford among the tenement buildings of Astoria remembers that baseball was once the most exciting thing in his life. Actually, Ford was born in Manhattan, but the family moved when he was still a baby. Jim Ford, his father, now tends bar at the Ivy Room, underneath a large photograph of his son.

"Whitey used to be out of the house all day playing ball," Jim Ford says. "He'd miss dinner sometimes, and he'd come home all scraped up from sliding in the dirt. The fields weren't like the big leagues."

As a youngster Ford had reason to be excited. He was small and he was left-handed, both of which worked against him. In Astoria, the 34th Avenue Boys were a first-rate team, and if Ford had been right-handed, he might have made the club easily as an infielder. If he had been bigger, he would have been offered first base. But as things were, he had to struggle. When he was young, older, stronger boys pitched. Ford didn't want to play the outfield. So he battled, and since he could hit and hustle, he became the best five-foot, four-inch first baseman the 34th Avenue Boys ever had.

Like his friends, Ford was tough; not in the sense that boys can be tough now with knives and zip guns, but tough in an unpretentious way. He was a subway kid. He thought a good, cheap way to kill time was to take a ride on the subway. Once when he was playing for the 34th Avenue Boys and Billy Loes was pitching for the Astoria Cubs, the two future big leaguers took the BMT subway from Astoria to Coney Island, a ride of perhaps an hour and a half. They stayed on the train until it turned around and came back to Astoria. It was one way to stretch a nickel in New York some fifteen years ago.

Ford was a fine ballplayer and partly because of this he became a leader of the 34th Avenue Boys. If he said the boys were going to the Valencia Theater in Jamaica, nobody argued. The boys went to the Valencia Theater in Jamaica. His friends looked up to Whitey as a good athlete, but no one guessed he was going to make the major leagues.

"Baseball," Ford says, "was my favorite game, but I never thought much about it as a career. I didn't know what I was going to do but I just never figured on baseball."

When Ford graduated from elementary school, he might have enrolled at Bryant High School near his home, just as Billy Loes did. But his best friend, Johnny Martin, who was a sandlot catcher, talked him into entering Manhattan High School of Aviation Trades, where the two could learn to become airplane mechanics.

Johnny Martin was once Astoria's hottest ballplayer, a fine hitter and a skilled receiver with a good arm. "We all figured that Johnny was going to make the majors," Ford says. (Martin never got past class D, and now drives limousines to the airports.)

At the first baseball tryout at Manhattan Aviation, Martin locked up the catching job. But Ford was troubled. The team already had a first baseman, and a good one. "Why don't you go out for pitcher?" Martin said. "That kid at first base might give you a rough time."

"I don't know," Ford said.

"These pitchers don't look like much," Martin said. "You can throw better than any of them." Ford respected Martin's baseball judgment. "Okay," he said.

When Ford talks about this now, he underplays it. "What a brainstorm that was," he says. "I didn't have anything on the ball. I just threw it and ducked line drives. I quit after a while and went back to first base."

Two things challenge this recollection. One is Martin's memory; the other is a listing of old high school records. "Whitey had good control even then," Martin says. "He did okay. He worked very good when he was behind. He used to scare the manager by getting guys on base, but he'd get out of it. He had a lot of change-up stuff and a good curve." The records show that one season Ford won six straight games at Aviation before being beaten in the vocational high school championship. . . .

When Ford was not pitching, he played first base. "I've never seen another boy with his intensity," [Mike] Chafetz [who coached Ford in high school] says. "We practiced on a public playground under the Queensboro Bridge. It was a long, narrow field, badly laid out. A left-hander who hit the ball solidly drove it into the structure of the bridge or onto the roof of a garage: across the street. My budget was so skimpy that I had to stop good left-handers from taking batting practice because I couldn't afford to lose the balls. Ford insisted on taking batting practice and promised that he'd retrieve whatever he knocked out of the field. Sure enough, he'd disappear for half an hour after taking his cuts and bring back all the balls."

Ford's early baseball intensity was put to even sterner tests. Once, pitching in a sandlot game at Woodside, Long Island, he noticed some confusion among his fielders. He looked around, and on the Long Island railroad tracks, he saw two girls, standing and beckoning. "Game called," suggested an outfielder.

"I can tell it's gonna rain," said an infielder, "because I got a crick in my neck. Let's stop playing."

"Bravo," said another infielder, in effect.

"Come on, you guys," Ford said. "Let's stay here and play ball. I can strike these guys out. Let's finish the game."

Ford struck out eight men in the last three innings, but despite his speed the girls were happily involved with some of the spectators before the game was over. Presently the girls and the spectators breached the peace and were arrested. This story is not intended to reflect harshly on girls who stand on railroad tracks, beckoning. Rather, it illustrates the fact that for a long time baseball was Whitey's one and only interest.

Two months after Ford finished high school in 1946, he wrote to the Yankees asking for a tryout. He applied as a first baseman—by this time he had grown to five-seven—and, of course, he got no serious consideration. But the late Paul Krichell, who was the most successful baseball scout of all time, saw something in the way Ford threw.

"Stop thinking about first base," Krichell said. "Think about pitching."

"I never saw a kid with a curveball like his," he said, "or one who could throw one so easy. Most of them you have to show how to throw one, but it just came natural to him. After he warmed up, I had him pitch to hitters and he looked like a pitcher. I didn't even have to show him how to stand on the rubber, and I could tell he had the guts to be a pitcher." But Krichell didn't sign Ford that day. The boy was small, and the scout wanted to learn more about him.

In September the 34th Avenue Boys met the Bay Ridge Cubs of Brooklyn in a city championship sandlot game at the Polo Grounds. Lou DeAngelis, the Bay Ridge pitcher, threw a no-hitter at Astoria for ten innings. Then Ford led off the eleventh with a double and scored on another hit. He struck out the side in the bottom of the inning, securing the 1–0 victory, then hurried to the clubhouse, ready to beat off scouts. An hour later, when no scout arrived, he took the subway back home to Astoria.

Later the Dodgers telephoned and offered Ford a $3,000 bonus. The Giants went to $4,000. After a week of extremely light bidding, he signed with the Yankees for $7,000. Krichell still wasn't certain.

Why was Ford ignored even then, ignored after a performance that comes straight from the dream book of boys who would like to be big leaguers? Size was the largest factor. Fresco Thompson, the Dodgers' vice president, has since pointed out that Ford would have been a bargain at $50,000. "I guess," Thompson said, "it's because everybody in the business is so hipped on getting big kids who can throw the ball through a brick wall, that we overlook other boys with qualifications that are a helluva lot harder to find. Ford had guts and poise and the curveball of a mature pro who had been pitching for ten years."

It is important here to realize that Thompson and Krichell both discussed Ford long after he had established himself as a Yankee. This itself may be part of a pattern. Scouts eventually recalled Ford the sandlotter as a genuinely outstanding prospect, but at the time they looked at him as a questionable investment. Perhaps eventually the fans who underrate him now will review the records and point out that during the third Yankee dynasty Ford was a superb pitcher.

Ford's minor-league career was brief. He was a .700-plus pitcher over three years, and in 1949, at Binghamton, he complained that the Yankees were making a mistake by forcing him to work in class A.

"Fundamentally," suggests Jim Turner, the Yankee pitching coach, "Whitey hasn't changed since he came up. He studies the batters. He knows what he's doing. He doesn't scare. He's gained experience, and if you want to say that that makes him a smarter pitcher, then he's a smarter pitcher."

Turner thinks Ford's success comes largely from relaxation. "The main thing," he says, "is that he's relaxed and he has ability. Without one, the other is wasted. There are lots of pitchers with just as much ability as Ford who don't know how to use it. Maybe they get tense. He doesn't. The ability to relax is useless if you don't have the ability to pitch. He does."

Ford's record is remarkably consistent. He has not won twenty games, but he won nineteen once and eighteen twice, and, as much as his victories, his losses are a yardstick. Ford has never lost as many as ten games in a season.

Any number of Ford's individual games stand out. There was the day in 1950 when he forgot the starting time and was finishing breakfast when he should have been taking batting practice. "Don't worry," he said. "As soon as I get a cup of coffee in me, I'll go out and handle those guys." He pitched a three-hitter against the White Sox.

There was the day in 1955 when the Dodgers were leading the World Series three games to two. "I go tomorrow," Ford announced on a network television show, "and Byrne pitches on Tuesday." Ford threw a four-hitter at the Dodgers and Byrne did pitch on Tuesday, when Johnny Podres beat him.

Then there was the 1957 afternoon in Milwaukee when Lew Burdette had suddenly become an invincible clutch pitcher. He drew Ford as his rival, and after a few innings it became evident that neither pitcher would give anything away. Burdette squirmed, licked his fingers, wet the ball, tried to dry it, and in between got the Yankees out. Ford neither squirmed nor spat. His lips tightened around his teeth, the way they do when he is working, and he kept the Braves hitting his curve into the dirt. When Gerry Coleman misjudged Ed Mathews's speed and played a ground ball into a single by neglecting to charge it, the Braves got their run and the ball game.

Afterward, all the publicity went to Burdette. Ford lost a game on another man's mistake without fuming, without turning on Coleman, without pointing out what baseball men knew. In short, he lost as befits a professional.

Ford still likes to return to Astoria, to sit in Donahue's, Astoria's Stork Club, with old friends, and there he talks baseball with noticeable excitement. It is as if he were recapturing the baseball of his boyhood, when he could play every day and the routine was not dull and his skills moved him for reasons he did not understand.

After one of the Yankees' road trips last season, Ford stopped in at Donahue's, on his way home to Glen Cove. He had left his old car, a 1950 Chevrolet, in the lot behind the restaurant before he left, and he had come to pick it up. Dropping off the car is part of Ford's routine. Now, with the Yankees back, word spread through Astoria that Whitey was coming.

His grandmother down the block knew that he would visit her. His in-laws, who live across the street from Donahue's, went to the restaurant because they knew Whitey would be there. Tom Slattery, a bartender at Donahue's, kept looking toward the door. Boys in the neighborhood crowded a nearby sporting goods store to buy baseballs for Ford to autograph.

When he reached Donahue's, Whitey sat in a large upholstered booth against a wall of the downstairs cocktail lounge. Behind him a design of black top hats and canes decorated pink wallpaper. In front an oval bar dominated the lounge. Johnny Martin came in to talk. Tom Cavanaugh and George Mueger, two of Ford's other 34th Avenue teammates, followed. "What a cinch you guys got," Johnny Martin said. "You guys got to win it by twenty games."

Ford nodded and grinned. He knew that pointed questions were coming.

"How's your elbow?" Mueger asked. "Still giving you trouble?"

"Nah, it's okay," Ford said. He had bought the first round of beers. The men drank quickly and he prepared to buy the second. "Just gotta get it loose. It'll be good," he said.

Pete Genussa, a local florist, wandered in. "Hey, Whitey," he said. "Why ain't Mantle hitting?"

"Little slump," Ford said. "He'll get out of it."

"How come the Tigers giving you guys so much trouble? [Pitcher Frank] Lary throws out his glove, you guys drop dead?"

The questions continued. Ford answered some, laughed at others, and ignored the rest. He was with men he understands, and he was happy. They knocked umpires and other players and second-guessed Stengel, and Ford grinned and paid for the beers. He is profoundly loyal to the old neighborhood and to the way things were.

"Whitey's a real soft touch for all the guys who used to know him," one of his friends says. "He's helped a lot of guys when they needed dough. He's even paid for lawyers to help out guys who had to have them. He hasn't forgotten any of the old gang. He's a helluva big man in Astoria."

Probably it comes down to this: because Ford is always going to be a big man in Astoria, he is never going to be quite as big a man in baseball as he otherwise might be.

It was a fascinating thing, growing up in a place like Astoria fifteen years ago. It was difficult and taxing and it made you rugged, but there weren't any juvenile gangs. You played in the streets and you didn't like school and you had to fight with your fists. But there were rules. You didn't threaten teachers and you steered clear of policemen because there was nothing quite so frightening as a cop at the door asking to see your father. You stayed out of trouble, and of all your rules that was the most important. Don't say too much and stay out of trouble and there won't be any policeman at the door.

You remember how you grew up. Ford grew into a five-foot, ten-inch 175-pounder, and he will be thirty years old before Christmas, but he remembers. He sasses a little and brags a little, the way he always has, but he keeps himself out of trouble, because that's the rule. Whitey Ford, who does not stop short of being a distinguished pitcher, stops just short of being a truly wild, a truly odd, and truly impertinent character.

It's hard to notice a tough New York kid who has learned to stay out of trouble. But ask the hitters around the American League. They've had to notice him. Aside from the gang from Astoria, they're the most important people in the world to Whitey Ford.

CHAPTER 17

JOE D'S STORMY MARRIAGE

A recent biography of the legendary Yankee Joe DiMaggio portrayed him as a reclusive, womanizing cheapskate. Kahn, who interviewed "Joe D" on a number of occasions, never saw that side of the "Yankee Clipper." But he did learn of DiMaggio's flash of anger when his wife, Marilyn Monroe, filmed her famous upskirt movie scene in New York City. Kahn's source was a photographer who was on the scene. This excerpt is from Kahn's 1986 Joe and Marilyn.

There's No Business Like Show Business, [Marilyn Monroe's] first film as Mrs. Joe DiMaggio, was advertised as a musical tribute to Irving Berlin. His songs are generally regarded as the best element in an unfortunate movie.

As Vicky, the hatcheck girl with theatrical ambitions, she played opposite Donald O'Connor, then a paradigm of boyishness. Marilyn's beauty was becoming more womanly. The pairing didn't work. Her costumes were so wildly overdone that they reminded one admirer of the rainbow skirts and fruit-salad hats that once adorned the hyperkinetic form of Carmen Miranda. Bosley Crowther in the *New York Times* pronounced Marilyn's "wriggling and squirming . . . embarrassing to behold."

Each day she brought to the set the troubles of a collapsing marriage. On several occasions she could not finish her work. DiMaggio liked her wriggling and squirming even less than Bosley Crowther would, and she felt fiercely conflicted. She insisted, she would always insist, that she wasn't lewd and that those who thought she was had lewd minds themselves. But she was playing a sexpot, she was selling sex. DiMaggio stayed away from the set.

He didn't care about show business, she complained to friends. The Toots Shor's advice he offered wasn't worth much. She was trying to reshape her career, and they just couldn't talk about that. It was beyond him. He retreated into silence, she would later testify, and not speak to her for days at a time.

She bought him books. He wouldn't read them. She tried to introduce him to poetry. He said he didn't get it. They had few mutual friends for play and evenings of good conversation. Sometimes Natasha Lytess visited to help with her lines, but most nights it was just Joe and Marilyn, alone, apart, and separate (and angry) in the big empty house on North Palm Drive.

When he did talk, she later claimed, his questions were intrusive. He was starting to suspect men she knew of being her lovers. The best evidence is that she had two or possibly three affairs, all brief, all casual, late in her marriage to Joe. She complained of loneliness and, with stardom, she had become defiant. A one-night stand, often as not, seems like an antidote to loneliness. DiMaggio's possessiveness also pushed her toward new beds. She was trying to get control of her own life. No one else, least of all the brooding and commanding man called Joe the Slugger, was going to control her.

Hot arguments took over their lives. She was sometimes away from home with no good explanation. When she returned, he questioned her. She pouted. He grew angrier. She walked away, fearful of his strength. Sometimes he bolted from the house.

According to Marilyn, Joe was "insanely jealous." According to DiMaggio's friends, he had good reason. It is a familiar story in divorce courts.

Charles K. Feldman, a prominent agent and reputedly one of her lovers, sent her the delicious script for *The Seven Year Itch*. In it, she would play a nameless enchantress called "The Girl Upstairs." Her performance as a not-very-bright blonde is a wonder of shimmering seductiveness. It was precisely the kind of role that troubled her husband the most.

The plot casts Tom Ewell as a summer bachelor. Marilyn, television model, sublets the apartment upstairs. Marilyn accidentally knocks a tomato plant onto Ewell's terrace, and he invites her down for a drink. He fantasizes passionate love, but when he actually makes a serious move they both fall off a piano bench. "Maybe we better send Rachmaninoff to the showers," he says.

She tells him how she caught her big toe in a faucet while taking a bath. She couldn't work it loose and had to call a plumber, who worked over her while she was naked in the tub. This sends Tom Ewell's fantasies running through arch, funny, sexy twists. He finally asks her to dinner and a movie, *The Creature from the Black Lagoon*. Marilyn empathizes with the creature, which is the sort of thing she might have done in real life. She is wholly bewitching, an original.

On the walk home, in that most famous of Marilyn's scenes, she pauses over a subway grating. Two trains pass. Marilyn's white skirt blows up toward her navel.

Since this was a 1950s film, Ewell ultimately hurries off to his wife in the country without ever having gotten Marilyn into bed, or even topless, if you can believe that in the 1980s. "This is the picture," wrote Phillip Strassberg in the *Daily Mirror*, "that every red-blooded American male has been awaiting." It was also a portrait of her as she could appear when the mood was right: innocence, seductiveness, blond fluff, and at the center, hidden among smiles and wonderment, awaiting only a proper touch, naked, undulating lust.

DiMaggio did not want her to play so sexual a part. She dismissed his objections. He may have known center field, but what the hell did he know about the movies? Nothing, that's what he knew. He didn't care about the movies; she wasn't even sure he cared about her. It was a wonderful role, and she was going to play it. It was her career. It was her life, not his.

She flew to New York for location shooting on September 9. The marriage was one week short of being nine months old. She flew without him.

Later, he joined her at the St. Regis Hotel in New York. Then he, who never visited a set, decided to show up for the scene in which her skirt blew high over her thin white panties.

Some say he made her change into more concealing underwear. Some say he simply stood in silent fury beside the Broadway columnist Walter Winchell. Everybody agrees that he left before the shooting was done, left the street scene on a rack of pain and horror.

Late that night they quarreled at the hotel. Stories persist of screaming, weeping, scuffling. A death watch settled upon the marriage. They were through.

He flew back to California, and when her New York work was finished, they managed to live together for a few crackling weeks. He wanted her to calm down. He was sorry he had been so rough. He loved her. She stammered in fright. He might get rough again. It was j-j-just too late.

He did care about movies, he told her. He would prove it. He'd come to see her on the set.

She couldn't stand that, the staring, the possessiveness, while she was working. She talked to Darryl Zanuck and, without publicity, Zanuck barred DiMaggio from the Twentieth Century lot. If the greatest center fielder of a generation tried to visit his wife at work, security men would collar him and, if necessary, call the police.

These were two people in pain, and their agony, like their passionate love, was major news. On October 4, Marilyn told somebody in the Fox production department that she was ill and could not appear at the studio. The production people informed Billy Wilder, who was directing *The Seven Year Itch*. Wilder made plans to shoot around her and passed the information to Harry Brand, the chief of publicity. Brand telephoned Marilyn at home. She began to cry. "Joe and I had a fight. We're splitting up." She told Brand she had hired Jerry Giesler, a Hollywood lawyer who became famous when he defended Errol Flynn in a paternity suit. Brand said there would have to be an announcement. He would handle it.

DiMaggio meanwhile telephoned his great friend Reno Barsochinni, the best man of only nine months before. Reno would travel from San

Francisco and help organize his things. He would move out on October 6.

[Joe DiMaggio never stopped loving Marilyn Monroe. She died on August 4, 1962.] Wrote Kahn: "She died at night naked and alone in a locked bedroom with the lights blazing."

Her half-sister, Bernice Miracle, of Gainesville, Florida, arrived. So did Joseph Paul DiMaggio. At Mrs. Miracle's request, DiMaggio organized a funeral at the Westwood Village Mortuary.

He invited fewer than thirty others, including her psychiatrist, Ralph Greenson, and her lawyer, Milton "Mickey" Rudin, but he pointedly kept out famous Hollywood people: Frank Sinatra, who had dated Marilyn briefly in her last years, Peter Lawford, and a panoply of famous movie types.

He wept and prayed.

Someone asked how he could have excluded the pantheon of names that were Hollywood.

"Because," said Joe the Slugger, no slouch at a final comment, "they killed her."

Then, with his beloved entombed in a crypt, he set off on the rest of his life alone.

CHAPTER 18

CATFISH IN
THE BIG APPLE

*He was the first major-league free agent, loosed from Oakland by a
contract mix-up and snared by George Steinbrenner's Yankees in
1975. When he arrived in New York, the media descended on him—
but the Yanks carved out special time for Kahn to hang out with
Catfish Hunter, the right-handed pitcher who eventually made the
Baseball Hall of Fame but died tragically young at the age of 53 in
1999.*

James Augustus Hunter is a Carolina sharecropper's son who does
not remember eating steak as a boy. "We ate what we grew," Hunter
was saying, on what would be the most overwhelming day of his life.
"Corn and turnips. We had some hogs. I got to eat a lot of pork. There
was plenty of food, but not enough money. At the end of one year of
farming, my dad showed a profit of seventy-five cents."

"Seventy-five dollars?"

"I said cents. My dad made seventy-five cents."

"That eliminates income tax problems," I suggested.

"Yep." Hunter offered a small smile. "But dad did some winter log-
ging. Pine and cypress. That way he was able to pick up a couple of
thousand dollars."

Hunter himself had just picked up a New York Yankee contract worth
a couple of million dollars. Across a few vertiginous weeks during which
he and a small-town law firm called Cherry, Cherry, Flythe and Evans

kept their collective balance, James Augustus Hunter realized that fero-
cious dry American dream: financial independence.

Jim Hunter is nicknamed Catfish, and baseball friends address him
as "Cat." According to a Yankee press release, "Hunter got his nickname as a boy in Hertford, North Carolina, when he ran away from
home and returned with two catfish." According to Jim Hunter, he got
his nickname when Charles O. Finley, the totalitarian proprietor of the
Oakland Athletics, said, in effect: "This baseball club needs colorful
nicknames. Yours is going to be Catfish. We're making up this story
that you ran away from home and returned with two catfish. I think it's
a great idea and so do you, don't you, Catfish."

"*Sieg heil*," Hunter replied, also in effect.

As the Catfish, Jim Hunter became the most consistent, though not
the most spectacular, of winning pitchers. He cannot throw as hard as
Nolan Ryan, nor does he possess that enormous, breathtaking curveball Sandy Koufax threw. Rather he works with a variety of breaking
pitches, with guile, and, most important, with control. Put simplistically, Catfish Hunter knows how to throw the right pitch to the right
spot at the right time. He knows how to get the hitters out.

For three consecutive years he won twenty-one games for Oakland.
Last season he won twenty-five. Pressure seems to prime his adrenal
glands. He has won seven of nine games in the championship playoffs
and won all five of his World Series decisions. In short, he's a consum-
mate professional.

His success at Oakland led to larger and larger contracts, and Hunter,
who by then had developed a taste for steak, instructed his lawyers to
arrange for certain annuities. Unaccountably, Charles O. Finley, who
made his first fortune in the insurance business, refused or neglected to
make an annuity payment due last year. At Hunter's urging, J. Carlton
Cherry, of Cherry, Cherry, Flythe and Evans, began demanding payment last August. Finley did not pay—the amount in question was
$50,0000—and Hunter charged Finley with breach of contract. Peter
Seitz, the arbitrator, found for Hunter. The contract was breached. It
was void.

Now something had happened that was unique in baseball history. A
superstar was a free agent. At the peak of his career, and not yet thirty,

Catfish Hunter was liberated from the so-called reserve clause, that feudal hangover which binds baseball players to the same organization indefinitely. On a fuzzy day, Justice Oliver Wendell Homes voted to uphold the legality of baseball's reserve clause "because of the peculiar nature of the business." Two subsequent Supreme Court decisions were equally equivocal. The Congress, which has made time to pass a law assuring congressmen the joys of watching the Washington Redskins on home television all autumn, shows no inclination to liberate baseball players from class discrimination.

"This Hunter thing is terrible," someone high in the baseball establishment assured me, when Peter Seitz announced the result of his arbitration. "It threatens the structure of the game." Baseball's rulers take pride in a tradition of free enterprise for owners. The same principle applied to the hired help smacks of revolution, atheism, and Lenin. One is reminded of doctors who demand federal support for medical schools and then argue, without a blush, that federal control of physicians' fees would destroy "the sacred doctor-patient relationship."

Still looking for his annuity, Catfish Hunter found himself emancipated. He sat on his 110-acre farm in Hertford, which lies close to Albermarle Sound or the Carolina coastal plain, and commuted fifty miles to the metropolis of Ahoskie, where Cherry, Cherry, Flythe and Evans maintain offices. One hears that baseball is troubled, that many franchises lose money, but it would be hard today to sell that point to Hunter. With a million dollars surely the lowest offer that he would consider, no fewer than twenty-three ball clubs entered the bidding. That is, twenty-three of baseball's impoverished club owners were able to find a spare million for one ballplayer. It is amazing what a man can find in the pockets of the suit he wore last Tuesday.

Some teams tried special pleas. The Dodgers had their best pitcher, Don Sutton, telephone and describe the glories of life in Los Angeles. Sutton seemed embarrassed. "I know you're busy," he said, "and you don't want to listen to my bull, but the Dodgers are a good organization." As Hunter recalls it, Sutton spoke for ten seconds, then hung up. Thurman Munson, the Yankee catcher, was more prolix. "Cat," he said, "you know I'm a good catcher. Would you rather throw to me or to catchers who're a hell of a lot worse?"

The Texas Rangers sent seven men into Ahoskie, each one bearing a checkbook. The San Diego Padres, the faltering orphans of the West, offered an exceptionally rich contract. Bids leapt almost geometrically and J. Carlton Cherry, the country lawyer, listened to everyone and said, "You and you can get back to us. We have to check out a few other clubs."

In the end the San Diego bid was highest. Hunter chose the Yankees because, he says, New York is only an hour's flight from his home and because he knows, in his country-cool way, that New York is the Big Turnip. The Yankees had to come back three times for their prize. At length, Hunter says, they agreed to pay him $150,000 a year for five years. In addition, they delivered a straight cash bonus, supposedly $1,000,000. Further, they provided extensive insurances and annuities. Newspapers have reported that the final Yankee offer totaled $3,700,000. The figure seems high. Hunter's contract probably is worth a mere $2,500,000. "What the hell," Marty Appel, the Yankees' publicity man, says. "We were looking for a right-handed pitcher anyway."

We met near dawn at the Essex House on Central Park South. This was the day when Hunter agreed to meet the media. He stands a solid six feet, and for his Yankee debut wore a tan double-knit leisure shirt that depicted hunting scenes.

"You like hunting?" I said.

He nodded. "When you hunt," Catfish drawled, "you get your mind off everything else. You just worry if your dog does good." Eleven years ago, Catfish was trampling in wetlands with one of his brothers when suddenly the other man's shotgun fired.

"It felt," he says, "like a hammer hit me in the boot. The impact knocked me into some water." Hunter called to his brother, "Get me the hell out of this hole."

After he climbed out, he glanced downward. Shotgun pellets had turned his right boot onto a sieve. "Dammit, dammit, dammit," Hunter said. "Ya done shot me." His brother fainted. The small toe had to be amputated and fifteen pellets still remain in the foot. Hunter, the best nine-toed right-hander in the history of baseball, walks without a limp and, indeed, the accident worked to a certain purpose. It kept Hunter out of the army and saved him a trip to Vietnam, where gunfire crackles more lethally.

Rusty Calley of Vietnam was discussing himself when Hunter arrived at the studios of the American Broadcasting Company for an interview on "AM America." Jesse Jackson, who would follow Hunter on the show, approached and said, "I thought you'd be bigger. When you beat the Dodgers in the World Series you looked twelve feet tall."

"I'm about as big as I have to be," Hunter said.

"I root for the Dodgers," Jackson said, "because they signed Jackie Robinson, but knowing about Finley I sort of rooted for you guys, too. You know. I'm against slavery."

Bill Beutel, the ABC interviewer, had been poorly briefed. He asked Hunter several times whether all baseball players would now make themselves free agents.

"They can't," Hunter explained patiently. "We all have contracts. To become a free agent, there's got to be a breach and you've got to prove that there was."

"Well, what is this going to mean?" Beutel said.

"It means owners are going to start reading the contracts they write," Hunter said.

We rode a cab to Shea Stadium, and I asked Hunter how he liked being interviewed. "During the season," he said, "I'll do anything the Yankees ask. Television, talks, anything else. But off-season, I'm really gonna be off. All that huntin' makes me do a lot of hard walkin', and the walkin' keeps my legs in shape, and a pitcher got to have strong legs. That's about how it's gonna be."

A blur of photographers loitered outside the ballpark. Fourteen Nikons chattered as Hunter walked into the bowels of Shea Stadium. He met Pete Sheehy, the Yankees' clubhouse man, and passed photographs of old Yankees in their glory: DiMaggio, Mantle, Whitey Ford, the marvelous old left-hander. Ford is the Yankee pitching coach, and someone asked whether, in view of the millions, he would treat Hunter differently from other Yankee pitchers.

"Not at all," Ford said. "Absolutely not. Except, of course, I'm gonna call him 'sir.'"

Hunter put on a Yankees uniform, while obeying a confusion of directions. "Look this way, Catfish. Smile Catfish. Look serious, Catfish." He walked onto the field, which was still patched with ice, and lobbed a baseball for twenty minutes. "Now look like you're really pitching," someone ordered.

Hunter went into a full windup and threw. Then he jerked his head and looked forlornly toward the right-field fence. It was a perfect pantomime of a pitcher who has just given up a home run.

We rode back to Manhattan for a luncheon press conference at the Americana, where a dozen reporters formed a circle around the quarry.

Had he heard from his old teammates?

"A few, but I've had to change my phone number. Some fan kept calling at three in the morning with advice. I've heard from three guys. They wished me well. Gene Tenace's wife cried because we wouldn't all be together anymore."

Didn't he feel any obligation toward Oakland?

"I played for them ten years. I gave them my best every game. We're square."

What about cards? Already some Yankees were talking about getting Hunter, or Hunter's contract, into a game of poker.

"They can play cards with me," Hunter said, "but only friendly games. They're not gonna get my money."

What about pressure? Everyone would be expecting everything from a million-dollar pitcher.

"I'm just gonna do what I always did. Take the games one game at a time and try to do my damn best. That's all I can do, What else *can* I do?"

He napped for half an hour, then went to The Royal Box, a nightclub at the Americana, where a squadron of television and radio people waited. I counted nine separate interviews, most repeating the same questions. Hunter answered and answered again. In time his eyelids drooped.

Toward four o'clock, he was finished, and celebrated by puffing a great sigh. "Did you expect all that?" I said.

"Nope."

"Would you like to go through it again tomorrow?"

"Tomorrow? Tomorrow I'm taking the telephone off the hook."

"How do you feel about Charlie Finley now?"

Hunter smiled a hard smile. "How do you expect you'd feel, when you're treated like an animal, and the keeper don't feed you when he's s'posed to?"

It had been a good beginning. We chatted on the street, and a dozen people asked Hunter for autographs. "This never happened on the streets in Oakland," he said, pleased.

The Big Turnip offers joys, but it is also the most demanding of cities. Hunter will be interviewed by legions of journalists day after day. He is expected to win and win and win. He is going to retain as much privacy as a blond streaker at an American Legion convention. Whether he knows it or not, the pressure has just begun to settle on his strong shoulders. Catfish Hunter, conquering hero, must now live up to his reputation and justify his salary and survive as the cynosure of every neighboring eye. It will not be an easy way in which to live.

Not at all. But it beats the hell out of sharecropping.

CHAPTER 19

PETE ROSE,
THE HIT MAN

When Kahn's son, Roger Jr., died in 1986, two people from baseball were at his funeral—Rachel Robinson, Jackie's widow, and Pete Rose, the major-league career leader with 4,256 hits. Kahn was touched. He had been working with Rose on a book, Pete Rose: My Story *(1989). It was a difficult book because Kahn was ghostwriting Rose's story. But Kahn was too famous and independent as a journalist to disappear from the book's pages. "What voice should tell the story?" Kahn asked. Working out a solution was problematic. The difficulty was compounded when Rose's gambling problems emerged as the book neared completion. In the end, the book reads smoothly, but it was a nightmare for Kahn to produce.*

Tyrus Raymond Cobb. The name rings with antique Roman grandeur and, perhaps, the hint of a bloody and sulphurous lord raging through Wales. (There is, in fact, a figure in Roman history named Tyrrhus, but he was a shepherd, not a warrior, in such ancient times that he seems about as mythic as he is real.) By most accounts, the Tyrus Cobb of the twentieth century was a man so full of fury, so brimming with bile, that some describe him as psychotic. Perhaps so. Assuredly he was mean, vindictive, paranoid, and in later years consistently drunk.

Near the end of his life—he died on July 17, 1961—Cobb was riding in a car beside a prolific California writer named Al Stump, who had been engaged to set down an authorized biography. "Have you got enough to finish?" Cobb asked.

"More than enough." (In fact the book, which Cobb approved, was somewhat bland, but Stump later composed a memoir written in blood.)

"Give 'em the word then," Ty Cobb told Al Stump. "I had to fight all my life to survive. They were all against me . . . tried every dirty trick to cut me down. But I beat the bastards and left them in the ditch."

By this time Cobb had reached the age of seventy-four. He was long since a Hall of Famer, secure at a summit of baseball history, and through tough contract bargaining and cold-eyed investing, he had amassed a personal fortune of $10 million. But Ty Cobb, that magnificent competitive ballplayer, would never, in this world, know a season of mellow mists.

Stories tumble down in a clattering slide of rock and metal. Before games Cobb was said to have sat in the dugout, sharpening his spikes with a file, where all the other teams could see. Unless you want to bleed, Cobb was saying, you'd better believe that the baselines belong to me. He once punched a roommate he found soaking in a tub. "Cobb," he announced, when quiet returned, "bathes first." He stepped in a patch of wet asphalt on the way to a ballpark, and responded by assaulting the workman who had been peacefully patching the road.

Arguments persisted whether Cobb was the greatest ballplayer of his time. Early in his major-league career, which spanned twenty-four years, some preferred Pittsburgh's great-fisted shortstop, John Peter "Honus" Wagner, nicknamed the Flying Dutchman. Later Yankee legions gathered behind that mighty flagon on stilts, Babe Ruth. But on one point there is no serious argument. Tyrus Raymond Cobb was the roughest son of a bitch who ever played the game.

In the last years, as he traveled about seeking treatment for cancer, Cobb always carried a brown bag which, he told Stump, contained "a million dollars in negotiable securities." All right. Don't leave home without security, particularly when you're feeling sick. But, as Cobb would say, you've got to watch the bastards. On top of the securities lay the Prussians' favorite pistol, a Luger, fully loaded.

Cobb's fury—some surely was innate—exploded after an August night in 1905 when his mother fired a shotgun and blew off his father's head. William Herschel Cobb of Royston, Georgia, was an editor, a state senator, and a scholar. He was also, he suspected, being cuckolded by his wife, Amanda Chitwood Cobb. He left the house one evening, by horse and buggy, then doubled back, hoping or fearing to catch his wife with a lover. In the dark Amanda noticed a figure climbing into her bedroom window. She was frightened; she didn't recognize her husband, or so the story is told. Mistaking William for an intruder, Amanda Cobb fired a shotgun and shot her husband dead.

Drunk or sober, Cobb himself never told this story in detail. He would mention, "My father had his head blown off by a member of my own family and I've never gotten over it." Then, without identifying his mother as the killer, he would move swiftly away from the particulars of that nightmare evening.

What Cobb did say—and Pete Rose says the same thing—was, "My father was a great man." Then Cobb would add in an oddly menacing way: "He was the only man who ever made me do his bidding."

Requiescat. Let the dead bury the dead. Ty Cobb hammered out 4,191 major-league hits, a record that virtually everyone, including Peter Edward Rose, believed would last as long as baseball.

"Mr. Rose," a young reporter asked not long ago, "what do you think Ty Cobb would hit today?"

Cobb's lifetime batting average was .367. Rose thought briefly and said, "Oh, about .333."

"That's all?" the reporter said.

"That's all," Rose said, "but that's not bad considering that Cobb's been dead for twenty-five years."

"I don't know just when I first heard about Ty Cobb," Rose says. "I'm good at dates and numbers, things like that. My own first hit: April 4, 1963, a triple off Bob Friend at Crosley Field. Four thousand one hundred and ninety-two? Well, I guess you know that. If you didn't, we wouldn't be working together on this book, am I correct?

"Remembering when I first heard Cobb's name, it must have been from Dad. To be truthful, I don't recall just when. Probably I was little. Probably I didn't appreciate how important the man's name was. And not just probably, I guarantee this, you could bet money on it and win, I didn't have any idea how important the name Cobb would end up being in my life.

"Even before I got close to the record, way before I thought I'd ever be able to break it, I did hear quite a bit about the man. There used to be a broadcaster of the Reds games when I first came up, named Waite Hoyt. He came from Brooklyn, like you, Rog, but maybe he could play the game a little better. He pitched in the majors for twenty years.

"Waite was a great storyteller and an outstanding man. I know he had trouble with his drinking for a time. Then he joined Alcoholics Anonymous and he never drank again. In fact he became one of those people they have in AA who are always on call to help somebody else fighting the booze. Like if it was three in the morning and an alcoholic was fighting to stay clean and felt he needed a drink, right then, at three, he'd call Hoyt. And Waite would get dressed and go over and calm the other person and stay right with him until that urge to drink was beaten. So even aside from his ball playing and his broadcasting, Waite was an outstanding person. A contributing person. He should be remembered.

"Waite liked to sit in the dugout and tell us about the old times and the big stars he played with. The stories about Babe Ruth were always funny. Babe Ruth was not the strictest-trained guy in the history of baseball, if I'm not mistaken. And the ones about Cobb were mean. Mean stories. Let me tell you two things about that.

"I don't like to hear about baseball books that are full of mean stories. You take that Jim Bouton, who wrote *Ball Four*. I been told there are a lot of mean stories in there about Mickey Mantle, Roger Maris— and I know that the publishers say you got to have controversy because controversy sells books. Well, I'll bet you today that Jim Bouton is sorry that he wrote *Ball Four* twenty years ago."

I broke in. "He isn't. His second wife is a psychologist, a beautiful psychologist. He's moved away from baseball with a whole new set of interests. He certainly seems happy and he's proud of *Ball Four*."

"Yeah? Well, is he proud he never gets invited back to an old-timers' game in Yankee Stadium or anywhere else? I guarantee you he isn't proud of that."

I conceded that Mr. Rose had a point.

"So to be honest, I could be wrong, but I don't believe I'm that controversial a guy. What's so controversial about me?"

"Your divorce," I said. "Your paternity suit."

"Maybe, but I'm not the first person who ever got divorced, and I'm not the first ballplayer to get named in a paternity suit. We're gonna talk about them things, too, but straight and honest."

He was following a thread and didn't want to lose it. "I was talking about 'mean.' Some people look at me, they see the way my face is when I'm determined—you can't be smiling all the time—and they figure that I'm mean. Pete Rose is mean. Now let me ask you. Did you ever see me turn down a little kid who wanted an autograph?"

I never had.

"I'm competitive. I'm enthusiastic. I play hard. But mean? That ain't me."

I mentioned two famous plays. In the 1970 All-Star Game, at Riverfront Stadium, Rose ran over an American League catcher named Ray Fosse. Rose scored the run, and Fosse was never again as physically sound as he had been. Three years later at Shea Stadium, Rose slid hard into second base and the New York Mets' skinny shortstop Derrel "Bud" Harrelson. He dumped Harrelson, who came up swinging and spitting. A brief bout ensued, matching cruiserweight Pete Rose against (to hear New York fans tell it) an amiable midget.

People uttered sour comments on each incident. Why crash into the opposing catcher during an All-Star Game which, when you snip through the hype and hoopla, is only an exhibition, as opposed to a championship game? "I only play baseball one way," Rose says. "The way my father taught me. I play hurt, I play tired, I play hard as hell. Don't tell me it's an exhibition or it's spring training. Don't tell me to take it easy between the lines. That's not me. That's not my dad. If I play a charity softball game, for nothing, not a dime, I go all out."

But to the critics . . . can there ever be a superstar without critics hopping in his footpaths? No, there cannot be. So some bad words on Pete held that he had broken up a catcher in an exhibition game and then, to show the mighty New York media how tough he was, he had picked a fight with an unarmed pigmy.

"Both times I made the right play. I wasn't trying to hurt anybody and I wasn't trying to get hurt myself. There was nothing mean, and there was nothing sissy. Play the game.

"Cobb must have been a very different feller from me, but I just wouldn't feel right spreading mean stories myself about a great ballplayer. Besides, there's one thing away from baseball that I have very much in common with Ty Cobb. We both thought the world of our fathers."

It can be said that Rose's epochal quarter-century pursuit of Cobb began on that April day in 1963, so long ago that few Americans had heard of Vietnam, when Pete lined a triple to right center field against the right-handed Pittsburgh pitcher named Bob Friend. (It might also be said that the pursuit began on the western edge of Cincinnati on scruffy little diamonds where children played at baseball in the 1940s. Pete has always been pursuing *something*; if not Cobb specifically, then excellence.)

But the major-league turns at bat, against the most wicked fastballs and sliders on earth, from hit number 1 to hit number 4,192, take the chronicler, as they took Rose, on a Homeric journey, past perils and prejudices and even through banishment until at last we see Ulysses coming home in a baseball reenactment of mankind's oldest story of the voyage from desolation to light.

From 1963 to 1978 Pete Rose played baseball in Cincinnati. As a free agent he then went to Philadelphia for five years. He began 1984 in Montreal, and then he returned home again that year after playing ninety-five games in Montreal.

On August 16, 1984, the Reds announced that Peter the Prodigal was coming home. Fans painted signs, in Cincinnati red: "YOU'RE BACK WHERE YOU BELONG."

The next day Ol' Pete walked into the lime green office at Riverfront Stadium and put on a Cincinnati uniform for the first time in six years. When Rose had last worn one, back in 1978, he told reporters that he knew about Ty Cobb's famous record of 4,191 hits, but that he really had no chance to reach it "because I won't be able to play that long." Now in Cincinnati, he pulled on his white uniform shirt, with the big red number 14 on the back. He was playing longer than he had dreamed he could.

In the early evening of August 17, Pete stood in the batter's box against a Chicago right-hander named Dick Ruthven. It was his first time up. There was one man on base. Rose took a strike and a ball. He likes to see "what the other feller's throwing." Then he lined a whistling shot to center field. Pete chugged round first and he chugged toward second, and when Bob Dernier threw the ball away, he kept chugging until he leaped into that marvelous headfirst slide that has split the air of so many summer nights. He dirtied his uniform, but he came up safe at third. (The hit was officially ruled a single and a two-base error.)

Peter Edward Franchise was back home.

"It was something coming home," Rose says. "I don't get too sentimental, but it was something. And the negotiations to get me were also something. At one point I called Bob Howsam [the Reds' owner] myself and told him I thought I could help as a player, and that I was willing to fill in and pinch-hit. As a manager I wasn't going to insist that I had to play every day because of Cobb or anything else. I told him I wanted to play because I could help the team. That took some talking. A lot of talking. We were on the phone for two hours. I should have called Howsam collect.

"But I guess not. You don't want to nickel-and-dime away the important things. And I got the job."

Rose had batted .259 for Montreal. For the balance of 1984 as player-manager of the Reds, he hit .365, not a bad major-league number for a forty-three-year-old who has lost his bat speed. He would be back with the Reds in 1985, and when that season began, he stood ninety-five hits short of the unreachable record.

"Baseball is peaks and valleys," Rose says. "You don't want to let yourself feel too high when you're on a peak, because then you're gonna feel too damn low when the valley comes. You try to keep your emotions as even as you can, although if you have any sense you recognize that it's an emotional game.

"There were two peaks ahead of me for '85. I couldn't help knowing they were there. The first was the team peak, a pennant, and that really is the first peak in the major leagues. Has to be. The team comes first. We finished fifth in '84, but I honestly thought with a few good moves we could win the division in '85. We didn't. The Dodgers did, but we came in second. That's as high as we went because that particular team didn't beat the Dodgers head-to-head. You've got to do that, beat the other contender one-on-one. We didn't, and we finished where we belonged.

"The second peak I had ahead of me was personal. On opening day, Monday, April 8, at Riverfront, I needed ninety-five hits to break Cobb's record. That was when they played the national anthem. When the game ended—we won it 4–1—I needed ninety-three. I doubled in the fifth and batted in two runs, and I singled in the second and knocked in another. I got my hits and we won the game. I hadn't seen a nicer major-league opener since 1963, when I was a rookie and most of the old Reds wouldn't talk to me. That was the way things were."

The 1985 Cincinnati Reds held first place for all of two days before a defeat by Bill Gullickson, then with Montreal, dropped them into second. They moved back into the lead for six days later in April. Then they lost to Houston, 8–3. The team would not occupy first place again. Eventually they finished five and a half games behind Los Angeles and the Dodgers' amiable, formerly pear-shaped manager, Tom Lasorda, who annoys certain Cincinnati fans so much that they carry signs into Riverfront Stadium denouncing "The Blue Tub of Goo."

So there was not much of a pennant race in Cincinnati, but 1985 may have been the most exciting of all baseball seasons in River City. Rose closed on Cobb slowly, persistently, bravely. By July 1, when he disturbed a commanding four-hitter worked by the Dodgers' Orel Hershiser IV with a sharp single, Rose stood only thirty-nine hits behind Cobb. By August 1, he was twenty-five hits back.

"That's about when the media began their pursuit. I was pursuing Cobb and the media was pursuing me. I almost always enjoy talking to the media. I like going back and forth with reporters. I like throwing them a good one-liner when I can think of one. Being with media, to tell the truth, gives me a chance to be as witty as I know how to be. Besides, long ago Sparky Anderson told me, 'When a reporter comes in with questions, don't go giving him any uncivilized answers. That man has a job to do. It's part of *your* job.'

"In the standard major-league contract, you have to promise that you'll promote the game. This isn't always enforced. My good friend Lefty [the pitcher Steve Carlton] would talk all about his collection of fermented juices. Wine. Lefty had a great collection of the grape, and he'd rap about that with anybody who would listen. So it isn't true he wouldn't talk to the press.

"But not about baseball. He wouldn't say a word about his pitching. I guess he figured he spoke with his left arm.

"I had one like Lefty last year. John Denny. A born-again Christian, he said he was. Born again and born again and born again. He said the media was corrupt because—he really said this—the media had convinced the world that America was not a Christian country.

"Hey, I'm a manager, not a philosopher, and I sure as hell can't be a dictator. That wouldn't work with today's players. So I listened to Lefty Carlton about the Chablis and I heard out Denny on his friend God and his enemy the press. After Denny had an up-and-down year in 1986, and got charged with assault by one writer, we released him. Contract or no; these fellers, Lefty and Denny, wouldn't talk to the writers. Well, I talk to the writers every day, and for as long as they need to hear me.

"Anyway, now I'm closing in on Cobb in 1985 and the media is closing in on me. A fellow named Rick Reilly from *Sports Illustrated* wanted to talk to me 'in depth.' All right I'll go as deep as I can, but he's doing a magazine story, not a book. Now he says he's got to talk to my wife, Carol, and my ex-wife, Karolyn. That's simply thrilling, setting up the two ladies, both named Mrs. Rose, so he could compare notes. But I went along with it. Leslie Stahl, who has that nice blow-dried hair, wanted me for the CBS show 'Face the Nation.' Somebody else and somebody else and somebody else. I even let a couple of fellers from NBC stay up at my house in Indian Hill. They wanted to see how I live.

"Pressure? Hell, getting up in the morning on a bad day is pressure. It's also attention. Dave Parker, our fine right fielder, said that players on my team actually enjoyed all the media. Every day's like the World Series, some of them said.

"As for me, I got to a point that season where I knew I would break the record. All I had to do was what I always done. See the ball, hit the ball, and it would come. See the ball, hit the ball, and don't get hurt. I'm pretty good at all three.

"All right. The total number of media covering me went higher and higher. It finally got up to four hundred, and it's September 11, 1985. Another press conference. Someone asks where I get my strength from. One of my commercials—I have been doing about ten—is for Wheaties, the breakfast cereal. They advertise 'Great out of the Box.' I don't say anything but I unbutton my jersey. All the reporters see my T-shirt that says 'Wheaties, Great out of the Box.' That broke them up.

"I have a good batting practice, hitting the ball hard. At seven forty-eight a small plane flies over Riverfront trailing a streamer. It read: 'Latonia [one of his favorite racetracks] is betting on Pete.' The crowd, 47,237, goes nuts. I'm actually feeling fairly calm.

"At seven fifty our left-handed starter, Tom Browning, gets them San Diego Padres out in order. At seven fifty-seven, we come to bat and Eddie Milner pops out against Eric Show. I follow, carrying my black Mizuno bat, Kentucky lumber milled in Japan. The crowd stands up and starts making noise. I take Show's first pitch. Fastball high. I foul one back and take another ball. The digital clocks say that it is eight oh one. See the ball. Hit the ball. The baseball is what I'm watching. Show throws and I line the hit, the big one, number 4,192, bouncing into the turf in left center field.

"Man. Fireworks light up the sky. I round first, clap hands with Tommy Helms, my coach. Steve Garvey of the Padres grins and says, 'Thanks for the memories.' I shake his hand, and he runs off the field. Garry Templeton, the shortstop, tosses over the ball as a memento. Some official takes the ball for safekeeping. Up above, a Goodyear blimp hovers with blinking lights that say: 'Pete Rose, 4,192.' Someone drives out a new red Corvette with a license plate, 'PR 4192.'

"And the people! They kept cheering and whistling and stomping. Almost all the other players leave the field. It's my moment. Some other official takes away first base, the base I touched for 4,192.

"And the people! They stand and cheer and cheer. Seven minutes. Now I got no ball, no glove, no bat, no base. For the first time in my life I don't know what to do on a ball field.

"I look up. I'm not a very religious person, but I see clear in the sky, my dad, Harry Francis Rose, and Ty Cobb.

"Ty Cobb was in the second row. Dad was in the first.

"That's when I went. I started crying, and Tommy Helms, the coach, put an arm around me and motioned for my son, Petey, the batboy. I hugged my son, and then I cried real hard.

"I think I know why. With Dad in the sky and Petey in my arms, you had three generations of Rose men together, in spite of time, in spite of change, in spite of death.

"So that's what it was that made me cry."

PART V

THE GLADIATORS FIGHT TO SUCCEED

CHAPTER 20

DEMPSEY: THE MANASSAS MAULER GOES DOWN

Jack Dempsey was a pioneer of modern boxing, one of the toughest men ever to enter the ring and the world heavyweight champion from 1919 to 1926 with forty-nine knockouts. In 1997, Kahn sifted through his old notes and determined that Dempsey deserved better. "I thought that he'd been overlooked," he explained. "There was too much written about Babe Ruth and not enough about Dempsey." The result was Kahn's first biography, A Flame of Pure Fire, *published in 1999. In this excerpt Kahn re-creates Dempsey's loss of the title to Gene Tunney.*

O n the morning of the Philadelphia bout, Mike Trent, the body-guard, gave Dempsey the usual small glass of olive oil. After that Trent disappeared. A few hours later, Dempsey began suffering from cramps. His intestines were hyperactive. Rumors spread that gamblers had paid Trent to add a nonlethal poison to Dempsey's olive oil. Nothing was substantiated. Dempsey might simply have eaten a bad clam. Whatever, his innards were chaotic and he looked pale at the weigh-in. "It's nothing," he said. "I just haven't been getting enough sun."

Tunney chartered a small plane to fly him from Stroudsberg to Philadelphia. He meant to demonstrate that he feared neither Dempsey nor flight in an open cockpit. But the weather was unsettled—a front was moving in—and the plane lurched about the sky. Tunney became airsick; he looked as pale as Dempsey at the weigh-in.

Federal tax records would put the paid attendance at 120,757. The *Times* estimated the crowd, including gate-crashers, ushers, reporters, and the rest, at 135,000. That may be generous, but not by much. This was, and still is, the greatest number of people ever assembled to see a boxing match. Gate receipts totaled $1,895,733. The *Times*, then two cents at the newsstand, proclaimed on its front page, "The biggest event in the history of sport."

One gets a measure of Dempsey's impact on boxing and on America by recalling that in 1919 paid attendance for Willard fell short of 20,000, and *that* was considered a pretty fair crowd. From 20,000 to 135,000 within eight years. From a gate of $450,000 to a gate of almost $2 million. From a sport scorned as immoral to a sport that had the leaders of the country tripping over one another in their rush for ringside seats. Neither before nor after has sport known a single individual attraction equal to the Mauler.

At introductions, the crowd cheered Tunney and hooted Dempsey. The jingoist press had turned a champion into a villain and lauded Tunney—who never saw combat—as the heroic manly marine. At the center of the ring, before the referee's instructions, Tunney said, "Hello, champion." Dempsey said, "Hello, Gene."

It was beginning to rain. Ruskin's famous opinion on "valueless books" notes that inept authors always create weather to match their scenes. Good things happen in sunshine. Funerals proceed through rain. Ruskin called this convergence "the pathetic fallacy." It rained so hard in Philadelphia on September 23 that the *Times* later ran a headline: "SOAKED FANS FLOOD TAYLORS WITH SUITS." Ruskin is unassailable in literary theory, but as the drizzle built into a downpour, Dempsey suffered a terrible battering. Pathetic to some, but not a fallacy to Dempsey's admirers. Tunney won every one of the ten rounds.

Tunney fought erect, even leaning backward as if to keep his face away from punches. His strategy was to retreat, always retreat, and counter Dempsey's charges with that dangerous snake of a left. The retreat was clockwise so that when Dempsey landed a left hook, Tunney was moving away from the punch, lessening impact. Tunney had noticed something when [Georges] Carpentier and later [Luis Angel]

Firpo tagged Dempsey with right hands. Sometimes, not often but sometimes, as Dempsey charged, he let his left drop a bit, as he was getting ready to hook. A boxer with fast-enough hands could slip a right cross over Dempsey's lowered left glove. That was how Carpentier connected to the cheekbone. That was how Firpo began the barrage that knocked Dempsey out of the ring.

Just describing this tactic diminishes it. You have to dare to get close to Dempsey and forget about pain and connect against the snorting, snarling roughhouse fighter. Miss the right, and Dempsey's hooks—swiveling from the hips, he could throw three or four in a seeming instant—will shatter you. Tunney, a ponderous fellow and a brave man, moved in close enough to shake Dempsey with a right to the cheekbone in each of the first two rounds. He could hit harder than Dempsey had imagined.

After that it was all pursuit, Dempsey pursuing as Tunney supposed he would, but not as recklessly and dangerously as he had pursued before Tunney landed the rights. The younger man moved backward, sometimes trotting. Dempsey tried to corner Tunney without success. As Tunney executed his remarkable footwork, he slashed Dempsey with small, repetitive, cutting blows to the nose and to the eyes.

Doc Kearns [Dempsey's manager] was sitting in the first row with [Hollywood writer] Gene Fowler and a Los Angeles sportswriter named Mark Kelly. In the sixth round, Kearns said, "He's gonna lose. His timing's off and his legs are gone. Still, there's something he could do." Over a moist and roaring crowd, Kelly said, "Get over to his corner and help him. The guys in there aren't any good at all."

Kearns shook his head. "No. Let him take it. That's the way he wanted it, and that's the way it will have to be."

Kelly looked at Kearns. "Doc, you're crying."

Kelly seized Kearns's arm. "You're not kidding me, you bum. You're crying. Get up in the corner and help the champion." Kearns would not. He watched Dempsey take a beating and cried into his right hand through the last four rounds. When the fight was over, Kearns dried his eyes. Then he found a speakeasy and drank himself into oblivion.

By most accounts Dempsey landed only one good punch. His left hook in the sixth round caught Tunney in the Adam's apple and left

Tunney hoarse. He even coughed up a little blood. But Dempsey could not land combinations. He said, "I was slower than I thought, or Tunney was faster. I was blaming the wet ring, but it didn't bother Tunney. He glided around like a great skater on ice." A twisting Tunney jab cut Dempsey over the right eye in the fourth round. By the eighth Tunney had punched Dempsey's left eye shut. Going out for the tenth, Dempsey was bleeding from the mouth and both his cheeks were bruised. The downpour continued, and Dempsey's face was streaked with rain and smeared with blood. Still he kept coming. His stomach ached and his legs wobbled and his visage looked like the thorn-raked face of a martyr. Still he kept coming. It was unforgettable, this raw and ghastly courage in the rain.

At the final bell, Dempsey fought back the pain and threw an arm over one of Tunney's shoulders. "Great fight, Gene," Dempsey said. "You won." He walked back to his corner. The judges gave Tunney all ten rounds. In the corner Dempsey heard cheering. People stood in the downpour and called his name. At last some of the people were beginning to realize what they'd had.

"You'll always be the champion," a man shouted. "You're our champion forever."

He had never heard words like that before in the ring. Rugged old Jack Dempsey blinked away tears. "I want you to get to the people," he told me forty-five years later, "that losing was the making of me."

"Not losing, Champ," I said. I was feeling proud for him. "Losing with guts."

He tapped a huge hand on my arm and looked embarrassed.

Estelle [Dempsey's second wife] had skipped the fight. She said she loved Jack so much she could not bear to see him hit. Fight night she caught a train to Philadelphia, and she was sitting in the living room of his hotel suite when Dempsey returned. Handlers walked with him, but only a few reporters. Most of the press was interviewing Tunney.

She gasped at the sight of his face, but recovered and gently touched his features, looking for a spot that was not bruised. She kissed him light and said, "What happened, Ginsberg?"

His answer was brief and droll and unforgettable. "Honey, I forgot to duck."

Dempsey earned $717,000. Kearns seldom failed to comment, "I woulda gotten him a million." Tunney made $200,000 for one fight, forty minutes, more than double Babe Ruth's salary for the year.

"Dempsey fought like the great champion he was," Tunney said. "He had the kick of a mule in his fists and the heart of a lion in his breast. I never fought a harder socker nor do I hope to meet one. I'm content to rest a while with the ambition I have nourished for seven years finally realized."

Dempsey said, "I have no alibis to offer. I lost to a good man, an American. A man who speaks the English language. I have no alibis."

CHAPTER 21

ALI

The record—fifty-six wins, thirty-seven knockouts, five losses—does little to describe the life and times of Muhammad Ali, the street-smart kid from Louisville, Kentucky, who held the heavyweight boxing title three times before finally losing it in 1980. Kahn visited the champ in 1976—two years after he regained the title and at a time when his popularity worldwide was greater than ever.

The fighter sat in semidarkness, talking in an urgent whisper. When you sit with Muhammad Ali, he talks in whispers. He knows that when the heavyweight champion speaks softly, you strain to hear.

"Why are you fighting this fight?" I asked. "Why are you going on?"

Rays of late-afternoon sunlight angled against an off-white wall. Ali, who wore black, had positioned himself in darkness.

"To do good works," he said. "I helped a Jewish nursing home. You know I go in the ghettos. Two, three days after this fight, I may be on the South Side of Chicago talking with people. What heavyweight champion before ever done that?" Ali stroked his brows, which are unmarked for all the punches crashed against them. "I gives a lot away. I got a mission. God, if there is a God, he's gonna judge me. That's when I die. And I'm gonna die. Sonny Liston. He died."

I nodded.

"And you," Ali said. "You gonna die. [Famous sportswriter] Jimmy Cannon, he was once sitting right where you are, and he died. You ever think about that?"

I had driven cheerfully into the Catskill Mountains to observe two black men readying themselves for a fight at Yankee Stadium. The Ali I remembered was brave, young, and handsome, and as remote from death as spring. But now this man had turned contemplative and grave. He was telling me something with great subtlety. Muhammad Ali was dying as a fighter.

Ken Norton, thirty-one, the opponent, is a child of the black middle class, a star in two dreadful movies, and the possessor of a body that Irving Rudd, a boxing publicist, called "mythologically hewn."

No rancor separated the fighters. Ali had been guaranteed $6 million. Norton would earn $1 million. September 28 was payday, but as they worked toward summits of conditioning, the world yawned. Ali is proud of his ability to sell tickets, and at the public prefight physical, he staged a vulgar, raucous demonstration.

"You a nigger," he screamed at Norton in a meeting room at Grossinger's Hotel. "You a yellow nigger. And your movies are bad." Ali lifted a poster displaying a photo of Norton that had appeared in the *Village Voice*. Posed next to a sink, Norton wore only a jockstrap. "You are a disgrace to athletics," Ali shouted. "You are a disgrace to your race. You are a disgrace to your country, posing for a picture with your balls hanging out."

Norton ignored the champion, and a doctor in a yellow-and-black sports jacket took pulses and blood pressures, complaining that he could not do his work unless Ali quieted down. Ali signaled to his retinue, and presently his seconds and Norton's seconds were calling each other flunkies.

"Both men are in superb condition," announced Harry Kleiman, the doctor.

"When Ali gets beat, you go on welfare," cried one of Norton's people.

"You're just a nigger," said Ali's man, Drew Brown.

The champion's eyes showed merriment. Privately he had given Joe Louis $10,000 to spend two weeks with him at the Concord Hotel.

Publicly he refused to notice Louis wince whenever the word "nigger" rang out.

Such alternations tax credulity, except for this: Ali is the champion and he is locked into a style. He turned professional during the last days of Dwight Eisenhower's administration, and he has fought well, sometimes brilliantly, through five presidencies. Young, he was Cassius Clay, the "Louisville Lip," establishing himself with his fists, his doggerel, and his outrageous predictions. Now, four months away from his thirty-fifth birthday, he is Muhammad Ali, the Muslim minister, pledged to peace and God. But he is also a ticket salesman. If vulgarity sells tickets, let it be.

Fight night broke chilly, and for all of Ali's noise, only thirty thousand people appeared in the cavernous stadium. There was more violence outside the ring than in. Ali still moves with a lithe beauty, but he no longer punches in flurries. He had predicted, "Norton must fall in five." After five rounds Norton stood strong. Across the whole fight, neither staggered the other. Ali reddened Norton's face. Norton bloodied Ali's nose. Eight-year-olds would do more.

Norton appeared to win narrowly, but a law of boxing holds that no heavyweight champion can lose by a narrow decision. Dutifully the referee and two judges gave the fight to Ali. Dutifully Norton's manager protested. Norton wept in frustration. Ali stole off into the night, frightened by hoodlums clawing at the windows of his car.

"Not exactly your classic fight," I said to Harold Conrad, a boxing scholar engaged by Ali as a personal aide.

"Dorian Gray," Conrad said. "The face is still beautiful, but what's gone on inside the body? The kidney punches. Shots to the liver. That stuff and time have taken a toll. It just doesn't show on the champion's face."

"This isn't the fighter who took on Joe Frazier in 1971."

Conrad puffed a cigarette. "Nobody," he said, "makes love as well as he did five years ago."

Ali sees his future in evangelism. He would become a cross between Billy Graham and William Jennings Bryan. To do that, to take care of his children and his divorces, to work his private charities, he has calculated that he needs $83,000 a month. That is why he has gone on boxing with eroded skills. That is why, his mind heavy with death, he shouted "nigger" into the face of a decent man like Kenny Norton.

But three days after the fight, Ali was not on the South Side of Chicago. He was in Istanbul. The dullness of his performance had sunk in. "As of now," he announced, "I am quitting boxing and will devote all my energy to the propagation of the Muslim faith."

He meant it. He means a lot of what he says. But six months from now, when he is hoarse from preaching and someone offers him $10 million to fight George Foreman, we will behold a mighty crisis of faith.

CHAPTER 22

BILLY VS. REGGIE

After a famous fight in a New York nightclub in 1957, Billy Martin
was as well known for his pugilistic inclinations as for his skill as a
baseball player and manager. Reggie Jackson, on the other hand, was
known for hitting important home runs in the spotlight (and 563 in
his career). But on one fateful day in 1977, under the glare of
national television cameras, "Battling Billy" squared off against
"Mr. October," as Kahn recounts in his 2002 book, October Men:
Reggie Jackson, George Steinbrenner, Billy Martin, and the
Yankees' Miraculous Finish in 1978.

M artin's technique for dealing with fires was a generous applica-
tion of gasoline. Now he could not restrain himself from
needling Jackson. "Reggie has to understand the way I do things. I'm
going to win or lose, but whatever happens I'm gonna do it my way. I
might bat Reggie fourth when he's hot, but with our running game it's
best to have a fourth-place hitter who does not strike out a lot." It was
common knowledge that Jackson had led, if that is the word, the American League in strikeouts four times. Still, his prodigious power always
dictated that he bats fourth, the cleanup spot. No fewer than seven big-
league managers had previously hit him cleanup. There had been no
issue about that before Martin. It was also common knowledge that
Jackson had been personally romanced by Steinbrenner. When reporters asked him to comment on Martin's comments, Jackson issued a

restrained and ambiguous response. "It's important for me to get along with my boss. I'm going to have to take a certain amount. Well, I'll take it, but I won't eat it." Ostensibly Jackson's boss was Martin, but the boss of bosses was Steinbrenner.

"I'm a driver," Steinbrenner told a reporter, as if doubt existed. "I'm a firm believer in the old adage that if you're going to lead. . . . You know, or don't you know, the saying? Lead, follow, or get the hell out of the way. I'm involved with everything from the ushers to the dining room to the players' equipment bags. I raise hell if the restrooms are dirty. On the field I've been letting Martin do things his way. But I know his record. I got Martin because he was what we needed at the time. His record has been instant success, and I knew he could put it together in a hurry. But then there's always been a drop. It's my job to see that Martin's drop is not allowed to happen here."

Following this resounding no-confidence vote, Martin led the Yankees to a 3–0 victory on opening day over a last-place team, the Milwaukee Brewers. He started Catfish Hunter and got a shutout. Neither McGraw nor Stengel could have managed better than that. Then, playing mostly the Brewers and an expansion club, the Toronto Blue Jays, Martin's Yankees lost eight out of their next nine. "I could see in spring training we had too many distractions," Lou Piniella said. "I could even see some players being complacent. I knew we weren't going to get off to a good start." By April 19, the Yankees had collapsed into last place, five and a half games behind the suddenly (and temporarily) competent Brewers. [*Sports Illustrated* reporter] Larry Keith summed up the groundswell of doubt: "A dream of New York's rivals seems to be coming true. . . . If the Yankees got off to a bad start, their explosive personalities would set off a disastrous chain reaction, with the players squabbling among themselves and Martin locking horns with Steinbrenner and eventually getting the axe."

Keith presented an essentially sound forecast, but he was just about fifteen months premature. No chain reaction developed, and on May 7, 1977, the Yankees defeated Oakland, 11–2, and moved into first place by half a game. [Catcher Thurmon] Munson explained the rapid turnaround as well as anyone: "People talk about our egos and our salaries, but they forget we're also ballplayers who've had success and care for what we do. Pride doesn't allow us to let down. When you start getting killed on the field [the team] and booed by the fans [Jackson], if you're a ballplayer who's had success, your pride takes over." Emotions aside, these were outstanding physical athletes, and another factor in the turnaround was talent. But few victories and even, as we would learn, a lot of victories did not end, or even muffle, the ragging.

On the day that the *Sport* magazine article [in which Jackson criticized teammate Munson] became public, Jackson hit a seventh-inning home run at the Stadium, a long drive to right that drew the Yankees even at 2 to 2 with their great rivals, the Boston Red Sox. It was only May, but first place hung in the balance. Suddenly Jackson's teammates forgot that they were angry and crowded to the home-plate side of the dugout to shake his hand. Jackson jogged toward the group, abruptly made a forty-five-degree turn, and entered the dugout from the first-base side, where nobody was waiting for him. Then he sat down. Jackson was refusing to accept congratulations. It may not be pure cause and effect, but the Yankees lost the game, 4–3, and they didn't get back into first place until June. Jackson's conduct was an oddly shocking, blatantly public illustration of the fratricidal aspect of this Yankee team. I'm reminded of Branch Rickey's comment on an earlier tempestuous character. "Leo Durocher," Ricky said, "had an infinite capacity to go into a bad situation and make it worse."

Six days later in Chicago first baseman Chris Chambliss, a soft-spoken "old-style black" Yankee, secured a victory over the White Sox by driving out a home run with Munson on base. Jackson, the on-deck hitter, moved toward home plate and extended a hand. Munson chugged right by it. Afterwards, Jackson tried to deflect reporters by saying, "Chris shook my hand. I guess Thurman just didn't see my hand out there."

"Sure I saw it," Munson said. He assumed an angry glare that foreclosed the questioning.

A writer remarked to Jackson that it was hard for him to grasp Jackson's real feelings toward Munson. What was Reggie's deep-down attitude, anyway? "My deep-down attitude toward Munson," Jackson said, "is that I'm trying to be a good Christian." (To play off Mike Nichols's phrase, Reggie regards his friend, God, as "a kind of nice guy.")

As the season proceeded, Martin batted Jackson fifth, sixth, third, every slot but fourth. This was needling, more than managing, and it was also an exercise in destructive behavior. The needling helped nothing and nobody, not Martin, not Jackson certainly, and not the team. Besides that, it riled Steinbrenner, who wanted Reggie batting cleanup. Steinbrenner had already broken up with Ralph Houk and Bill Virdon. In someone's hyperbolic, inelegant, but catchy phrase, George changed managers as often as a hooker changes partners. Martin was weaving the strands of his own noose.

The Yankees played the Red Sox in Boston on Saturday, June 18, with first place on the line. The NBC network was televising the game; executives estimated that "thirty, maybe fifty million" people would be watching. It was a hot, sunny afternoon and 34,603 paying customers jammed Fenway Park, the largest daytime crowd gathered there in twenty years.

Jackson had hit safely in thirteen straight games and was feeling ebullient. Bucky Dent missed a bunt the night before on an early inning squeeze play, and a few minutes before the first pitch Jackson sat next to him in the dugout to show support. Martin nodded. Martin looked at Jackson. "I thought I made a good call. What do you think?"

"If you really want my opinion," Jackson said, "I think he feels that when you make him bunt that early in the game you take the bat out of his hand." (Translation: in essence, you destroy his confidence. You make him feel as though he doesn't know how to hit.) Martin stalked away. He may have wanted a Jackson opinion, but he did not want the one he had just heard. In the game the Red Sox pounded the big right-hander Mike Torrez; Carl Yastrzemski, Bernie Carbo, and George Scott hit homers and the Red Sox were leading, 7–4, in the sixth inning. With Fred Lynn on first base, Jim Rice checked his swing on an outside fastball, but made contact and lifted a soft fly into short right field. Jackson looked toward the infield, as though expecting second baseman Willie Randolph to race down the looper. Then he broke slowly, picked up the ball on a few bounces, and soft-tossed it toward the pitcher's mound. Rice pulled into second base. The ball was not catchable. There was no call for Jackson to make a frantic, diving lunge. But had he broken smartly, he could have held Rice to a single. It was a poor play, the play of a ballplayer whose mind was out of focus.

Martin walked to the mound. He was lifting Torrez for Sparky Lyle. He also dispatched Paul Blair, a gifted outfielder but a mediocre hitter, to right field. He told Torrez, who had not asked, "I'm pulling that son of a bitch for not hustling." Munson nodded in agreement. Martin was benching Jackson during an inning in plain view of a sellout crowd and an enormous television audience. When Blair reached right field, Jackson said, "You coming in for me?"

"Yeah."

"What the hell is going on?"

Blair, sometimes called "Motormouth," turned laconic. "You got to ask Billy that."

Jackson set his jaw and began running toward the dugout with powerful, purposeful strides. The television cameramen in center field and alongside the Yankee dugout followed him, step by jolting step. Martin leaned forward on the bench, waiting, a coil of anger. Jackson closed with him, spread his hands as though bewildered, and said, "What did I do? What did I do?"

Martin rose and said through a snarling look, "What do you mean, what did you do? You know what the fuck you did." (Lip-readers, including nuns and precocious children, picked up these syllables from their television sets.) Jackson moved past Martin as if he had heard nothing. Then he said, "Why did you take me out? You have to be crazy to embarrass me in front of fifty million people."

Martin said, "You want to show me up by loafing? Then I'm going to show *your* ass up. Anybody who doesn't hustle, doesn't play for me."

Reggie said he hadn't been loafing. "Confused, maybe. But that doesn't matter to you. Nothing I could do would please you. You never wanted me on this team. You don't want me now. Why don't you just admit it?" On the mound Sparky Lyle threw warmup pitches. The ten or twelve Yankees in the dugout sat silent. They were watching, just like the Fenway crowd, just like the television millions. In the truck, one of the NBC men said, "We're getting one helluva show. This should be prime-time." (It would make pretty much every evening news show in the country.)

Martin moved toward Jackson, who stood his ground. The veins bulged in Martin's neck. He screamed, "I ought to kick your fucking ass."

"Who the fuck do you think you're talking to, old man?"

"What? Who's an old man? Who are you calling an old man?"

"You're forty-nine years old and you weigh one hundred sixty. I'm thirty and I weigh two hundred ten. Let me tell you something, Martin. You aren't going to do shit. What you are is plain crazy."

Coach Elston Howard had quickly marshaled a peace corps. He and Berra grabbed Martin from behind. The wiry, thick-armed outfielder Jimmy Wynn grabbed Jackson. Nobody got to throw a punch. (Although some claim to have seen Martin launch a roundhouse right, the tape replays I've watched show tempers, but no punches.) Reggie shook free and tramped into the clubhouse. By the time he got there, he says, he decided that after the game he would punch Martin silly.

Mike Torrez, six-foot-five and 220, sat on a stool in front of his locker. He'd heard the encounter described on Boston radio. "Why don't you go back to the hotel?" he said to Jackson. "Just keep away from Billy for a while."

"Maybe," Reggie said, and walked into the trainer's room, where he found Bucky Dent dressed in street clothes. Earlier Martin had lifted Dent for a pinch hitter. "I can't take any more of this," Dent said. He had made a plane reservation to Chicago, where his son was still attending school, and had called his wife, Karen, asking her to meet him at O'Hare. "Martin never lets me swing with men on base," Dent said. "I've had enough. I'm jumping the club." (Reggie's pregame comment on the consequences of taking that bat out of Dent's hands were coming true in a whirlwind rush and in spades.) Big Fran Healy, the bullpen catcher who was named after three saints, Francis, Xavier, and Paul, appeared and in the next few minutes earned his season's pay. Jackson spoke to him about the humiliations he was suffering. "He wants me to make a hard throw on a nothing play like that? I've had three cortisone shots this season. I have to save my arm for when it counts." Jackson went on with his litany. Healy said sincere, placating things. Listening, Bucky Dent felt less isolated, less the lone victim of a strange and willful manager. He called Karen, a spirited young woman nicknamed

"Stormy," in Chicago for a second time. He loved her, he said, and he had decided to stick with the club.

Steinbrenner missed the game. He was in Cleveland attending a funeral. But he saw the encounter on television and immediately telephoned the Fenway Park press box and demanded to talk to Phil Rizzuto. There was no phone connection between the press box and the radio booth, and Bill Browley of the Red Sox, who answered the call, assumed the loud character on the other end was "some nut." He hung up. He hung up on George M. Steinbrenner III. The phone rang again. A frightened Fenway operator began, "I have to know who it was that just hung up." A strong voice drowned her out. "This is George Steinbrenner." In the end, Steinbrenner reached not Rizzuto, but a Yankee publicity man. "Have Gabe Paul [the Yankees' president] call me right away," he ordered.

Paul recalled that Steinbrenner was distraught and wanted to fire Martin "immediately, if not sooner." The man was a disgrace, Steinbrenner said. He had completely lost control of himself on national television. His language was disgusting, "a terrible example for American youth." Paul said he couldn't disagree, but there were other factors to consider. If Martin were fired, it could seem that Jackson was running the team. Munson might organize, or anyway try to organize, some sort of nasty rebellion. "We don't need a *firing* right now, George. What we need is a *cease-fire*. Let me meet with Martin and Jackson in the morning." Then, speaking slowly and clearly, Paul said, "If you fire Martin now, I won't be able to deal with the consequences. If you fire Martin, I'll resign." This would have left the Yankees without a manager or a president. Like Hannibal, Caesar, and Patton, Steinbrenner knew that not often, but every once in a great while, one beats a strategic retreat.

In Paul's suite at the Sheraton, Martin again challenged Jackson to fight. "I'm going to kick the shit out of you right here. Get up, boy."

"Hey, Gabe," Jackson said, "You're a smart guy. Why won't you tell me what you think when he called me 'boy'?" Martin started toward the door. Paul rose and ordered him to sit. After a while, Jackson said to Paul, "I know you're not trading me because you would have done that already. I know I'm going to be staying. I assume Billy is staying, too. I've talked to some friends and my father. The only recourse I have

is to bust my ass for this guy regardless of what he tries to do to me."
As Jackson was leaving the suite, he remembers Paul sounding his sec-
ular anthem: "Don't look at the hole in the doughnut. Look at the
doughnut as a whole."

The Red Sox swept the series from the Yankees, who fell two and a
half games out, into third place. The team flew to Detroit, where Steinbrenner was waiting at the Ponchartrain Hotel, breathing heavily
between growls. He called Martin to his suite. "I thought Jackson was
dogging it," Martin said. "If I let Jackson get away with it, they all will.
I'll lose my team." (Twenty-five players, the storied New York Yankees,
Munson, Piniella, Nettles, Randolph, Dent, and the rest, all loafing on
the job in midseason? That may have been possible in the fantasies of
Billy Martin. It was not possible in reality.) Martin continued, "You're
just mad, George, because we got swept by the Red Sox. You're the only
owner that wants to fire the manager every time the team drops out of
first place." Still considering Paul's counsel that a cease-fire was the best
course, Steinbrenner suspended judgment. He encountered Jackson
walking through the lobby, and in a few intense minutes Jackson told
him that firing Martin would cause more problems than it would solve.
"It will make it look as though I'm running the club." At length Steinbrenner called over Martin and issued a command. Martin and Jackson
were to ride out to Tiger Stadium in the same taxi. "And," Steinbrenner said, fiercely, "make sure all the sportswriters see the two of you
getting into one cab." Later Gabe Paul told me, "Actually George
wanted Martin to take a taxi to the Sahara Desert by himself. He never
entirely forgave me for not agreeing with him."

Paul left the team in Detroit and flew to his home in Tampa. He was
the president of the Yankees. He was giving himself a little vacation;
surely he had earned it. Quiet, temperate Gabe—it was said no one had
ever seen him lose his temper, except perhaps his wife, Mary—was worn
out by all the ranting, but quiet, temperate Gabe was at his core a
shrewd, audacious man. He was acutely aware that he was leaving the
team at a time of crisis. The players were difficult, the manager was on
the way to becoming a full-time drunk, but Paul felt that he could handle these matters. What bothered him were reports that Steinbrenner
was saying vituperative things behind his back. "I'd been hearing," he

told me, "and you know I have a lot of sources, I'd messed up with Martin and that George had had to bail me out. And I heard he was telling people that I was over the hill, that I was getting senile, that my mind had been affected by a stroke. I'll put up with a lot, but there are limits even for me." The Yankees lost two more games in Detroit, falling four and a half behind the Red Sox. They came home and managed to lose the Mayor's Trophy game to the New York Mets, 6 to 4. That was a charity exhibition, devoid of championship significance, but in the years before interleague play it was heavy with local symbolism. As it happened the '77 Mets were one of the weakest teams in baseball. They would finish last, thirty-seven games out of first place, with a rookie manager widely regarded as an ambulatory disaster. As [legendary sports columnist] Red Smith remarked, "The only apprentice who seems less suited for managing than the Mets' novice, Joe Torre, is the Atlanta amateur, Ted Turner." Turner had managed the Braves, which he owned, for a single game in 1977. The Braves lost it and, just like the Mets, finished thirty-seven games out of first place.

After Detroit and the lost exhibition game, the Yankees were to play three more against the Red Sox, this time at the Stadium. Another Boston sweep would just about end their season. From Detroit, Steinbrenner flew to Tampa, following Paul. He owned a team of renegade ballplayers, with a captain wrapped up in himself and a manager increasingly erratic. Deep down, within the macho, three layers underneath the bravado, Steinbrenner knew he needed help. He asked Paul when he would come back. Paul said when he was assured that the backbiting would stop. Steinbrenner apologized, or at least apologized sufficiently to placate the Yankees' president, and Paul agreed to go back to work on June 24, when the Yankees opened against the Red Sox at night in the Stadium.

Jackson had been swinging at some bad pitches, and he had misplayed a line drive in Detroit. At Martin's suggestions, he visited an ophthalmologist on June 23. His eyes turned out to be fine. It surprised him the next night to see his name missing from the lineup. The Red Sox were starting the left-handed Bill Lee, and at first Martin told reporters that Jackson had been having trouble with left-handers. Someone pointed out that in nine turns at bat against Lee so far this season, Jackson had belted five hits, including two homers. "But his eyes," Martin said. "He had them dilated by the doctor. The trainer says they still look dilated. I'm sitting Reggie because I don't want him getting hurt. I'm doing this for his good." Hearing that, Jackson jogged to the outfield without a glove. He didn't want to be pressed by the sportswriters.

During the second inning Gabe Paul arrived at the Stadium. The Red Sox were leading, 3 to 1, and Jackson was sitting on the bench. After listening to explanations, Paul summoned the Yankees' team doctor, Maurice Cowen, and told him to check out Jackson's eyes. Not long afterward, Paul telephoned the dugout. He told Martin: "I've just talked to Cowen, Billy. Reggie is *available*." Not needing to listen further, or so he hoped, Paul hung up. Martin sent Jackson up to pinch-hit in the ninth inning with the Yankees down by two runs. The Stadium crowd numbered 54,940. Jackson drew a fortissimo of boos. The substantial redneck element on the Yankee fan base, often identified a bit simplistically as beer drunks from New Jersey, didn't care for the outspoken and, dammit, snooty black guy. Jackson grounded out. Then Carl Yastrzemski misplayed Willie Randolph's fly into a triple, and Roy White hit a hanging screwball into the left-field seats, tying the score. Jackson came to bat in the eleventh inning with runners on first and second and rocketed the first pitch into right field for a run-scoring single. Reggie (and Gabe Paul) had won a very big game in eleven, 6 to 5. The Yankees went on and swept the Red Sox.

CHAPTER 23

STEINBRENNER: A YANKEE DOODLE DANDY

Long before he became a household name and a television caricature, George Steinbrenner was the subject of a Roger Kahn profile. Kahn found the owner and force behind the New York Yankees to be mercurial, feisty, and obsessive, but also, surprisingly, a lover of fine literature. The article, from Sport *magazine in 1981, won Kahn a best-article-of-the-year award, one of five he has won for his magazine work.*

He stepped from the 1981 Cadillac immaculate in white and blended shades of blue; and the earth rose slightly to meet his feet. "It's him," people said in the sunlit afternoon. "It's George. It's him. Hiya, George."

As he strode toward the little minor-league ballpark at Pompano Beach, a retinue materialized and grew. A crew from the television program "60 Minutes." Yankee officials. Policemen. Ushers. But most of the swarming people were fans.

"Hey, George, would you sign this?" "Hey, George, how about an autograph?" "You really gonna fine Reggie?" "Hey, George, are the Yankees gonna win?'"

He slowed his pace, the better to sign his name on scorecards and the backs of tickets, and uttered pleasantries to the idolaters. His path crossed that of a ballplayer, Bob Watson, the Yankee first baseman, who was headed toward the field. "Isn't anybody under thirty-eight working today?" he asked. Watson, actually a lad of thirty-five, trudged on, ignored by the fans and the television people.

"I'll sign," George said. "I'm glad to sign. Thank you for asking. Hello, son. How's the schoolwork going?"

About him people chattered and beamed, the way people beam in the presence of a superstar, a sun king. George Mitchell Steinbrenner, principal owner of the New York Yankees, basked in his own glory, a happy, restless man.

He is fun and business, charm and fury, a remorseless tyrant in the boardroom and a particularly compassionate friend. "I work twelve-hour days," he says, "and I never ask anybody I hire to work any harder than I do. But I guess I am a sonofabitch to work for. I don't know if I'd want to work for me."

His rages at poor performance have left at least one major-league pitcher weeping in the clubhouse and have driven former business associates to move a thousand miles away. Talking about Steinbrenner's full, ranting wrath, Reggie Jackson cringes like a battered child. "When he really rips me and Gossage and Nettles," Jackson says, "you know how I feel? Screw it. I don't care if we win or lose. I just want to get away." But after Elston Howard, the first of the black Yankees, died last December, Steinbrenner quietly, indeed discreetly, paid all the medical bills.

Like all men of powerful passions, Steinbrenner evokes powerful passions in return. When Al Rosen was president of the Yankees—a limited presidency under Steinbrenner's absolute monarchy—he was afraid that one of their baseball arguments would explode into a fistfight. Although he admired George, Rosen could not continue working for him.

Steinbrenner's anger can be severe and charged with personal expletives, and it knows no time clock. One former Yankee staff man fired several times during Steinbrenner outbursts but always rehired within hours, eventually resigned. Steinbrenner later invited him to lunch and made him a generous offer to return.

"I just can't take those 3 a.m. calls from you anymore," the man said.

Steinbrenner pointed to his own World Series ring. "That," he said, "is the price you pay for this."

The man did not return. The price, he thought, was too high.

"Look," Steinbrenner says, "I'm like a fan, I live with the Yankees and I die with the Yankees. I'm an involved owner, and one way baseball brought itself trouble was with owners who were not involved." His talk is quick, sometimes gruff, always urgent. "I'm an involved owner, and we've finished first four times and won the Series twice since I've been here. Our attendance has gone up for eight consecutive seasons. That's a record."

He is a master at milking the media, at keeping the Yankees in the news. It apparently took him weeks to decide to retire Manager Dick Howser last fall. Meanwhile, Yankee stories won space away from New York's dreary pro football teams, the Giants and the Jets. Last March, when Jackson reported to spring training two days late, Steinbrenner fined him $5,000. Stories about that won space away from the Rangers and the Knickerbockers. Of course, milking the media, like milking a cow, exposes a man to knifing hooves. The press file on Steinbrenner is a harvest of wormwood.

The case for Steinbrenner is nicely made by William Denis Fugazy, a New York entrepreneur best known for the huge limousine service that bears his name. "I call him the Commander," Fugazy says, "and sure he's a powerful guy with strong opinions. But he's a tremendous civic asset, even beyond bringing the Yankees back to life. He's always working for causes, good government, a dozen charities. The charitable work is private with no publicity. The Commander is one tremendous man."

Steinbrenner tries to be careful with the media. By decree his family—a wife and four children—is off-limits to the press. He cooperated with Harry Reasoner on a segment for "60 Minutes," but a friend says George would not have agreed to appear had the interviewer been Mike Wallace.

"George," the man comments, "doesn't need Mike the Knife." It is, however, a bit late for Steinbrenner to lower his strong-jawed profile. He has become a thundering presence, a water buffalo in Bowie Kuhn's patch of summer flowers.

"George Steinbrenner," Dave Winfield mused on a pleasant spring afternoon. "I read more than I know from experience, but I've picked up this. Some love him. Some hate him. Most fear him."

It is surprising to learn that the object of so much intense feeling was once an English major at Williams College, among the maples and white-pine trees of western Massachusetts, and that he wrote his senior thesis on the heroines of Thomas Hardy's novels, whose lust always lay between the lines.

"We're going to be wired for '60 Minutes,'" Steinbrenner said in Florida.

"They want to pick up a little of our banter. It'll be great exposure for you."

Not everything had been proceeding according to plan. I'd wanted to spend a few days with George, watching him at play and at work in three or four of his businesses. I'd have to settle for a few full hours, George had said cheerfully. He really couldn't conduct his business with readers listening in. Now some of the time we did have would be wired into the second most popular television program (after "Dallas") on earth.

"We'll respect anything you want to keep for yourself or use for background," Harry Reasoner promised.

"We work with little wireless transmitters," one of the technicians said. "You'll forget you have them on. We've even used them with First Ladies, and four of them, four presidential wives, actually wore transmitters into the bathroom. You ought to hear those tapes." (This was about the time some in the media were criticizing Steinbrenner's taste.)

George and I settled into a box. On the field the Yankees and the Texas Rangers went through final warm-ups.

"This seems to be the spring of moaning millionaires," I said. "Rudy Carpenter can't afford the Phillies. Is Roy Kroc going broke in San Diego?"

"The day Kroc goes broke, the country goes broke," Steinbrenner said. "And don't worry about the Yankees. We don't need a benefit luncheon."

"Some blame you for the high cost of free agents."

"I didn't start free agency, but as an involved owner I've had to figure out how to live with it. How do I know how much to offer a Jackson, a Winfield? There's some talk with my financial people, some talk with my baseball people, and there's a little bit of intuition.

"Too many noninvolved owners treated baseball like a hobby. Now, understand Marvin Miller of the players association. When he was with the steel union he didn't get publicity because he was a second-row guy, a mastermind. But Miller is more than capable. He's brilliant. What happened when baseball bargained with him? They gave away the house. They locked the barn door after both the horse and the wagon were gone. You can't leave the business of baseball to baseball people. What does a brilliant baseball man necessarily know about business, about who to hire to bargain with Miller?

"The owners, the businessmen, should have been more involved. I'm a damn involved owner with twenty-five years' experience in labor negotiation. The current baseball situation, where certain clubs don't have money problems—well there are ways in which free-agency negotiations could be reopened, but you have to know what you're doing." He did not say it, but clearly George's choice as baseball's best negotiator with Miller is George M. Steinbrenner III.

He glanced up. Doc Medich was starting for the Rangers. "What a fine young man," Steinbrenner said. "I was really pleased to have him on the Yankees." Oscar Gamble reached the young doctor for a soaring three-run homer to right. "Hey, Oscar," George bellowed in delight. "Attaway, Oscar."

A young Yankee right-hander named Gene Nelson began blowing away the Rangers. George watched and signed more autographs and went from topic to topic with great agility. On shipbuilding: "How much is a pound of steel going to cost? If I make a mistake it can cost a million dollars."

Bowie Kuhn: "He's going to become a good commissioner. Sometimes he acts pompous, but he's a smart man, a good leader. There's been talk that some people want to replace him and that they expect me to help. Wrong. I am a supporter of the commissioner."

The Yankees: "I walk out of a hotel in New York and my energy gets going. It's a battler's city, battles all day long. My ego feeds on that competition. I love it. I want the team to be like the city. I didn't think they battled hard enough in the playoffs against Kansas City last year, and that's why I got worked up. After we lost the third game I called a staff meeting for eight thirty the next morning. Work! Battle!

"And owning the Yankees is just unique. I've had offers, big offers, to sell the team. No way. Owning the Yankees is like owning the *Mona Lisa.*"

I was beginning to run short of breath. That happens, of course, when you talk long and hard and fast. With Steinbrenner, you run out of breath listening.

The roots of all this hammering intensity lie in a prosperous Cleveland suburb, Bay Village, where Steinbrenner was born into comfortable, sedate circumstances in 1930. The family business, Kinsman Marine Transit, a Great Lakes shipping company, dates from the 1840s. Fireworks, loud and flamboyant as a Yankee press conference, accompanied George's arrival. His birth date: July 4.

As a boy, George went without an allowance. His father, Henry, a graduate of MIT, was severe and disciplined. He bought his son a variety of chickens and ordered him to look after them. "You can make your spending money selling the eggs." The boy worked tirelessly and prospered. He called his egg business the George Company.

To this day Steinbrenner can and will describe the differences that distinguish a guinea hen from a Plymouth Rock and from a Buff Wine Dot. At thirteen, when he was shipped to Culver Military Academy in Indiana, Steinbrenner was ordered to sell the George Company to his two sisters. "I don't remember the price," he says, "but it must have been pretty good. My sisters still don't talk to me." Other sources report that it was $50 cash.

At Culver, George played end, ran hurdles, and won an award for all-around excellence. He still expresses abiding respect for military men. "He's the only guy I know," says Bill Fugazy, "who walks around humming the theme from Patton."

At Williams, one of New England's prestigious Little Three colleges, George ran varsity hurdles and developed a fondness for Hardy, Shelley, and Keats, and a passion for Shakespeare. He became president of the glee club. He wrote a sports column for the Williams Record. "As a columnist I was not a knocker," he says.

He spent his service hitch in peacetime as a general's aide in Columbus. After that, had George stayed with family tradition, he would have gone into the shipping business and settled into a life of disciplined, affluent obscurity. But sport tugged at him as strongly as it tugged at Stan Musial or, for that matter, Reggie Jackson. It was something clean and exciting that attracted crowds. It was a way to break new ground, to establish, in the current phrase, an identity. For George, who actually favors blue, sport seems to be something like that beckoning green light Gatsby saw and sought on a dock he could not reach.

He briefly coached high school football and basketball in Columbus and in 1955 signed as an assistant to Lou Saban, then head football coach at Northwestern and now Rosen's successor as president of the Yankees. Steinbrenner moved on to Purdue as backfield coach, but life as a Big Ten assistant was limited, insecure, and poorly paid. Besides, his family was calling him back to the Great Lakes.

As the giant steel companies acquired fleets of their own, Kinsman Transit ran into buffeting days. After three years "when my father and I really beat the bushes for business," Kinsman signed a contract with Jones & Laughlin guaranteeing a considerable annual tonnage.

George had helped rescue the family business; he was then thirty.

Still, sport beckoned. Against family advice, Steinbrenner borrowed and scratched and organized a $125,000 partnership that bought an industrial basketball team, the Cleveland Pipers. But with pro basketball beginning to rise, the industrial league was doomed. The Pipers won two championships and went bankrupt, with George shouting and scrambling to cover his payroll.

He turned his energy back towards the waters and became part of a group that purchased the American Ship Building Company, a sprawling enterprise with shipyards in Tampa, Cleveland, and half a dozen other cities. American Ship prospered, but it wasn't sport. "Actually, George was trying to buy the Cleveland Indians," recalls his longtime associate Marsh Samuel, "but Vernon Stouffer, who owned the Indians, was taking his time on deciding on selling. Patience has never been George's long suit. Then the Yankee thing came up."

On January 3, 1973, it was announced that a group headed by George M. Steinbrenner of Cleveland had purchased the Yankees from CBS for $10 million, or about $3 million less than CBS paid in 1964.

No one has found a better bargain in sports. The Yankees, purchased for a reported $10 million in 1973, showed a net profit of about $7.5 million in 1980.

Why would CBS sell at a loss? The late 1960s had been an inglorious Yankee era. The team finished tenth in 1966, and on one September day that year the Yankees played the White Sox at the old Stadium before a crowd of 413 paid.

The finest achievement of Michael Burke, who ran the team for the CBS conglomerate, was convincing New York City politicians to rebuild Yankee Stadium. Cost overruns were enormous, but today we have the New York Yankees, not the New Jersey Meadowland Yankees.

"About a year before the sale," Burke says, "it became apparent that Willie Paley [the chairman of CBS] would want to sell the club. He asked if I'd be interested in putting together a syndicate, and I went about New York talking to people, including some financial exotics. The interest was zero. Absolute zip. But Gabe Paul learned what I was doing and put me in touch with George. We had lunch and we agreed to try to buy the team together. George spoke to certain people . . . and we came up with the $10 million."

Burke and Steinbrenner also agreed to run the club together. "But it was early apparent," Burke says, "that George and I could not be compatible, so we elected to part in an adult fashion." Burke, who retained a 9 percent interest in the Yankees, announced his withdrawal from the day-to-day operations of the club with great style. He quoted lines from a William Butler Yeats poem called "An Irish Airman Foresees His Death."

In the plays of Shakespeare, Steinbrenner's favorite dramatist, triumph and tragedy work in magical alternation. So it is in Steinbrenner's life. Before he had time really to enjoy the ball club he had won, the *Mona Lisa* he had found in the South Bronx, he was caught in a backwash of Watergate.

Steinbrenner is an independent Democrat. Among his good friends today are Ted Kennedy and [Democratic congressman] Tip O'Neill. At Cleveland in 1969 and '70 Steinbrenner organized fund-raising dinners for Democratic congressional candidates and, George being George, raised almost $2 million. Then as the 1972 presidential election approached, President Nixon's infamous men, angered by his fund-raising for Democrats, sprang at him from all sides. They threatened an antitrust investigation of American Ship Building. His steamers might lose vital port licenses. Steinbrenner, his companies, and all those close to him, would undergo Internal Revenue audits that would be "memorable."

Steinbrenner decided to buy his way out. He personally gave $75,000 to CREEP—the Committee to Re-elect the President—and gave "bonuses" of $25,000 each to eight American Ship executives. The bonuses, also, were donated to CREEP. That sort of forced contribution is illegal, although not unheard of in American executive suites, according to Steinbrenner associates.

The $275,000 was not enough. Nixon's people wanted whatever dirt Steinbrenner had discovered as a Democratic fund-raiser. George kept silent. In April of 1973 he was indicted on fourteen counts alleging conspiracies to violate the campaign-funding law. Still silent, he pleaded guilty to two of the charges a year later and paid a $15,000 fine. Kuhn suspended him for the season of 1975 but let him return to baseball in 1976. Coincidentally, that was the year in which the remodeled Yankee Stadium opened. Less coincidentally, that was the year in which the Yankees won the pennant for the first time since 1964.

Under the benign Florida sun, I said to Steinbrenner: "The conviction means that you can't run for president."

Steinbrenner's response was so quick that the same thought must have previously crossed his mind. "Unless," he said, grinning, "I get a pardon."

His performance as Commander of the Yankees has been innovative, tireless, impulsive, loud, and most of all effective. He was the first man to react to the possibilities, as opposed to the perils, of free agency. He has expanded the Yankee scouting program and brought a measure of intelligence to the farm systems. By irrational tradition, minor-league clubs have generally been supervised by one man, the manager, who pitches batting practice, teaches hitting, works with infielders and outfielders, and in some instances drives the team bus. All Yankee farms now, from Triple A Columbus to Paintsville, Kentucky, in a rookie league, employ at least two full-time coaches, in addition to a manager.

Yankee minor leaguers, who are supposed to be learning the professional game, now have reasonable teaching staffs to help them. No fewer than six of the Yankees' seven farm teams won the pennant in 1980.

How do you get results like that? You learn the game. You hire the best people and you drive them as you drive yourself; drive, drive until your staff works harder than anyone else's staff.

Up close some consequences are unsettling. A Yankee secretary, asked recently what kind of sandwich she wanted at her desk for lunch, abruptly replied, "I can't eat," she said. "He's here. Mister Steinbrenner is here."

A new backwash threatens Steinbrenner these days. Those who see baseball as an American art form profess to be offended by his fortissimo chatter. I believe baseball is an art form, and I believe major-league baseball is a business. Ten years ago the business was in trouble. So William Paley felt when he elected to sell the Yankees at a loss.

Now, among the moaning millionaires, franchises sell for ever-greater sums. The one executive who shows us all what you can do with a franchise is George Michael Steinbrenner of Bay Village, Ohio, Tampa, Florida, and the South Bronx.

At Pompano the Yankees defeated the Rangers 9–2. George signed a final autograph. Next day Reggie Jackson would ask what Steinbrenner had said. "He didn't knock you, Reggie," I said. He looked surprised—and disappointed.

"I have some ship business in Tampa tomorrow," Steinbrenner told me, "but I'll be back the next day and we can spend more time together. Don't be a stranger. Is your hotel room okay? I really like your books. Don't forget to bring your kids to the stadium. They'll be my guests. It will be great spending more time together."

I am trying to give a sense of what one feels like sitting beside him. Unfettered energy. A whirlwind. An earth force, lightly filtered through a personality.

The winter had been cold, and my new novel was proceeding at a slow, strangely exhausting tempo. Now the world excited me anew. If Steinbrenner survived bankruptcy in basketball and Nixon's troops and still found his *Mona Lisa*, is there any reason why the rest of us can't find our *Mona Lisa*, too?

Meeting tomorrow, 8:30 a.m.

Neckties. Jackets. Pressed pants. (No jeans, please.)

Have your presentation cogent and complete.

Be prepared to work harder than you've ever worked before.

Work! Battle! Or be prepared to work for someone else.

PART VI

HEROES OFF THE FIELD

CHAPTER 24

JACKIE ROBINSON: LIKE NO ONE ELSE

Roger Kahn came to know—and love—Jackie Robinson when he covered the Dodgers in the early 1950s, when they were in the process of winning six pennants in Robinson's ten years with the team. Kahn knew that Robinson "could hit and bunt and steal and run," as he wrote in The Boys of Summer. *"He wanted passionately to win." More important, Kahn learned that the man who broke baseball's color line in 1947 "bore the burden of a pioneer, and the weight made him stronger. If one can be certain of anything in baseball, it is that we shall not look upon his like again." Kahn recollected the ten years of Robinson's major-league career in this 1955 article for* Sport *magazine.*

When the Dodgers were still in Brooklyn and were playing at home, Jackie Robinson might visit the United Nations on a Monday afternoon and discuss sociology with a delegate. "There is still a little prejudice in baseball," he would remark, "but we have reached the point where any Negro with major-league ability can play in the major leagues." That Monday night, Robinson might travel to Ebbets Field and discuss beanballs with an opposing pitcher. "Listen, you gutless obscenity," he was apt to suggest, "throw that obscene baseball at my head again and I'm gonna cut your obscene legs in half." Jackie could converse with Eleanor Roosevelt and curse at Sal Maglie with equal intensity and skill.

During Robinson's ten years in major-league baseball, he was known in many ways by many people.

Because in the beginning Robinson endured outrage and vituperation with an almost magic mixture of humility and pride, there were those who knew him as a saint.

Because later Robinson fought mudslinging with mudslinging, there were those who knew him as a troublemaker.

Because Robinson destroyed baseball's shameful racial barrier, there are those who know him as a hero.

Because in the ten seasons Robinson turned not one shade lighter in color, there are those who know him as a villain.

The world of baseball is essentially simple. The men in the light uniforms—the home team—are the good guys. They may beat little old ladies for sport, they may turn down requests to visit children in hospitals, but on the field, just so long as their uniforms are white, they are the good guys. The fellows in the dark uniforms are bad. They may defend the little old ladies and spend half their time with the sick, but as soon as they put on gray traveling uniforms, they become the bad guys.

The one modern player who did not fit the traditional pattern is Robinson. He was booed while wearing his white uniform at Ebbets Field. He was cheered as a visiting player in Crosley Field, Cincinnati, or Busch Stadium, St. Louis. Robinson was a marvelously effective Dodger ballplayer but, first and foremost, he always remained, as he still does to this day, the Negro who opened the major leagues to his race.

As a ballplayer, Robinson created one overwhelming impression. "He comes to win," Leo Durocher summed it up. "He beats you."

It was not as a Dodger star but rather as a man that Jackie aroused controversy. Ask one hundred people about Robinson as an individual, and you are likely to get one hundred different impressions.

"They told me when I went to Brooklyn that Robinson would be tough to handle," said Chuck Dressen, who managed the Dodgers from 1951 through 1953. "I don't know. There never was an easier guy for me to manage, and there never was nothing I asked that he didn't do. Hit-and-run. Bunt. Anything. He was the greatest player I ever managed."

Walter O'Malley, who replaced Branch Rickey as Dodger president in 1951 but did not replace Rickey as Robinson's personal hero, has a different view. "Robinson," he once insisted in an off-guard moment, "is always conscious of publicity and is always seeking publicity. Maybe it's a speech he's about to make, or a sale at his store, but when Robinson gets his name in the headlines, you can be sure there's a reason."

"I'll say this for Jack," Duke Snider declared. "When he believes something is right, he'll fight for it as hard as anybody I ever saw."

"I got fed up with Robinson fights and Robinson incidents and Robinson explanations," admitted a widely syndicated columnist. "He's boring. I heaved a great sigh of relief when he got out of baseball. Now I don't have to bother with him any more."

"When I first came up, I was pretty scared by the big leagues," Carl Erskine recalls. "I remember how friendly Jackie was. I was just a kid. It's something you appreciate a whole lot."

"He was always the loudest man around," an umpire said. "No, maybe Durocher was just as bad. But Robinson had to second-guess every call and keep his big mouth going all the time."

"I've got to admire him," Ralph Kiner said. "He had a tough time when he was younger, and he was a pretty rough character. That's no secret out on the coast. But he got over all that. You have to hand it to Robinson. He has come a long way, and he's taken a hell of a lot, but he's never stopped."

On the Brooklyn Dodgers, his last few seasons, Jackie held a peculiar position. In point of years he was an elder statesman, and in point of spirit he was a club leader. Yet he had no truly close friends among either white or Negro Dodgers.

Jackie is an inveterate card player, and when the Dodgers traveled, this passion seemed to bring him near players with whom he couldn't have much else in common. Frequently he played with Billy Loes, a pitcher who walked out of the blackboard jungle and into the major leagues. Loes is interested in girls and, to a lesser degree, in baseball; he is interested in little else. Jackie's conversations with him occasionally ran two sentences long.

"Boy, am I havin' lousy luck," Loes might offer.

"Your deal, Billy," was a typical Robinson reply.

Jackie roomed with Jim Gilliam, the young second baseman who usually has less to say than any other Dodger. Even when he might have roomed with Joe Black, who, like himself, is a fluent and fairly sophisticated college man, he roomed with Gilliam. Robinson and Gilliam, in a sense, were strictly business associates rather than friends, but Gilliam, during a burst of conversation, was able to cast a great deal of light on Robinson's relationship with other Negroes both in and out of baseball. "Some of my friends, when they heard I roomed with Jack, they say 'Boy, you room with him? Ain't he stuck up?'" Gilliam reported. "I tell them the truth. He was wonderful to me. He told me about the pitchers and stuff like that, and how much I should tip and where I should eat and all that. He wasn't stuck up at all."

Inside the Brooklyn clubhouse, Robinson's position was more of what one would expect. He was a dominant figure. His locker was next to that of Gil Hodges. Next to Hodges's locker was a space occupied by a small gas heater, and on the other side of that sat Pee Wee Reese. As captain, Reese was assigned the only locker in the entire clubhouse that had a door.

Duke Snider was nearby, and Reese's locker was one of the gathering points in the clubhouse. (The television set was another, and that wasn't far from Robinson's locker, either.) During clubhouse conversations, Jackie, like Reese and Erskine, was a club leader.

In many ways Jackie, after ten years, was the natural captain of the Dodgers. He was the team's most aggressive ballplayer, and it has been suggested that had Robinson been white he would have ended up the captain. Reese was the most respected of all Brooklyn players, but he didn't have Robinson's fire.

Right up to the end of Robinson's time, a few Dodgers made occasional remarks about color. "Don't you think they're gonna take over baseball in ten years?" a player challenged a newspaperman after a long and obviously fruitless conversation. "They can run faster; they'll run us white guys right out of the game." The player spoke sincerely. He had been happy to have Robinson on his side, but he was afraid that Robinson represented a threat. This ambivalent feeling was not uncommon on the Dodgers.

"The players were the easiest part of all," Jackie himself insisted once when reviewing his struggle. "The press and fans made things a whole lot tougher." Robinson tends to say what he wishes were true and offer his wish as truth. The resentment of players obviously was among the most difficult obstacles he had to surmount. Robinson's introduction into the major leagues prompted Dixie Walker to ask that he be traded, and brought the St. Louis Cardinals to the verge of a player strike. A great deal of player resentment against the Negroes still remains, and in Jackie's case, his success made it even stronger. Naturally, players who resented Robinson did not tell him so. Public proclamations of bigotry have virtually ended in baseball. Integration is a fact, and Jackie Robinson did more than anybody else to make it so.

We talked one morning on a bumpy bus that carried the Dodgers from the Chase Hotel in St. Louis to the city's airport. Robinson was permitted to stay at the Chase for his last few seasons. It is interesting to note that when the hotel management first suggested to the club that it was time the Negro players checked in at the Chase along with the rest of the Dodgers, certain qualifications were laid down. "They'll have to eat in their rooms," the hotel official said, "and they'll have to agree not to hang around the lobbies and the other public rooms." Told about the offer, Roy Campanella said he would pass it up. Roy wasn't going to stay anywhere he wasn't wanted. Don Newcombe, Jim Gilliam, and Joe Black agreed with Roy. But Jackie Robinson said he guessed the terms were all right with him, he would stay at the Chase. It was a wedge, anyway. So he did, and within an amazingly short time the hotel lifted all the bars and quietly passed the word that Jackie should consider himself just another guest and go where he pleased in the hotel and eat where everybody else ate. Jackie, eight years after he hit the big leagues, long after the "pioneering" days were supposed to be ended, was still willing to humble himself in order to advance the larger cause. Another barrier came down. Wherever Jackie goes, he encounters reminders of barriers that no longer exist because of himself.

"We feel," he began, "that . . ."

"Who is we?"

"Rachel and me," Robinson explained. Rachel, his wife, played a tremendous role in the ten years of Jackie Robinson.

"Anyway," he said, "we feel that those barriers haven't been knocked down because of just us. We've had help. It isn't even right to say I broke the color line. Mr. Rickey did. I played ball. Mr. Rickey made it possible for me to play."

Of all the men Robinson met in baseball, he considers Rickey "the finest, in a class by himself." Before the 1952 World Series, Jackie made a point of specifying that he wanted to win the Series for two people: "Rae and Mr. Rickey." Rickey was then general manager of the Pittsburgh Pirates, and O'Malley had succeeded him as Dodger president. "But I wanted to let Mr. Rickey know where he stood in my book," Jackie explained.

Robinson was carrying two large packages on his lap, juggling them as the bus swayed. "I don't think I can be any more contented than I am now," he said. "I've been awfully lucky. I think we've been blessed." He nodded toward the packages. "These are for Rae. Presents. We're very close. Probably it's because of the importance of what I've had to do. We've just gotten closer and closer. A problem comes up for me, I ask Rae. A problem for her, she asks me."

"What does she say about all the fights you get into?"

Jackie grinned. This had come up before. "Whenever I get in a real bad argument, I don't care about O'Malley or anything like that. I'm kinda worried about coming home. What's Rae gonna say? My real judge of anything is my family relations. That's the most important. The house, you know, it wasn't so important to me. Rae, it's something she always wanted for the kids. It's no real mansion. I mean there's only four bedrooms."

"Do you think you get involved in too many incidents?"

"If I stayed in a shell," Robinson said, "personally I could be maybe 50 percent better off in the minds of the little people. You know, the people that feel I should mind my place. But people that I know who aren't little, you know, people who are big in their minds, I've lost nothing by being aggressive. I mean that's the way I am, and am I supposed to try to act different because I'm Negro? I've lost nothing being myself. Here in St. Louis, you know how much progress in human relations we've made? Aggressiveness hasn't hurt."

"Suppose, Jack, you were to start in again. Would you be less aggressive? Would you act differently?"

Around Robinson on the bus, his teammates chattered among themselves. None bothered to eavesdrop. "I'll tell you one thing that would be different," Jackie said. "I sort of had a chip in the beginning. I was looking for things. Maybe in the early years I kept to myself more than I should have because of that chip. I think maybe I'd be more—what's the word?—outgoing. Yeah. I know that. I'd try and make friends quicker."

Jackie looked at his shoes, then glanced out the bus window. It was a factory neighborhood. The airport was still twenty minutes away. "I wouldn't be different about aggressiveness if I was doing it over again," he said. "I guess I'm an aggressive guy." Robinson stopped as if he were waiting for a refutation. "Funny thing," he said when none was offered, "about this whole business. A lot of times you meet white fellows from the South who never had a chance to mix. You find them more friendly than a lot of northerners. It's the northerners sometimes who make the fuss about aggressiveness."

The bus pulled onto a concrete highway and, quite suddenly, the bouncing stopped. The sun had risen higher, and heat was beginning to settle on St. Louis. It was going to be good to escape. There was only one other question I wanted to ask Jackie. His answer was not really satisfactory.

"The toughest stretch since I came into baseball?" he said. "I guess it was that Williams thing. I ran into Davey Williams at first base, and there I was right in the middle of a big obscene mess again, and I figured when I get home Rachel's gonna be sore and what the hell am I doing this for? I don't need it. I don't need the money. What for?" Jackie sometimes gets excited when he recalls something that is important to him, and he seemed about to get angry all over again. Sal Maglie had thrown at a few Brooklyn hitters one game in May, and Robinson bunted to get Maglie within spiking distance. Maglie stayed at the mound and, instead, Davey Williams covered first after Whitey Lockman fielded the bunt. Jackie was out easily, but he bowled over Williams as he crossed the base. Thereafter Maglie threw no more beanballs, and the Dodgers won the game, but Robinson, praised by some and damned by others, was a storm center again. As he thought of it, his anger rose.

"Wasn't it tougher in the early years?" I asked quickly.

"No," Jackie said. "In the early years I never thought of quitting. There was too much to fight for. With that Williams thing, I was fighting for nothing except to win. That was the toughest stretch I ever had to go through. I mean it." If Robinson's evaluation of the Williams affair was valid, then he is the recipient of a lot of misplaced credit. Actually, his evaluation was wrong. The hardest thing Robinson ever had to do in baseball was the first thing he had to do—just be the first Negro in modern history to play organized ball. Almost willingly, he seems to have forgotten a great deal of his difficult past. Rarely now is there talk in baseball of the enormously courageous thing which Jackie accomplished.

On a train between Milwaukee and Chicago, Rube Walker, a reserve Dodger catcher from Lenoir, North Carolina, was talking about beanballs. "I don't like 'em nohow," he said.

"But what we see isn't so bad," said Dixie Howell, the Dodgers' number-three catcher, who lived in Louisville. "I was at Montreal when Robinson first broke in. Man, you never saw nothin' like that. Every time he come up, he'd go down. Man, did they throw at him."

"Worst you ever saw?" asked Walker.

"By a long shot," Howell said.

Ballplayers are not demonstrative, and Walker did not react further. This was in a dining car, and his next words were merely "pass the salt, please." But he and Howell felt a matter-of-fact professional admiration for one of Jackie Robinson's many talents—his ability to get up from a knockdown pitch unfrightened.

To make a major point of a North Carolinian and a Kentuckian sharing admiration for a Negro would be wrong. After Jackie Robinson's ten years, Walker and Howell are not unique. The point is that after the ten years, Howell still regards the beanballs directed at Robinson by International League pitchers during the 1946 season as the most vicious he has ever seen. Jackie himself never mentions this. He cannot have forgotten it, nor is it likely that he has thrust the memory into his subconscious. But he would like to forget it.

It is no small part of the ten years of Jackie Robinson that nobody any longer bothers to count the number of Negro players who appear on the field in a big-league game. There once was much discussion of what John Lardner called "the 50-per-cent color line." Branch Rickey described it as "the saturation point." When a major-league club first attempted to field a team of five Negroes and four white players it was whispered, there would be trouble. There seemed to be an enormous risk in attempting to topple white numerical supremacy on a major-league diamond. Today the Giants can start Sam Jones, Willie Mays, Orlando Cepeda, Willie McCovey, and Willie Kirkland without so much as a passing comment.

In October 1945, William O'Dwyer was mayor of New York City, and Harry Truman was a rookie president. Dwight D. Eisenhower was wondering what new field he should try, because World War II had been over for two months. On the twenty-third day of the month, Branch Rickey announced that the Brooklyn Dodgers had signed a twenty-six-year-old Negro named Jackie Robinson and had assigned him to play for their Montreal farm team.

On the twenty-fourth day of October, the late William G. Bramham, commissioner of minor-league baseball, had a statement to make. "Father Divine will have to look to his laurels," Bramham told a reporter, "for we can expect Rickey Temple to be in the course of construction in Harlem soon." Exercising iron self-control, Bramham called Rickey no name worse than a carpetbagger. "Nothing to the contrary appearing in the rules that I know of," Bramham said with open anger, "Robinson's contract must be promulgated just as any other."

The day he announced the signing, Rickey arranged for Jackie to meet the press. "Just be yourself," he told him. "Simply say that you are going to do the best you can and let it go at that." Since more than twenty-five newspapermen flocked to the press conference, Robinson could not let it go at that.

"He answered a dozen questions," wrote Al Parsley in the *Montreal Herald*, "with easy confidence but no cocksureness. His was no easy chore . . . he was a lone black man entering a room where the gathering, if not frankly hostile, was at least belligerently indifferent." Robinson handled his chore splendidly; press reaction was generally favorable, although frank hostility was evident throughout much of baseball and in some newspaper columns.

Alvin Garner, the president of the Texas League, announced: "I'm positive you'll never see any Negro players on any teams in the South as long as the Jim Crow laws are in force."

Happy Chandler, commissioner of baseball, refused to comment.

Clark Griffith, president of the Washington Senators, who had long ignored clamor urging him to hire a Negro, suddenly accused Rickey of attempting to become "dictator of Negroes in baseball"!

Jimmy Powers, sports editor of the *New York Daily News*, a tabloid with the largest circulation of any newspaper in America, predicted: "Robinson will not make the grade in the big leagues this year or next . . . Robinson is a 1000–1 shot."

Red Smith, writing in the now dead *Philadelphia Record*, summarized: "It has become apparent that not everybody who prattles of tolerance and racial equality has precisely the same understanding of the terms."

There was precious little prattling about tolerance in Florida that winter. In late February, Robinson flew from his California home to Daytona Beach, where the Montreal Royals were to train after a week of early drills at Sanford, a smaller town twenty miles distant. Jackie was cheerfully received by newspapermen, Dodger officials, and Clay Hopper, the Mississippi-born manager of the Royals, but he was received in the established southern tradition by the white citizens of Sanford. After two days of practice at Sanford, Robinson was forced to return to Daytona Beach. Before running him out of town, Sanford civic groups explained: "We don't want no Nigras mixing with no whites here."

At Daytona Beach, Jackie lived with a Negro family and encountered only isolated resistance. When the Royals traveled to Deland for an exhibition game with Indianapolis some weeks later, he was given another taste of democracy as it was practiced in Florida during mid-March of 1946. As Robinson slid across home plate in the first inning of the game, a local policeman bolted onto the field.

"Get off the field right now," he ordered Robinson, "or I'm putting you in jail!"

Robinson claims that his first reaction was to laugh, so ludicrous did the situation seem. But he did not laugh. Then, as always in the South, Robinson had attracted a huge crowd, and as he faced the policeman, the crowd rose to its feet. The Indianapolis players, in the field, stood stark still, watching. Then Jackie turned and walked toward the dugout, and Clay Hopper emerged from it.

"What's wrong?" Hopper asked.

"We ain't havin' Nigras mix with white boys in this town," the policeman said. "You can't change our way of livin'. Nigras and white, they can't sit together and they can't play together and you know damn well they can't get married together."

Hopper did not answer.

"Tell that Nigra I said to git," the policeman said. And Jackie left.

Spring training ended on April 14, and when it did, the burden of living in the South was lifted from Jackie's shoulders. He had made the team, and when the 1946 International League season began, his job was pretty much limited to the field. Jackie had played shortstop for the Kansas City Monarchs when Clyde Sukeforth scouted him for Rickey in 1945, and he had tried out for the Royals as a shortstop. But the Royals owned a capable shortstop named Stan Breard, and that, coupled with some questions about the strength of Robinson's arm, prompted a switch. As the 1946 season opened, Jackie Robinson was a second baseman.

This was the season of the beanballs Dixie Howell remembers. It was the season in which a Syracuse player held up a black cat and shouted, "Hey, Robinson! Here's one of your relatives!" It was the season in which Baltimore players greeted Jackie with vile names and profanity.

But it was also the season in which beanballs so affected Robinson that he batted .349. And rather than answer the Syracuse player with words, Robinson replied with a double that enabled him to score the winning run. Rather than match names with the Baltimore players, he stole home one night and drew an ovation from the Baltimore fans. Probably 1946 was baseball's finest year, for in 1946 it was proved that democracy can work in baseball when it is given a chance.

At times during the 1946 season, Branch Rickey would travel from Brooklyn to Montreal for talks with Robinson.

"Always," Rickey once said, "for as long as you are in baseball, you must conduct yourself as you are doing now. Always you will be on trial. That is the cross you must bear."

"I remember the meeting when Rickey said that," a man in the Dodger organization said. "Jackie agreed, too." The man chuckled. "I guess Jack's sort of changed his mind over the years." But it wasn't until the place of Negroes in baseball was assured that Robinson's conduct changed.

Late in the 1946 season, the Dodgers found themselves involved in a close race with the St. Louis Cardinals, and there was pressure applied to Rickey to promote Robinson in August and September. For a while Rickey held his peace, but finally he announced: "Robinson is the property of Montreal, and that is where he will stay. Montreal is going to be involved in a playoff, and we owe it to our Montreal fans to keep Robinson there." Montreal, with Robinson, won the Little World Series. The Dodgers, without him, lost a pennant playoff to the Cardinals in two consecutive games.

There was little connection between the reason Rickey gave for not promoting Robinson and the reasons that actually existed. As far as he could, Rickey wanted to make Robinson's task easy. To do that he needed time. All through the winter of 1946–47, Rickey met with leaders of the American Negro community. Just as Robinson would be on trial as a major leaguer, he explained, so would Negroes be as major-league fans. Working directly with Negro groups and indirectly through Negro leaders, Rickey worked to make sure there would be as little friction in the grandstand as possible. While barring Negroes from play, owners had not refused to allow them to buy tickets, of course, and the idea of Negroes in big-league stadiums was nothing new. Yet, with Robinson on the Dodgers, a whole new set of circumstances applied to the old idea. Rickey's caution was rewarded in 1947, and in Robinson's first major-league season there was not one grandstand incident worthy of note.

In another foresighted move, Rickey shifted the Dodger and Montreal training camps to Havana, where the air was free of the fierce racial tensions that throbbed in America's South. Finally Rickey did not place Robinson on the Dodger roster before spring training started. He wanted the Dodgers first to see Jackie and to recognize what a fine ballplayer he was. Then, Rickey hoped, there would be a sort of mass demand from Dodger players: "Promote Robinson." This just was not to be. Leo Durocher, who was then managing the Dodgers, is a man totally devoid of racial prejudice, but some of Durocher's athletes thought differently.

Dixie Walker wanted to be traded and wanted other Dodgers to join with him in protest against Robinson. Eddie Stanky wasn't sure. Happily, Walker found few recruits, and his evil influence was countered by that of Pee Wee Reese, a Kentucky gentleman. "The first time I heard Robinson had been signed," Reese said, "I thought, what position does he play? Then I found out he was a shortstop and I figured, damn it, there are nine positions on the field and this guy has got to be a shortstop like me. Then I figured some more. Maybe there'd be room for both of us on the team. What then? What would the people down around home say about me playing with a colored boy? I figured maybe they wouldn't like it, and then I figured something else. The hell with anyone that didn't like it. I didn't know Robinson, but I knew he deserved a chance, same as anybody else. It just didn't make any difference what anybody else had to say."

While the Dodgers trained in the city of Havana, Montreal drilled at Havana Military Academy, fifteen miles away. The team was quartered at the school dormitory, but Robinson, who had been accompanied by a Negro pitcher named John Wright during 1946 and now was one of four Negroes in the Brooklyn organization, was booked into a Havana hotel. This meant thirty miles of travel daily, and Robinson, unable to understand the reason for a Jim Crow pattern in Cuba, asked Rickey about it. "I can't afford to take a chance and have a single incident occur," Rickey answered. "This training session must be perfectly smooth."

For two weeks Montreal played exhibitions with a Dodger "B" squad, and then the Royals and the Dodger regulars flew to Panama for a series of exhibitions. Shortly before the trip, Mel Jones, then business manager of the Royals, handed Robinson a first-baseman's mitt. "Listen,"

Robinson said, "I want to play second base. Didn't I do all right there last year?" Jones said he was sorry. "Just passing an order down from the boss," he said. "Mr. Rickey wants you at first base." Robinson did not do badly at first base in the Panama series, and in the seven games he batted .625 and stole seven bases. This was the demonstration Rickey had awaited. Unprejudiced Dodgers said they were impressed. Prejudiced Dodgers insisted that they were not. "I've seen hot-hittin' bushers before," one said. After the series the teams flew back to Cuba, and late one night Rickey passed along word to Robinson that on April 10 he was to become a Dodger. Eddie Stanky was the Dodger second baseman. Robinson would have to play first.

Happy Chandler's suspension of Leo Durocher had taken the spotlight away from Robinson by the time April 10 arrived, and in retrospect Jackie insists he was just as glad to have a respite from publicity. The Dodgers had not asked for his promotion, and as a whole their reception was cool. Robinson in turn remained aloof.

Jack has dark memories of 1947. He was reading in the club car of a train once while several other Dodgers played poker. Hugh Casey, the pitcher, was having a hard time winning a pot, and finally he got up from the table and walked over to Robinson. Without a word Casey rubbed Robinson's head, then turned and went back to his card game.

In 1947, Burt Shotton, who replaced Durocher, put Robinson second in the Brooklyn batting order. On several occasions Dixie Walker hit home runs with Robinson on base, but at no time did Jackie follow baseball custom and shake Walker's hand at home plate. "I wasn't sure if he'd take my hand," Robinson said, "and I didn't want to provoke anything."

In 1947 the Philadelphia Phillies, under Ben Chapman, rode Robinson so hard that Commissioner Chandler interceded.

But there are other memories of 1947 for Robinson; more pleasant ones. Jeep Handley, a Philadelphia infielder, apologized for Chapman's name-calling. Clyde Sukeforth, a coach under Shotton, never once left Robinson's corner. Hank Greenberg told him: "Let's have a talk. There are a few things I've learned down through the years that can help make it easier for you."

One player on the Chicago Cubs attempted to organize a strike against Robinson, but was unsuccessful. The situation on the St. Louis

Cardinals was more serious. Only splendid work by Stanley Woodward, a magnificent newspaperman who was sports editor of the *New York Herald Tribune*, brought the story to light. Only forthright work by Ford Frick, the president of the National League who has since become baseball commissioner, killed the Cardinal strike aborning.

The original Cardinal plan, as exposed by Woodward, called for a strike on May 6, date of the team's first game against the Dodgers. "Subsequently," Woodward wrote, "the St. Louis players conceived the idea of a general strike within the National League on a certain date." An uncompromising mandate from Frick to the players who were threatening to strike went like this: "If you do this, you will be suspended from the league. You will find that the friends you think you have in the press box will not support you, that you will be outcasts. I do not care if half the league strikes. All will be suspended. . . . This is the United States of America and one citizen has as much right to play as any other."

If, in all the ten years of Jackie Robinson, there was a single moment when the success of his mission became assured, then it was the instant Frick issued this directive. It is impossible to order people to be tolerant, but once the price of intolerance becomes too high, the ranks of the bigots tend to grow slim.

For Robinson, 1947 was very much like 1946. He never argued with an umpire. When Lenny Merullo, a Chicago infielder, kneed him, Jackie checked the punch he wanted to throw. When Ewell Blackwell stopped pitching long enough to call him a long series of names, Robinson said only: "Come on. Throw the ball." Then he singled.

But gradually the web of tension in which Robinson performed began to loosen. In the spring of 1948, the Ku Klux Klan futilely warned him not to play in Atlanta. But by the summer of '48, Robinson had relaxed enough to argue with an umpire. This was in Pittsburgh, and he was joined by Clyde Sukeforth. The two argued so violently that they were thrown out of the game.

Robinson became a major-league second baseman in 1948, but, except for an appearance before the House Committee on Un-American Activities, it was not a notable year for him. Called to Congress to refute Paul Robeson's statement that American Negroes would never fight against the Soviet Union, Robinson delivered an eloquent speech.

Rickey and Lester Granger, head of the Urban League, a National Negro organization, helped him write it, and applause came from all sides. On the field, however, Robinson slumped. He had grown fat over the winter, and not until 1949 was Jackie to regain top form.

The Dodgers finished third in 1948, but in 1949, when Robinson won the batting championship and a most valuable player award, they won the pennant. By '49 Robinson felt free to criticize umpires whenever the spirit moved him, and by '50 he was feuding with umpires and Leo Durocher, and by '51 he was probably the most controversial player in the game. He learned to call a newspaperman down when he felt the reporter had been biased or inaccurate. He had his most interesting argument with a reporter, Dick Young, of the *Daily News*, who had written somewhat sharply about Robinson and then made a customary visit to the dugout before a Dodger game in Philadelphia. A few minutes before game time nearly all the Dodgers were seated in the dugout and Young was standing nearby talking. "If you can't write the truth, you shouldn't write," Robinson shouted quite suddenly from his seat.

Unaware that Robinson was shouting at him, Young continued talking. "Yeah, you, Young," Robinson hollered. "You didn't write the truth."

George Shuba, the Dodger sitting next to Robinson, was studying the floor. Other Dodgers were staring at left field. None was saying anything.

"Ever since you went to Washington, Robinson," Young screamed as he attempted to seize the offensive, "your head has been too big."

"If the shoe fits," Robinson shouted, "wear it."

"Your head is big," Young screamed.

"If the shoe fits wear it," Robinson shouted.

The screaming and shouting continued until game time, when Young left for the press box and Robinson devoted his attention to his job. "I couldn't let him get away with yelling at me in front of the whole team," Young said later. Relations between the two were cool for a while, but time healed the rift.

Another season Robinson called down Francis Stann, a Washington columnist, before an exhibition game in Griffith Stadium. Stann had quoted an anonymous third party as saying that Robinson was about through, and Robinson lashed him mercilessly and profanely.

"What good can that possibly do?" someone asked Jackie. "You'll only make an enemy."

"I can't help it," Robinson said. "I get so mad I don't know what I'm saying."

Why get so angry at newspapermen, who as a class are not more bigoted or biased than lawyers, congressmen, or physicians? Well, newspapermen have hurt Robinson, and in his lifetime Robinson has been hurt more than any man should be.

When a Dodger kicked in the door to the umpires' dressing room at Braves Field late in 1951, a Boston reporter blamed Robinson for the kicking. "I'm sorry, Jackie," the reporter said when he was told the truth. "It was right on the deadline and I didn't have time to check."

Another newspaperman once stole Robinson's name to use as a byline on a story consisting of lies and opinions with which Robinson did not agree. This was during a period of racial tension on the Dodgers, and the reporter's piracy put Robinson in the position of lying about the most important cause in his life. No one could take this in stride, of course, but Robinson took it particularly badly.

Jackie's rantings at reporters are well known in the newspaper business, and possibly because they made him a formidable target for all but the most bull-voiced of critics, Robinson almost reveled in his notoriety. But he got along with most reporters most of the time, and all of them knew he would always answer them openly and candidly, and never deny what he had told them just because somebody put the heat on.

Jackie Robinson always spoke his mind. This American Negro born in Georgia, bred in California, loved and hated everywhere, will not sit in the back of a bus or call all white men "Mister." He does not drawl his words, and he isn't afraid of ghosts, and he isn't ashamed of his skin, and he never ever says "Yowsah, boss." This American Negro, this dark symbol of enlightenment, is proud and educated and sensitive and indiscreet and hot-tempered and warmhearted. Those who do not know Robinson will call him "troublemaker." Those who do not understand him will call him "pop-off guy." Perhaps both terms are right. Robinson has made trouble for bigots, more trouble than they could handle.

Branch Rickey, who supposedly is the finest scout in baseball history, chose Robinson with wisdom that borders upon clairvoyance, to right a single wrong. Robinson had the playing ability to become a superstar, plus the intelligence to understand the significance of his role. He had the fighting temperament to wring the most from his ability, and he had the self-control to keep his temper in check. His ten years in major-league baseball will never be forgotten.

CHAPTER 25

ROBERTO CLEMENTE'S TRIUMPH AND TRAGEDY

Roberto Clemente was the first great Latino player in the major leagues. Playing for the Pittsburgh Pirates from 1955 to 1972, the outfielder was the National League batting champion four times, was awarded twelve Gold Gloves, and selected most valuable player in 1966. Like Jackie Robinson, he died young. On New Year's Eve of 1972, his plane—loaded with relief supplies for earthquake victims in Nicaragua—crashed into the Atlantic Ocean. He was inducted into the Baseball Hall of Fame a year later. In this excerpt from A Season in the Sun, *Kahn finds that his legacy is the joy of baseball that has permeated Puerto Rico.*

On a flat Puerto Rican plain, beside Avenida Iturregui and a pleasant subdivision called Country Club, four hundred barren acres stretched under a pitiless sun. Part of the land lay fried and caked; part still was marsh. This was Ciudad Deportiva, sports city, the last dream Roberto Clemente voiced before a DC-7, overloaded and undermanned, carried him to death in the Caribbean Sea on the rainy night of December 31, 1972. He had lined his three thousandth major-league hit, a double riding deep into left center field, three months before. He was thirty-eight years old.

I suppose sociologists would find Clemente's dream naïve. He wanted to build a Puerto Rican sports camp, free to all but open to the very poor, so that, as he said, "every single child from poverty can learn to play sports and maybe make some success as I did." By now more than $800,000 has been collected for Ciudad Deportiva and three and a half years have passed since Clemente's death. On the barren plain two bulldozers worked at a languorous pace inimical to Roberto Clemente.

Certain rumors persist about the death of Clemente, neither a saint nor a tramp, only a gifted ballplayer with a social conscience. "Bobby had a broad in Nicaragua," someone insists. "That's the real reason he took that flight." Another Puerto Rican suggests that his plane contained gold, or U.S. dollars, which Clemente was going to sequester beyond the grasp of tax authorities.

These are the facts. During November of 1972 Clemente had taken an amateur Puerto Rican baseball team to play a series of games in Nicaragua. He had liked riding in oxcarts as a boy in Carolina, his home village, and in Nicaragua he saw oxcarts again. He also met a hospitalized child without legs. He asked why the child had no artificial legs.

"We don't have any money," the boy said, in Spanish. "Legs would cost $800. When I go back to Puerto Rico, I will raise the money," Clemente promised.

Five weeks later Managua was flattened by six violent shocks. Howard Hughes flew away at the first tremor. In Puerto Rico, Clemente organized a relief campaign. He appeared on television and radio, pleading for money, morphine, sugar. Although his back ached, he helped load supplies on trucks in a staging area near Hiram Bithorn Stadium. Then word reached him that soldiers in the Nicaraguan Army were stealing the supplies and selling sugar to people who were starving, and morphine to people who writhed in agony.

Clemente remembered the oxcarts and the crippled boy. He was the finest of Latin ballplayers, and he had a strong sense of his own fame. "If I go to Nicaragua, the stealing will stop," he said, beating a palm against his iron chest. "They would not steal from Roberto Clemente."

A palm on his chest was Clemente's way of displaying earnest pride. His career, he liked to say, was proof "the Latin ballplayer is no hot dog." The Dodger organization let him go to Pittsburgh in 1955 for confusion of motives. What troubled Clemente was his suspicion of a quota system. The Dodger roster was already heavy with black ballplayers. "And me," he would say, "I am black and a nigger because I am Puertorriqueno."

In 1971, when the Pirates defeated Baltimore in an exciting World Series, Clemente batted .414 and hit a home run in the sixth game and the seventh. He was chosen Most Valuable Player by *Sport* magazine. With the honor comes a luncheon and a free car. For the honor, a man must make a speech.

A politician from San Juan introduced Clemente. He was a puffy, rotund man, and whiskey had made him prolix and maundering. The audience sat in boredom and embarrassment. But when Clemente rose, it was as if he had been introduced by Demosthenes.

"I am thirty-seven years old," he began, "and I was a poor boy in the village of Carolina, and I have always played hard and run out every hit, and this is the first time I have ever been asked to speak in New York City." Hearing him, one listened to an overflowing heart.

"I've been to a lot of these luncheons," I told him afterward, "and that was the best speech I've heard."

Clemente did not smile. The palm beat on the left side of his chest. "From here," he said. "It was good and true because it came from here."

After the earthquake the next year, a jet was available to ferry supplies from San Juan to Managua. The DC-7 would be cheaper, leaving more money to purchase medicines. During Christmas week, the DC-7 crashed into a cyclone fence after its brakes failed. Clemente said he did not care. "The brakes can be fixed."

A DC-7 is a big, four-engine turboprop plane, usually flown by a trained crew of three. The pilot, a man named Hill, was fully licensed. The copilot, Arthur Rivera, owned the aircraft, but he did not have a valid certificate to act as first officer, a fact he never revealed to Clemente. Instead, he said, "Would I myself take off if anything were wrong? Above all people, I value myself most."

The third seat in the cockpit properly is occupied by a flight engineer. Arthur Rivera could not find an engineer willing to work on New Year's Eve. He hired an aircraft mechanic. The plane was loaded in haste until its gross takeoff weight totaled 4,193 pounds more than the maximum allowed by the Federal Aviation Authority. At least sixteen sixty-pound sacks of sugar were piled behind the cockpit. According to Cristobal Colon, who accompanied Clemente to the plane, the sugar sacks were not lashed down.

As the plane accelerated down the runway at 9:20 P.M., one engine began to sputter. A flight engineer, studying the analyzers that show the condition of each engine, can make an instant diagnosis. If necessary, he shouts, "Abort, abort." A mechanic lacks the training and experience to make such a decision.

The plane took off. Another engine coughed. On the tape of the plane's transmission to the tower you can hear the pilot say, without panic, "this is NC 500, comin' back around." The pilot banked steeply. Perhaps the bags of sugar shifted. In the blackness of a winter rainstorm, NC 500 continued to bank and slipped sideways into twelve-foot waves at approximately 150 miles an hour. The aircraft might as well have flown into a wall of concrete.

"It was so sad for all of us," said Luis Rodriguez Mayoral, a Pittsburgh Pirate scout who guided me about his island. "In one year we lost two great heroes. Roberto and Don Pablo Casals. But do people remember? If they did, wouldn't Ciudad Deportiva be more that this by now?" He gestured toward the plain, simmering in a tropic summer.

Latinos have a gift for patient melancholy, but Mayoral brightened quickly. "I will show you, amigo, that there is nothing else sad about baseball on our island. Our island baseball is wonderful, *tu sabe?*"

Puerto Rican baseball is a joyous pastime, played mostly for the wonder of the game. Stateside one hears that Puerto Ricans play ball because anything, even catching a doubleheader in July, is preferable to cutting sugar in the canebrakes. That was true in Clemente's boyhood when, as he liked to recount, he earned a few pennies a day carrying jugs of milk to sweltering field hands. But Puerto Rico has become a relatively prosperous island. Attracted by tolerant tax laws, American electronics firms (GTE-Sylvania) and cosmetic companies (Avon Products) have moved factories there. Beyond rum and tourism, the island boasts scores of varied industries. Most willing workers can find jobs. Puerto Ricans play baseball now because they love the game. It is their national fanaticism.

The island's seventy-six towns and barrios are organized into an end-less summer of baseball. Boys from four to eight are grouped into a cat-egory called Piruli. They play with plastic balls and bats. Then, those with ability move successively to Little Leagues, Boys' Baseball, and Babe Ruth Leagues. After that, as in the continental United States, the best athletes sign with scouts like Mayoral. Boys with good but lesser skills remain. Many play amateur baseball until their thirties.

The season of the Puerto Rican Central Amateur League lasts from July to January. The Puerto Rican Amateur Federation begins its sched-ule in February and runs through autumn. Unlike the continental United States, every Puerto Rican town has its team, peopled by local semipros. Like Mayoral, most dreamed of being Clemente. But when the dream failed, they kept on playing. Town ball, not sugar cane, cov-ers the island. For nine months a year Puerto Rico glows with lights shining on a hundred baseball fields.

Mounting Mayoral's Volkswagen beetle, we bounced about San Juan and the village called Guaynabo and into Caguas, a small city settled under hills along a road lined by flamboyants, a tree blossoming with rust-red flowers. We watched Little League ball in Carolina, now a sub-urb in the San Juan sprawl, and we saw amateurs play in Las Piedras, The Rocks, a town so small that it does not appear on tourist maps, and where the single saloon is called, for reasons nobody knows, the Guadalcanal Bar.

"We have a problem," Vic Power, the old major league first baseman, said as he studied fourteen-year-olds on a cloudy day at a dusty little field in Caguas. "We have much participation. *Too* much participation. *Too* many dreams of the major leagues. I see a good ballplayer. I have to tell him, it is ten thousand to one that he will not make the major leagues. Sometimes I have to tell them it is one hundred thousand to one, because if you are both black and Puertorriqueno, they will not easily accept you. It will be very much more difficult."

Power's memories of playing as a black are cold and somewhat bit-ter, an opposite of the genial recollections you find in Artie Wilson [a black ballplayer who was denied entry to the major leagues before Jackie Robinson broke the color line in 1947].

"It was very bad when I got to the States," Power said. "I am strong and not afraid, but I do not want to be murdered, and when I first came to Florida for training in Fort Myers, I was afraid to cross the street. One night, three white men stood on the other side. I could see from the way they held themselves that it would be bad if we came close together.

"The light was green. They walked across the street. I stood in a doorway, and as you see I am very black. I hoped they would not notice me. They did not. They passed. When the light was red, I went across the street.

"The policeman came from nowhere. He held my shoulder, and he had a gun, and he said I was arrested for crossing against the light. He took me to court, and the judge looked at me in a hard way, and this is what I said:

" 'I am Puertorriqueno and a ballplayer, and I do not know how it is in the continental States. I thought the green light meant for whites to cross and the red light meant black people could cross the street.' "

"What did the judge tell you?" I asked Power.

"He said he didn't believe me and the case was dismissed and that I should never again appear before him in court."

Power told harder stories then, mostly sexual and bellicose. But Ted Williams liked him, and he was proud of that. When Jimmy Peirsall called him a black bastard, Power recognized Peirsall's intensity and his own strength and withdrew. And Early Wynn, oh Early Wynn. He lived in Florida, where the police had been cruel to blacks, but he was a very good pitcher.

You watch the shortstop. When you are looking at a team you have not seen before, watch the shortstop, who must move laterally and charge slow, twisting ground balls and make the play. Neither fourteen-year-old shortstop before Power and myself looked promising to me. Vic Power agreed, we were not seeing the best of Puerto Rican ball games. "In New York," he said, "in what you call Spanish Harlem, do they still remember the Gold Gloves I won for fielding?"

The baseball case is always changing, and in Spanish Harlem now, people talk of Felix Millan and John Candelaria and Willie Montanez. "Sure they remember your Gold Gloves," I told Power.

He beamed. "This one team," he said "is called Café Crema, after a big coffee company which gives them uniforms. It is not the best team, and Café Crème is not the best coffee. When you have lunch, order our other coffee, Café Rico."

Mayoral drove me to the development called Country Club for a Little League playoff. At Parque Angel Ramos, a manicured field set among tidy suburban homes, two hundred people cheered and listened to Carlos de Jesus broadcast over loudspeakers. Country Club defeated Valle Ariba, 9–0, and the Country Club shortstop, Jorge Burgos, played impressively.

In the fifth inning, with the Country Club's victory already safe, a Valle Ariba base runner reached second. The next pitch bounded five feet from the catcher. The runner did not try to advance, but when I looked up, there was shortstop Jorge Burgos backing up third.

"Good play," I told the twelve-year-old after the game.

"Not a good play," he corrected me in Spanish. "Just the play you're supposed to make." His face was long and bronze and free of lines.

"Would you like to be a major leaguer?"

"In my short life," Jorge Burgos said, "I have accomplished little aside from baseball. So my answer is, yes, I would like to play there. But perhaps later, when I accomplish other things, my answer would be different."

When Guaynabo played Cayey, two town teams meeting at the modern ballpark at Guaynabo, two thousand fans showed up at 9:45 Saturday morning. Guaynabo's uniforms were blue and white. Cayey wore orange. The game stayed close. The visiting Cayey squad was leading by two runs. Then a cloudburst struck. The home team's ground crew moved so slowly that the field was drenched. The fans chattered and applauded and sipped beer. A drunk began to curse and wave his arms. Four children started a game of punchball, using a crushed paper cup as their *pelota*. The drunk shouted at the children. A policeman grabbed him from behind and shoved him toward a gate and out of the park. The Cayey manager announced that he was protesting the game "because of Guaynabo's lazy ground crew." The people of Guaynabo hooted and laughed. "If we were ahead at Cayey and it rained," a man said to me in Spanish, "would not their ground crew be even lazier than ours?"

"Cayey is a pretty town," Mayoral said, "among mountains and not far from lakes."

The downpour continued. The fans sat chattering. The ballpark was their own town meeting hall. When the game was called, two hours later, and everyone went home, they were still chattering in good cheer.

Near a barren field in Las Piedras, on the narrow road that twists toward Humacao Beach, a young man was playing pepper with his son. Their names were Jose Soto, junior and senior, and after Mayoral introduced us, Mr. Soto said, "Vic Power tells me my child's swing is so good I should not touch it."

"*Tu eres de Nueva York?*" the boy asked. Was I from New York?

"Yes."

Had I seen the Yankees? Would I watch him?

The father gabbled like a salesman, and Jose Soto, who was seven, swung wildly and then missed six ground balls out of eight.

"He moves well," I told the father.

"If you come back to Las Piedras," Mr. Soto said, "understand you always will be welcome."

That night I attended a bicentennial banquet at the Caribe Hilton sponsored by the Association of the U.S. Army. The room was thick with braid and brass, and the menu included such dishes as Yankee Pot Roast, Revere Cheese Pie, and Liberty Tomato. The guest of honor was an astronaut and Marine officer named Jack Robert Lousma, who piloted Skylab 2 and said he had logged fourteen hundred hours in space.

Colonel Lousma presented the governor of Puerto Rico with a photo of San Juan taken from a height of 270 miles. Then he made a curious speech. It was strange and beautiful in space, Lousma said, and one thing he'd noticed was that you could not see the boundary lines between countries. Nevertheless, none of us should forget the constant peril of godless atheistic Communism. The military men, some Puerto Rican but mostly continental Americans, cheered. "Our space technology," Lousma said, "benefits every single person on this island." The band played "Dixie." A hundred officers sprang to attention.

I don't think Jose Soto, Jr., would have been able to make any more sense than I out of Lousma's speech.

Puerto Rico is not poor compared to Haiti, but the median income is $2,328 per person. In the barrios, the billions we invest in space appear irrelevant.

But baseball came to Puerto Rico in 1900, introduced by occupation soldiers after the Spanish-American War. That is the single continental export almost every islander understands and watches and plays.

"My friend," Mayoral said at the airport, "what you should help continental Americans understand is not only that we love baseball but that we are good players and we are proud that we are good. We are a tiny island, and some of our politics is crazy, but you know how all of us want to feel? Before he died, flying into the rain, Roberto Clemente said, 'I would like to be remembered as a ballplayer who gave all he had to give.' That is it. The opposite of lazy. Our dedication. *Tu sabe?*"

I said I thought I did.

CHAPTER 26

REMEMBERING RING

Ring Lardner Jr. was known as one of "the Hollywood 10," the writers who refused to answer the government's questions in 1947 about their relationships with the Communist Party. Kahn recollected his friend, who went to jail for his refusal and also won two Academy Awards for screenplay writing, in an article that appeared in The Nation *in 2000.*

The quiet grace of Ring Lardner Jr., who died the other week at eighty-five, seemed at odds with these noisy, thumping times. I cannot imagine Ring playing "Oprah" or composing one of those terribly earnest essays, "writers on writing," that keep bubbling to the surface of the *New York Times*. He was rightly celebrated for personal and political courage but underestimated, it seems to me, as a protean writer who was incapable of composing an awkward sentence. It ran against Ring's nature to raise his voice. Lesser writers, who shouted, drew more acclaim, or anyway more attention.

The obituaries celebrated his two Academy Awards, but made less of other achievements. Ring's novel, *The Ecstasy of Owen Muir*, begun in 1950 while he was serving his now-famous prison sentence for contempt of Congress, drew a transatlantic fan letter from Sean O'Casey. Ring felt sufficiently pleased to have the longhand note framed under glass, which he then slipped into a shirt drawer. He was not about advertisements for himself. In 1976 he published *The Lardners: My Family*

Remembered. Garson Kanin commented, "In the American aristocracy of achievements, the Lardners are among the bluest of blue bloods. In Ring Lardner Jr. they have found a chronicler worthy of his subject. *The Lardners* is a moving, comical, patriotic book."

The progenitor was, of course, Ring Lardner Sr., the great short-story writer, who sired four sons, each of whom wrote exceedingly well. James Lardner was killed during the Spanish Civil War; David died covering the siege of Aachen during World War II; a heart attack killed John in 1960, when he was forty-seven. Add Ring's prison term to the necrology and you would not have what immediately looks to be the making of a "moving, comical" book. But *The Lardners* was that and more because of Ring Jr.'s touch and slant and his overview of what E. E. Cummings called "this busy monster, manunkind."

From time to time, Ring published splendid essays. The one form he avoided was the short story. He wrote, "I did not want to undertake any enterprise that bore the risk of inviting comparison with my father or the appearance of trading on his reputation."

We became close in the days following the death of John Lardner, who was, quite simply, the best sports columnist I have read. I set about preparing a collection, *The World of John Lardner*, and Ring, my volunteer collaborator, found an unfinished serio-humorous "History of Drinking in America." He organized random pages with great skill. Reading them I learned that the favorite drink of the Continentals, shivering at Valley Forge, was Pennsylvania rye called Old Monongahela. George Washington called it "stinking stuff." At headquarters the general sipped Madeira wine.

A year or so later, with the blacklist still raging, I picked up Ring for lunch at the Chateau Marmont, an unusual apartment hotel on Sunset Boulevard near Hollywood. Outside the building, a fifty-foot statue of a cowgirl, clad in boots and a bikini, rotated on the ball of one foot, advertising a Las Vegas hotel. I asked the room clerk for Mr. Robert Leonard. Ring was writing some forgotten movie, but could not then work under his own name. "Robert Leonard" matched the initials on his briefcase.

This was a pleasant November day, but the blinds above Ring's portable typewriter were drawn. When I asked why, he opened them. His desk sat facing the bikinied cowgirl, bust high. Every eighteen seconds those giant breasts came spinning round. "Makes it hard to work," Ring said and closed the blinds.

The *Saturday Evening Post* was reinventing itself during the 1960s, on the way to dying quite a glorious death, and with my weighty title there, editor at large, I urged Clay Blair, who ran things, to solicit a piece from Ring about the blacklist. Ring responded with a touching, sometimes very funny story that he called "The Great American Brain Robbery." He explained, "With all these pseudonyms, I work as much as ever. But the producers now pay me about a tenth of what they did when I was allowed to write under my own name."

Clay Blair lived far right of center, but Ring's story conquered him, and he said, "Marvelous. Just one thing. He doesn't say whether he was a member of the Communist Party. Ask him to put that in the story."

"I won't do that, Clay."

"Why not?"

"He chose jail, rather than answer that question."

"Then, if he still won't, will he tell us why he won't?"

Ring composed a powerful passage.

The impulse to resist assaults on freedom of thought has motivated witnesses who could have answered no to the Communist questions as well as many, like myself, whose factual response would have been yes. I was at that time a member of the Communist party, in whose ranks I found some of the most thoughtful, witty and generally stimulating men and women in Hollywood. I also encountered a number of bores and unstable characters. . . . My political activity had already begun to dwindle at the time [Congressman J. Parnell] Thomas popped the question, and his only effect on my affiliation was to prolong it until the case was finally lost. At that point I could and did terminate my membership without confusing the act, in my own or anyone else's head, with the quite distinct struggle for the right to embrace any belief or set of beliefs to which my mind and conscience directed me.

These words drove a silver stake into the black heart of the blacklist.

Ring won his first Oscar for *Woman of the Year* in 1942, and when he won his second, for *M*A*S*H* in 1970, numbers of his friends responded with cheering and tears of joy. The ceremony took place early in 1971, and Ring accepted the statuette with a brief speech. "At long last a pattern has been established in my life. At the end of twenty-eight years I get one of these. So I will see you all again in 1999."

Indeed. Early in the 1990s I lobbied a producer who had bought film rights to my book *The Boys of Summer* to engage Ring for the screenplay. Ring, close to eighty, worked tirelessly. A screenplay is a fictive work, and Ring moved a few days and episodes about for dramatic purposes. His scenario ended with the Brooklyn Dodgers winning the 1955 World Series from the Yankees and my account of that ball game landing my byline on the front page of the *New York Herald Tribune*. The sports editor is congratulating me on a coherent piece when the telephone rings. My father has fallen dead on a street in Brooklyn; I am to proceed to Kings County Hospital and identify his body.

As I, or the character bearing my name, moves toward the morgue, I bump into two beer-drunk Dodgers fans. One says, "What's the matter with him?" The other says, "He's sober. That's the matter with him." The body is there. It is my father's body. Beer drunks behind us, my mother and I embrace. *Fin.*

I can only begin to suggest all that Ring's scene implies. I would start with the point that winning the World Series is not the most important thing on earth, or even in Brooklyn. I was always careful not to embarrass Ring with praise, but here I blurted out, "This is the best bleeping screenplay I've ever read, Ringgold. Oscar III may come true in '99."

"Curious," Ring said. "I seem to have had the same curious thought myself."

The blacklisting bounders were now dead, but a new generation of Hollywood hounds refused to shoot Ring Lardner's scenario. The grounds: "a father-son angle" was not commercial. "It worked in *Hamlet*," Ring said, but to unhearing ears. And then we were talking about Ring writing a screenplay for a book I published in 1999 about Jack Dempsey and the Roaring Twenties. "Have to cut it back a bit," Ring said. "Following your text would give us the first billion-dollar picture."

Years ago, the critic Clifton Fadiman wrote that Ring Lardner Sr. was an unconscious artist and that his power proceeded from his hatred of the characters he created. Ring told me: "If my father hated anyone or anything, it was a critic like Fadiman. Unconscious artist? My father knew perfectly well how good he was and—better than anyone else—how hard it was to be that good."

Ring Jr. knew the very same thing about himself. Or so I believe. Yeats writes, "the intellect of man is forced to choose/perfection of the life, or of the work." As well as anyone in our time, my suddenly late friend Ring Lardner came pretty damn close to achieving perfection in both.

CHAPTER 27

THE CAPTAIN

Jackie Robinson was Kahn's unabashed hero, but Hall of Famer Pee Wee Reese, the captain of the Dodgers, became his great friend, as this 1999 article from the Los Angeles Times *shows.*

We were working on a film, Pee Wee Reese, his son Mark, and myself, five years ago, and we were trying to get one memorable story right. The film was a one-hour documentary on the old Dodger captain and shortstop, which Mark had titled, *The Quiet Ambassador*.

The story we sought recounted a single brief, moving deed. But it had been told and retold and mistold so many times, we had a hard time reconstructing the scene. Was it Boston, that old abolitionist center, where the Red Sox practiced apartheid baseball until 1959? Was it St. Louis, the old major-league city that was closest to the heart of the Confederacy? In the end it turned out to be neither. The place was the river town, Cincinnati, and that made the story all the stronger.

Pee Wee Reese grew up in the Louisville area, when segregation reigned, and whenever the Dodgers traveled to play the Reds some of his old ball-playing friends from Kentucky made the easy drive up the Ohio River valley to watch Reese work his trade at Crosley Field. The year 1947 was different from what had gone before. The Dodgers were starting a black man at first base, the first to play in the major leagues since 1884. Now after sixty years, the Cotton Curtain was coming down. That was not to everyone's satisfaction.

As the Dodgers moved into infield practice, taunts began. Fans started calling Jackie Robinson names: "Snowflake," "Jungle Bunny," and worse. Very much worse. Some Cincinnati players picked that up and began shouting obscenities at Robinson from their dugout. There Jackie stood, one solitary black man, trying to warm up and catching hell.

Reese raised a hand and stopped the practice. Then he walked from shortstop to first base and put an arm around Jackie Robinson's shoulders. He stood there and looked into the dugout and into the stands, stared into the torrents of hate, a slim, white Southerner, who wore number 1, and just happened to have an arm draped in friendship around a black man, who wore number 42.

Reese did not say a word. The deed was beyond words. "After Pee Wee came over like that," Robinson said years afterward, "I never felt alone on a baseball field again."

Reese detested bigotry, hatred against blacks or Jews or Latinos, whatever. I never knew anyone whose life was a more towering example of decency. "With malice toward none; with charity for all; with firmness in the right as God gives us to see the right. . . ." The words are Lincoln's. The character that comes to mind is that of Harold Henry Reese, who died Saturday at eighty-one. A funeral service was held for Reese on Wednesday in Louisville.

After starring in a Presbyterian church league, Reese turned professional in 1938, when he was twenty. He had to quit his job as a line splicer for the telephone company, and the foreman said sternly that the phone company would always be there, that by leaving it, Pee Wee was making a terrible mistake. "I'm young, sir," Reese said. "I can afford to take a chance."

Recounting this, he gave me a gentle smile before he added, "Where that foreman might be today I do not know." He joined the Brooklyn Dodgers in 1940, when Larry MacPhail was restoring a ball club that had been more famous for gag lines than base hits. The Dodgers had not won a pennant since 1920, and John Lardner wrote of one star slugger: "Floyd Caves Herman, known as Babe, did not always catch fly balls on the top of his head, but he could do it in a pinch."

Another Dodger outfielder, Frenchy Bordagaray, came home standing up one afternoon and was tagged out. "Why the hell didn't you slide?" asked the manager, Casey Stengel. "I was gonna, Case," Bordagaray said, "but I was afraid I'd crush my cigars."

Reese was droll and often very funny, but after he moved in as Dodger shortstop in 1940, comedy came only after winning. The Dodgers beat a fine Cardinal team for the pennant in 1941 and, after World War II, Branch Rickey picked up from MacPhail and assembled the team I called "The Boys of Summer." Reese was a very fine shortstop, a great base runner, and a superb clutch hitter. He played every inning of every game in seven Dodger World Series. He was a captain who led by civility, however difficult the circumstances.

Panama City, Florida, 1947. Spring training was winding down, and Rickey was about to promote Robinson from the Triple-A Montreal Royals. Some veteran Dodgers—Hugh Casey, Dixie Walker—prepared a petition that said, in effect, "If you promote the black man, trade us. We won't play."

Walker brought the document to Reese confident that, Southerner to Southerner, Pee Wee would sign. Reese refused. Five or six older players pressed him. Was he gonna let Rickey make him play with one of them? "I'm not signing," Reese said, and the petition died.

As it happened, I rooted for the Dodgers and Pee Wee Reese when I attended a Brooklyn prep school, and kept rooting from secondary school and college, and even when the *New York Herald Tribune* hired me to write sports, which meant that I was professionally neutral. I was neutral all right. Neutral for Brooklyn. When I was twenty-three, the *Tribune* assigned me to cover the Dodgers, and I walked into the clubhouse, trying to choke back awe, and introduced myself to Reese.

"It's a pleasure to meet you," he said, "but you don't want to hang around me."

"Why not, Mr. Reese?"

"I'm not good copy."

We became closer than the journalism textbooks say is right. One night in Brooklyn, the late Joan Kahn, my first wife, was sitting in a photographer's booth when a foul ball bounced out of the upper deck onto a metal support that held up the big lenses on the old-fashioned cameras and the ball spun backward, hitting her and breaking her nose. As she was being cared for in the first-aid room, Walter O'Malley sent me a message in the press box: "Don't bother to sue. Courts have held we don't have to protect that location. If you sue me, you will lose."

Pee Wee's comment in the clubhouse was different: "How's your wife getting home?"

"I'll drive her," I said, "but I have to write my story first."

"Take your time with the story," Reese said. "I'll drive Joan home."

When I finally arrived, he was applying soothing talk and an ice pack to a patient who was in pain, but delighted with the company.

The next spring at Vero Beach Reese said, "You've played a little ball. Why don't you go out to left and shag a few?" When I got to left field, Gil Hodges stood in the cage. He slashed a nasty line drive over Reese's head and the baseball came bouncing toward me, looking curiously like a hand grenade. Who else was on the field? Reese, of course, Robinson, Duke Snider, Carl Furillo.

"If there is a God," I thought, "please don't let this one go through the wickets." I moved up slowly, dropped down to one knee, and the ball plunked into my glove. Whew! Then the shortstop called my name.

"Yes, Captain?"

"You're supposed to pick up the ball before it stops." Reese could say things few others dared.

Once, Robinson was raging against the steady run of knockdown pitches he had to endure.

Jackie was, in fact, a fierce competitor and a withering, sometimes unpleasant needler, hardly the bland saint baseball celebrates today.

"Jack," Pee Wee said, "some guys are throwing at you because you're black and that's a terrible thing. But there are other guys, Jack, throwing at you because they plain don't like you."

Robinson blinked. No one but Reese could talk to him that way. Then Robinson nodded and said, "You've got a point."

Reese had some rules. After he'd caught a pop fly, he never held up, say, two fingers signaling two outs. "This is the major leagues," he said. "You're supposed to be able to keep track of the outs by yourself. Besides, they're on the scoreboard."

Once, the Dodgers' backup catcher, Rube Walker, won a game at Ebbets Field with a home run, and in the clubhouse a photographer took one picture after another. Finally Walker snapped, "That's it. I got a bridge date with my wife." Reese bounded up from the captain's chair beside his locker.

"Rube, you had a job to do on the field and you did it," he said. "This man has a job to do here. You'll stay in the clubhouse until he has all the pictures he needs."

At length the New York baseball writers voted Reese their "Good Guy" award. He told me on the phone from Louisville that he was nervous about making a speech at the Waldorf Astoria and maybe I could meet him there and look over and edit the text. "I'm getting some help here," he said, "from a friend that knows the classics."

Here is the speech that Reese presented to me—and delivered to an audience of two thousand. I didn't change a word: "Gentlemen, if I possessed the oratorical fire of Demosthenes, or the linguistic elasticity of Branch Rickey, I would wow you with superlatives. But frankly, fellers, I ain't got it. Thank you very much."

He was playing shortstop at Yankee Stadium on October 4, 1955, when the Brooklyn Dodgers won their only World Series. Fittingly, the final out was Elston Howard's ground ball to short, and some said Reese choked and threw the baseball in the dirt and only Gil Hodges's great pickup saved him and all of Brooklyn. Nonsense. The throw was shin high, an easy catch for a big-league first baseman.

Somehow Reese and I ended up late that night, toasting the universe on West 57th Street. Pee Wee's face was shining, a child's face on Christmas morning. "Can I ask you something?" I said. "Sure."

"Two out in the ninth. You've played on five [up until then] losing Series teams. You're one out from winning a Series. Howard's up. What are you thinking."

"I'm thinking," said the bravest shortstop I've ever known, "I hope he doesn't hit the ball to me."

Reese probably didn't want to manage the Dodgers. He was semi-offered the job in 1954. He told me: "They said, 'You don't want to manage the team, do you, Pee Wee?' Probably not, and certainly not when they made the offer the way they did."

He became a broadcast partner to Dizzy Dean and then an executive at Hillerich and Bradsby, the company that manufactures Louisville Sluggers, and gloves and hockey sticks. He invested sensibly. He never earned more than $35,000 playing shortstop, but he became comfortable.

We stayed close, and on a terrible night in the summer of 1987, he rallied to my side. That July, I lost a child to heroin. He was twenty-two. When I buried my boy and came home, I knew deep crevices of despair. Toward midnight the phone rang.

"Do you remember," Pee Wee said, "that I was the captain of the team?"

"Of course."

"Well, I just want to say for all the fellers, we are very, very sorry."

Now, as Mark Reese was creating his documentary, *The Quiet Ambassador*, he brought Reese, Bobby Thomson, and myself together on Bedford Avenue, the street that runs behind the late but well-remembered right-field wall at Ebbets Field. After some baseball talk, Mark said, "I'd like you to talk about your late son and Pee Wee's phone call."

"I'd rather not," I said. "It's very emotional. I don't want to go misty in front of your camera."

"You ought to get over that," Mark said. "It's not the way it used to be, the macho nonsense. Guys are allowed to cry." I looked at Pee Wee. The captain's expressive face said—again no words—it's your call.

The camera rolled and I told the story, and there was Pee Wee right in front of me and I said, "So, I will be very, very grateful to you for all the rest of my days."

I blinked away a little mist, and kept control, but there on Bedford Avenue, Pee Wee Reese burst into tears. They were for my dead son, Roger Laurence Kahn, and they were for my grief, but they were for more than that. They were for all the bereaved, the stricken, the bereft, all mankind. As I compose these lines, Pee Wee Reese, the immortal shortstop, has moved past tears.

One dreams of heaven, and, of course, no one is sure. But I know this: Pee Wee Reese is alive in the minds and hearts of everyone who knew him. And I also know that the atoms that were the man remain. Now we shall hear him in the thunder and see him in the lightning and feel him in the rain.

Facing the fatal hemlock, Socrates said, "To a good man, no evil can come, either in life or after death."

Pee Wee is safe.

PART VII

ON GETTING OLD

CHAPTER 28

THE YOUNG WRITER
MEETS THE AGED POET

*Roger Kahn first met Robert Frost, the winner of four Pulitzer
Prizes for poetry, when he studied with him at Vermont's Bread Loaf,
the oldest writing center in America. When Kahn proposed a story on
Frost to his editors at the* Saturday Evening Post *in 1960, they
sneered. But Kahn convinced them, and the result is a charming
encounter between the aspiring writer, then thirty-three years old,
and Frost, who was eighty-six.*

To find Robert Frost, the great poet who wrote so fondly of New
Hampshire, one drove deep into the Green Mountains of Vermont. The paradox amused Mr. Frost. It made his green eyes twinkle
and moved him to soft laughter. Beyond his eighty-fifth birthday, Frost
wore the seasons lightly and humor ran strong and young within him.

If America anointed poets laureate, Robert Frost, of course, would
have been chosen. His poems won him four Pulitzer Prizes, a special
congressional medal, and, more important, earned for him and the craft
of poetry the admiration of millions who found Pound, Stevens, and
Eliot obscure and puzzling.

"I never like to read anyone who seems to be saying, 'Let's see you
understand this, you damn fool,'" Frost said. "I haven't any of that spirit,
and I don't like to be treated with that spirit." The spirit Frost did possess, scholarly, independent, questioning, sage, reached out, a golden
beacon across an uncertain land.

What sort of talk did one hear on paying Frost a visit? Talk about poetry, to be sure; good talk that stirred the mind. But more that that, one heard about scores of other things: Fidel Castro's revolution and John Thomas's high jumping; the feel of farming and the sight of beatniks; loneliness and love and religions and Russia, and how important it is for a man to know how to live poor. Somewhat sadly, too, one heard about the Boston Red Sox. Frost rooted for the Red Sox, but cheerlessly. He felt that they played baseball in the manner of Boston gentlemen and, although Frost appreciated Boston gentlemen in their place, he did not feel that their place is on a ball field. "Spike 'em as you go around the bases," he suggested.

Frost was not a poet by accident, and much of what one heard came in phrases, which, like his poems, were vivid and exciting. It was not surprising to find here such sure command of English, but what may surprise you is the freshness with which the patriarchal Frost looked at the world. He once wrote:

> *I never dared be radical when young*
> *For fear it would make me conservative when old.*

At eighty-six he was neither radical nor conservative. He was simply Robert Frost, one man unique in his time and ours.

Come with me then backward in time to the year 1960 on a cool pleasant afternoon when Vermont summer is changing into fall. The route, up from the south, leads past mountains and farmland almost into Middlebury, the college town. Then you turn off the main highway into a side road that runs through the village of Ripton and, for a time, follows the course of a swift-running stream. A few miles beyond Ripton, approaching a spine of the Green Mountains, you turn down a dirt road, and when the dirt road stops, you get out of the car and walk up to the brow of a hill. There, in an unpretentious house of weathered timber, Frost lives by himself.

Two old friends, Mr. and Mrs. Theodore Morrison, occupy a large farmhouse at the bottom of the hill. Morrison is a novelist and a member of the English faculty at Harvard. Mrs. Morrison is unofficial secretary to Frost, handling his correspondence, screening visitors, helping the poet with such mundane matters as income-tax returns. The Ripton farm is Frost's home from May until October. During the winter he lives by himself at Cambridge, Massachusetts, when he is not traveling to recite and talk about poetry.

"Are you going to use a tape recorder?" Mrs. Morrison asked in the farmhouse. She is a sprightly, cultured lady who has been close to, and perhaps suffered, writers for most of her life.

"No, I thought I'd set up my typewriter and just type as he talks."

"Good," Mrs. Morrison said. "He's had a lot to do with tape recorders, and he doesn't like them very much. He feels they make one watch every word, make every word permanent, whether it's really meant to be permanent or not. Come. Let's start up the hill."

Entering Frost's home, one walks into a small, screened porch. The porch leads to a rectangular living room, with a stone fireplace in one long wall and a window, opening onto the countryside, opposite. Above the hearth, two red roses sat in tiny vases. "We're here," Mrs. Morrison called.

Frost emerged from the bedroom, walking very straight, and shook hands firmly. He was wearing blue slacks, a gray sweater, and a white shirt, open at the throat. He is not tall, perhaps five-feet-seven, but his body is strong and solid as one might expect in a man who has spent years behind a plow. His hair, once red, is white and luxuriant. His face, its broad nose and resolute chin, is marked by time, but firm. It is a memorable face, mixing as it does strength and sensitivity.

"No tape recorder," Mrs. Morrison said.

"Good," Frost said. "Very good."

Mrs. Morrison helped set up my typewriter on a table she uses when taking dictation and excused herself. The poet walked to one of the large chairs in the room and motioned for me to sit on the other. "You're a journalist?" Frost asked.

"Yes, mostly. I write a few other things, too."

"Nearly everybody has two lives," Frost said, smiling. "Poets, sculptors. Nearly everybody has to lead two lives at the least."

"What life have you been leading recently?" I asked. "What have you been doing?"

"I never am doing anything, really," Frost said, "and I can't talk about my plans until I see how the plans work out. If I were writing a novel or an epic I could tell you what I've been doing, but I don't write novels or epics."

"I don't have any routine," Frost said. "I don't have any hours. I don't have any desk. I don't have any letter business with people, except I dictate one once in a while. Lectures? 'Lecture' is the wrong word. I'm going to about twenty or twenty-five places from here to California, but 'lecture' is the wrong word. I talk, and then I read. I never wrote out a lecture in my life. I never wrote a review, never a word of criticism. I've possibly written a dozen essays, but no more. You couldn't call mine a literary life." Frost chuckled and gestured at the typewriter.

"You use that thing pretty well," he said.

"Thanks," I said.

"Never learned to type, myself," Frost said.

"The world," I said. "Khrushchev and Castro—what do you think about what the world's been doing lately?"

"I wonder," Frost said, "if God hasn't looked down and turned away and said, 'Boys, this isn't for me. You go ahead and fight it out with knives and bombs.'"

Frost runs a conversation as a good pitcher runs a baseball game, never giving you quite what you expect. There are semi-humorous answers to serious questions and serious answers to semi-humorous questions. Frost is a master of the conversational change of pace.

"The world," he said, earnest now, "is being offered a choice between two kinds of democracy. Ours is a very ancient political growth, beginning at one end of the Mediterranean Sea and coming westward, tried in Athens, tried in Italy, tried in England, tried in France, coming westward all the way to us. A very long growth, a growth through trial and error, but always with the idea that there is some sort of wisdom in the mob. Put a marker where the growth begins, at the eastern end of the Mediterranean, and there's never been a glimmer of democracy south of there. Over east, in Asia, there have been interesting ideas, but none bothered by the wisdom of the mob.

"Our democracy is like our bill of fare. That came westward, too, with wheat and so on, adding foods by trial and error and luck. I think, when corn comes in good and fresh, what would I have done if Columbus hadn't discovered America?" Again the change of pace.

"What is the Russian democracy?" Frost said. "Ours, I say, is like our bill of fare, kills a few people every year probably, but most of us live with it. The Russian democracy is like a doctor's prescriptions or a food fad. That's all there is to that. That finished them off." Frost laughed.

"I have pretty strong confidence that our kind of democracy is better than a trumped-up kind," he said. "I'm pretty sure we're going to win. I'm on our side, anyway."

After Boris Pasternak, the late Russian poet and novelist, won the Nobel Prize for *Dr. Zhivago* but was prevented by commissars from accepting the prize, Frost was asked to issue a personal protest. "I couldn't do that," he said. "I understood what it was he wanted. He wanted to be left alone. He could have gotten out and gotten the [Nobel Prize] money, but he didn't want to. He had done what he wanted. He'd made his criticism. He lived in a little artists' colony outside of Moscow, and that was where he wanted to live and be left alone, and I had to respect that. I'm a nationalist myself."

Frost paused then to ask a question. "Have you noticed," he said, "that every bill up before Congress lately, bills on horses, men, everything, winds up: 'This would tend to promote international peace'?"

It was a short hop from Pasternak and Khrushchev to Castro. "I'd be in favor of leaving Castro alone for a time," Frost said, "and seeing if he can make it. We've gone past the time when we can fight to protect foreign investments. You know what I do? I'm protected up to $10,000 on what I put in the savings bank. We could protect anyone who wants to invest in foreign countries up to half a million. A sort of insurance. Then we beg these investors to behave themselves. Try to make friends. Explain to Castro, 'I want to help you help me and your people make money.' If that doesn't work, pack up, come home, prove your failure, and collect your insurance."

The idea delighted Frost. "I'm going to propose that," he said, "the next time I'm in Congress. The general policy of the past—backing foreign investments—is over. Protect them with insurance, but not with army, navy, and diplomacy. That doesn't work anymore.

"Belgium was the most selfish of all nations. They're getting their reward for that in the Congo now. England was a little loftier. The English brought nice Indian boys back to Oxford to see what freedom was. Castro is a puzzle to me, but he ought to see that we are a well-meaning nation. He needn't blackguard us all the time."

Frost places one hand before his eyes, and when he spoke again, his voice was soft. "Unfinished business," he said. "I'm very much in favor of unfinished business. Some of them aren't, but every single heading in the newspaper represents a whole lot of things that have got to stay unfinished, that can't be finished. Us and Russia, that might take a couple of hundred years before it's finished. That's one of the hard things about dying, wondering how unfinished business will come out.

"Oh, you could go crazy with too much unfinished business. You'd feel unfulfilled. You make a finished article out of this, and I make a finished poem. But talk about anyone's career. That has got to be suspended and thought about a great deal, and you're not saying much about it till you see how it comes out. You suspend judgment and go to bed." Outside, beyond the window, a lawn stretched down the hill. To the far right lay a brown field, newly turned by the plow. Beyond the valley, mountains rose, deep, green. "Three things have followed me," Frost said. "Writing, teaching a little, and farming. The three strands of my life."

"About writing," I said.

"A boy called on me the other day and said, 'I'm a poet,'" Frost went on. "I said, that's a praise word. I'd wait until somebody else called me that.'" Frost laughed a little now. It had been a long and lonely time before many people called Robert Frost a poet.

"I started by the ocean," Frost said. "San Francisco. My father was a newspaperman there. He went to Harvard, finished first in his class, but never talked much about that. Once he got West he put the East behind him, never mentioned it, drank enough for three generations of Frosts, died young. My mother was born in Scotland, raised in Ohio."

"Did you grow up amid books?" I asked.

"Didn't you? Didn't you?" Frost said, his voice almost a chant. "Oh, I never got the library habit much. I have an interest in books, but you couldn't call me a terribly bookish man."

There are two bookcases in Frost's living room, and on the window seat between our chairs books rested in three small stacks. His recent reading ranged from Latin poetry to a work about contemporary architecture. But the room was not overrun with books. The average pub-lishing-house editor lives among more books than does Robert Frost.

"We came to southern New Hampshire after my father died," Frost said. "I escaped school until I was twelve. I'd try it for a week, and then the doctor would take me out. They never knew what the matter was, but I seemed to be ailing. I got so I never wanted to see school. The first time I liked it was in New Hampshire. I liked the noon hour and so I became interested in the rest of it, the studies.

"It was a little country school. There was no grading. I could go as fast as I wanted, and I made up the whole eight years in a year and a half without realizing I was doing it. Then they sent me down to Lawrence [Massachusetts] to live with my grandfather and go to the high school where my father had gone. It was just the luck of that year in the coun-try, that country school. Otherwise, I might not have made it.

"In high school I had only Greek, Latin, and mathematics. I began to write in my second year, but not for any teacher. There were not English teachers. We had an active school magazine that the teachers had nothing to do with. I must have been reading Prescott's *Conquest of Mexico* because my first poem was a ballad about the night the Indi-ans fought Cortez. People say, 'You were interested in Indians the way children are interested in cops and robbers.' But it wasn't that at all. I was interested in Indians because of the wrongs done to them. I was wishing the Indians would win all the battles.

"The magazine would surprise you if you saw it. We did it for pleas-ure. When they do it nowadays, they have teachers, and that spoils the whole thing. They say, 'I can't finish this, teacher, help me.' That spoils it. We had poems, stories, editorials, and we did it all ourselves. I edited the magazine the last year, and I had eighteen assistant editors. One day I got mad at them. They weren't giving me enough material. I got sore and went down to the printing room, and in a day or two I wrote the whole damn thing. I wrote it all. I even made up a story about the debat-ing union and wrote the whole debate. I wrote it all, the whole thing, then I resigned." Frost smiled at me as he remembered something he had done seventy years before of which he was still proud.

"Dartmouth is my chief college," he said, "the first one I ran away from. I ran from Harvard later, but Dartmouth first. In a little library at Dartmouth I saw a magazine, and on the front page there was a poem. There was an editorial inside about the poem, so evidently that magazine was in favor of poetry. I sent them a poem, 'My Butterfly.' It's in the big collection. They bought it so easily I thought I could make a living this way, but I didn't keep selling 'em as fast as that. The magazine was called the *New York Independent*, and after they bought the poem they asked that when I sent them more, would I please spell the name of the magazine correctly. I'd made a mistake, but they bought my poem.

"When I told Grandfather Frost I wanted to be a poet, he wasn't pleased. He was an old-line Democrat, the devil take the hindmost, and here I was, making good grades, and wanting, he thought, to waste my life. 'I give you one year to make it, Rob,' he said. I put on an auctioneer's voice. 'I'm offered one, give me twenty, give me twenty, give me twenty,' I said. My grandfather never brought up poetry again."

Frost married Elinor White, his co-valedictorian at Lawrence High, in 1895, and set about rearing a family and dividing his life among poetry, teaching, and farming. "I had to find other means than poems," he said. "They didn't sell fast enough, and I didn't send my poems out much. Oh, I wanted them to want my poems. Some say, 'So you write for yourself entirely?' 'You mean into the wastebasket?' I say, but I had pride there. I hated rejection slips. I had to be very careful of my pride. Love me little, love me long. Did you hear that? Were you brought up on that? Love me little, love me long." Frost smiled. "But not too little," he said.

He places a hand before his eyes again. "One of the most sociable virtues or vices is that you don't want to feel queer. You don't want to be too much like the others, but you don't want to be clear out in nowhere. 'She mocked 'em and she shocked 'em and she said she didn't care.' You like to mock 'em and to shock 'em but you really do care.

"You are always with your sorrows and your cares. What's a poem if it is not to share them with others? But I don't like poems that are too crudely personal. The boy writes that the girl has jilted him, and I know who the boy is and who the girl is, and I don't want to know. Where can you be personal and not in bad taste? In poetry, but you have to be careful. If any-body tries to make you say more, they have to stop where you stop.

"'What does this poem mean?' some ask.

"'It means what it says.'

"'I know what it means to me, but I don't know just what it means to you,' they say.

"Maybe I don't want you to."

Frost was sitting back comfortably, his mind at work. "We have all sorts of ways to hold people," he said. "Hold them and hold them off. Do you know what the sun does with the planets? It holds them and holds them off? The planets don't fall away from the sun, and they don't fall into it. That's one of the marvels. Attraction and repulsion. You have that with poetry, and you have that with friendships."

For a time in his youth, guarding his pride, developing his art, Frost expected to work as a New England farmer for the rest of his life. "But people asked me out to read," he said, "and that kind of checked that. Then, when I was teaching in academies, having a successful time, it would be eating me all up, taking me away from poetry too much. Whenever it got like that, I'd run away.

"I didn't have any foundation to help me, but I had a tiny little bit of money saved up, and I went to England. Not for the literary life. I didn't want that. But we could live cheaper there. The six of us [including his wife and four children] went to England, and we stayed for three years for thirty-six hundred dollars, fare and everything. We lived poor, but we had a little garden, and we got something out of it, and we had some chickens. We lived very much like peasants. I was thirty-six years old or so, and I never offered a book. My poems were scattered in maga-zines, but not much. Then one day I thought I'd show a little bunch of poems. I left them with a small publisher, and three days later I signed the contract. Funny, it had never occurred to me to try a book here. *A Boy's Will*, that was the book."

This was a time when beatniks, masquerading as poets, recited their work at you, pinning you to the ground when necessary. Frost, men-tioning his first book, which brims with classics, offered no recitations.

Only when I urged him did he nod. Then, looking at me intently, he spoke this stanza from his poem "Reluctance":

Ah, when to the heart of man
Was it ever less than a treason
To go with the drift of things,
To yield with a grace to reason,
And bow and accept the end
Of a love or a season?

He spoke his poetry surely, clearly, with perfect command of the cadences. It is poetry written to be heard aloud, and when you heard it in Frost's voice, you felt that it reached its final measure of beauty in those fine New England tones.

"I once thought I'd like to have my lyrics seen as well as heard," Frost said. "I had some booklets made up and given out to audiences who came to hear me. That lasted two nights. The second night so many wanted me to sign the booklets that the police had to get me away. Now I sign anything of mine that they type out or write out. Without money and without price, you see. There's quite a little of that in me."

After Frost returned from England with his family, he had to go back to farming and teaching. He was forty before he gained much recognition as a poet, and he was nearly fifty before his volume *New Hampshire* won him his first Pulitzer Prize. It struck me then, sitting in the little living room, that Frost has gone from complete obscurity to great fame without changing his way of life. The Vermont house was as simple as the houses where he dwelled when there was no choice but to live simply. One difference is that by 1960 a sizable portion of the world had tried to beat a path through the wood and up to Frost's door.

"You have to be careful about idolizers," Frost said. "Emerson calls an unwanted visitor a devastator of a day. It's a cranky Yankee poem, but I suppose he was pestered all the time by people who wanted to go deeper into him than he could go himself, and, goodness, he was such an artist they should very well have left it where he did. They think, the idolizers, that you've injured them. Whether they injure you or not, the idolizers always think you've injured them.

"How much do you need someone who always thinks you're a hero? How much do you need being thought a hero all the time? People say, 'I got over this, I got over that.' They are a lot of fools, the people who say you get over your loves and your heroes. I never do. I don't change very much."

"Has your method of writing changed?"

"I'm not in shape so I can't strike it out, like a good golf stroke or a good stroke of the bat, there's not much I can do," Frost said. "Oh, you get so that some days you can play a beautiful game, but there are always days when you can't. Those days, I can't redo them. They're done. Down the sink.

"What some seem to do is worry a thing into shape and have others worry with them. Not to say I don't have the distress of failure, but the worry way isn't for me. There are the days you can and the days you can't, and both are training toward the future days you can. Do you know the story about how the bear is born?"

I didn't.

"The bear is born shapeless, says the story, and the mother licks it into shape. That's the way it is with some people's writing. But no good piece is worried into shape. A child is unfortunate that needs to be reshaped just after it's born. Is a poet made? A poet might be through all the years of trial and error, but any good poem is not made. It's born complete."

In many of Frost's poems, loneliness is a strong theme. His wife died in 1938, and only two of his five children survive. I wondered how he had come to terms with solitude.

"In the big newspaper office," Frost said, "where everyone sits alongside the other and writes—I couldn't do that. Even reading. I've got to be totally absorbed when I read. Where there are other people reading, too, I don't feel very happy.

"Alone you take all your traits as if you were bringing 'em to market. You bring them from the quiet of the garden. But the garden is not the marketplace. That's a big trouble to some: how you mix living with people with not living with people; how you mix the garden with the marketplace.

"I like the quiet here, but I like to have a big audience for my talks, to have a few turned away. I like to feel all that warmth in the room. At Kansas City once they told me, 'You see that hazy look down the end of the hall? That's whiskers. Them's beatniks.' They came to wish me well. But I do like some form in the things that I read."

Suddenly Frost sat up straight. "I'm sorry I can't entertain you," he said. "I'm not set up here for that sort of thing."

He meant drinks, and I asked if he took a drink himself.

"A daiquiri once in awhile," he said. "But not much, and not serious. I don't care for those parties where everyone goes. They take just a little too much, and they say just a little too much. I've always been shy. I get uncomfortable."

Outside, in the later afternoon sun, the grass looked bright and fresh. "Used to play softball out past there," Frost said. "I pitched. They don't let me do all the things I want to anymore, but if we had a ball, I'd pitch to you a little, and I'd surprise you." He grinned.

"You like sports?"

"Oh, yes," he said. "You get a certain glory out of being translated, but no, no, it doesn't work. So much is lost. There are other arts that are international. Boxing, and high-jumping seven feet two inches. Anyone can understand that. Just think of that boy from Boston [John Thomas] going right up in the air higher than anybody but a basketball player."

Then we were serious again. I asked about another strong theme in Frost's work, the theme of God. "Don't make me out to be a religious man," Frost said. "Don't make me out to be a man who has all the answers. I don't go around preaching God. I'm not a minister. I'm always pleased when I see people comfortable with these things. There's a rabbi near here, a friend of mine, who preached in Cincinnati in the winter. He talks at the Methodist church here sometimes and tells the people in Cincinnati that he's a summer Methodist.

"People have wondered about him at the Methodist church. One lady was troubled and said to me, 'How do they differ from us?'

" 'What you got there on that table?' I said.

" 'That's a Bible,' she said.

"I didn't say any more.

" 'Oh,' she said, 'Oh, the Old Testament. Why can't you have a Jew in church?' she said, and she understood."

Frost's voice was strong. "There's a good deal of God in everything you do," he said. "It's like climbing up a ladder, and the ladder rests on nothing, and you climb higher and higher and you feel there must be God at the top. It can't be unsupported up there. I'd be afraid, though, of any one religion being the whole thing in one country, because there would probably come a day when they would take me down to the cellar and torture me—just for my own good."

He smiled briefly. "There is more religion outside church than in," Frost said, "more love outside marriage than in, more poetry outside verse than in. Everyone knows there is more love outside the institutions than in, and yet I'm kind of an institutional man."

We turned back to poetry then. "They ask me if I have a favorite," Frost said, "but if a mother has a favorite child, she has to hide it from herself, so I can't tell you if I have a favorite, no."

"Is there one basic point to all fine poetry?" I asked.

"The phrase," Frost said slowly, clearly, "and what do I mean by a phrase? A clutch of words that gives you a clutch at the heart."

His own phrases, his own words, were all about me in the little house. Afternoon was fading, and I realized how much we had discussed, and how Frost had ranged from the profound to the simple, as his own life, which seems so simple, has in reality been so profound. I remembered his poems, too.

Some summing up seemed in order and, for want of a better term, I intended to say that this visit had brought me into the presence of greatness. "I feel as though . . ." I began.

"Now, none of that," Frost said, anticipating. "We've had a fine talk together, haven't we? And we've talked to some purpose. Come now, and I'll walk with you down the hill." He got up from his chair and started out the door and down the steep path, pausing to look at the sunset as he went. . . .

I brought my son to see him a year later, on a day when Frost wanted to talk politics. I listened, disappointed. I wanted to talk writing. The child ran out into a cornfield and played. Then it was time to go and I gathered the child, hiked him onto my shoulder, and started down the steep hill. Frost ran to the porch, calling, "The boy, the boy, I have to say good-bye to the boy." I turned and then the boy stared at Frost, who was eighty-seven, all wonder, and Frost looked at the boy with a face I read as love.

Down the hill I heard Robert Frost cry after me, "Come back again, if you'd care to." Because trivialities crowded my time, I never did.

CHAPTER 29

THE LAST SUMMER OF "STAN THE MAN"

Kahn once told a friend that no one hit better at Ebbets Field than the St. Louis Cardinals' Stan Musial. And to prove it Musial went out and got five hits in a game that Kahn and his friend witnessed. No surprise. Musial had 3,630 hits, 475 homers, 1,951 RBI, and a .331 batting average in twenty-two seasons. With three MVP awards and seven batting titles, he was one of the game's greatest hitters. But even the great ones have trouble when age creeps up, as Kahn found when he visited with Musial for a 1960 Sports Illustrated *article. By the way, Musial played two more years, retiring in 1963. With his last swing he singled sharply to right and drove home the run that proved decisive in a 3–2 victory for the Cardinals.*

Disturbing paradoxes surround an aging baseball player. He is old but not gray; tired but not short of breath; slow but not fat as he drives himself down the first-base line. Long after the games, when the old ballplayer thinks seriously, he realizes that he has become obsolete at an age when most men are still moving toward their prime. It is a melancholy thing, geriatrics for a forty-year-old.

To Joe DiMaggio age meant more injuries and deeper silences. To Bob Feller it meant months of forced jokes, with nothing to pitch but batting practice. To more fine ballplayers than anyone has counted, age has meant Scotch, bourbon, and rye. Athletes seldom bow out gracefully.

Amid the miscellaneous excitements of the current National League pennant race, the most popular ballplayer of his time is trying desperately to overcome this tradition. Stanley Frank Musial of the St. Louis Cardinals, now thirty-nine and slowed, intends to end his career with dignity and with base hits. Neither comes easily to a ballplayer several years past his peak, and so to Musial, a man accustomed to ease and to humility, this has been a summer of agony and pride.

Consider one quiet June evening in Milwaukee when Musial walked toward the batting cage to hit with the scrubs, dragging his average (.235) behind him. He had been riding the bench for two weeks.

"Hey, what a funny-looking ballplayer," called Red Schoendienst of the Braves, who was Musial's roommate on the Cardinals for five years. Musial grinned wide. It was an old joke between friends. Then he stood silently among anonymous second-liners, attempting to act as though he were used to the company.

"Stash," someone said, while George Crowe, a St. Louis pinch hitter, was swinging, "did you know that Preacher Roe was using a spitball when he pitched against you?"

The question snapped Musial to life. "Sure," he said enthusiastically. "We had a regular signal for it. One day Preacher goes into his motion, and Terry Moore, who's coaching at third, picks off the spitter and gives me the signal. Preacher knows I've got it, so he doesn't want to throw the spitter. But he's halfway through his windup, and all he can change to is a lollipop [a nothing ball]. I hit it into the left-field seats, and I laughed all the way around the bases."

Musial laughed again at the memory, then stepped in to hit. He swung three times but never got the ball past the batting-practice pitcher. A knot of Milwaukee fans jeered as Musial stepped out of the cage, and the sound, half boos, half yahs, was harsh. Musial blushed and began talking very quickly about other games against Roe and the old Brooklyn Dodgers. "Yeah, I could really hit those guys," he said. It was strange and a little sad to see so great a figure tapping bouncers to the pitcher and answering boos with remembrances of past home runs.

Why was he doing it, one wondered. He was long since certain of election to the Baseball Hall of Fame. He was wealthy, independent of the game. (One friend estimates that Musial earns $200,000 a year, no more than half of that from the Cardinals.) He was a man who had always conducted himself sensibly. Now here was sensible old Stan Musial reduced to a benchwarmer as he waged trench warfare against time.

The answer, of course, is pride: more pride than most of us suspected Musial possessed, more pride than Musial ever displayed when he was Stan the Man, consistent .350 hitter, owner and proprietor of most National League pitching staffs.

The issues in the case of Stan Musial versus time have cleared considerably since his May benching and his dramatic July comeback. He was not through in June, as many suspected but, because Musial is well loved, few put into words. But neither was he the young Musial in July, as many said loudly, and few, I imagine, really believed. Both the benching and the comeback represent skirmishes in the continuing battle Musial joins whenever he puts on a pair of spikes and heads out toward left field, trotting a shade more slowly than he once did.

After a career in which he had never batted lower than .310, Musial hit .255 in 1959. Since he was thirty-eight, the wise conclusion was that he was finished, and most baseball men assumed he would retire. In fact, most hoped he would choose retirement instead of the awkward exit that seemed inevitable if he played this season. "No," Musial insisted during the winter. "I want to go out on a good year. I'm not quitting after a lousy year like that." Athletes, like chorus girls, are usually the last to admit that age has affected them, and Musial appeared to be following the familiar unhappy pattern. His timing seemed gone—change-ups made him look foolish—and he appeared to be the only man who didn't realize it.

During the winter Musial enrolled in a physical education program at St. Louis University. The exercises were orthodox—pushups and such—but the emphasis was on tumbling.

He arrived at spring training splendidly conditioned, and he hit well, if not sensationally, during exhibition games. For the first three weeks of the regular season he played first base, batted about .300, and fielded poorly. Then his hitting dropped sharply, and for the next three weeks his average drifted toward .200. Finally, on May 27, Solly Hemus, the Cardinal manager, benched Musial. The decision brought pain to

Musial and pain to Hemus, too, since what the manager did, after all, was bench a legend.

"He'll be back," Hemus said vaguely. When? Solly wasn't quite sure. "I'll play whenever they want me to," Musial said cheerlessly. But he didn't start another game for almost a month.

Hemus is a conscientious, combative man of thirty-six, who joined the Cardinals in 1949 when Musial was already a star, a factor that later complicated the manager-ballplayer relationship. "I'd never pulled much," Hemus recalls, "and when I first came up Stan gave me some tips. He told me to concentrate on hitting that right-field screen—it's close—at Busch Stadium. I admired him, and I guess he liked me." It got so that when Stan came home, his daughter, Janet, wouldn't start by asking if he got any hits. First she'd say, "Did Solly get any hits?"

Discussing the Musial benching troubles Hemus. He was buffeted in St. Louis sports pages for the move, and beyond that it strained a friendship. But he talked about the benching at some length and with tremendous earnestness after one recent Cardinal night game.

"What's my obligation as manager?" Hemus said, staring darkly into a glass of light beer. "It's not to a friendship, no matter how much I like a guy. My obligation is to the organization that hired me and to twenty-five ballplayers. I have to win. Stan was hurting the club. He wasn't hitting, and balls were getting by him at first base. It wasn't something I wanted to do. I had to do it."

For all his attempts to show indifference, Musial hated the bench. He confided to a few friends that he wouldn't mind being traded to a club that would play him every day. Hints appeared in the press that he and Hemus were feuding. They weren't; they were just miserable about the situation. But Musial still says, in the closest he comes to a grumble, "Don't let anyone tell you they were resting me. I was benched."

On June 19, after Musial had spent three weeks in the dugout, Hemus said before a doubleheader, "Maybe I'll use you in the second game." The Cards won the first. In the clubhouse afterward Hemus announced simply: "Same lineup."

Later Musial, deadly serious, approached him. "There's one thing you shouldn't ever try to do, Solly," he said. "Don't ever try to kid me along." Hemus said nothing. There wasn't anything to say. "He caught me," the manager remarked over his beer. "He knew me well and he caught me. I was wrong to kid him, but I did."

Hemus paused and gathered his thoughts. "I spent a lot of time, a lot of nights worrying about this thing," he said finally, "and I got to remember the coffin. What does he want to take with him to his coffin? Records. Something that people will remember. As many records as he can. Now what do I want to take to my coffin? Honesty. I always wanted to manage, and I want to know I managed honestly. I was right to bench him when I did, but I was wrong to kid him, and I know it makes me look bad to admit it, but I was wrong."

Hemus never evolved a plan to work Musial back into the lineup. While benched, Musial pinch-hit nine times but batted safely only once. There was no indication he was going to hit any better than he had.

On June 16 Bob Nieman, who had been hitting well, pulled a muscle, and suddenly Hemus needed a left fielder. He alternated Walt Moryn and rookie John Glenn, but neither hit. Then he turned to Musial, hoping for batting but not really confident that he would get it. What would have happened to Musial if Nieman hadn't been hurt, or if Glenn or Moryn had started slugging? Again Hemus speaks with frankness. "I really don't know," he says. "I just got no idea."

On June 24 Musial started in left field against the Phils and got one hit in four times at bat. On June 25 he was hitless, but on June 26 he started again and that day took off on a devastating hitting tear (fifteen games, .500 average) that surprised everyone except, possibly, The Man.

What brought Musial back to batting form? "Well, one reason I didn't quit," he says, "is that they weren't throwing the fast one by me. Last year they were giving me changes, and I wasn't going good, so I kept swinging too hard. I figured that one out. Now I'm going to left real good on lots of the changeups."

Musial has also changed the unique stance that was his trademark. Remember the old crouch? Now Musial stands closer to the plate, a change that gives him better control of fastballs over the outside corner. He still crouches, but less markedly. His stance remains unusual, but it is no longer radical. He always concentrated when he hit, but Musial's concentration seems to have deepened further. It must make up for what age has taken from his reflexes, and he now plots his swings with great care.

Nobody around the league has an easy explanation of Musial's great hitting in July, because there is no easy way to explain great hitting by a washed-up thirty-nine-year-old ballplayer. "Hell," Musial himself says, "just use that old line of Bosco Slaughter's. Just say I never been away."

One night before the Cardinals played the Braves, Charlie Dressen, a man who has more explanations than newspapermen have questions, agreed to study the revivified Musial and report on what he saw. Musial lined one of Bob Buhl's inside changeups high into the right-field bleachers.

"Ah," Dressen said later. "I know how to pitch to him."

"How?"

"Same as always," Dressen said. "Changeups."

"But he hit the home run off the change."

"Wrong kinda change," Dressen said.

Fred Hutchinson, who manages Cincinnati and once managed the Cardinals, took up the Musial question several days later. "What can you say?" Hutchinson asked, shrugging. "He's hitting like hell, that's all. He's hitting all kinds of pitches, just like he used to."

On the field during workouts, he tries to be as he once was, too, filled with small jokes and with laughter. "Do you know what sex is?" he may ask. "That's what Poles put potatoes into." Then, lest he offend, "You know I'm Polish."

Sometimes, while playing catch, he shows his pitches—he was a pitcher in the low minor leagues twenty-three years ago. "Forkball," he'll say. "Me and [Elroy] Face. Next time I come back it's gonna be as a pitcher."

Since his July blaze, Musial has slipped somewhat. "One thing I know about him now," Hemus says, "is that when he gets real tired, one day's rest isn't enough. If he needs it, he'll get a week off. If he goes real bad, he'll get plenty of time to get strong again."

The old 154-game-a-year Musial has vanished. The swift base runner, whose sloped shoulders suggested the contours of a greyhound, has slowed. The great batter, whose forte was consistency, now hits in spurts. Yet, in sum, this season makes for a glorious exit. Musial wanted to go out with a respectable year, and by concentrating on pitchers and conserving his energies, he seems likely to achieve this.

But ahead lies one more trap—another season. Musial has not formally committed himself to 1961, but informally he drops hints that he may play again. He relishes his life in baseball, and when he hits well he seems to feel that he can go on hitting indefinitely. "Maybe my wheels are gone," he says, "but I'll be able to hit like hell for a long time."

Perhaps, but anyone who watched his prideful struggle this summer must wonder. Time presses. The benchings can only get longer, the comebacks still more labored. He has been a fine and gracious man, Stan Musial. It would be nice to see him say farewell with a wave, a grin, and a double lined up the alley in right center field.

CHAPTER 30

PAST THEIR PRIME

The cliché that every sportswriter hears from the aging ballplayer is, "I will know when it is time to retire." Most do not, however. Joe DiMaggio knew when; Muhammad Ali did not. Kahn located aging athletes with declining skills and aching bodies in this article for Playboy, *which won Kahn an award for the best magazine article of 1979.*

The pitcher telephoned me, which should inform you that he was a veteran athlete. Young baseball players do not waste change telephoning writers who are male.

He was coming to town, the pitcher said, and he was going to start a baseball game in Yankee Stadium. There weren't many games left in his arm, and I knew he had become afraid of the rest of his life. But mostly his fear was stoic, wreathed in resignation, like the fear of certain brave, old, dying men. Anyway, after the game, he wanted a woman.

The pitcher felt a fulminating lust for a particular tennis star. When I called her, she agreed to meet him, with one proviso: I would have to date someone she called her "new best friend." That was the woman superintendent of the brownstone house where the tennis player cohabited with cats and fantasies. The building super, I thought. A woman who spends days stacking garbage bags and reaming toilet drains. Dating her would be some enchanted evening. We would all turn into frogs, I thought. But I owed the pitcher certain favors.

"What should I know about the tennis player?" he asked me on the morning of the game. He didn't have to ask about opposing hitters anymore. He knew all their rhythms and their weaknesses. "I mean, gimme a little scouting report on the lady, so I can plan my moves."

"Miss Center Court," I said, "loves to talk dirty, and if you don't press hard, she gets wild and delicious. But she has one peculiarity. She has to be the one to talk dirty first. If the man comes on raunchy, Miss Center Court turns off."

"Got ya," the pitcher said, with a confident nod. He then lost to the Yankees, 3–2, in punishing sunlight.

When the ballplayer marched into an East Side bar at seven thirty that night, he was swaggering bravado. Actually, of course, he was covering up. He had always despised losing, and he hated losses even more now that so few afternoons of stadium sunlight were left. Technically, he suffered from an irreversible chronic tendonitis in one shoulder. The condition would be annoying, but not much more than that, for an accountant. But this man was a major-league pitcher, and chronic tendonitis meant something more extreme. His major-league arm was all but dead.

He looked at the tennis player and blinked and smiled. She was attractive, not merely for a lady jock. She was large-eyed and lissome, and she wet her lips before she spoke. Abruptly the ballplayer became desperately cheerful.

"Say," he said, dropping into a captain's chair, "you all know about the city boy and the country girl and the martinis? This here country girl had never heard of martinis, and the city boy got her to drink a batch." The pitcher's tongue was brisker than his slider. "Finally, the country girl says, 'Them cherries in them maranas gimme heartburn.'

"The city boy, he says, 'You're wrong on all three counts. They're not cherries, they're olives. They're not maranas, they're martinis. And you don't have heartburn, your left tit is in the ashtray.' "

The pretty tennis player made a face like a dried apricot. Then she and my date, the woman superintendent, went to the washroom.

"Dead," I told the pitcher. "The German word is *tot*. I believe the French say *mort*. The Yankees knocked you out this afternoon, and you just knocked yourself out now."

"It's a good joke," the pitcher said. "I used it at a supermarket opening in Largo, Florida, and they loved it, even the mothers with kids."

"We're north of Largo. Didn't you listen to me? Miss Center Court has to set the tone herself. If she lets guys start the rough talk, it might seem as though she's an easy lay."

"Isn't she?"

"That isn't the question. The question is style."

The women dismissed us civilly after dinner, and the pitcher said the hell with them. He knew a Pan Am stewardess who could do unusual things with a shower nozzle. He called, and an answering machine reported that his mistress was in Rome.

"Forget it," I told the big pitcher. "Everybody has nights like this. John Kennedy had nights like this. The dice are cold. Let's go to sleep."

"Stay with me," the pitcher said. We rode down to a Greenwich Village club that was cavernous and loud with bad disco and empty of talent except for a dark-haired teenaged girl from Albany. The pitcher was quite drunk by now. He scribbled love notes and sexual suggestions on cocktail napkins, which a small Spanish waiter delivered. The girl from Albany paid her check and fled in fright.

A serious thought suddenly made the pitcher sober. "I can't pitch big-league ball no more," he said.

"You knew this was going to happen," I said.

His voice was naked. "But now it's happening."

One tear, and only one, rolled down the man's right check, "Shee-yit," he said, embarrassed. "Shee-yit."

"Like hell, shee-yit," I said. "You've got something to cry about."

He was thirty-nine, hardly old. He was well conditioned and black-haired, and every movement he made suggested physical strength. Most would have called him a young man. But because he was an athlete, his time was closing down. He had won premature fame at twenty-two, and now he was paying with a kind of senility at thirty-nine. The adulatory press conferences were ending. He would not again travel as grandly as he had; he would never again earn as much money as he had been making. Already his manner with attractive women had regressed. He was finished, or he *thought* he was finished. The two often are the same.

In the usual curve of ascendancy, the American male completes so-called formal education in his twenties and spends the next fifteen years mounting a corporate trapeze. If he is good and fortunate and very agile, he will be soaring by forty. Athletes follow wholly different patterns. They soar almost with puberty. Life for a great young athlete is different from other children's lives, even as he turns fourteen. Already he is the best ballplayer of his age for blocks or miles around. He is the young emperor of the sandlot.

With enough toughness, size, nutrition, and motivation, the athlete will feel his life expanding into a diadem of delights. He does not have to ask universities to consider his merits and tolerate his college board scores. A brawl of jock recruiters solicits him. If necessary, they offer him a free year at a prep school, finally to master multiplication tables.

Assuming certain basic norms, the athlete has a glorious pick of women. Pretty wives are not an exception around ball clubs; they are characteristic. It is all a kind of knightly beginning to life, isn't it? Doing high deeds, attended by squires, moving from stately courts to demi-mondes? But most knightly tales conclude with the hero full of youth.

I remember a marvelous quarterback named Ben Larsen, who dominated high school football in Brooklyn. His passing was splendid, and he ran with a deceptive gliding style. Perhaps thirty colleges offered him scholarships. He chose one in the Big Ten, where the wisdom of football scouts proved finite. Ben was suddenly pressed harder than he had ever been, by athletes of comparable skills. He wilted quickly and never finished college. He was the first of my acquaintances to become an alcoholic.

Ben Larsen's life reached its peak while he was a schoolboy. For many the climax comes in college or as a young professional. Others (Carl Yastrzemski and Fran Tarkenton) can play well and enthusiastically as they approach forty. Once an eon a Satchel Paige or a Gordie Howe makes it to fifty. Technical literature doesn't yet tell us much. Studying human behavior is still a science of inexactitude. But broadly, and obviously, we're dealing with two elements.

The first is physical. An athlete must be granted a good body, a durable body, and—I hate to be the one to make this point—he'd better take care of it. I don't know whether or not all those careless nights cut short Mickey Mantle's career, but unwillingness to do proper pregame calisthenics and to perform therapeutic drills on all those hungover mornings sure as hell cut off his legs.

Then there is emotion, world without end. How long can an athlete hold all his passion to be an athlete? How long can he retain all his enthusiasm for repetitive experiences?

One hot afternoon last spring, Johnny Bench, Tom Seaver, and I were riding together to make an appearance at a book fair in Atlanta. Bench at twenty-six was the best catcher baseball has known. Not perhaps, not one of, just the best. Last spring, at thirty, he was in decline. Bench's batting average lounged below his old standard. He was getting hurt frequently. His matchless play, his Johnny Bench–style play, seemed limited to spurts. "You get bored, John?" I asked in the car.

"With what?"

"Catching a baseball game every day."

"Do I?" Bench has a broad, expressive face, and he lifted his eyebrows for emphasis. "You know why I envy him?" he said, elbowing Seaver.

"For my intellect," Seaver said. "My grooming and my skills at doing the *New York Times* crossword puzzle."

"Because he's a fucking pitcher," Bench said. "He doesn't have to work a ball game but one day in four. All that time off from playing ball games. That's why I envy Tommy."

Seaver grew serious and nodded. Both men are intelligent, curious, restless. As they grow older and recognize that the universe is larger than a diamond, it becomes increasingly difficult to shut out everything else and play a game. It also hurts more. The human body was not designed to play catcher from April to October.

It was not designed to fight for the heavyweight championship at the age of thirty-six either.

Last September I flew to New Orleans to watch Muhammad Ali make a fight he really did not want to fight. He won easily over Leon Spinks, but a new sourness invaded Ali's style. "It's murder, how hard he's got to work," said Angelo Dundee, the sagest of Ali's seconds.

The motivated athlete responds to the physical effects of age by conditioning himself more intensively. "That Spinks, he looks like Dracula, but he's only twenty-five," Ali said, in a house he had rented near Lake Pontchartrain. "So I have to make myself twenty-five. I been up every morning, running real long, real early for five months. Five months. I've done the mostest exercises ever, maybe three hundred and fifty different kinds, so's I could become the first man ever, in all history, to win back the heavyweight championship twice."

For the first two rounds in the New Orleans Superdome, Ali toyed with a dream of knocking out Spinks. But all the roadwork and the sparring could not bring back the snake-tongue quickness of the hands. Ali missed badly with two hard rights. Then, yielding to reality, he made a perfect analysis of Spinks's style and how to overcome it.

Spinks had no style, really. Move in standing up, move in, move in, punch, lunge. Devoid of style, he still is strong and dangerous. From the third round Ali simply moved around and about Spinks, flicking punches, holding, sliding, holding, always staying three moves ahead. It was a boring and decisive victory, and it must've hurt like hell.

Afterward, at a press conference in the Superdome, Ali spoke in the crabbed tones of age. First of all, this huge crowd—seventy thousand, give or take a few thousand—had come to a black promotion. "Wasn't no blond hair or blue eyes doing no promoting," the champion said. That is accurate, but only in a lawyerly way. The man who put together Ali-Spinks II (and the marvelous undercard) is Robert Arum, whose hair is black and whose eyes are brown. He is, however, white. Under the Arum umbrella, so to speak, two blacks and two whites, all from Louisiana, were subsidiary promoters. They are now suing each other.

Having stretched truth until it snapped, Ali offered a brief return to his old form. "Was that a thirty-six-year-old man out there, fighting tonight? And not only fighting but dancing? Was that dancing man out there thirty-six?"

"Thassright," chirped a parliament of votaries.

"That *Time* magazine," Ali said, "that great *Time* magazine, goes all over the world, they wrote Ali was through. Could *Time* magazine be wrong . . . ?"

Crabby again, he was settling an account he had already closed in the ring, treating a buried story as though it were alive. It was a graceless effort from a man Dundee says now has to work too hard. Why, then, does Ali drive on past his prime? Supporting himself and his children and his wife and former wives and his retinue and properties, Ali said not long ago, costs about $60,000 a month after taxes. His investment income is short of that. He fights on because he believes he needs the money.

Over three recent months I explored cash and credit, concentration and distraction, professional life and professional death—in short, how the jock grows older—with thirty-one remarkable athletes. They have worked their trades—baseball, boxing, basketball, football, hockey—from San Diego to New England. One (Tarkenton) was sufficiently sophisticated to evoke Thomas Jefferson. "Doing a variety of things, like Jefferson did, keeps you fresh." Others (Lou Brock, Merlin Olsen, Brooks Robinson) showed positively Viennese instincts for self-analysis.

"Did anyone say that money had nothing to do with why he kept on playing?" asked Fred Biletnikoff. He's been a wide receiver at Oakland for fourteen seasons.

"Some said the money wasn't primary."

Biletnikoff drew a breath to prepare his own comment. "You know," he said, "they're full of shit."

Generally the athletes were honest and direct. Away from cameras, one on one, athletes speak more honestly than entertainers or politicians. Most shared annoyance at America's blinding obsession with youth. They found subtle prejudice against age in certain executive suites. "In the front office I have to put up with," one veteran baseball player said, "they're always looking for a reason to replace me. Maybe it's because a young guy would cost less, but I think it's not just that. They got a mind-set on the axiom that baseball is a young man's game."

Willie McCovey, the mighty first baseman who reached forty-one in January, is discomfited by a particular fan in Chicago. "There's this dude who sits behind the on-deck circle in Wrigley Field," McCovey reported, "and when I get a hit, he doesn't make a sound. But every time I swing and miss, I hear the joker holler, 'You're getting old, McCovey. You're washed up.'"

McCovey shook his head in annoyance. "That's shit," he said. "Doesn't the guy know I missed pitches years ago? Does he think I never made an out until I was thirty-five?"

"He's just needling," I said.

"Well, I say needle with a little intelligence. Judge me by my performance. Forget my age. I try to forget my age myself. Too much thinking about your age can psych you. It can make you press and panic and retire before your time." McCovey believes that is what happened to his friend Willie Mays.

Every geriatric athlete that I talked to maintained an unabated passion for the game. It was a passion to win, to prove certain points, to keep on making money. To those men, sport was no small sliver of the consciousness; it dominated them.

Brooks Robinson, the fine third baseman who played until he was forty, said, "My whole life had been baseball. Passion? It sure was for me. In the eighth grade back in Arkansas, I wrote a whole booklet about how I wanted to be a ballplayer. That never changed. I kept on wanting to be a ballplayer until my reflexes told me it was time to stop. By then I'd played almost as many big-league games as Ty Cobb."

"Didn't age hit you like a rabbit punch?" I asked.

"The first time something was written about my age, I was thirty. 'The aging Brooks Robinson,' the story said. I thought, What do they mean by 'aging'? I'm a young man. And I went out to play harder. When they called me aging at thirty-five, it didn't hit me either way. I knew they were accurate in sports terms. But then, when I was called aging at thirty-nine, the thing became a challenge all over again. It stayed a challenge until I accepted what time can do and got out."

A few old athletes remain absolutely juvenile in their enthusiasms. George Blanda, the quarterback and placekicker, was forty-eight when he played his last game in the National Football League. "Hell, I didn't retire even then," Blanda said. "*They* retired me. I enjoyed it. I always enjoyed it. Proving myself week after week. Ego-building week after week. Who wouldn't enjoy all that?"

A generation ago, major-league baseball extended only from St. Louis to Boston. The professional hockey season was half the present schedule. Pro football was a secondary sport. The sporting life, the sporting pace, was leisurely and more conducive to longevity than today's Sunday afternoon and Monday night fever.

I was fortunate enough to begin covering sports before the disappearance of the American train. Going from New York to St. Louis was a twenty-four-hour hegira. You traveled in a private car and you ate in a private diner, and a drink was never farther away than a porter's call button. Moving at double-digit speeds, trains gave your body a chance to adjust as you crossed time zones.

"But jet travel now is part of the package," said Lou Brock, a major-league outfielder since 1961 and the man who broke Ty Cobb's record for stolen bases. "Mentally it doesn't make sense to eliminate or separate different aspects of a ballplayer's life. If you want the cheers and the fame and the money and the victories, you've got to accept the two A.M. jet rides. They go together."

I first traveled a sports circuit in high excitement. I had never seen the Golden Triangle in Pittsburgh or the lakeshore north of Milwaukee or the drained malarial swamps around Houston, for that matter. Like the young men in the old stories, I ached for travel. Then, very quickly, sports travel—as distinct from a pleasure trip to Cozumel— became a mini-hell.

"I don't look at travel like that," said Brock. "Not like that at all. To me, travel is still exciting. When I think of travel, I ask myself, How else can I get to my opponent? Get to where he is and whip him?"

Various athletes play tactical games with time. Phil Esposito, the hockey forward, keeps his weight twelve pounds lower than it was a decade ago. Tony Perez, the first baseman, says that at thirty-six he is far better at anticipating pitches than he was when younger. If you guess low slider and the pitcher throws a low slider, you stay in business. "You can sometimes beat the younger guys with your head," said Dave Bing, the basketball player, who decided to retire last August when he was thirty-five. "You figure their weaknesses and you play into them. But in the end . . ."

Major sport is American trauma. Crumpled knees drive halfbacks into early retirement; pitchers' arms go dead; hockey players slammed to the ice twist in convulsion. Before this onslaught both the body and the psyche tremble.

The complete athlete measures pain against glory, risk against profit. He considers what is left of his body and then, I believe, he subconsciously decides whether or not he wants to go on. In the end, the difference between Carl Yastrzemski, a star at thirty-nine, and Mickey Mantle, an assistant batting coach at that age, is that Yaz wanted it more.

It is tempting to conclude with too much certitude on so-called qualitative distinctions among the experiences of various athletes aging into other men's prime time. Is Tony Perez, who grew up in the balmy poverty of Cuba, markedly afraid hard times will come now in the North? He says not. Is Gordie Howe, who still works hockey at the age of fifty, clutching the withered stump of his boyhood? Hell, no, Howe says. His wrists hurt and his legs are gone, but he loves playing pro hockey on the same team as his sons.

This temptation to conclude too much persists. To me, the core here is rather like what the saucy, lissome tennis player was to the veteran pitcher. The object looks so damned attainable: then, in a blink of too-bright eyes, it is gone.

My journalistic interviews are not excursions into therapy. You ask. The athlete answers. You press a little. He tries to be honest. You press harder. He thinks of his image. He also tries to be macho. He tries to keep his dignity. You ask some more. You think. And you move on.

So I fight temptations to write glibly about predictable crises, self-flagellation, or variable testosterone levels. If I can hear and share a little of the heartbeat of another man, I have my accomplishment.

The bravest and most competitive athlete I knew was Jackie Robinson. Breaking the major-league color line in 1947, he played with teammates who called him nigger. Rivals from at least four teams tried to spike him. The best I can say for the press is that it was belligerently neutral.

What Jack did—his genius and his glory—was to make obstacles work for him. Call him nigger and he'd get mad. Mad, he'd crush you. Misquote him out of laziness or malice and he'd take his disgust out on rival pitchers, as though they were the boozy press. Barred from the dining room of your hotel in Cincinnati at lunch, he'd dominate your ballpark in Cincinnati after dinner.

It was a cruel, demanding way to have to live. His career burned out in a decade, and his life ended when he was fifty-three. "This man," the

Reverend Jesse Jackson intoned from the funeral pulpit, "turned a stumbling block into a stepping-stone."

Only a few extraordinary athletes—Stan Musial and Joe DiMaggio—are able to prevail in retirement. Their glory intact, they move from the ballpark to other arenas, still special heroes. Some, like Jack Dempsey and Casey Stengel, even achieve Olympian old age. All these men learned how to transform obstacles into stepping-stones.

"Did Robinson know he was dying?" my friend Carl Erskine, once a Dodger pitching star, asked after the funeral.

"I think maybe he did."

"How did he bear up?"

"It was amazing. He was getting blinder and lamer every day and working harder and harder for decent housing for blacks."

"He was a hero," Erskine said.

"Apart from baseball," I said.

"But don't you think," Erskine said, "that disciplining himself the way he had to and mastering self-control and commanding a sense of purpose—don't you think the things he had to do to keep making it in baseball taught him how to behave in the last battle?"

Before that moment I had a distaste for people who saw sports as a metaphor for life. Where I grew up, life was less trivial than a ball game. "I never thought of that till now," I said, still learning.

CHAPTER 31

EVEN SPORTSWRITERS GET OLD

The scribes last longer than the gladiators they observe and chronicle. But even the writers get old, as Kahn learns when he turns the tables and muses about the likes of newspaper columnists Red Smith, Jimmy Cannon, and Paul Gallico as their bodies begin to creak. Kahn was forty-six when he wrote this 1974 article for Esquire. *He was seventy-five when he wrote his 2002 book,* October Men.

Somewhere Ring Lardner is supposed to have offered, among wry sours, "There isn't anything on earth as depressing as an old sportswriter." Nothing in my first encounter with the breed refuted the great sportswriter, who himself did not live to be old.

There was a man on the *New York Post* who drank three meals a day, deified Leo Durocher, cadged money from anyone who moved, and used to fall asleep while smoking. He started several hotel fires and became a professional joke until he set fire to the bed in his apartment. Most of his body was charred, but the man required no anesthetic for hours. Alcohol had immunized him from pain, although not from death. Three days after his admission to a hospital, the sportswriter died, stone sober for the first time in years.

The *Brooklyn Eagle* had a writer past seventy who dragged after young athletes, barely able to tote his typewriter, loathing the work but having nothing else to sustain his life. "They'll break you, kid," he said. "I used to write short stories, but they broke me, and you'll get broken, too." He tripped over a small step in a hotel lobby, fractured a hip, and died on the road.

Some old writers felt trapped by the insignificance of what they were reporting. During World War II one complained, "The world is blowing up and what do I write? Zeke Bonura got two hits today. That's no work for a grown man, is it?"

Others reacted to the trivia of games by taking unshakable, mindless postures on more important things. "Anyone who sympathized with the Loyalists during the Spanish Civil War," an old *New York Times* man told me, "was a fool."

"Well, Ernest Hemingway supported the Loyalists," I said. "Means nothing," the reporter insisted. "A man can be a great writer and still be a fool."

Back of the dining room at Vero Beach, Florida, the old sportswriters sat in wicker chairs and played poker with baseball officials who were earning five times as much as they. Betting their rent against someone else's tip money, the writers were constantly bluffed out of pots, forever defeated.

One writer tried to recoup by drinking brandy supplied by the ball club. In a desperate reach toward elegance, he ordered ponies of Courvoisier, dipped his cigar in the drink, lit it, threw out the brandy, and ordered a fresh shot. "Goddamnit," said Buzzy Bavasi of the Dodgers. "Do you think that hundred-fifty-dollar-a-week slob does that at home?"

Without lusting to find out personally, I suppose that everyone's later years are sapped endurance, uncertain sleep, and failing memory. It was Yeats who complained, "What shall I do with this absurdity . . . decrepit age that has been tied to me as to a dog's tail." But old poets—Frost, Masefield, Sandburg—achieve the blessing of patriarchy. Old physicians, who may still believe in leeches, perfect an authoritative look, practice less, and charge more. Old lawyers—well I've heard of one in Bridgeport who has just married at seventy-five and is moving toward his second million.

The old sportswriters I knew drew no rewards for vintage. They still had to meet the guillotine of deadlines. They had to argue with room clerks, struggle with baggage, and climb the interminable steps at Princeton that lead to a press box called Thrombosis Terrace. The athletes, young and intolerant, laughed at the sportswriters' salaries. It was said that a football player on a good Big Ten scholarship earned more than a crack reporter for United Press.

Finally, the writers were constantly instructed on their unimportance. A generation of editors preached anti-ego sermons. Nobody cares about you, your ulcer, your bent dreams. Write about hook slides. Indeed, the protean sports editor Stanley Woodward, explaining why a prospect failed, observed, "He single-spaces his copy and he uses the first person." Not a happy group, I thought, on many nights, hearing old sportswriters tell flat stories in a prolix way.

A few years ago Jerry Holtzman, a Chicago baseball writer in middle years, mentioned an idea for a book. He wanted to record the reminiscences of old sportswriters, he said, and did I think he'd be able to find a publisher.

"A dumb one," I said.

"What do you mean?"

"Well, most of these people are going to be dull."

Holtzman, a stocky, intense man, nodded, but I could see from his eyes that he intended to go on. Now, forty-four interviews later, his publisher, Holt, Rinehart and Winston (smart enough, incidentally, to hold the rights to Frost's poems), has sent me *No Cheering in the Press Box*. The finished product staggers and corrects me. *No Cheering in the Press Box* is a splendid work of oral history, on a par with Lawrence Ritter's *The Glory of Their Times*.

Out of the forty-four men he interviewed, Holtzman prints the memoirs of eighteen. (When last we met, he was concerned that he might be making twenty-six enemies.) By rejecting what is maundering, he gives us a book of pace, interest, and even a certain consistency. These old journalists, mean age seventy-five, appear to have come to terms with the toughness of life. It wasn't easy, it isn't easy, and it won't become easy. Yet as Faulkner said, one tries to prevail. That is the sense of the book. Have you ever heard of a man called Richard Vidmer? He wrote a sports column in the *New York Herald Tribune* called "Down Front," which he abandoned to marry a rajah's daughter. They traveled, lived in Barbados, played golf. But Vidmer had a need to work. The rajah's daughter disapproved. Holtzman found him in Orlando, Florida, still handsome, married for a third time, and newly philosophical. "Two people, you and I as voting men, go into business together and we hit it off fine. We are twenty-one. But when we're thirty five, your life has changed and my life has changed and we're not good business partners anymore. That's what happens to marriages."

John R. Tunis, eighty-four, has composed a score of books on young athletes struggling and winning. A sample title is *The Kid Comes Back*. In Essex, Connecticut, Tunis says, "I've written what I wanted and tried to explain there is more to life than throwing a football. You can say my books have been read, but only by kids. Nobody has paid any attention. Still my books are the most important thing I did. Damn right. I just sent back the proofs on my latest, *The Grand National*. I doubt I'll do another one. I've always been busy, and this is the first time I haven't another book to begin. Now I may have time to read Flaubert."

Fred Lieb, eighty-six, says he was "in the foremost freshman class that ever broke into the New York press box." That was in 1911, and the other rookies were Grantland Rice, Damon Runyon, Heywood Broun. Lieb talks about his friendship with Lou Gehrig and Gehrig's wife and about "a falling out after Lou died. I found that Lou's grave— he's buried in Westchester County—was very much neglected, a ton of weeds, bird shit all over it." After Lieb complained to a third party, Mrs. Gehrig called him one three A.M. Apparently the two no longer speak.

The most prosperous of Holtzman's writers is Paul Gallico, whom Holtzman traces to a forty-five-year-old house in Antibes. During the 1920s Gallico suggested to Jack Dempsey that they spar.

"What's the matter, son," the champion said. "Don't your editor like you no more?"

Jack Kearns, who managed Dempsey, protested. "Listen. You don't know this kid. He might be a ringer."

Dempsey said, "Well, I promised the kid and I don't break a promise."

"All right, but don't be a fool," Kearns said. "Get him quick." Dempsey threw a left hook and Gallico went down. He heard Kearns saying 'six, seven, eight.' "Like a goddamn fool, I got up. By then Dempsey knew I was a bum. He whispered, 'Hang on, kid, till your head clears.' But he couldn't stop. He hit me with six straight rabbit punches on the neck, and the next thing I knew, Kearns was saying, 'thirty-eight, thirty-nine, forty.' A half hour later I was writing my story."

Gallico still fences, enjoys a solitary life with his fourth wife, and relishes Antibes, which he says is a working town, not like Cannes and Nice. "We're sort of locals. We live a very quiet life. You have to concentrate to write. You can't be disturbed. You can't do a lot of running around. You can't stay up too late at night. You can't drink too much. I'm seventy-six, but I don't feel old. I'll write as long as my brain is able to put together two sentences."

Red Smith, now sixty-nine, meditates on glory. "When you go through Westminster Abbey, you find that excepting for that little Poets' Corner, almost all the statues are of killers. Of generals and admirals whose specialty was human slaughter. I don't think they're such glorious heroes. I've tried not to exaggerate the glory of athletes."

Finally, Holtzman gives us Jimmy Cannon, just before Cannon died at sixty-three. I remember Cannon on a night in The Little Club when he was dating Judy Garland. I can't recall what anybody said, but everyone kept talking. As Cannon spoke, Miss Garland's eyes glazed. When Judy spoke, Cannon fumbled for his cigarettes. Cannon's own epitaph makes me wish I'd watched the self-involvement less and listened more.

Sitting in a wheelchair, where a stroke prisoned him, Cannon is hard, exciting, brave. He says, "Sportswriting has survived because of the guys who don't cheer." He would rather have been with Hemingway than with Babe Ruth. He feels that "the great athletes are fortunate that they met me." The best newspaper writers were Ben Hecht, Westbrook Pegler, Damon Runyon. The most neglected writer in America is Nelson Algren. He "wrote better about Chicago than anybody—including Carl Sandburg." Cannon can't stand politicians. "They lie more than football coaches." At the end, crippled and solitary, Cannon sums up his life, this book:

"I've had a great life. I sat at glad events. And I've liked some of the people. My two favorite people in sports were Joe Louis and Joe DiMaggio. They were my friends, and I think explaining friendship is like explaining pain. It's impossible after it's subsided. I have terrible pain right now." But what a legacy.

CHAPTER 32

CARL FURILLO, 1922–1989

His nickname was "Skoonj," short for scungili, *which is Italian for snail. In 1953 he led the National League in hitting with a .344 batting average. He was best known for his rifle arm, and once he threw out a runner at first base from his position in right field. But when he died in 1989, Kahn movingly remembered not his exploits on the green pastures but the strangely solitary man who was Carl Anthony Furillo.*

G il Hodges was the first to go. Then Jackie Robinson. Next—after a brief remission from death, Billy Cox. And suddenly there stood a journalist asking Pee Wee Reese, "How does it feel to be the last person alive from the great Brooklyn Dodger infield?"

I gasped. I was next to the one who asked that wicked question. Reese stood his ground and said, in the full flower of his poise, "I don't think about things that way. If I did, I might go crazy."

Carl Furillo's death commands such memories to mind. Even as it does, I cannot believe Carl Furillo is dead. He was so skilled, so handsome, and so strong, I thought he'd be throwing out base runners, some smart, some dumb, until he passed his one hundredth birthday. Furillo was granted sixty-six birthdays. That was enough time to brighten life for everyone who took the time to know him.

Quite simply, he was a great player. Some write about his arm, the human cannon. He was not the man you'd ask to join you in a casual game of catch. Or how he played the right-field wall at Ebbets Field. That wall, a mystery of dead spots, bounces, angles, and planes, was a wonder of baseball before the dream destroyers wrecked it. Furillo never attended high school. Plane geometry remained a mystery to him. But he knew every angle, every carom. The way Furillo played the wall describes an art form.

Carl Erskine says he was a "Bible hitter." First pitch anywhere, in the dirt or at the eyes, Furillo took his mighty swing. Why, then, was he a Bible hitter? Erskine says, "Thou shalt not pass" (Numbers 20).

Furillo gathered 1,910 hits in fifteen major-league years. He pulled the ball sometimes, or went to right. No one ever banged a baseball harder up the middle. If Furillo ever misjudged a fly I never saw it.

In the whispering rush of memory I hear my father saying: "We'll go out to the ballpark early, son. They have a feller who can throw." And so the Dodgers did. A young center fielder. Others came out, thousands of others, long before formal competition started, to watch the warm-up throws. You could hear gasps at Ebbets Field and sometimes, an hour before game time, bursts of applause.

The Dodgers moved Furillo into right field, making him yield center to the exuberant grace of Duke Snider. Where a dandelion could not grow—right field in Brooklyn—Furillo flowered.

George (Shotgun) Shuba said that when Billy Herman hit fungoes in warm-up, he told Herman, "You better hit to left field first. *I'm not going to throw after that guy.*"

Doing a retrospective radio program with Roy Campanella I said, "Campy, how did you like that throw off wet grass?"

Campanella remembered certain moist nights. "You know," he said, "I had to go to Carl one time and tell him: 'Please bounce the ball closer to first base. No one in the world can handle that one-hopper the way you're giving it to me.'"

So there was, I suppose, an element of awe. Beyond that, there stood an extraordinary person. I knew Furillo for thirty-seven years. I do not believe he was capable of telling a lie.

Early on he had a hard time accepting the integration of baseball. He grew up in all-white country and was never schooled beyond the eighth grade. But Furillo changed and grew, a quiet man learning from his times. In 1953 the Dodgers added Jim Gilliam to the roster, and a few players complained about another black in an ugly way. I wrote a story using no names, and Buzzy Bavasi, running the Brooklyn Dodgers, said, "Who talked to you?"

"We don't work that way, Buzzy."

"I'll find out," Bavasi said.

By this point Furillo was warming up each night by playing catch with Campanella. He had surpassed his boyhood and grown color-blind. Into the clubhouse I went, and Furillo called me over. "That stuff was years ago," he said. "I was wrong. I got nothing against the colored."

"I didn't write that you had anything against the colored."

"Bavasi says you did."

"Carl, I swear I never wrote that. I'll show you the story."

"You don't have to swear and you don't have to show me the story, just giving me your word is good enough."

Such seems to be the stuff of friendship, even love. Long afterward, a career later, he mentioned that he was afflicted by chronic leukemia. "Some of the tests are bad," he said, "but you know I never made real money playing ball. So what can I do? I always worked. I got to work."

When I last saw this elegant gentleman, he was putting in four nights a week as a night watchman, fighting off leukemia, and not complaining. Hell, Carl said, we all have to work, even writers.

In 1987 I lost a gifted son to heroin. Roger Lawrence Kahn had just passed his twenty-second birthday. The telephone rang a few days later, and the caller said, "This is Pee Wee. You remember I was captain of the team."

"I do remember."

"I just want to say," Reese said, "for all the fellers, that we are very, very sorry."

Our turns come and go. I mean only to say, for all the fellers, Carl, may you walk in green pastures.

ACKNOWLEDGMENTS

The idea of preparing an anthology of Roger Kahn's work began in the fall of 2002 after Kahn visited my university. I had begun to read some of his books, beyond his 1972 classic, *The Boys of Summer*, which I—and everyone else—had already read. And I began to see that he had written so much good nonfiction, as well as two novels. I started then to delve into his magazine pieces, of which there are hundreds. I had only a vague recollection of his 1950s articles written for *Sport*, then the top sports magazine in the country. I was more familiar with his entrancing *Esquire* columns of the early 1970s, articles that I used to look forward to as a respite from the turbulent and exhausting politics of that era. Someone, I thought, had to collect a representative selection of his work. And that is when Kahn and I began to plan *Beyond the Boys of Summer*, which for me has been a labor of love. How could it not be? His work is always lyrical, literary, biting, amusing and interesting.

Kahn was patient and helpful in the preparation of this book. He consented to three long interviews as I prepared to write my introductory essay. He also guided me to various articles and answered many follow-up questions, as we became friends and colleagues. I appreciate his time, but I'm most appreciative that readers will get to see the breadth of his work as viewed here in the selected articles and book chapters and in this first-ever bibliography.

Various people at the State University of New York's College at New Paltz helped me. The interlibrary loan staff at the Sojourner Truth

Library was patient and diligent as I searched out Kahn articles. Various librarians helped find citations for missing Kahn articles. Linda Smith of my college's computer center was most important as she and a student helper scanned Kahn articles to prepare them for publication. The bibliography was helped tremendously by James L. Gates Jr., library director, National Baseball Hall of Fame and Museum. And Alan Silverman helped keep my computer virus-free and in playing shape while the manuscript was prepared.

As always, my wife, Mary Beth Pfeiffer, listened and encouraged and became enthusiastic as the book unfolded. And my children, Robert Michael and Sara Elspeth, both became Kahn enthusiasts along the way, listening to his stories and reading his work.

ROGER KAHN
BIBLIOGRAPHY

1953

"What White Big Leaguers REALLY Think of Negro Players," *Our Sports*, 10–14.

1954

Mutual Baseball Almanac, eds., Roger Kahn and Al Helfer (Garden City, N.Y.: Doubleday).

"The Curious Case of Joe Black," *Sport*, May, 16–17.

"Durocher Has to Win or Else," *Sport*, August, 10–11.

"Twilight of the Baseball Gods," *Sports Illustrated*, September 20, 10–13.

"One . . . Two . . . Three . . . Four & Bingo Sports," *Sports Illustrated*, October 11, 16–24.

"Forget Something, Boys?" *Sports Illustrated*, December 20, 10–13.

"The World Series Is a Wonderful Moment—New York Proudly Presents: Those Giants," *Sports Illustrated*, September 27, 11–13.

"Baseball 1954," *Sports Illustrated*, October 4, 14–18.

"Here's Tap Day," *Sports Illustrated*, November 22, 70–72.

1955

Mutual Baseball Almanac, Roger Kahn and Harry Wismer. Paul Lapolla, ed. (Garden City, N.Y.: Doubleday).
"The Ten Years of Jackie Robinson," *Sport*, October, 12–21.
"Big Newk and His Psyche," *Sport*, August, 22–23.

1956

"What's Wrong with the American League," Al Silverman, ed., *True's 1956 Baseball Yearbook* (Greenwich, Conn.: Fawcett), 66–72.
"Oklahoma's Mickey Mantle: Can the Young Yankee Beat the Babe?" *Newsweek*, June 25, 63–67.
"The Four Sides of the Beanball Argument," *Sport*, January, 10–11.
"The Life and Death of Howie Morenz," *Sport*, February, 23–27.
"Where Does Big Newk Go from Here?" *Sport*, March, 26–27.
"Early Wynn: The Story of a Hard Loser," *Sport*, March, 52–61.
"Life with a Manager," *Newsweek*, March 24, 79–80.
"Marty Marion: The Philosopher of the Dugout," *Sport*, May, 58–64.
"The Bewildering World of Willie Mays," *Sport*, June, 52–63.
"I Play Baseball for Money—Not Fun," *Collier's*, May 25, 44.
"Halfbacks Carry the Mortgage," *The Nation*, December 22, 539–41.

1957

"Why Birds Fly High," *Sport*, July 1, 69–74.
"Sports in America," *The Nation*, "Money, Muscles—and Myths," July 6, 9–11.
"The Boswells of Baseball," *The Nation*, August 3, 49–51.
"Nice Guys Finish Last," *The Nation*, September 7, 108–10.
"Case of the Erudite Jockey," *Saturday Evening Post*, February 23, 77–79.
"Pee Wee and the Fountain of Youth," *Sport*, June, 52–61.
"Intellectuals and Ball Players," *The American Scholar*, Summer, 342–49.

1958

"Money, Muscles—and Myths," Eric Larrabee and Rolf Meyersohn, eds., *Mass Leisure* (New York: Free Press), 264–68.
"The Man—Stan Musial Is Baseball's No. 1 Citizen," *Sport*, February, 52–67.

"Turn Back the Clock: Chicago White Sox," *Newsweek*, March 17, 94.

"Little Nellie's a Man Now," *Sport*, April, 52–67.

"Red Smith of the Press Box," *Newsweek*, April 21, 77–80.

"Rookie of the Year," *Cosmopolitan*, June, 74–77.

"The Art of Warren Spahn," *Sport*, June, 56–67.

"Headaches of Notre Dame," *Saturday Evening Post*, September 28, 42–44.

"Control Is Seventeen Inches Wide," *Coronet*, September, 135–39.

"Milwaukee's Man on Third," *Sport*, September, 52–62.

"How the Other Half Lives," *Sport*, October, 32–36.

"Whitey Ford Is His Own Boss," *Sport*, December, 52–61.

1959

"Intellectuals and Ballplayers," introduction to Harold P. Simpson, ed. *Cross Currents* (New York: Harper), 126–34.

"Soldiers Are His Game," in *Best Sports Stories 1959 Edition: A Panorama of the 1958 Sports Year*, Irving T. Marsh and Edward Ehre, eds. (New York: Dutton), 127–30.

"Lew Burdette, Professional Pitcher," *Sport*, February, 52–62.

"Something's Changing About Baseball," *New York Times Magazine*, April 5, 49–50.

"Man with the Brainy Arm," *New York Times Magazine*, May 31, 22–25.

"Inside the Clubhouse: What the Yankees Think of Mickey Mantle," *Sport*, June, 16–19.

"Don Newcombe's Good Days and Bad," *Sport*, July, 56–71.

"Toonder on the Right," *The Nation*, July 18, 29–31.

"Salute to Baseball's Elder Statesman," *New York Times Magazine*, July 26, 13.

"The Crucial Part Fear Plays in Sports," *Sport*, August, 20–24.

"Brains in Their Arms," *Baseball Digest*, September, 35–41.

"Hank Aaron's Success Story," *Sport*, September, 52–71.

"Olympic for Thoroughbreds," *Saturday Evening Post*, November 7, 31.

"The Elder Statesman Near the End of the Road," *Baseball Digest*, December, 35–40.

"The Real Babe Ruth," *Baseball Digest*, October, 23–32.

1960

"Willie Mays," Ed Fitzgerald, ed., *Heroes of Sport* (New York: Bartholomew House), 72–79.

"Salute to Baseball's Elder Statesman," ibid., 5–22.

"Jackie Robinson," ibid., 137–54.

"The Elder Statesman Near the End of the Road," *Baseball Digest*, January, 35–41.

"Shakeup at Yankee Stadium," *Sport*, January, 16–17.

"Dodgers, We Love You," *Sport*, February, 48–57.

"Right That Failed," *The Nation*, July 9, 28–30.

"Does Charley Dressen Talk Too Much?" *Saturday Evening Post*, August 27, 25.

"Special Report: The Fans' Favorite," *Sport*, September, 16–17.

"Benching of a Legend," *Sports Illustrated*, September 12, 1–6.

"The Day Bobby Hit the Home Run," *Sports Illustrated*, October 10, 40–59.

"Visit with Robert Frost," *Saturday Evening Post*, November 19, 26–27.

1961

The World of John Lardner, Roger Kahn, ed., with a preface by Walt Kelly (New York: Simon and Schuster).

"Football's Taking Over," in *Best Sports Stories: A Panorama of the 1960 Sports Year*, Irving T. Marsh and Edward Ehre, eds. (New York: Dutton), 115–22.

"Nellie Fox," in Ed Fitzgerald, ed., *Heroes of Sport* (New York: Bartholomew House), 64–77.

"Actor Without an Ego," *Saturday Evening Post*, January 21, 22–23.

"Advantage, Mr. Kramer," *The Nation*, February 18, 146–47.

"Success and Ned Irish," *Sports Illustrated*, March 27, 39–40.

"Baseball's Secret Weapon, Terror," *Sports Illustrated*, July 10, 22–25.

"Eleanor Powell's Comeback," *Good Housekeeping*, October, 32.

"Pursuit of No. 60: The Ordeal of Roger Maris," *Sports Illustrated*, October 2, 22–28.

1962

Inside Big League Baseball (New York: Macmillan).

"The Ten Years of Jackie Robinson," *Editors of Sport, World of Sport* (New York: Holt, Rinehart and Winston), 43–60.

"The Real Babe Ruth," *Great Men and Moments in Sports* (New York: Harper), 45–52.

"Early Wynn's Struggle," *Sport*, July, 14–17.

1963

"The Time of the Hustler," in *Best Sports Stories 1963 Edition: A Panorama of the 1962 Sports Year*, Irving T. Marsh and Edward Ehre, eds. (New York: Dutton), 255–63.

"Robert Frost: A Reminiscence," *The Nation*, February 9, 121.

"Is There a Doris Day?" *Ladies Home Journal*, July, 62–65.

"Pursuit of No. 60: The Ordeal of Roger Maris," in *Editors of Sports Illustrated* (New York: McGraw Hill), 101–15.

1964

"Harlem Sketchbook: White Man, Walk Easy," *Saturday Evening Post*, January 13, 26–28, 34–38.

"Bill Miller: The GOP's Tough, Shrewd Pro," *Saturday Evening Post*, August 8, 81–83.

"Yankees: Descent from Olympus," *Saturday Evening Post*, September 12, 80–83.

"Our Davis Cup Runneth Over," *Saturday Evening Post*, September 26, 66–69.

"Speaking Out: Let's Pull Out of the Olympics," *Saturday Evening Post*, October 10, 64.

"Goldwater's Desperate Battle," *Saturday Evening Post*, October 24, 81–83.

1965

"The Case of the Dead Bookie," *Saturday Evening Post*, March 13, 34–38, 40, 42–43.

"House of Adolph Ochs," *Saturday Evening Post*, October 9, 32–38, 41–42, 46–49, 54–56, 58–60.

"Frank Ryan," *Saturday Evening Post*, November 20, 92, 95, 96.

1966

"Willie Mays, the Boy Who Came to Play," Herbert W. Wind, ed., *The Realm of Sport* (New York: Simon and Schuster), 72–79.

"Arthur Goldberg: I'm Not Discouraged, Got It?" *Saturday Evening Post*, January 29, 85–89.

"Durocher: They Ain't Getting No Maiden," *Saturday Evening Post*, June 18, 97–101.

"Baseball's Score: Tumult, Arrogance, Anarchy, and Some Magnificent Games," *Sport*, September, 62–69.

1967

"Game Without Ball," *Saturday Evening Post*, December 16, 79–83.

1968

The Passionate People: What It Means to be a Jew in America (New York: Fawcett).

"Revolt Against LBJ," *Saturday Evening Post*, February 10, 17–21.

"On the Brink of Chaos," *Saturday Evening Post*, July 27, 22–23.

"They Shall Have Music," *Saturday Evening Post*, September 7, 68–71.

"Sixty Years of Feuding: How the Giants and Dodgers Got That Way," *Sport*, January, 52–63.

"Glenn Hall: An Hour or So of Hell," *Saturday Evening Post*, March 23, 86–89.

1969

"Willie Mays, Yesterday and Today," *Sport*, August, 54–66.

"The Collapse of the S.D.S.," *Esquire*, October, 140–44.

"Fiddler on the Shelf," *Life*, October 31, 58.

1970

Battle for Morningside Heights: Why Students Rebel. Foreword by Eugene McCarthy. (New York: William Morrow & Co.).

"How About a New TV Deal for Baseball," *Life*, March 20, 10.

"Our Sports" column in *Esquire*: "Writing Sports," August, 32, 34, 36;
  "Ron Bloomberg," September, 58, 60; "Bill Veeck," October, 34,
  38–39; "The Rhinoceros Hypothesis," November, 78; "Baseball
  Books," December, 14, 16, 18, 22.
"Perfect Toy," *Esquire*, December, 172–76.

1971

"The Life and Hard Times of Jim Bouton," in *Best Sports Stories 1971:
  A Panorama of the 1970 Sports World*, Irving T. Marsh and Edward
  Ehre, eds. (New York: Dutton), 247–56.
"Willie Mays, Yesterday and Today," Al Silverman, ed., *The Best of
  Sport, 1946–1971* (New York: Viking Press), 472–89.
"The Ten Years of Jackie Robinson," ibid., 114–30.
"Our Sports" column in *Esquire*: "Derek Sanderson," January, 50–51;
  "Joe Frazier," February, 18–20; "Willis Reed," March, 34, 38, 40;
  "Television," April, 22; "The Mick," May, 16–17; "Roy Emerson,"
  June, 30–31; "Bob Gibson," July, 16–17; "Michael Burke," August,
  20; "Jimmy the Greek," September, 14–15, 21–22; "John Rotz,"
  October, 24, 30, 32, 34; "Jackie Robinson Jr.," November, 24, 26,
  30; "Bob Lilly," December, 14, 16.
"The Hard Hat Who Sued Baseball," *Sport*, September, 56–62.
"One Stayed in Brooklyn," *Sport*, October, 54–56.
"The Road to Viola," *Sport*, November, 54–56.
"Jackie Robinson," *Sport*, December, 64–87.

1972

The Boys of Summer (New York: Harper & Row).
"Our Sports" column in *Esquire*: "Jim Plunkett," January, 11, 22, 30;
  "Emile Francis," February, 33, 38; "Earl Monroe," March, 13–14;
  "The Sports Draft," April, 24, 29; "Basketball vs. Football," May,
  16, 18, 22, 40; "Gardner Mulloy," June, 21–22, 24, 34; "A Parting
  Column," July, 13, 16, 18.
"Fragile Genius of a Virtuoso," *Life*, August, 49–52.

1973

How the Weather Was (New York: Harper & Row).

"Leo Durocher: 'They Ain't Getting No Maiden,' " in Jim Bouton, ed., *I Managed Good but Did They Play Bad* (Chicago: Playboy Press), Chapter 10.

"Why Football?" *New York Times Magazine*, October 7, 22.

"Our Sports" column in *Esquire*: "The St. Louis Cardinals," September, 34; "Robert G. Woolf, Agent," November, 114, 116, 121; "Nick Bouniconti," December, 31, 34, 37, 118.

1974

"One Stayed in Brooklyn," in Tom Seaver, ed., *How I Would Pitch to Babe Ruth* (Chicago: Playboy Press), 24–27.

"Background: Roy Campanella," *TV Guide*, February 16, 19–20.

"Babe Ruth: A Look Behind the Legend," *Reader's Digest*, August, 136–40.

"In the Catbird Seat," *Sports Illustrated*, 41:34–40, August 5.

"Our Sports" column in *Esquire*: "On Diving," January, 42, 44; "Off-Track Betting," February, 48, 50, 52; "Brad Park," March, 32, 36, 38, 42; "Vito Antuofermo," April, 36, 38; "Lee Arthur, Sportscaster," May, 54, 56, 58; "Stephen Blass," June, 24, 26, 28; "The Old Neighborhood," July, 14, 18, 20, 22, 62; "Old Sportswriters," September, 32, 34, 38, 64; "Where Have All Our Heroes Gone? Gone to Television, Everyone," October, 141–43; "Notre Dame Football," November, 54, 65, 61; "Julie Heldman's Tennis," December, 76, 80, 82.

1975

"Where Have All Our Heroes Gone?" in *Best Sports Stories 1975: A Panorama of the 1974 Sports World*, Irving T. Marsh and Edward Ehre, eds., (New York: Dutton), 254–65.

"Our Sports" column in *Esquire*: "J. Walter Kennedy," January, 38, 40; "The Brawling Flyers," February, 41–42, 44; "Kareem's First Year," March, 20, 24; "Catfish Hunter," April, 30, 33–34; "Remembering Leo Durocher," May, 48, 50; "The Charitable Muhammad Ali," June, 47; "Lou Brock: When He Walked He

Ran," July, 46–48; "Connors vs. Newcombe," August, 14, 16, 26; "First Things First: Can Sports Survive Money?" October, 105–9; "The Good and Bad Times of Don King," November, 65–66, 71; "Russell Francis at Tight End," December, 51, 54, 56.

1976

"Emperors and Clowns," *Time*, January 10, 34.

"Our Sports" column in *Esquire*: "Supercoach Fred Shero," January, 13, 16; "All Hail the Commissioner of Roundball," February, 52, 54; "Iconoclasm of the Long Distance Runner," March, 14, 16; "The Quickest Hands in All of Sport," April, 34, 36; "George Foreman Is Down but Not Out," May, 51, 53; "Angel Cordero's Luck," June, 11–12, 20; "Baseball: The State of the Game," July, 20–22; "Martina? A Big, Tough Competitive Kid," August, 9–10.

Sports Illustrated articles: "Still a Grand Old Game," August 16, 56–60; "Of Galahad and Quests That Failed," August 23, 28–32; "Golden Triumphs, Tarnished Dreams," August 30, 32–36.

"Doing It Just One More Time," *Time*, October 11, 74–75.

"Sing One Happy Song, Johnny," *Time*, November 1, 71.

"Aboard the *Lusitania* in Tampa Bay," *Time*, November 22, 54–55.

1977

A Season in the Sun (New York: Harper & Row).

"Les Canadiens of Pucks," *Time*, February 14, 63–64.

"Our Treasurer's Report," *Time*, March 21, 62, 78.

"The Cincinnati Kid," *Time*, April 11, 78.

"Bill Veeck: The Happy Hustler," *Time*, April 25, 90.

"Who Needs the Derby," *Time*, May 9, 60.

"Encountering the Yankees," *Time*, June 6, 79.

"The Joy of Deprogramming Sport," *Time*, August 22, 50.

1979

But Not to Keep (New York: Harper & Row).

"A Visit with Red Smith," *Notre Dame Magazine*, December, 32–34.

1980

"My Movie Option; 8 Years of Strikeouts," *New York Times*, May 4, D1.

"Hurry! Hurry! Hurry!" The Dodgers Are in Town," *Sport*, June, 30–37.

"Cooperstown Takes Two," *Sport*, August, 73.

"Crowning the Dodgers' Duke," *Sport*, August, 73–74.

"Roger Kahn's All-Time Dodger Team," *Sport*, 36.

1981

"Lafleur," *Sport*, December, 61.

"A Farewell to Heroes," *Sports Illustrated*, November 16, 16.

"Gibson, the Hungry Lion, Approaches the Hall," *New York Times*, July 26, 19.

"Whitey's Redbirds," *Sport*, July, 26.

"He's a Yankee Doodle Dandy," *Sport*, June, 36–40.

"Pray for a Great World Series," *Sport*, November, 77.

1982

The Seventh Game (New York: New American Library).

"He's a Yankee Doodle Dandy," in *Best Sports Stories 1982: A Panorama of the 1981 Sports World*, Edward Ehre, ed. (New York: Dutton), 15–23.

"Take Me Out to the (a) Ballgame or (b) Armchair," *TV Guide*, October 9, 24–26.

"Sunshine Boy," *Reader's Digest*, July, 118–25.

1983

"Bums' Rush Turns into a Big Bonanza: 25 Years Ago Baseball Headed West," in Dick Kaegal, ed., *1983 Baseball Yearbook* (St. Louis. Mo.: *Sporting News*), 20.

1985

Good Enough to Dream (Garden City, N.Y.: Doubleday).

"Dodger Verities Span the Seasons," *New York Times*, October 6, S1, 25.

1986

Joe & Marilyn: A Memory of Love (New York: William Morrow & Co.).

"Lords of the Flies," *Esquire*, June, 69–73.

"A Dodger Generation, Always in Season," *Los Angeles Times*, October 19, 1.

"A Tribute to Roger Maris: The Reporter," *Spitball*, Spring, 28–29.

1987

"The Bishop's Brother," in Charles Einstein, ed., *The Fireside Book of Baseball* (New York: Simon and Schuster), 191–97.

"Baseball vs. Football: the Winner Is . . . Roger Kahn and Frank Ryan," *New York Times*, September 13, S5, 12.

"Rose Manages Headfirst, Too," *New York Times*, May 4, S3, 41.

1988

"Roger Kahn on Jackie Robinson," *The Baseball Hall of Fame 50th Anniversary Book* (New York: Prentice–Hall), 214–27.

"The Return of Hardball Economics?" *New York Times*, February 28, 11.

"You Are What You're Rated in the League-Tennis System," *New York Times*, June 27, C13.

1989

Pete Rose: My Story, by Pete Rose and Roger Kahn (New York: Macmillan).

"Carl Furillo, 1922–1989," *New York Times*, January 29, S1, 8.

"Two Years Later, Neither Friends nor Causes Have Been Won," *Los Angeles Times*, March 14, III, 1.

1990

"Rose Book Was a Story in Itself," *Los Angeles Times*, July 29, C1.

"Can TV Capture the Magic of the World Series?" *TV Guide*, October 13, 12–14.

1991

"A Rose by Another Name," *Playboy*, December, 174.

1992

Games We Used to Play: A Lover's Quarrel with the World of Sport (New York: Ticknor & Fields).

"The Ten Years of Jackie Robinson," in *The Twentieth Century Treasury of Sports*, Al Silverman and Brian Silverman, eds. (New York: Viking), 334–51.

"Awesome Sights? The Sistine Chapel . . . and a Sandy Koufax Fastball," *New Choices for Retirement Living*, September, 46.

"Can TV Capture the Magic of the World Series?" *TV Guide*, October 13, 12.

1993

The Era: 1947–1957, When the Yankees, the Giants, and the Dodgers Ruled the World (New York: Ticknor & Fields).

1994

"Pursuit of No. 60: The Ordeal of Roger Maris," (reprint of 1961 article) *Sports Illustrated*, September 26, 54–56.

1995

"Remembering Mickey," *The Sporting News*, August 21, 8.

1996

"Biography: Jackie Robinson," *Los Angeles Times*, December 29, B9.

"American Hero," *Los Angeles Times*, September 22, B1.

1997

Memories of Summer: When Baseball Was an Art and Writing About It a Game (New York: Hyperion).

"What I Wrote for Love: Your Passion," *Writer's Digest*, November, 31–36.

"Take Me Back to the Ballgame," *Los Angeles Times*, June 19, B9.

"Tough Act to Follow," *Los Angeles Times*, January 8, D1.

1998

"Is There Life After Immortality?" *Los Angeles Times*, September 4, D9.

"Cautionary Tales: History's Baseball Gods Fell to Tragic Depths," *Denver Post*, September 13, G4.

"The Boys Turn 26," *Los Angeles Times*, February 22, D1.

1999

A Flame of Pure Fire: Jack Dempsey and the Roaring '20s (New York: Harcourt, Brace & Co.).

"A Tribute to . . . Captain Courageous," *Los Angeles Times*, August 19, 1.

"Opinions and Fax, There's More to It than Simply Calling Legendary Dodger the Greatest Pitcher of the Century," *Los Angeles Times*, July 15, 5.

"Joltin' Joe Has Gone," *Los Angeles Times*, March 9, D1.

2000

Head Game: Baseball Seen from the Pitcher's Mound (New York: Harcourt).

A Season in the Sun (Lincoln: University of Nebraska Press).

"Remembering Ring," *The Nation*, December 4, 38.

"The Revenge of Flatbush, New York Aboard for Series sans Dodgers," *Los Angeles Times*, October 20, D1.

"Baseball Town, Again," *New York Times*, October 14, A19.

2001

"Deja Whew; Kim Is Living Proof that Lightning Can Strike Twice in Same Place," *Los Angeles Times*, November 3, D1.

"Most Valuable (Gentleman) from Japan: Ichiro Suzuki Did More than Win Some Hardware—He Destroyed a Stereotype," *Time International*, December 3, 65.

2002

October Men: Reggie Jackson, George Steinbrenner, Billy Martin, and the Yankees' Miraculous Finish in 1978 (New York: Harcourt).

Foreword to Howard Bryant, *Shut Out: A Story of Race and Baseball in Boston* (Boston: Beacon Press, 2002) ix–xiii.

"Bonds Not Necessarily Chip off His Godfather," *Los Angeles Times*, October 25, D1.

"Country Played Hardball," *Los Angeles Times*, August 13, D1.

"Joe Black, 1924–2002; Hard Thrower, Soft Heart," *Los Angeles Times*, May 18, D1.

"Give Him One Last Summer," *Los Angeles Times*, May 26, D6.

2003

"We All Know It's Only a Game, but Still . . . Say It Ain't Sosa," *Los Angeles Times*, June 5, B15.

"Scorecard: Mind over Batter," *Sports Illustrated*, December 8, 23.

INDEX